Praise for

'His child's voice is immensely powerful and is an extraordinary testament to the human desire for survival. Not only did Dave Pelzer survive, he triumphed . . . Essentially, *The Lost Boy* is a story of regeneration and resilience, as well as harrowing pain . . . What has made Dave Pelzer's story a bestseller is that it is also a story of redemption. It is a story where love, kindness, patience and endurance triumph' *Daily Mail*

'The tale of how he survived the really bad abuse of his early life makes for inspirational, if incredibly sad, reading'
Manchester Evening News

'It takes a personal testimony like Dave Pelzer's to bring home the horrors of child abuse – the secrecy, the shame, the struggle to survive' Bel Mooney, *Mail on Sunday*

'The three books tell a harrowing tale with vast dignity – and not a trace of psychobabble' *Independent*

'Pelzer is able to continue his dreadful story in an admirably dispassionate style. He lets you see what was going on through the eyes of the child he once was but, because he has doggedly taught himself not to hate, his voice is never shrill or hysterical. It is this cool tone that makes what he has to say even more compelling' *The Times*

'The raw simplicity of this honest account keeps the pages turning as the reader stays abreast with David's recovery. If ever a book demonstrated the power of the human spirit to triumph in adversity, this is it. An inspirational book which reaches resilience and forgiveness' *Birmingham Post*

'This heartfelt true story of one child's courage to survive cannot fail to move you' *Heat*

My Story

A Child Called 'It'

The Lost Boy

A Man Named Dave

Dave Pelzer

An Orion paperback

A Child Called 'It'
First published in Great Britain in 2000
The Lost Boy
First published in Great Britain in 2000
by Orion Media
A Man Named Dave
First published in Great Britain in 2001
by Orion

This paperback edition published in 2004
by Orion Books Ltd,
Carmelite House, 50 Victoria Embankment
London EC4Y ODZ

An Hachette UK company

43 45 47 49 50 48 46 44

A CIP catalogue record for this book is
available from the British Library

ISBN 978-0-7528-6401-3

Typeset at The Spartan Press Ltd,
Lymington, Hants

Printed in Great Britain by
Clays Ltd, Elcograf S.p.A.

The Orion Publishing Group's policy is to use papers that
are natural, renewable and recyclable products and
made from wood grown in sustainable forests. The logging
and manufacturing processes are expected to conform to
the environmental regulations of the country of origin.

www.orionbooks.co.uk

Contents

This book is dedicated to my son Stephen, who, by the grace of God, has taught me the gift of love and joy through the eyes of a child.

This book is also dedicated to the teachers and staff members of Thomas Edison Elementary School to include:

Steven E. Ziegler, Athena Konstan, Peter Hansen, Joyce Woodworth, Janice Woods, Betty Howell and the School Nurse.

To all of you, for your courage and for putting your careers on the line that fateful day, March 5, 1973. You saved my life.

Contents

ACKNOWLEDGMENTS

After years of intensive labor, sacrifice, frustration, compromises and deception, this book is finally **published** and available in bookstores everywhere. I wish to take a moment to pay homage to those who truly believed in this crusade.

To Jack Canfield, co-author of the phenomenal best-seller *Chicken Soup for the Soul*, for his extreme kindness and for opening a big door. Jack is indeed a rare entity who, without reservation, assists more individuals in a single day than many of us can help in a lifetime. Bless you, sir.

To Nancy Mitchell and Kim Wiele at the Canfield Group for their enormous enthusiasm and guidance. Thank you, ladies.

To Peter Vegso at Health Communications, Inc., as well as Christine Belleris, Matthew Diener, Kim Weiss and the entire friendly staff at HCI for their honesty, professionalism and everyday courtesy that make publishing a pleasure. Kudos galore to Irene Xanthos and Lori Golden for their tenacious drive and for picking up the slack. And a gargantuan thank you to the Art Department for all your hard work and dedication.

A special thank you to Marsha Donohoe, editor extraordinaire, for her hours of reediting and eradicating 'the Wahoo' out of the tome (that's 'book' for those of you who reside in Yuba/Sutter Counties in Northern CA), so to provide the reader with a clear, precise sense of this story through the eyes of a child. For Marsha, it was a matter of '. . . Farmer's Trust'.

To Patti Breitman, of Breitman Publishing Projects, for her initial work and for giving it a good run for the money.

To Cindy Adams for her unwavering faith when I needed it the most.

A special thank you to Ric and Don at the Rio Villa Resort, my then home away from home, for providing the perfect sanctuary during the process of this project.

And lastly, to Phyllis Colleen. I wish you happiness. I wish you peace. May God bless you.

AUTHOR'S NOTE

Some of the names in this book have been changed in order to maintain the dignity and privacy of others.

This book, the first part of the trilogy, depicts language that was developed from a child's viewpoint. The tone and vocabulary reflect the age and wisdom of the child at that particular time.

This book is based on the child's life from ages four to twelve.

The second part of the trilogy, *The Lost Boy*, is based on his life from ages twelve to eighteen.

chapter 1

THE RESCUE

March 5, 1973, Daly City, California – *I'm late. I've got to finish the dishes on time, otherwise no breakfast; and since I didn't have dinner last night, I have to make sure I get something to eat. Mother's running around yelling at my brothers. I can hear her stomping down the hallway towards the kitchen. I dip my hands back into the scalding rinse water. It's too late. She catches me with my hands out of the water.*

SMACK! Mother hits me in the face, and I topple to the floor. I know better than to stand there and take the hit. I learned the hard way that she takes that as an act of defiance, which means more hits, or worst of all, no food. I regain my posture and dodge her looks, as she screams into my ears.

I act timid, nodding to her threats. Please, *I say to myself,* just let me eat. Hit me again, but I have to have food. *Another blow pushes my head against the tile countertop. I let the tears of mock defeat stream down my face as she storms out of the kitchen, seemingly satisfied with herself. After I count her steps, making sure she's gone, I breathe a sigh of relief. The act worked. Mother can beat me all she wants, but I haven't let her take away my will to somehow survive.*

I finish the dishes, then my other chores. For my reward I receive breakfast – leftovers from one of my brothers' cereal bowls. Today it's Lucky Charms. There are only a few bits of cereal left in a half of a bowl of milk, but as quickly as I can, I swallow it before Mother changes her mind. She has done that before. Mother enjoys using food as her weapon. She knows better than to throw leftovers in the garbage can. She knows I'll dig them out later. Mother knows most of my tricks.

Minutes later I'm in the old family station wagon. Because I'm so late with my chores, I have to be driven to school. Usually I run to school, arriving just as class begins, with no time to steal any food from other kids' lunch boxes.

Mother drops my oldest brother off, but keeps me for a lecture about her plans for me tomorrow. She is going to take me to her brother's house. She says Uncle Dan will 'take care of me'. She makes it a threat. I give her a frightened look as if I am truly afraid. But I know that even though my uncle is a hard-nosed man, he surely won't treat me like Mother does.

Before the station wagon comes to a complete stop, I dash out of the car. Mother yells for me to return. I have forgotten my crumpled lunch bag, which has always had the same menu for the last three years – two peanut butter sandwiches and a few carrot sticks. Before I bolt out of the car again, she says, 'Tell 'em . . . Tell 'em you ran into the door.' Then in a voice she rarely uses with me, she states, 'Have a nice day.' I look into her swollen red eyes. She still has a hangover from last night's stupor. Her once beautiful, shiny black hair is now frazzled clumps. As usual, she wears no makeup. She is overweight, and she knows it. In all, this has become Mother's typical look.

Because I am so late, I have to report to the administrative office. The gray-haired secretary greets me with a smile. Moments later, the school nurse comes out and leads me into her office, where we go through the normal routine. First, she examines my face and arms. 'What's that above your eye?' she asks.

I nod sheepishly, 'Oh, I ran into the hall door . . . by accident.'

Again she smiles and takes a clipboard from the top of a cabinet. She flips through a page or two, then bends down to show me. 'Here,' she points to the paper, 'you said that last Monday. Remember?'

I quickly change my story, 'I was playing baseball and got hit by the bat. It was an accident.' Accident. I am always supposed to say that. But the nurse knows better. She scolds me so I'll tell the truth. I always break down in the end and confess, even though I feel I should protect my mother.

The nurse tells me that I'll be fine and asks me to take off my clothes. We have been doing this since last year, so I immediately obey. My long-sleeved shirt has more holes than Swiss cheese. It's the same shirt I've worn for about two years. Mother has me wear it every day as her way to humiliate me. My pants are just as bad, and my shoes have holes in the toes. I can wiggle my big toe out of one of them. While I stand clothed only in my underwear, the nurse records my various marks and bruises on the clipboard. She counts the slash-like marks on my face, looking for any she might have missed in the past. She is very thorough. Next, the nurse opens my mouth to look at my teeth that are chipped from having been slammed against the kitchen tile countertop. She jots a few more notes on the paper. As she continues to look me over, she stops at the old scar on my stomach. 'And that,' she says as she takes a deep swallow, 'is where she stabbed you?'

'Yes, ma'am,' I reply. Oh no! *I tell myself,* I've done something wrong . . . again. *The nurse must have seen the concern in my eyes. She puts the clipboard down and hugs me.* God, I tell myself, she is so warm. I don't want to let go. I want to stay in her arms forever. I hold my eyes tightly shut, and for a few moments nothing else exists. She pats my head. I flinch from the swollen bruise Mother gave me this morning. The nurse then breaks the embrace and leaves the room. I rush to put my clothes back on. She doesn't know it, but I do everything as fast as possible.

The nurse returns in a few minutes with Mr Hansen, the principal, and two of my teachers, Miss Woods and Mr Ziegler. Mr Hansen knows me very well. I've been in his office more than any other kid in school. He looks at the paper, as the nurse reports her findings. He lifts my chin. I'm afraid to look into his eyes, which is mostly a habit from trying to deal with my mother. But it's also because I don't want to tell him anything. Once, about a year ago, he called Mother to ask about my bruises. At that time, he had no idea what was really going on. He just knew I was a troubled kid who was stealing food. When I came to school the next day, he saw the results of Mother's beatings. He never called her again.

Mr Hansen barks he's had enough of this. I almost leap out of my skin with fear. He's going to call Mother again! *my brain screams. I break down and cry. My body shakes like jello and I mumble like a baby, begging Mr Hansen not to phone Mother.* 'Please!' *I whine,* 'not today! Don't you understand, it's Friday?'

Mr Hansen assures me he's not going to call Mother, and sends me off to class. Since it's too late for homeroom class, I sprint directly to Mrs Woodworth's English class. Today's a spelling test on all the states and their capitals. I'm not prepared. Usually I'm a very good student, but for the past few months I have given up on everything in my life, including escaping my misery through my schoolwork.

Upon entering the room, all the students plug their noses and hiss at me. The substitute teacher, a younger woman, waves her hands in front of her face. She's not used to my smell. At arm's length she hands my

11

test to me, but before I can take my seat in the back of the class by an open window, I'm summoned back to the principal's office. The entire room lets out a howl at me – the reject of the fifth grade.

I run to the administration office, and I'm there in a flash. My throat is raw and still burns from yesterday's 'game' Mother played against me. The secretary leads me into the teachers' lounge. After she opens the door, it takes a moment for my eyes to adjust. In front of me, sitting around a table, are my homeroom teacher Mr Ziegler, my math teacher Miss Woods, the school nurse, Mr Hansen and a police officer. My feet become frozen. I don't know whether to run away or wait for the roof to cave in. Mr Hansen waves me in, as the secretary closes the door behind me. I take a seat at the head of the table, explaining I didn't steal anything . . . today. Smiles break everyone's depressed frowns. I have no idea that they are about to risk their jobs to save me.

The police officer explains why Mr Hansen called him. I can feel myself shrink into the chair. The officer asks that I tell him about Mother. I shake my head no. Too many people already know the secret, and I know she'll find out. A soft voice calms me. I think it's Miss Woods. She tells me it's all right. I take a deep breath, wring my hands and reluctantly tell them about Mother and I. Then the nurse has me stand up and show the policeman the scar on my chest. Without hesitation, I tell them it was an accident; which it was – Mother never meant to stab me. I cry as I spill my guts, telling them Mother punishes me because I am bad. I wish they would leave me alone. I feel so slimy inside. I know after all these years there is nothing anyone can do.

A few minutes later, I am excused to sit in the outer office. As I close the door, all the adults look at me and nod their heads in an approving way. I fidget in my chair, watching the secretary type papers. It seems forever before Mr Hansen calls me back into the room. Miss Woods and Mr Ziegler leave the lounge. They seem happy, but at the same time worried. Miss Woods kneels down and wraps me in her arms. I don't think I will ever forget the smell of the perfume in her hair. She lets go, turning away so I won't see her cry. Now I am really worried. Mr Hansen gives me a lunch tray from the cafeteria. My God! Is it lunch-time already? I ask myself.

I gobble down the food so fast I can hardly taste it. I finish the tray in record time. Soon the principal returns with a box of cookies, warning me not to eat so fast. I have no idea what's going on. One of my guesses is that my father, who is separated from my mother, has come to get me. But I know it's a fantasy. The policeman asks for my address and telephone number. That's it! *I tell myself.* It's back to hell! I'm going to get it from her again!

The officer writes down more notes as Mr Hansen and the school nurse look on. Soon he closes his notepad and tells Mr Hansen that he has enough information. I look up at the principal. His face is covered with sweat. I can feel my stomach start to coil. I want to go to the bathroom and throw up.

Mr Hansen opens the door, and I can see all the teachers on their lunch break staring at me. I'm so ashamed. They know, *I tell myself.* They know the truth about my mother; the real truth. *It is so important for them to know that I'm not a bad boy. I want so much to be liked, to be loved.* I turn down the hall. Mr Ziegler is holding Miss Woods. She is crying. I can hear her sniffle. She gives me another hug and quickly turns away. Mr Ziegler shakes my hand. 'Be a good boy,' he says.

'Yes, sir. I'll try,' is all I can say.

The school nurse stands in silence beside Mr Hansen. They all tell me goodbye. Now I know I am going to jail. Good, *I tell myself.* At least she won't be able to beat me if I'm in jail.

The police officer and I walk outside, past the cafeteria. I can see some of the kids from my class playing dodge ball. A few of them stop playing. They yell, 'David's busted! David's busted!' The policeman touches my shoulder, telling me everything is okay. As he drives me up the street, away from Thomas Edison Elementary School, I see some kids who seem to be fazed by my departure. Before I left, Mr Ziegler told me he would tell the other kids the truth – the real truth. I would give anything to have been there in class when they found out I'm not so bad.

In a few minutes, we arrive at the Daly City Police Station. I sort of expect Mother to be there. I don't want to get out of the car. The officer opens the door and gently takes me by the elbow, into a big office. No other person is in the room. The policeman sits in a chair, in the corner, where he types several sheets of paper. I watch the officer closely as I slowly eat my cookies. I savor them as long as I can. I don't know when I will be eating again.

It's past 1:00 P.M. when the policeman finishes his paperwork. He asks for my telephone number again.

'Why?' I whine.

'I have to call her, David,' he says gently.

'No!' I command. 'Send me back to school. Don't you get it? She mustn't find out I told!'

He calms me down with another cookie, as he slowly dials 7-5-6-2-4-6-0. I watch the black dial turn as I get up and walk towards him, straining my whole body while trying to hear the phone ringing on the other end. Mother answers. Her voice scares me. The policeman waves me away, and takes a deep breath before saying, 'Mrs Pelzer, this is Officer Smith from the Daly City Police Department. Your son David will not be coming home today. He will be in the custody of the San Mateo Juvenile Department. If you have any questions, you can call them.' He hangs up the phone and smiles. 'Now that wasn't so hard, was it?' he asks me. But the look on his face tells me he is assuring himself, more than he is me.

A few miles later, we are on Highway 280, heading towards the outskirts of Daly City. I look to my right and see a sign that reads, 'THE MOST BEAUTIFUL HIGHWAY IN THE WORLD'. The officer smiles with relief, as we leave the city limits. 'David Pelzer,' he says, 'you're free.'

'What?' I ask, clutching my only source of food. 'I don't understand. Aren't you taking me to some kind of jail?'

Again he smiles, and gently squeezes my shoulder. 'No, David. You have nothing to worry about, honest. Your mother is never going to hurt you again.'

I lean back against the seat. A reflection from the sun hits my eyes. I turn away from the rays as a single tear runs down my cheek.

I'm free?

chapter 2

GOOD TIMES

In the years before I was abused, my family was the 'Brady Bunch' of the 1960s. My two brothers and I were blessed with the perfect parents. Our every whim was fulfilled with love and care.

We lived in a modest two-bedroom house, in what was considered a 'good' neighborhood in Daly City. I can remember looking out of our living-room bay window on a clear day, to gaze at the bright orange towers of the Golden Gate Bridge and the beautiful skyline of San Francisco.

My father, Stephen Joseph, supported his family as a fireman, working in the heart of San Francisco. He stood about five feet ten inches tall, and he weighed about a hundred and ninety pounds. He had broad shoulders and forearms that would make any muscle man proud. His thick black eyebrows matched his hair. I felt special when he winked at me and called me 'Tiger'.

My mother, Catherine Roerva, was a woman of average size and appearance. I never could remember the color of her hair or eyes, but Mom was a woman who glowed with love for her children. Her greatest asset was her determination. Mom always had ideas, and she always took command of all family matters. Once, when I was four or five years old, Mom said she was sick, and I remember feeling that she did not seem to be herself at all. It was a day when Father was working at the fire station. After serving dinner, Mom rushed from the table and began painting the steps that led to the garage. She coughed as she frantically brushed the red paint onto every step. The paint had not fully dried, when Mom began tacking rubber mats to the steps. The red paint was all over the mats and Mom. When she finished, Mom went into the house and collapsed on the couch. I remember asking her why she had put the mats down before the paint dried. She smiled and said, 'I just wanted to surprise your dad.'

When it came to housekeeping, Mom was an absolute clean fiend. After feeding my two brothers, Ronald and Stan, and I breakfast, she would dust, disinfect, scour and vacuum everything. No room in our house was left untouched. As we grew older, Mom made sure we did our part by keeping our room neat. Outside, she meticulously attended a small flower garden, which was the envy of the neighborhood. With Mom, everything she touched turned to gold. She didn't believe in doing anything halfway. Mom often told us that we must always do the best we could, in whatever we did.

Mom was truly a gifted cook. Of all the things she did for her family, I think creating new and exotic meals was her favorite. This was especially true on those days when Father was home. Mom would spend the better part of the day preparing one of her fantastic meals. On some days when Father was working, Mom would take us on exciting sight-seeing tours around the city. One day, she took us to Chinatown in San Francisco. As we drove around the area, Mom told us about the culture and history of the Chinese people. When we returned, Mom started her record player, and our home was filled with beautiful sounds from the Orient. She then decorated the dining room with Chinese lanterns. That evening, she dressed in a kimono and served what seemed to us a very exotic but delicious meal. At the end of dinner, Mom gave us fortune cookies and read the captions for us. I felt that the cookie's message would lead me to my destiny. Some years later, when I was old enough to read, I found one of my old fortunes. It said, 'Love and honor thy mother, for she is the fruit that gives thou life.'

Back then our house was full of pets – cats, dogs, aquariums filled with exotic fish and a gopher tortoise named 'Thor'. I remember the tortoise best because Mom let me pick a name for it. I felt proud because my brothers had been chosen to name the other pets and it was now my turn. I named the reptile after my favorite cartoon character.

The five- and ten-gallon aquariums seemed to be everywhere. There were at least two in the living-room, and one filled with guppies in our bedroom. Mom creatively decorated the heated tanks with colored gravel and colored foil backs; anything she thought would make the tanks more realistic. We would often sit by the tanks while Mom told us about the different species of fish.

The most dramatic of Mom's lessons, came one Sunday afternoon. One of our cats was behaving in an odd way. Mom had us all sit down by the cat while she explained the process of birth. After all the kittens had slipped safely out of the mother cat, Mom explained in great detail the wonder of life. No matter what the family was doing, she somehow came up with a constructive lesson; though we were not usually aware that we were being taught.

For our family – during those good years – the holidays started with Halloween. One October night, when the huge harvest moon was in full view, Mom hurried the three of us out of our house, to gaze at the 'Great Pumpkin' in the sky. When we returned to our bedroom, she told us to peek under our pillows where we found Matchbox race cars. My two brothers and I squealed with delight as Mom's face was flushed with pride.

The day after Thanksgiving, Mom would disappear to the basement, then bring up enormous boxes filled with Christmas decorations. While standing on a ladder, she tacked strings of ornaments to the ceiling beams. When she was finished, every room in our house had a seasonal touch. In the dining room Mom arranged different sizes of red candles on the counter of her prized oak hutch. Snowflake patterns graced every window in the living-room and dining room. Christmas lights were draped around our bedroom windows. Every night I fell asleep while staring at the soft, colorful glow of the Christmas lights that blinked on and off.

Our Christmas tree was never ever an inch under eight feet, and it took the whole family hours to decorate it. Each year one of us was honored by being allowed to place the angel at the top of the tree, while Father held us up in his strong arms. After the tree was decorated and dinner was finished, we would pile into the station wagon and cruise the neighborhood, admiring the decorations on other homes. Mom always rambled on about her ideas of bigger and better things for the next Christmas, even though my brothers and I knew our house was always the best. When we returned home, Mom sat us down by the fireplace to drink egg nog. While she told us stories, Bing Crosby sang 'White Christmas' on the stereo. I was so excited during those holiday seasons that I couldn't sleep. Sometimes Mom would cradle me, while I fell asleep listening to the crackle of the fire.

As Christmas Day came nearer, my brothers and I became more and more excited. The pile of gifts at the base of the tree grew day by day. By the time Christmas finally arrived, there were dozens of gifts for each of us.

On Christmas Eve, after a special dinner and caroling, we were allowed to open one gift. Afterwards, we were sent to bed. I always strained my ears as I laid in bed, waiting for the sound of Santa's sleigh bells. But I always fell asleep before I heard his reindeer land on the roof.

Before dawn, Mom would creep into our room and wake us, whispering, 'Santa came!' One year she gave each of us a yellow, plastic, Tonka hard hat and had us march into the living-room. It took us forever to rip the colorful paper from the boxes, to discover our new Christmas toys. Afterwards, Mom had us run to the backyard in our new robes, to look back in through the window at our huge Christmas tree. That year, standing in the yard, I remember seeing Mom cry. I asked her why she was sad. Mom told me she was crying because she was so happy to have a real family.

Because Father's job often required him to work twenty-four-hour shifts, Mother often took us on day trips to places like the nearby Golden Gate Park in San Francisco. As we slowly drove through the park, Mom explained how the areas were different and how she envied the beautiful flowers. We always visited the park's Steinhart Aquarium last. My brothers and I would blaze up the stairs and charge through the heavy doors. We were thrilled as we leaned over the brass, sea-horse-shaped fence, looking far below at the small waterfall and pond that were home to the alligators and large turtles. As a child, this was my favorite place in the entire park. I once became frightened, as I thought about slipping through the barrier and falling into the pond. Without speaking a word, Mom must have felt my fear. She looked down at me and held my hand ever so softly.

Spring meant picnics. Mom would prepare a feast of fried chicken, salads, sandwiches and lots of desserts the night before. Early the next day, our family sped off to Junipero Serra Park. Once there, my brothers and I would run wild on the grass and pump higher and higher on the park's swings. Sometimes we would venture off on a new trail. Mom always had to pry us away from our fun, when it came time for lunch. We wolfed down our food, hardly tasting it, before my brothers and I blitzed off for parts unknown, in search of high adventure. Our parents seemed happy to lie next to each other on a blanket, sip red wine and watch us play.

It was always a thrill when the family went on summer vacation. Mom was always the mastermind behind these trips. She planned every detail, and swelled with pride as the activities came together. Usually we traveled to Portola or Memorial Park, and camped out in our giant, green tent for a week or so. But whenever Father drove us north across the Golden Gate Bridge, I knew we were going to my favorite place in the world – the Russian River.

The most memorable trip to the river for me, happened the year I was in kindergarten. On the last day of school, Mom asked that I be excused a half-hour early. As Father honked the horn, I rocketed up the small hill from the school, to the waiting car. I was excited because I knew where we were going. During the drive, I became fascinated at the seemingly endless fields of grapes. When we drove into the quiet town of Guerneville, I rolled my window down to smell the sweet air from the redwood trees.

Each day was a new adventure. My brothers and I either spent the day climbing an old, burnt tree stump with our special whomper-stomper boots or swimming in the river at Johnson's Beach. Johnson's Beach was a whole day's event. We would leave our cabin by nine and return after three. Mom taught each of us to swim in a small, trenched hole in the river. That summer Mom taught me how to swim on my back. She seemed so proud when I was finally able to do it.

Every day seemed sprinkled with magic. One day after dinner, Mom and Dad took the three of us to watch the sunset. All of us held hands, as we crept past Mr Parker's cabin to get to the river. The green river water was as smooth as glass. The bluejays scolded the other birds, and a warm breeze blew through my hair. Without a word, we stood watching the fireball-like sun as it sank behind the tall trees, leaving bright blue and orange streaks in the sky. From above, I felt someone hug my shoulders. I thought it was my father. I turned and became flushed with pride to find Mom holding me tightly. I could feel her heart beat. I never felt as safe and as warm as that moment in time, at the Russian River.

chapter 3

BAD BOY

My relationship with Mom drastically changed from discipline that developed into a kind of lifestyle that grew out of control. It became so bad at times, I had no strength to crawl away – even if it meant saving my life.

As a small child, I probably had a voice that carried farther than others. I also had the unfortunate luck of getting caught at mischief, even though my brothers and I were often committing the same 'crime'. In the beginning, I was put in a corner of our bedroom. By this time, I had become afraid of Mom. Very afraid. I never asked her to let me come out. I would sit and wait for one of my brothers to come into our bedroom, and have him ask if David could come out now and play.

About this time, Mom's behavior began to change radically. At times while Father was away at work, she would spend the entire day lying on the couch, dressed only in her bathrobe, watching television. Mom got up only to go to the bathroom, get another drink or heat leftover food. When she yelled at us, her voice changed from the nurturing mother to the wicked witch. Soon, the sound of Mother's voice began to send tremors down my spine. Even when she barked at one of my brothers, I'd run to hide in our room, hoping she would soon return to the couch, her drink and her TV show. After a while, I could determine what kind of day I was going to have by the way she dressed. I would breathe a sigh of relief whenever I saw Mom come out of her room in a nice dress with her face made up. On these days she always came out with a smile.

When Mother decided that the 'corner treatment' was no longer effective, I graduated to the 'mirror treatment'. In the beginning, it was a no-notice form of punishment. Mother would simply grab me and smash my face against the mirror, smearing my tear-streaked face on the slick, reflective glass. Then she would order me to say over and over again, 'I'm a bad boy! I'm a bad boy! I'm a bad boy!' I was then forced to stand, staring into the mirror. I would stand there with my hands locked to my sides, weaving back and forth, dreading the moment when the second set of television commercials aired. I knew Mother would soon be stomping down the hall to see if my face was still against the mirror, and to tell me what a sickening child I was. Whenever my brothers came into the room while I was at the mirror, they would look at me, shrug their shoulders and continue to play – as if I were not there. At first I was jealous, but soon I learned that they were only trying to save their own skins.

While Father was at work, Mother would often yell and scream while forcing my brothers and I to search the entire house for something she had lost. The quest usually started in the morning and lasted for hours. After a while, I was usually sent to search in the garage which was under part of the house – like a basement. Even there, I trembled upon hearing Mother scream at one of my brothers.

The searches continued for months, and finally, I was the only one singled out to look for her things. Once, I forgot what I was looking for. When I timidly asked her what it was that I was to find, Mother smacked me in the face. She was lying on the couch at the time, and she didn't even stop watching her television show. Blood gushed from my nose and I began to cry. Mother snatched a napkin from her table, tore a piece and rammed it up my nose. 'You know damn well what you're looking for!' she screamed. 'Now go find it!' I scurried back down to the basement, making sure I made enough noise to convince Mother I was feverishly obeying her command. As Mother's 'find the thing' became more common, I began to fantasize that I had found her missing item. I imagined myself marching upstairs with my prize and Mom greeting me with hugs and kisses. My fantasy included the family living happily ever after. But, I never found any of Mother's lost things, and she never let me forget that I was an incompetent loser.

As a small child, I realized Mom was as different as night and day when Father was home from work. When Mom fixed her hair and put on nice clothes, she seemed more relaxed. I loved it when Dad was home. It meant no beatings, mirror treatments or long searches for her missing things. Father became my protector. Whenever he went to the garage to work on a project, I followed him. If he sat in his favorite chair to read the newspaper, I parked myself at his feet. In the evenings, after the dinner dishes were cleared from the table, Father would wash them, and I would dry. I knew that as long as I stayed by his side, no harm would come to me.

One day before he left for work, I received a dreadful shock. After he said goodbye to Ron and Stan, he knelt down, held my shoulders tightly and told me to be a 'good boy'. Mother stood behind him with her arms folded across her chest, and a grim smile on her face. I looked into my father's eyes and knew right then that I was a 'bad boy'. An ice-cold chill rushed through my body. I wanted to hold on to him and never let go, but before I could give Father a hug, he stood up, turned and walked out the door, without saying another word.

For a short time after Father's warning, things seemed to calm down between Mother and I. When Dad was home, my brothers and I played in our room or outside, until about 3:00 P.M. Mother would then turn on the television so we could watch cartoons. For my parents, 3:00 P.M. meant 'Happy Hour'. Father would cover the kitchen countertop with bottles of alcohol and tall fancy glasses. He cut up lemons and limes, placing them in small bowls beside a small jar of cherries. They often drank from mid-afternoon, until my brothers and I climbed into bed. I remember watching them dance around the kitchen to music from the radio. They held each other close, and they looked so happy. I thought I could bury the bad times. I was wrong. The bad times were only beginning.

A month or two later, on a Sunday, while Father was at work, my brothers and I were playing in our room when we heard Mother rush down the hall, yelling at us. Ron and Stan ran for cover in the living room. I instantly sat down in my chair. With both arms stretched out and raised, Mother came at me. As she came closer and closer, I backed my chair towards the wall. Soon, my head touched the wall. Mother's eyes were glazed and red, and her breath smelled of booze. I closed my eyes as the oncoming blows began to rock me from side to side. I tried to protect my face with my hands, but Mother would only knock them away. Her punches seemed to last forever. Finally, I snaked my left arm up to cover my face. As Mother grabbed my arm, she lost her balance and staggered back a step. As she jerked violently to regain her stability, I heard something pop, and felt an intense pain in my shoulder and arm. The startled look on Mother's face told me that she had heard the sound too, but she released her grip on my arm, and turned and walked away as if nothing had happened. I cradled my arm as it began to throb with pain. Before I could actually inspect my arm, Mother summoned me to dinner.

I plopped down at a TV tray to try to eat. As I reached for a glass of milk, my left arm did not respond. My fingers twitched upon command, but my arm tingled and had become lifeless. I looked at Mother, trying to plead with my eyes. She ignored me. I knew something was very wrong, but I was too afraid to utter a word. I simply sat there, staring at my tray of food. Mother finally excused me and sent me to bed early, telling me to sleep in the top bunk. This was unusual because I had always slept on the bottom. Sometime near morning I finally fell asleep, with my left arm carefully cradled in the other.

I hadn't slept long when Mother awakened me, explaining that I had rolled out of the top bunk during the night. She seemed to be deeply concerned about my condition, as she drove me to the hospital. When she told the doctor about my fall from the top bunk bed, I could tell by the look he gave me that he knew my injury was no accident. Again, I was too afraid to speak up. At home, Mother made up an even more dramatic story for Father. In the new version, Mother included her efforts to catch me before I hit the floor. As I sat in Mother's lap, listening to her lie to Father, I knew my mom was sick. But my fear kept the accident our secret. I knew if I ever told anyone, the next 'accident' would be worse.

School was a haven for me. I was thrilled to be away from Mother. At recess I was a wild man. I blitzed through the bark-covered playground, looking for new, adventurous things to do. I made friends easily and felt so happy to be at school. One day in late spring, when I returned home from school, Mother threw me into her bedroom. She then yelled at me, stating I was to be held back from the first grade because I was a bad boy. I did not understand. I knew I had more 'happy face' papers than anybody in the class. I obeyed my teacher and I felt she liked me. But Mother continued to roar that I had shamed the family and would be severely punished. She decided that I was banned from watching television, forever. I was to go without dinner and accomplish whatever chores Mother could dream up. After another thrashing, I was sent to the garage to stand until Mother called me to go to bed.

That summer, without warning, I was dropped off at my Aunt Jose's house on the way to the campsite. No one told me about this and I could not understand why. I felt like an outcast as the station wagon drove away, leaving me behind. I felt so sad and hollow. I tried to run away from my aunt's house. I wanted to find my family, and for some strange reason, I wanted to be with Mother. I didn't get far, and my aunt later informed my mother of my attempt. The next time Father worked the twenty-four-hour shift, I paid for my sin. Mother smacked, punched and kicked me until I crumpled to the floor. I tried to tell Mother that I had run away because I wanted to be with her and the family. I tried to tell her that I had missed her, but Mother refused to let me speak. I tried once more and Mother dashed to the bathroom, snatched a bar of soap and crammed it down my throat. After that, I was no longer allowed to speak unless I was instructed to do so.

Returning to the first grade was really a joy. I knew the basic lessons and was instantly dubbed the class genius. Since I was held back, Stan and I were in the same grade. During recess, I would go over to Stan's first-grade class to play. At school we were the best of friends; however, at home, we both knew I was not to be acknowledged.

One day I rushed home to show off a school paper. Mother threw me into her bedroom, yelling about a letter she had received from the North Pole. She claimed the letter said that I was a 'bad boy' and Santa would not bring me any gifts for Christmas. Mother raged on and on, saying that I had embarrassed the family *again.* I stood in a daze, as Mother badgered me relentlessly. I felt I was living in a nightmare that Mother had created, and I prayed she would somehow wake up. Before Christmas that year, there were only a couple of gifts for me under the tree, and those came from relatives outside the immediate family. On Christmas morning, Stan dared to ask Mother why Santa had brought me only two paint-by-number pictures. She lectured him saying, 'Santa only brings toys to *good* boys and girls.' I stole a glance from Stan. There was sorrow in his eyes, and I could tell that he understood Mother's freakish games. Since I was still under punishment, on Christmas Day I had to change into my work clothes and perform my chores. While I was cleaning the bathroom, I overheard an argument between Mother and Father. She was angry with him for 'going behind her back' to buy me the paintings. Mother told Father that *she* was in charge of disciplining 'The Boy' and that he had undermined her authority by buying the gifts. The longer Father argued his case, the angrier she became. I could tell he had lost, and that I was becoming more and more isolated.

A few months later, Mother became a den mother for the Cub Scouts. Whenever the other kids came to our home, she treated them like kings. Some of the other kids told me how they wished their mothers would be like mine. I never responded, but I wondered to myself what they would think if they knew the real truth. Mother only kept the den mother job for a few months. When she gave it up I was so relieved because it meant I could go to other kids' homes for the Wednesday meetings.

One Wednesday, I came home from school to change into my blue and gold Cub Scout uniform. Mother and I were the only ones in the house, and I could tell by the look on her face that she was after blood. After smashing my face against the bedroom mirror, she snatched my arm and dragged me to the car. During the drive to my den mother's house, Mother told me what she was going to do with me when we got home. I scooted to the far side of the front seat of the car, but it didn't work. She reached across the seat and seized my chin, lifting my head towards hers. Mother's eyes were bloodshot and her voice sounded as if she were possessed. When we arrived at the den mother's house, I ran to the door crying. I whined to her that I had been a bad boy and could not attend the meeting. The den mother smiled politely, saying that she would like me to come to the next meeting. That was the last time I saw her.

Once home, Mother ordered me to strip off my clothes and stand by the kitchen stove. I shook from a combination of fear and embarrassment. She then revealed my hideous crime. Mother told me that she had often driven to school to watch my brothers and I play during our lunch period recess. Mother claimed that she had seen me that very day playing on the grass, which was absolutely forbidden by her rules. I quickly answered that I never played on the grass. I knew Mother had somehow made a mistake. My reward for observing Mother's rules and telling the truth was a hard punch in the face.

Mother then reached over and turned on the gas burners to the kitchen stove. Mother told me that she had read an article about a mother who had her son lie on top of a hot stove. I instantly became terrified. My brain became numb, and my legs wobbled. I wanted to disappear. I closed my eyes, wishing her away. My brain locked up when I felt Mother's hand clamp my arm as if it were in a vice grip.

'You've made my life a living hell!' she sneered. 'Now it's time I showed *you* what hell is like!' Gripping my arm, Mother held it in the orange-blue flame. My skin seemed to explode from the heat. I could smell the scorched hairs from my burnt arm. As hard as I fought, I could not force Mother to let go of my arm. Finally I fell to the floor, on my hands and knees, and tried to blow cool air on my arm. 'It's too bad your drunken father's not here to save you,' she hissed. Mother then ordered me to climb up onto the stove and lie on the flames so she could watch me burn. I refused, crying and pleading. I felt so scared I stomped my feet in protest. But Mother continued to force me on top of the stove. I watched the flames, praying the gas might run out.

Suddenly I began to realize the longer I could keep myself off the top of the stove, the better my chances were for staying alive. I knew my brother Ron would soon be coming home from his scout meeting, and I knew Mother never acted this bizarre when anyone else was in the house. In order to survive, I had to buy time. I stole a glance at the kitchen clock behind me. The second hand seemed to creep ever so slowly. To keep Mother off balance, I began to ask whining questions. This infuriated her even more, and Mother began to rain blows around my head and chest. The more Mother slugged me, the more I began to realize I had won! Anything was better than burning on the stove.

Finally I heard the front door fly open. It was Ron. My heart surged with relief. The blood from Mother's face drained. She knew she had lost. For a moment in time, Mother froze. I seized that instant to grab my clothes and race to the garage, where I quickly dressed. I stood against the wall and began to whimper until I realized that *I* had beaten her. *I* had bought a few precious minutes. *I* had used my head to survive. For the first time, *I* had won!

Standing alone in that damp, dark garage, I knew, for the first time, that I could survive. I decided that I would use any tactic I could think of to defeat Mother or to delay her from her grizzly obsession. I knew if *I* wanted to live, *I* would have to think ahead. I could no longer cry like a helpless baby. In order to survive, *I* could never give in to her. That day I vowed to myself that I would never, ever again give that bitch the satisfaction of hearing me beg her to stop beating me.

In the coldness of the garage, my entire body trembled from both the cold anger and intense fear. I used my tongue to lick the burn and soothe my throbbing arm. I wanted to scream, but I refused to give Mother the pleasure of hearing me cry. *I* stood tall. I could hear Mother talking to Ron upstairs, telling him how proud she was of him, and how she didn't have to worry about Ron becoming like David – a bad boy.

chapter 4

THE FIGHT FOR FOOD

The summer after the burn incident, school became my only hope of escape. Except for the short duration of a fishing trip, things with Mother were touch and go, or smash and dash – she would smash me, and I would dash to the solitude of the basement/garage. The month of September brought school and bliss. I had new clothes and a shiny, new lunch pail. Because Mother had me wear the same clothes week after week, by October my clothes had become weathered, torn and smelly. She hardly bothered to cover my bruises on my face and arms. When asked, I had my ready-made excuses Mother brainwashed into me.

By then, Mother would 'forget' to feed me any dinner. Breakfast wasn't much better. On a good day, I was allowed leftover cereal portions from my brothers, but only if I performed all of my chores before going to school.

At night I was so hungry, my stomach growled as if I were an angry bear. At night I lay awake concentrating on food. *Maybe tomorrow I'll get dinner*, I said to myself. Hours later, I would drift off to sleep, fantasizing about food. I mainly dreamt of colossal hamburgers with all the fixings. In my dreams I seized my prize and brought it to my lips. I visualized every inch of the hamburger. The meat dripped with grease, and thick slices of cheese bubbled on top. Condiments oozed between the lettuce and tomato. As I brought the hamburger closer to my face, I opened my mouth to devour my prize, but nothing happened. I'd try again and again, but no matter how hard I struggled, I could not taste a morsel of my fantasy. Moments later I would wake up, with my stomach more hollow than before. I could not satisfy my hunger; not even in my dreams.

Soon after I had begun to dream about food, I started stealing food at school. My stomach coiled with a combination of fear and anticipation. Anticipation because I knew that within seconds, I would have something to put in my stomach. Fear because I also knew that at any time, I could get caught stealing. I always stole food before school began, while my classmates were playing outside the building. I would sneak to the wall, right outside my homeroom, drop my lunch pail by another pail and kneel down so nobody could see me hunting through their lunches. The first few times were easy, but after several days, some students began to discover Twinkies and other desserts missing from their lunches. Within a short time, my classmates began to hate me. The teacher told the principal, who in turn informed Mother. The fight for food became a cycle. The principal's report to Mother led to more beatings and less food for me at the house.

On weekends, to punish me for my thefts, Mother refused to feed me. By Sunday night, my mouth would water as I began to plot new, fool-proof ways to steal food without getting caught. One of my plots was to steal from other first-grade rooms, where I wasn't known as well. On Monday mornings I would dash from Mother's car to a new first-grade classroom to pick through lunch boxes. I got away with it for a short time, but it didn't take long for the principal to trace the thefts back to me.

At the house, the dual punishment of hunger and violent attacks continued. By this time, for all practical purposes, I was no longer a member of the family. I existed, but there was little or no recognition. Mother had even stopped using my name; referring to me only as The Boy. I was not allowed to eat meals with the family, play with my brothers, or watch television. I was grounded to the house. I was not allowed to look at or speak to anybody. When I returned to the house from school, I immediately accomplished the various chores Mother assigned me. When the chores were finished, I went directly to the basement, where I stood until summoned to clean off the dinner table and wash the dishes. It was made very clear that getting caught sitting or lying down in the basement would bring dire consequences. I had become Mother's slave.

Father was my only hope, and he did all he could to sneak me scraps of food. He tried to get Mother drunk, thinking the liquor might leave her in a better mood. He tried to get Mother to change her mind about feeding me. He even attempted to make deals, promising her the world. But all his attempts were useless. Mother was as solid as a rock. If anything, her drunkenness made it worse. Mother became more like a monster.

I knew Father's efforts to help me led to stress between he and Mother. Soon, midnight arguments began to occur. From my bed I could hear the tempo build to an ear-shattering climax. By then they were both drunk, and I could hear Mother scream every vulgar phrase imaginable. It didn't matter what issue started the fight, I would soon be the object of their battle. I knew Father was trying to help, but in bed I still shivered with fear. I knew he would lose, making things worse for me the next day. When they first began to fight, Mother would storm off in the car with the tires screeching. She usually returned home in less than an hour. The next day, they would both act as if nothing had happened. I was grateful when Father found an excuse to come down to the basement and sneak me a piece of bread. He always promised me he would keep trying.

As the arguments between Mother and Father became more frequent, he began to change. Often after an argument, he would pack an overnight bag and set off in the middle of the night for work. After he left, Mother would yank me out of bed and drag me to the kitchen. While I stood shivering in my pyjamas, she'd smack me from one side of the kitchen to the other. One of my resistance techniques was to lay on the floor acting as though I didn't have the strength to stand. That tactic didn't last long. Mother would yank me up by the ears and yell into my face with her bourbon breath, for minutes at a time. On these nights, her message was always the same: I was the reason she and Father were having problems. Often I became so tired, my legs would shake. My only escape was to stare at the floor and hope that Mother would soon run out of steam.

By the time I was in the second grade, Mother was pregnant with her fourth child. My teacher, Miss Moss, began to take a special interest in me. She began by questioning me about my attentiveness. I lied, saying I had stayed up late watching television. My lies were not convincing, and she continued to pry not only about why I was sleepy, but also about the condition of my clothes and the bruises on my body. Mother always coached me on what to say about my appearance, so I simply passed Mother's story to the teacher.

Months crept by and Miss Moss became more persistent. One day, she finally reported her concerns to the school principal. He knew me well as the food thief, so he called Mother. When I returned to the house that day, it was as if somebody had dropped an atomic bomb. Mother was more violent than ever. She was furious that some 'hippie' teacher had turned her in for child abuse. Mother said that she would meet with the principal the very next day to justify all the false accusations. By the end of the session, my nose bled twice and I was missing a tooth.

When I returned from school the next afternoon, Mother smiled as if she had won a million-dollar sweepstake. She told me how she had dressed up to see the principal, with her infant son Russell in her arms. Mother told me how she had explained to the principal how David had an overactive imagination. Mother told him how David had often struck and scratched himself to get attention, since the recent birth of his new brother Russell. I could imagine her turning on her snake-like charm as she cuddled Russell for the benefit of the principal. At the end of their talk, Mother said that she was more than happy to cooperate with the school. She said they could call her any time there was a problem with David. Mother said the staff at school had been instructed to pay no attention to my wild stories of child beating or not being fed. Standing there in the kitchen that day, listening to her boast, gave me a feeling of total emptiness. As Mother told me about the meeting, I could sense her heightened confidence, and her new confidence made me fear for my life. I wished I could dissolve and be gone forever. I wished I would never have to face another human being again.

That summer, the family vacationed at the Russian River. Although I got along better with Mother, the magical feeling had disappeared. The hayrides, the weenie roasts and story telling were things of the past. We spent more and more time in the cabin. Even the day trips to Johnson's Beach were rare.

Father tried to make the vacation more fun by taking the three of us to play on the new super slide. Russell, who was still a toddler, stayed in the cabin with Mother. One day, when Ron, Stan and I were playing at a neighbor's cabin, Mother came out onto the porch and yelled for us to come in immediately. Once in the cabin, I was scolded for making too much noise. For my punishment, I was not allowed to go with Father and my brothers to the super slide. I sat on a chair in a corner, shivering, hoping that something would happen so the three of them wouldn't leave. I knew Mother had something hideous on her mind. As soon as they left, she brought out one of Russell's soiled diapers. She smeared the diaper on my face. I tried to sit perfectly still. I knew if I moved, it would only be worse. I didn't look up. I couldn't see Mother standing over me, but I could hear her heavy breathing.

After what seemed like an hour, Mother knelt down beside me and in a soft voice said, 'Eat it.'

I looked straight ahead, avoiding her eyes. *No way!* I said to myself. Like so many times before, avoiding her was the wrong thing to do. Mother smacked me from side to side. I clung to the chair, fearing if I fell off she would jump on me.

'I said eat it!' she sneered.

Switching tactics, I began to cry. *Slow her down*, I thought to myself. I began to count to myself, trying to concentrate. Time was my only ally. Mother answered my crying with more blows to my face, stopping only when she heard Russell crying.

Even with my face covered with defecation, I was pleased. I thought I might win. I tried to wipe the shit away, flicking it onto the wooden floor. I could hear Mother singing softly to Russell, and I imagined him cradled in her arms. I prayed he wouldn't fall asleep. A few minutes later my luck ran out.

Still smiling, Mother returned to her conquest. She grabbed me by the back of the neck and led me to the kitchen. There, spread out on the countertop, was another full diaper. The smell turned my stomach. 'Now, you are going to eat it!' she said. Mother had the same look in her eyes that she had the day she wanted me to lie on top of the gas stove back at the house. Without moving my head, I moved my eyes, searching for the daisy-colored clock that I knew was on the wall. A few seconds later, I realized the clock was behind me. Without the clock, I felt helpless. I knew I needed to lock my concentration on something, in order to keep any kind of control of the situation. Before I could find the clock, Mother's hands seized my neck. Again she repeated, 'Eat it!' I held my breath. The smell was overpowering. I tried to focus on the top corner of the diaper. Seconds seemed like hours. Mother must have known my plan. She slammed my face into the diaper and rubbed it from side to side.

I anticipated her move. As I felt my head being forced down, I closed my eyes tightly and clamped my mouth shut. My nose struck first. A warm sensation oozed from my nostrils. I tried to stop the blood from escaping by breathing in. I snorted bits of defecation back up my nose with the blood. I threw my hands on the countertop and tried to pull myself out of her grip. I twisted from side to side with all my strength, but she was too powerful. Suddenly Mother let go. 'They're back! They're back!' she gasped. Mother snatched a wash cloth from the sink and threw it at me. 'Clean the shit off your face,' she bellowed as she wiped the brown stains from the countertop. I wiped my face as best I could, but not before blowing bits of defecation from my nose. Moments later, Mother stuffed a piece of napkin up my bloody nose and ordered me to sit in the corner. I sat there for the rest of the evening, still smelling traces of the diaper through my nose.

The family never returned to the Russian River again.

In September I returned to school with last year's clothes and my old, rusted, green lunch pail. I was a walking disgrace. Mother packed the same lunch for me every day: two peanut butter sandwiches and a few limp carrot sticks. Since I was no longer a member of the family, I was not allowed to ride to school in the family station wagon. Mother had me run to school. She knew I would not arrive in time to steal any food from my classmates.

At school I was a total outcast. No other kid would have anything to do with me. During the lunch recesses, I stuffed the sandwiches down my throat as I listened to my former friends make up songs about me. 'David the Food Thief' and 'Pelzer-Smellzer' were two of the playground favorites. I had no one to talk to or play with. I felt all alone.

At the house, while standing for hours in the garage, I passed the time by imagining new ways to feed myself. Father occasionally tried to sneak scraps of food to me, but with little success. I came to believe if I were to survive, *I* would have to rely on myself. I had exhausted all possibilities at school. All the students now hid their lunch pails, or locked them in the coat closet of the classroom. The teachers and principal knew me and watched me carefully. I had little to no chance of stealing any more food at school.

Finally I devised a plan that might work. Students were not allowed to leave the playground during lunch recess, so nobody would expect me to leave. My idea was to sneak away from the playground and run to the local grocery store, and steal cookies, bread, chips or whatever I could. In my mind, I planned every step of my scheme. When I ran to school the next morning, I counted every step so I could calculate my pace and later apply it to my trip to the store. After a few weeks, I had all the information I needed. The only thing left was finding the courage to attempt the plan. I knew it would take longer to go from the school to the store because it was up a hill, so I allowed fifteen minutes. Coming back downhill would be easier, so I allowed ten minutes. This meant I had only ten minutes at the store.

Each day when I ran to and from school, I tried to run faster, pounding each step as if I were a marathon runner. As the days passed and my plan became more solid, my hunger for food was replaced with daydreaming. I fantasized whenever performing my chores at the house. On my hands and knees while scrubbing the bathroom tiles, I imagined I was the Prince in the story 'The Prince and the Pauper'. As the Prince, I knew I could end the charade of acting like a servant any time I wanted. In the basement, I stood perfectly still with my eyes closed, dreaming I was a comic-book hero. But my daydream was always interrupted by hunger pangs, and my thoughts soon returned to my plan of stealing food.

Even when I was sure my plan was foolproof, I was too afraid to put it into action. During the lunch recess at school, I strolled around the playground making excuses to myself for my lack of guts to run to the store. I told myself I would get caught or that my timing calculations were not accurate. All through the argument with myself, my stomach growled, calling me a 'chicken'. Finally, after several days without dinner and only the small leftover portions for breakfast, I decided to do it. A few moments after the lunch bell rang, I blitzed up the street, away from the school, with my heart pounding and my lungs bursting for air. I made it to the store in half the time I allowed myself. Walking up and down the aisles of the store, I felt as if everybody was staring at me. I felt as though all the customers were talking about the smelly, ragged child. It was then that I knew my plan was doomed because I had not taken into account how I might look to other people. The more I worried about my appearance, the more my stomach became seized with fear. I froze in the aisle, not knowing what to do. I slowly began to count the seconds away. I began to think about all the times I had been starving. Suddenly without thinking, I grabbed the first thing I saw on the shelf, ran out of the store and raced back to school. Clutched tightly in my hand was my prize – a box of graham crackers.

As I came near the school I hid my possession under my shirt, on the side that didn't have any holes, as I walked through the schoolyard. Inside, I ditched the food in the garbage can of the boys' restroom. Later that afternoon, after making an excuse to the teacher, I returned to the restroom to devour my prize. I could feel my mouth begin to water, but my heart sank as I looked into an empty trash can. All my careful plans and all the pain of convincing myself that I would eat, were wasted. The custodian had emptied the trash can before I could slip away to the restroom.

That day my plan failed, but on other attempts I was lucky. Once, I managed to hide my treasure in my desk in homeroom, only to find on the next day that I had been transferred to the school across the street. Except for losing the stolen food, I welcomed the transfer. Now, I felt I had a new license to steal. Not only was I able to snitch food from my classmates again, but I also sprinted to the grocery store about once a week. Sometimes at the grocery store, if I felt things weren't just right, I didn't steal anything. As always, I finally got caught. The manager called Mother. At the house, I was thrashed relentlessly. Mother knew why I stole food and so did Dad, but she still refused to feed me. The more I craved food, the more I tried to come up with a better plan to steal it.

After dinner, it was Mother's habit to scrape the leftovers from the dinner plates into a small garbage can. Then she would summon me up from the basement, where I had been standing while the family ate. It was my function to wash the dishes. Standing there with my hands in the scalding water, I could smell the scraps from dinner in the small garbage can. At first my idea was nauseating, but the more I thought about it, the better it seemed. It was my only hope for food. I finished the dishes as fast as I could and emptied the garbage in the garage. My mouth watered at the sight of the food, and I gingerly picked the good pieces out while scraping bits of paper or cigarette butts away, and gobbled the food as fast as I could.

As usual, my new plan came to an abrupt halt when Mother caught me in the act. For a few weeks I quit the garbage routine, but I finally had to return to it, in order to silence my growling stomach. Once I ate some leftover pork. Hours later I was bent over in extreme pain. I had diarrhea for a week. While I was sick, Mother informed me she had purposefully left the meat in the refrigerator for two weeks, to spoil before she threw it away. She knew I couldn't resist stealing it. As time progressed, Mother had me bring the garbage can to her so she could inspect it while she lay on the couch. She never knew that I wrapped food between paper towels and hid them in the bottom of the can. I knew she wouldn't want to get her fingers dirty, digging in the bottom of the trash can, so my scheme worked for a while.

Mother sensed I was getting food some way, so she began sprinkling ammonia in the trash can. After that, I gave up on the garbage at the house and focused my sights on finding some other way to get food at school. After getting caught stealing from other kids' lunches, my next idea was to rip off frozen lunches from the school cafeteria.

I timed my restroom break so that the teacher excused me from the classroom just after the delivery truck dropped off its supply of frozen lunches. I crept into the cafeteria and snatched a few frozen trays, then I scurried to the restroom. Alone in the restroom, I swallowed the frozen hot dogs and tater tots in huge chunks so fast I almost choked myself in the process. After filling my stomach I returned to the classroom, feeling so proud *I* had fed myself.

As I ran to the house from school that afternoon, all I could think about was stealing food from the cafeteria the next day. Minutes later Mother changed my mind. She dragged me into the bathroom and slugged me in the stomach so hard that I bent over. Pulling me around to face the toilet, she ordered me to shove my finger down my throat. I resisted. I tried my old trick of counting to myself, as I stared into the porcelain toilet bowl, 'One . . . two . . .' I never made it to three. Mother rammed her finger into my mouth, as if she wanted to pull my stomach up through my throat. I squirmed in every direction in an effort to fight her. She finally let me go, but only when I agreed that I would vomit for her.

I knew what was going to happen next. I closed my eyes as chunks of red meat spilled into the toilet. Mother just stood behind me, with her hands on her hips and said, 'I thought so. Your Father's going to hear about this!' I tensed myself for the volley of blows that I knew was coming, but nothing happened. After a few seconds I spun around to discover that Mother had left the bathroom. I knew the episode wasn't over. Moments later she returned with a small bowl, ordered me to scoop the partially digested food out of the toilet and put it in the bowl. Since Father was away shopping at the time, Mother was gathering evidence for his return.

Later that night, after I finished all of my evening chores, Mother had me stand by the kitchen table while she and Father talked in the bedroom. In front of me was the bowl of hot dogs that I had vomited. I couldn't look at it, so I closed my eyes and tried to imagine myself far away from the house. A short time later Mother and Father stormed into the kitchen. 'Look at this, Steve,' Mother barked, thrusting her finger in the direction of the bowl. 'So you think The Boy is through stealing food, do you?'

By the look on Father's face, I could tell he was getting more and more tired of the constant 'What has The Boy done now' routine. Staring at me, he shook his head in disapproval and stammered, 'Well, Roerva, if you would just let The Boy have *something* to eat.'

A heated battle of words broke out in front of me, and as always, Mother won. 'EAT? You want The Boy to eat, Stephen? Well, The Boy is going to EAT! He can eat this!' Mother yelled at the top of her lungs, shoving the bowl towards me and stomping off to the bedroom.

The kitchen became so quiet I could hear Father's strained breathing. He gently placed his hand on my shoulder and said, 'Wait here, Tiger. I'll see what I can do.' He returned a few minutes later, after trying to talk Mother out of her demand. By the saddened look on his face, I knew immediately who had won.

I sat on a chair and picked the clumps of hot dogs out of the bowl with my hand. Globs of thick saliva slipped through my fingers, as I dropped it in my mouth. As I tried to swallow, I began to whimper. I turned to Father, who stood looking through me with a drink in his hand. He nodded for me to continue. I couldn't believe he just stood there as I ate the revolting contents of the bowl. At that moment I knew we were slipping further and further apart.

I tried to swallow without tasting, until I felt a hand clamp on the back of my neck. 'Chew it!' Mother snarled, 'Eat it! Eat it all!' she said, pointing to the saliva. I sat deeper in my chair. A river of tears rolled down my cheeks. After I had chewed the mess in the bowl, I tilted my head back and forced what remained, down my throat. I closed my eyes and screamed to myself to keep it from coming back up into my mouth. I didn't open my eyes until I was sure my stomach wasn't going to reject my cafeteria meal. When I did open them, I stared at Father who turned away to avoid my pain. At that moment I hated Mother to no end, but I hated Father even more. The man who had helped me in the past, just stood like a statue while his son ate something even a dog wouldn't touch.

After I finished the bowl of regurgitated hot dogs, Mother returned in her robe and threw a wad of newspapers at me. She informed me the papers were my blankets, and the floor under the table was now my bed. Again I shot a glance at Father, but he acted as though I was not even in the room. Forcing myself not to cry in front of them, I crawled, completely dressed, under the table, and covered myself with the newspapers, like a rat in a cage.

For months I slept under the breakfast table next to a box of kitty litter, but I soon learned to use the newspapers to my advantage. With the papers wrapped around me, my body heat kept me warm. Finally Mother told me that I was no longer privileged enough to sleep upstairs, so I was banished downstairs to the garage. My bed was now an old army cot. To stay warm, I tried to keep my head close to the gas heater. But after a few cold nights I found it best to keep my hands clamped under my arms and feet curled towards my buttocks. Sometimes at night I would wake up and try to imagine I was a real person, sleeping under a warm electric blanket, knowing I was safe and that somebody loved me. My imagination worked for a while, but the cold nights always brought me back to my reality. I knew no one could help me. Not my teachers, my so-called brothers or even Father. I was on my own, and every night I prayed to God that I could be strong both in body and soul. In the darkness of the garage, I laid on the wooden cot and shivered until I fell into a restless sleep.

Once, during my midnight fantasies, I came up with the idea of begging for food on my way to school. Even though the after-school vomit inspection was carried out every day when I returned to the house from school, I thought that any food I ate in the morning would be digested by the afternoon. As I began my run to school, I made sure I ran extra fast so I would have more time for my hunt for food. I then altered my course – stopping and knocking on doors. I would ask the lady who answered if she happened to find a lunch box near her house. For the most part, my plan worked. I could tell by looking at these ladies that they felt sorry for me. Thinking ahead, I used a fake name so nobody would know who I really was. For weeks my plan worked, until one day when I came to the house of a lady who knew Mother. My time-tested story, 'I lost my lunch. Could you make me one?' fell apart. Even before I left her house, I knew she would call Mother.

That day at school I prayed for the world to end. As I fidgeted in the classroom, I knew Mother was lying on the couch, watching television and getting more drunk by the hour, while thinking of something hideous to do to me when I arrived at *her* house after school. Running to the house from school that afternoon, my feet felt as though they were encased in blocks of cement. With every step I prayed that Mother's friend had not called her, or had somehow mistaken me for another kid. Above me the skies were blue, and I could feel the sun's rays warm my back. As I approached Mother's house, I looked up towards the sun, wondering if I would ever see it again. I carefully cracked the front door open before slipping inside, and tiptoed down the stairs to the garage. I expected Mother to fly down the stairs and beat me on the cement floor any second. She didn't come. After changing into my work clothes, I crept upstairs to the kitchen and began washing Mother's lunch dishes. Not knowing where she might be, my ears became radar antennae, seeking out her exact location. As I washed the dishes, my back became tense with fear. My hands shook, and I couldn't concentrate on my chores. Finally, I heard Mother come out of her bedroom and walk down the hall towards the kitchen. For a fleeting moment I looked out of the window. I could hear the laughter and screams of the children playing. For a moment I closed my eyes and imagined I was one of them. I felt warm inside. I smiled.

My heart skipped a beat when I felt Mother breathing down my neck. Startled, I dropped a dish, but before it could hit the floor I snatched it out of the air. 'You're a quick little shit, aren't you?' she sneered. 'You can run fast and find time to beg for food. Well . . . we'll just see how fast you really are.' Expecting Mother to bash me, I tensed my body, waiting for her to strike. When it didn't happen, I thought she would leave and return to her TV show, but that didn't happen either. Mother remained inches behind me, watching my every move. I could see her reflection in the kitchen window. Mother saw it too, and smiled back. I nearly peed my pants.

When I finished the dishes, I began cleaning the bathroom. Mother sat on the toilet as I scoured the bathtub. While I was on my hands and knees scrubbing the tile floor, she calmly and quietly stood behind me. I expected her to come around and kick me in the face, but she didn't. As I continued my chores, my anxiety grew. I knew Mother was going to beat me, but I didn't know how, when or where. It seemed to take forever for me to finish the bathroom. By the time I did, my legs and arms were shaking with anticipation. I could not concentrate on anything but her. Whenever I found the courage to look up at Mother, she smiled and said, 'Faster, young man. You'll have to move much faster than that.'

By dinner-time, I was exhausted with fear. I almost fell asleep as I waited for Mother to summon me to clear the table and wash the evening dishes. Standing alone downstairs in the garage, my insides became unglued. I so badly wanted to run upstairs and go to the bathroom, but I knew without Mother's permission to move, I was a prisoner. *Maybe that is what she has planned for me*, I told myself. *Maybe she wants me to drink my own pee.* At first the thought was too crude to imagine, but I knew *I* had to be prepared to deal with anything Mother might throw at me. The more I tried to focus on my options of what she might do to me, the more my inner strength drained away. Then an idea flashed in my brain; I knew why Mother had followed every step I took. She wanted to maintain a constant pressure on me, by leaving me unsure of when or where she would strike. Before I could think of a way to defeat her, Mother bellowed me upstairs. In the kitchen she told me that only the speed of light would save me, so I had better wash the dishes in record time. 'Of course,' she sneered, 'there's no need to tell you that you're going without dinner tonight, but not to worry, I have a cure for your hunger.'

After finishing the evening chores, Mother ordered me to wait downstairs. I stood with my back against the hard wall, wondering what plans she had for me. I had no idea. I broke out in a cold sweat that seemed to seep through to my bones. I became so tired I fell asleep while standing. When I felt my head roll forward, I snapped it upright, waking myself. No matter how hard I tried to stay awake, I couldn't control my head that bobbed up and down like a piece of cork in water. While in my trance-like state, I could feel the strain lift my soul away from my body, as if I too were floating. I felt as light as a feather until my head rolled forward again, jolting me awake. I knew better than to fall into a deep slumber. To get caught could be deadly, so I escaped by staring through the molded garage window, listening to the sounds of the cars driving by and watching the red flashes of planes flying overhead. From the bottom of my heart I wished that I could fly away.

Hours later after Ron and Stan had gone to bed, Mother ordered me to return upstairs. I dreaded every step. I knew the time had come. She had drained me emotionally and physically. I didn't know what she had planned. I simply wished Mother would beat me and get it over with.

As I opened the door, a calmness filled my soul. The house was dark except for a single light in the kitchen. I could see Mother sitting by the breakfast table. I stood completely still. She smiled, and I could tell by her slumped shoulders that the booze had her in a deep-six. In a strange way, I knew she wasn't going to beat me. My thoughts became cloudy, but my trance broke when Mother got up and strolled over to the kitchen sink. She knelt down, opened the sink cabinet and removed a bottle of ammonia. I didn't understand. She got a tablespoon and poured some ammonia into it. My brain was too rattled to think. As much as I wanted to, I could not get my numbed brain into gear.

With the spoon in her hand, Mother began to creep towards me. As some of the ammonia sloshed from the spoon, spilling onto the floor, I backed away from Mother until my head struck the counter-top by the stove. I almost laughed inside. *That's all? That's it? All she's going to do is have me swallow some of this?* I said to myself.

I wasn't afraid. I was too tired. All I could think was, *Come on, let's go. Let's get it over with.* As Mother bent down, she again told me that only speed would save me. I tried to understand her puzzle, but my mind was too cloudy.

Without hesitation I opened my mouth, and Mother rammed the cold spoon deep into my throat. Again I told myself this was all too easy, but a moment later I couldn't breathe. My throat seized. I stood wobbling in front of Mother, feeling as if my eyes were going to pop out of my skull. I fell on the floor, on my hands and knees. *Bubble!* my brain screamed. I pounded the kitchen floor with all my strength, trying to swallow, and trying to concentrate on the bubble of air stuck in my esophagus. Instantly I became terrified. Tears of panic streamed down my cheeks. After a few seconds I could feel the force of my pounding fists weaken. My fingernails scraped the floor. My eyes became fixed on the floor. The colors seemed to run together. I began to feel myself drift away. I knew I was going to die.

I came to my senses, and felt Mother slapping me on the back. The force of her blows made me burp, and I was able to breathe again. As I forced huge gulps of air back into my lungs, Mother returned to her glass of booze. She took a long drink, gazed down at me and blew a mist of air in my direction. 'Now, that wasn't so hard, was it?' Mother said, finishing her glass before dismissing me downstairs to my cot.

The next evening was a repeat performance, but this time in front of Father. She boasted to him, 'This will teach The Boy to quit stealing food!' I knew she was only doing it for her sick, perverted pleasure. Father stood lifeless as Mother fed me another dose of ammonia. But this time, I fought back. She had to pry my mouth open, and by thrashing my head from side to side, *I* was able to make her spill most of the cleaner onto the floor. But not enough. Again I clenched my fingers together, beating the floor. I looked up at Father, trying to call out to him. My thoughts were clear, but no sound escaped from my mouth. He simply stood above me, showing no emotion, as I pounded my hands by my feet. As if she were kneeling to pet one of her dogs, Mother again slapped me on the back a few times before I blacked out.

The next morning while cleaning the bathroom, I looked in the mirror to inspect my burning tongue. Layers of flesh were scraped away, while remaining parts were red and raw. I stood, staring into the sink, feeling how lucky I was to be alive.

Although Mother never made me swallow ammonia again, she did make me drink spoonfuls of Clorox a few times. But Mother's favorite 'game' seemed to be dishwashing soap. From the bottle she would squeeze the cheap, pink liquid down my throat and command that I stand in the garage. My mouth became so dry, I sneaked away to the garage faucet and filled my stomach full of water. Soon I discovered my dreadful mistake, and diarrhea took hold. I cried out to Mother upstairs, begging her to let me use the toilet upstairs. She refused. I stood downstairs, afraid to move, as clumps of the watery matter fell through my underwear and down my pant legs, onto the floor.

I felt so degraded; I cried like a baby. I had no self-respect of any kind. I needed to go to the bathroom again, but I was too afraid to move. Finally, as my insides twisted and turned, I gathered the last of my dignity. I waddled to the garage sink, grabbed a five-gallon bucket and squatted to relieve myself. I closed my eyes trying to think of a way to clean myself and my clothes when suddenly, the garage door opened behind me. I turned my head to see Father, looking on dispassionately, as his son 'mooned' him and as the brown seepage spilled into the bucket. I felt lower than a dog.

Mother didn't always win. Once, during a week when I was not allowed to attend school, she squeezed the soap into my mouth and told me to clean the kitchen. She didn't know it, but I refused to swallow the soap. As the minutes passed, my mouth became filled with a combination of soap and saliva. *I* would not allow myself to swallow. When I finished the kitchen chores, I raced downstairs to empty the trash. I smiled from ear to ear, as I closed the door behind me and spat out the mouthful of pink soap. At the trash cans by the garage door, I reached into one of the cans and plucked out a used paper towel, and wiped out the inside of my mouth ensuring that I removed every drop of soap. After I finished, I felt as though I had won the Olympic Marathon. I was so proud for beating Mother at her own game.

Even though Mother caught me in most of my attempts to feed myself, she couldn't catch me *all* of the time. After months of being confined for hours at a time in the garage, my courage took over and I stole bits of frozen food from the garage freezer. I was fully aware that I could pay for my crime at any time, so I ate every morsel as if it were my last meal.

In the darkness of the garage I closed my eyes, dreaming I was a king dressed in the finest robes, eating the best food mankind had to offer. As I held a piece of frozen pumpkin pie crust or a bit of a taco shell, *I* was the king, and like a king on his throne, I gazed down on my food and smiled.

chapter 5

THE ACCIDENT

The summer of 1971 set the tone for the remainder of the time that I lived with Mother.

I had not yet reached my eleventh birthday, but for the most part, I knew what forms of punishment to expect. To exceed one of Mother's time limits on any of my multiple chores, meant no food. If I looked at her or one of her sons without her permission, I received a slap in the face. If I was caught stealing food, I knew Mother would either repeat an old form of punishment or dream up something new and hideous. Most of the time Mother seemed to know exactly what she was doing, and I could anticipate what she might do next. However, I always kept my guard up and tensed my entire body if I thought she might come my way.

As June turned to early July, my morale dwindled. Food was little more than a fantasy. I rarely received even leftover breakfast, no matter how hard I worked, and I was *never* fed lunch. As for dinner, I averaged about one evening meal every three days.

One particular July day began like any other mundane day, in my now slave-like existence. I had not eaten in three days. Because school was out for the summer, my options for finding food vanished. As always during dinner, I sat at the bottom of the stairs with my buttocks on top of my hands, listening to the sounds of 'The Family' eating. Mother now demanded that I sit on my hands with my head thrust backward, in a 'prisoner of war' position. I let my head fall forward, half dreaming that I was one of them – a member of 'The Family'. I must have fallen asleep because I was suddenly awakened by Mother's snarling voice, 'Get up here! Move your ass!' she yelled.

At the first syllable of her order I snapped my head level, stood up and sprinted up the stairs. I prayed that tonight I would get something, anything, to soothe my hunger.

I had begun clearing the dishes from the dining-room table at a feverish pace, when Mother called me into the kitchen. I bowed my head as she began to babble her time limits to me. 'You have twenty minutes! One minute, one second more, and you go hungry again! Is that understood?'

'Yes, ma'am.'

'Look at me when I'm talking to you!' she snapped.

Obeying her command, I slowly raised my head. As my head came up, I saw Russell rocking back and forth on Mother's left leg. The harsh tone of Mother's voice didn't seem to bother him. He simply stared at me through a set of cold eyes. Even though Russell was only four or five years old at the time, he had become Mother's 'Little Nazi', watching my every move, making sure I didn't steal any food. Sometimes he would make up tales for Mother so he could watch me receive punishment. It really wasn't Russell's fault. I knew Mother had brainwashed him, but I had begun to turn cold towards him and hate him just the same.

'Do you hear me?' Mother yelled. 'Look at me when I'm talking to you!' As I looked at her, Mother snatched a carving knife from the countertop and screamed, 'if you don't finish on time, I'm going to kill you!'

Her words had no effect on me. She had said the same thing over and over again for almost a week now. Even Russell wasn't fazed by her threat. He kept rocking on Mother's leg as if he were riding a stick pony. She apparently wasn't pleased with her renewed tactic because she continued to badger on and on as the clock ticked away, eating up my time limit. I wished she would just shut up and let me work. I was desperate to meet her time limits. I wanted so much to have something to eat. I dreaded going to sleep another night without food.

Something looked wrong. Very wrong! I strained to focus my eyes on Mother. She had begun to wave the knife in her right hand. Again, I was not overly frightened. She had done this before too. *Eyes*, I told myself. *Look at her eyes.* I did, and they seemed normal for her – half glazed over. But my instincts told me there was something wrong. I didn't think she was going to hit me, but my body began to tense anyway. As I became more tense, I saw what was wrong. Partly because of Russell's rocking motion, and partly because of the motion of her arm and hand with the knife, Mother's whole body began to weave back and forth. For a moment I thought she was going to fall.

She tried to regain her balance, snapping at Russell to let go of her leg, while she continued to scream at me. By then, her upper body looked like a rocking chair that was out of control. Forgetting about her useless threats, I imagined that the old drunk was going to fall flat on her face. I focused all of my attention on Mother's face. Out of the corner of my eye I saw a blurred object fly from her hand. A sharp pain erupted from just above my stomach. I tried to remain standing, but my legs gave out, and my world turned black.

As I regained consciousness, I felt a warm sensation flowing from my chest. It took me a few seconds to realize where I was. I sat propped up on the toilet. I turned towards Russell who began chanting, 'David's going to die. The Boy's going to die.' I moved my eyes towards my stomach. On her knees, Mother was hastily applying a thick wad of gauze to a place on my stomach where dark red blood pumped out. I tried to say something. I knew it was an accident. I wanted Mother to know that I forgave her, but I felt too faint to speak. My head slumped forward again and again, as I tried to hold it up. I lost track of time as I returned to darkness.

When I woke up, Mother was still on her knees wrapping a cloth around my lower chest. She knew exactly what she was doing. Many times when we were younger, Mother told Ron, Stan and I how she had intended to become a nurse, until she met Father. Whenever she was confronted with an accident around the home, she was in complete control. I never doubted her nursing abilities for a second. I simply waited for her to load me in the car and take me to the hospital. I felt sure that she would. It was just a matter of time. I felt a curious sense of relief. I knew in my heart it was over. This whole charade of living like a slave had come to an end. Even Mother could not lie about this one. I felt the accident had set me free.

It took Mother nearly half an hour to dress my wound. There was no remorse in her eyes. I thought that, at the very least, she would try to comfort me with her soothing voice. Looking at me with no emotion, Mother stood up, washed her hands and told me I now had thirty minutes to finish the dishes. I shook my head, trying to understand what she had said. After a few seconds, Mother's message sunk in. Just as in the arm incident a few years ago, Mother was not going to acknowledge what had happened.

I had no time for self-pity. The clock was running. I stood up, wobbled for a few seconds, then made my way to the kitchen. With every step, pain ripped through my ribs and blood seeped through my ragged T-shirt. By the time I reached the kitchen sink, I leaned over and panted like an old dog.

From the kitchen I could hear Father in the living-room, flipping through his newspaper. I took a painfully deep breath, hoping that I could shove off and make my way to Dad. But I breathed too hard, and fell to the floor. After that I realized I had to take short, choppy breaths. I made my way into the living-room. Sitting on the far end of the couch was my hero. I knew he would take care of Mother and drive me to the hospital. I stood before Father, waiting for him to turn his page and see me. When he did, I stuttered, 'Father . . . Mo . . . Mo . . . Mother stabbed me.'

He didn't even raise an eyebrow. 'Why?' he asked.

'She told me if I didn't do the dishes on time . . . she'd kill me.'

Time stood still. From behind the paper I could hear Father's labored breathing. He cleared his throat before saying, 'Well . . . you ah . . . you better go back in there and do the dishes.' My head leaned forward as if to catch his words. I couldn't believe what I had just heard. Father must have sensed my confusion when I saw him snap his paper and heard him raise his voice saying, 'Jesus H. Christ! Does Mother know that you're here talking to me? You better go back in there, and do the dishes. Damn it, boy, we don't need to do anything that might make her more upset! I don't need to go through that tonight . . .' Father stopped for a second, took a deep breath and lowered his voice, whispering, 'I tell you what; you go back in there and do the dishes. I won't even tell her that you told, okay? This will be *our* little secret. Just go back in the kitchen and do the dishes. Go on now, before she catches the both of us. Go!'

I stood before Father in total shock. He didn't even look at me. Somehow I felt if he could at least turn a corner flap of the paper and search into my eyes, he would know; he would feel my pain, how desperate I was for his help. But, as always, I knew that Mother controlled him like she controlled everything that happened in her house. I think Father and I both knew the code of The Family – if we don't acknowledge a problem, it simply does not exist. As I stood before Father, not knowing what to do next, I looked down and saw droplets of blood staining the family's carpet. I had felt in my heart that he would scoop me up in his arms and take me away. I even imagined him ripping off his shirt to expose his true identity, before flying through the air like Superman.

I turned away. All my respect for Father was gone. The savior I had imagined for so long was a phony. I felt more angry at him than I did at Mother. I wished that somehow I could fly away, but the throbbing pain brought me back to reality.

I washed the dishes as fast as my body would let me. I quickly learned that moving my forearm resulted in a sharp pain above my stomach. If I sidestepped from the wash basin to the rise basin, another pain raced through my body. I could feel what little strength I had, draining away. As Mother's time limit passed, so did my chances of getting fed.

I wanted to just lie down and quit, but the promise I made years ago kept me going. I wanted to show The Bitch that she could beat me only if I died, and I was determined not to give in, even to death. As I washed the dishes, I learned that by standing on my toes and leaning my upper body towards the countertop, I could relieve some of the pressure on my lower chest. Instead of sidestepping every few seconds, I washed a few dishes at a time, then moved over and rinsed them all together. After drying the dishes, I dreaded the task of putting them away. The cupboards were above my head, and I knew reaching for them would cause great pain. Holding a small plate, I stretched my legs as far as I could and tried to raise my arms above my head to put the dish away. I almost made it, but the pain was too great. I crumbled to the floor.

By now my shirt was saturated with blood. As I tried to regain my footing, I felt Father's strong hands helping me. I brushed him away. 'Give me the dishes,' he said. 'I'll put them away. You better go downstairs and change that shirt.' I didn't say a word as I turned away. I looked at the clock. It had taken me nearly an hour and a half to complete my chore. My right hand clamped tightly onto the railing, as I slowly made my way downstairs. I could actually see the blood seep from my T-shirt with every step I took.

Mother met me at the bottom of the stairs. As she tore the shirt from my body, I could see Mother was doing it as gently as she could, however, she gave me no other comfort. I could see it was just a matter of business to her. In the past, I had seen her treat animals with more compassion than she did me.

I was so weak that I accidentally fell against her as she dressed me in an old, oversized T-shirt. I expected Mother to hit me, but she allowed me to rest against her for a few seconds. Then Mother set me at the bottom of the stairs and left. A few minutes later Mother returned with a glass of water. I gulped it down as fast as I could swallow. When I finished, Mother told me that she couldn't feed me right away. She said she would feed me in a few hours when I felt better. Again her voice was monotone – completely without emotion.

Stealing a glance, I could see the California twilight being overtaken by darkness. Mother told me I could play outside with the boys, on the driveway in front of the garage door. My head was not clear. It took me a few seconds to understand what she had said. 'Go on, David. Go,' she persisted. With Mother's help, I limped out of the garage to the driveway. My brothers casually looked me over, but they were much more interested in lighting their Fourth-of-July sparklers. As the minutes passed, Mother became more compassionate towards me. She held me by the shoulders as we watched my brothers make figure eights with their sparklers. 'Would you like one?' Mother asked. I nodded yes. She held my hand as she knelt down to light the sparkler. For a moment I imagined the scent of the perfume Mother wore years ago. But she had not used perfume or made up her face for a long time.

As I played with my brothers, I couldn't help but think about Mother and the change in the way she was treating me. *Is she trying to make up with me?* I wondered. *Are my days living in the basement finally over? Am I back in the family fold?* For a few minutes I didn't care. My brothers seemed to accept my presence, and I felt a feeling of friendship and warmth with them that I thought had been buried forever.

Within a few seconds my sparkler fizzled out. I turned towards the retreating sun. It had been forever since I had watched a sunset. I closed my eyes, trying to soak up as much heat as I could. For a few fleeting moments my pain, my hunger and my miserable way of life disappeared. I felt so warm, so alive. I opened my eyes, hoping to capture the moment for the rest of eternity.

Before she went to bed, Mother gave me more water and fed me some small bites of food. I felt like a disabled animal being nursed back to health, but I didn't care.

Downstairs in the garage I laid on my old army cot. I tried not to think of the pain, but it was impossible to ignore as it crept throughout my body. Finally exhaustion took over and I drifted off to sleep. During the night I had several nightmares. I startled myself, waking up in a cold sweat. Behind me I heard a sound that scared me. It was Mother. She bent down and applied a cold wash cloth to my forehead. She told me that I had been running a fever during the night. I was too tired and weak to respond. All I could think about was the pain. Later, Mother returned to my brothers' downstairs bedroom, which was closer to the garage. I felt safe knowing she was nearby to watch over me.

Soon I drifted back into darkness, and with the fitful sleep came a dreadful dream of sheets of red, hot rain. In the dream I seemed to drench in it. I tried wiping the blood off my body only to find it quickly covered again. When I awoke the next morning, I stared at my hands which were crusted with dried blood. The shirt covering my chest was entirely red. I could feel the dried blood on parts of my face. I heard the bedroom door behind me open, and I turned to see Mother walking towards me. I expected more sympathy like she had given me the night before, but it was an empty hope. She gave me nothing. In a cold voice, Mother told me to clean myself up and begin my chores. As I heard her march up the stairs, I knew nothing had changed. I was still the bastard of the family.

About three days after the 'accident', I continued to feel feverish. I didn't dare ask Mother for even an aspirin, especially since Father was away at work. I knew she was back to her normal self. I thought the fever was due to my injury. The slit in my stomach had opened up more than once since that night. Quietly, so Mother wouldn't hear me, I crept to the garage sink. I picked up the cleanest rag I could find in my heap of rags. I cracked the water faucet open just enough to let a few drops of water spill onto the rag. Then I sat down and rolled up my red, soggy shirt. I touched my wound, flinching from the pain. I took a deep breath and as gently as possible, pinched the slit. The pain was so bad I threw my head back against the cold concrete floor, almost knocking myself out. When I looked at my stomach again, I saw a yellowish-white substance begin to ooze from the red, angry slash. I didn't know much about such things, but I knew it was infected. I started to get up to go upstairs and ask Mother to clean me up. When I was half-standing, I stopped. *No!* I told myself. *I don't need that bitch's help.* I knew enough about basic first-aid training to clean a wound, so I felt confident that I could do it alone. I wanted to be in charge of myself. I didn't want to rely on Mother or give her any more control over me than she already had.

I wet the rag again and brought it down towards my wound. I hesitated before I touched it. My hands were shaking with fear, as tears streamed down my face. I felt like a baby and hated it. Finally I told myself, *You cry, you die. Now, take care of the wound.* I realized that my injury probably wasn't life-threatening; I brainwashed myself to block out the pain.

I moved quickly before my motivation slipped away. I snatched another rag, rolled it up and stuffed it into my mouth. I focused all my attention on the thumb and first finger of my left hand, as I pinched the skin around my slit. With my other hand I wiped away the pus. I repeated the process until blood seeped through, and I was wiping away only blood. Most of the white stuff was gone. The pain from the pinching and wiping was more than I could stand. With my teeth clamped tightly on the rag, my screaming was muffled. I felt as though I was hanging from a cliff. By the time I finished, a river of tears soaked the neck of my shirt.

Fearing Mother would catch me not sitting at the bottom of the stairs, I cleaned up my mess then half-walked, half-crawled to my assigned place at the foot of the staircase. Before I sat on my hands, I checked my shirt; only small drops of blood escaped from the wound to the rag bandage. I willed the wound to heal. Somehow I knew it would. I felt proud of myself. I imagined myself like a character in a comic book, who overcame great odds and survived. Soon my head slumped forward and I fell asleep. In my dream, I flew through the air in vivid colors. I wore a cape of red . . . I was Superman.

chapter 6

WHILE FATHER IS AWAY

After the knife incident, Father spent less and less time at home and more at work. He made excuses to the family, but I didn't believe him. I often shivered with fear as I sat in the garage, hoping for some reason he might not leave. In spite of all that had happened, I still felt Father was my protector. When he was home, Mother only did about half the things to me that she did when he was gone.

When Father was home, it became his habit to help me with the evening dishes. Father washed and I dried. While we worked, we talked softly so neither Mother nor the other boys could hear us. Sometimes several minutes would pass without us talking. We wanted to make sure the coast was clear.

Father always broke the ice. 'How ya doin', Tiger?' he would say.

Hearing the old name that Father used when I was a little boy, always brought a smile to my face. 'I'm okay,' I would answer.

'Did you have anything to eat today?' he often asked. I usually shook my head in a negative gesture.

'Don't worry,' he'd say. 'Some day you and I will both get out of this madhouse.'

I knew Father hated living at home, and I felt that it was all my fault. I told him that I would be good and that I wouldn't steal food any more. I told Father I would try harder and do a better job on my chores. When I said these things, he always smiled and assured me that it wasn't my fault.

Sometimes as I dried the dishes, I felt a new ray of hope. I knew Father probably wouldn't do anything against Mother, but when I stood beside him I felt safe.

Like all good things that happened to me, Mother put an end to Father helping me with the dishes. She insisted that The Boy needed no help. She said that Father paid too much attention to me and not enough to others in the family. Without a fight, Father

52

gave up. Mother now had complete control over everybody in the household.

After a while, Father didn't even stay home on his days off. He would come in for only a few minutes. After seeing my brothers, he would find me wherever I was doing my chores and say a few sentences, then leave. It took Father no more than ten minutes to get in and out of the house, and be on his way back to his solitude, which he usually found in a bar. When Father talked to me, he'd tell me that he was making plans for the two of us to leave. This always made me smile, but deep inside I knew it was a fantasy.

One day he knelt down to tell me how sorry he was. I looked into his face. The change in Father frightened me. He had dark black circles around his eyes, and his face and neck were beet red. Father's once rigid shoulders were now slumped over. Gray had begun to take over his jet-black hair. Before he left that day, I threw my arms around his waist. I didn't know when I would see him again.

After finishing my chores that day, I rushed downstairs. I had been ordered to wash my ragged clothes and another heap of smelly rags. But that day, Father's leaving had left me so sad that I buried myself in the pile of rags and cried. I cried for him to come back and take me away. After a few minutes of self-comfort, I settled down and began scrubbing my 'Swiss-cheese' clothes. I scrubbed until my knuckles bled. I no longer cared about my existence. Mother's house had become unbearable. I wished I could somehow manage to escape the place I now called the 'Madhouse'.

During one period of time when Father was away, Mother starved me for about ten consecutive days. No matter how hard I tried to meet her time limits, I couldn't make it. And the consequence was no food. Mother was completely thorough in making sure I was unable to steal any food. She cleared the dinner table herself, putting the food down the garbage disposal. She rummaged through the garbage can every day before I emptied it downstairs. She locked the freezer in the garage with her key and kept it. I was used to going without food for periods up to three days, but this extended time was unbearable. Water was my only means of survival. When I filled the metal ice-cube tray from the refrigerator, I would tip the corner of the tray to my mouth. Downstairs I would creep to the wash basin and crack the faucet tap open. Praying that the pipe would not vibrate and alert Mother, I would carefully suck on the cold metal until my stomach was so full I thought it would burst.

By the sixth day I was so weak when I woke up on my army cot, I could hardly get up. I worked on my chores at a snail's pace. I felt so numb. My thought responses became unclear. It seemed to take minutes for me to understand each sentence Mother yelled to me. As I slowly strained my head up to look at Mother, I could tell that to her it was a game – a game which she thoroughly enjoyed.

'Oh, poor little baby,' Mother sarcastically cooed. Then she asked me how I felt, and laughed when I begged for food. At the end of the sixth day, and those that followed, I hoped with all my heart that Mother would feed me something, anything. I was at a point that I didn't care what it was.

One evening, towards the end of her 'game', after I had finished my chores, Mother slammed a plate of food in front of me. The cold leftovers were a feast to my eyes. But I was wary; it seemed too good to be true. 'Two minutes!' Mother barked. 'You have two minutes to eat. That's all.' Like lightening I picked up the fork, but the moment before the food touched my mouth, Mother snatched the plate away from me and emptied the food down the garbage disposal. 'Too late!' she sneered.

I stood before her dumbstruck. I didn't know what to do or say. All I could think of was *Why?* I couldn't understand why she treated me the way she did. I was so close that I could smell every morsel. I knew she wanted me to cave in, but I stood fast and held back the tears.

Alone in the garage, I felt I was losing control of everything. I craved food. I wanted my father. But more than anything, I wanted just an ounce of respect; one little bit of dignity. Sitting there on my hands, I could hear my brothers opening the refrigerator to get their desserts, and I hated it. I looked at myself. My skin had a yellowish tint, and my muscles were thin and stringy. Whenever I heard one of my brothers laugh at a television show, I cursed their names. *Lucky bastards! Why doesn't she take turns and beat up on one of them for a change?* I cried to myself as I vented my feelings of hatred.

For nearly ten days I had gone without food. I had just finished the dinner dishes when Mother repeated her 'you have two minutes to eat' game. There were only a few bits of food on the plate. I felt she would snatch the plate away again, so I moved with a purpose. I didn't give Mother a chance to snatch it away like she had the past three evenings. So I grabbed the plate and quickly swallowed the food without chewing it. Within seconds I finished eating all that was on the plate and licked it clean. 'You eat like a pig!' Mother snarled. I bowed my head, acting as though I cared. But inside I laughed at her, saying to myself, *Fuck you! Say what you want! I got the food!*

Mother had another favorite game for me while Father was away. She sent me to clean the bathroom with her usual time limits. But this time, she put a bucket, filled with a mixture of ammonia and Clorox, in the room with me and closed the door. The first time she did this, Mother informed me she had read about it in a newspaper and wanted to try it. Even though I acted as if I were frightened, I really wasn't. I was ignorant about what was going to happen. Only when Mother closed the door and ordered me not to open it, did I begin to worry. With the room sealed, the air began to quickly change. In the corner of the bathroom I dropped to my hands and knees and stared at the bucket. A fine gray mist swirled towards the ceiling. As I breathed in the fumes, I collapsed and began spitting up. My throat felt like it was on fire. Within minutes it was raw. The gas from the reaction of the ammonia and Clorox mixture made my eyes water. I was frantic about not being able to meet Mother's time limits for cleaning the bathroom.

After a few more minutes, I thought I would cough up my insides. I knew that Mother wasn't going to give in and open the door. To survive her new game, I had to use my head. Laying on the tiled floor I stretched my body, and using my foot, I slid the bucket to the door. I did this for two reasons: I wanted the bucket as far away from me as possible, and in case Mother opened the door, I wanted her to get a snoot full of her own medicine. I curled up in the opposite corner of the bathroom, with my cleaning rag over my mouth, nose and eyes. Before covering my face, I wet the rag in the toilet. I didn't dare turn on the water in the sink for fear of Mother hearing it. Breathing through the cloth, I watched the mist inch its way closer and closer to the floor. I felt as if I were locked in a gas chamber. Then I thought about the small heating vent on the floor by my feet. I knew it turned on and off every few minutes. I put my face next to the vent and sucked in all the air my lungs would hold. In about half an hour, Mother opened the door and told me to empty the bucket into the drain in the garage before I smelled up *her* house. Downstairs I coughed up blood for over an hour. Of all Mother's punishments, I hated the gas chamber game the most.

Towards the end of the summer Mother must have become bored with finding ways to torture me around the house. One day, after I had completed all my morning chores, she sent me out to mow lawns. This wasn't an altogether new routine. During the Easter vacation from school the spring before, Mother had sent me out to mow. She had set a quota on my earnings and ordered me to return the money to her. The quota was impossible for me to meet, so, in desperation, I once stole nine dollars from the piggy bank of a small girl who lived in our neighborhood. Within hours, the girl's father was knocking on the front door. Of course, Mother returned the money and blamed me. After the man left, she beat me until I was black and blue. I only stole the money to try to meet her quota.

The summer mowing plan turned out no better for me than the one during Easter vacation. Going from door to door, I asked people if they cared to have their lawns mowed. No one did. My ragged clothes and my thin arms must have made me a pathetic sight. Out of sympathy, one lady gave me a lunch in a brown bag and set me on my way. Half a block down the street a couple agreed to have me mow their lawn. When I finished, I started running back to Mother's house, carrying the brown bag with me. I intended to hide it before I turned onto her block. I didn't make it. Mother was out cruising in her car, and she pulled over and caught me with the bag. Before Mother screeched the station wagon to a stop, I threw my hands into the air, as if I were a criminal. I remember wishing that lady luck would be with me just one time.

Mother leaped out of the car, snatched the brown bag in one hand and punched me with the other. She then threw me into the car, and drove to the house where the lady had made the lunch for me. The woman wasn't home. Mother was convinced that I had sneaked into the lady's house and prepared my own lunch. I knew that to be in the possession of food was the ultimate crime. Silently I yelled at myself for not ditching the food earlier.

Once home, the usual 'ten-rounder' left me sprawled on the floor. Mother then told me to sit outside in the backyard while she took 'her sons' to the zoo. The section where Mother ordered me to sit was covered with rocks about an inch in diameter. I lost circulation in much of my body, as I sat on my hands in my 'prisoner of war' position. I began to give up on God. I felt that He must have hated me. *What other reason could there be for a life like mine?* All my efforts for mere survival seemed futile. My attempts to stay one step ahead of Mother were useless. A black shadow was always over me.

Even the sun seemed to avoid me, as it hid in a thick cloud cover that drifted overhead. I slumped my shoulders, retreating into the solitude of my dreams, I don't know how much time had passed, but later I could hear the distinctive sound of Mother's station wagon returning into the garage. My time sitting on the rocks was over. I wondered what Mother had planned for me next. I prayed it was not another gas chamber session. She yelled from the garage for me to follow her upstairs. She led me to the bathroom. My heart sank. I felt doomed. I began taking huge breaths of fresh air, knowing that soon I would need it.

To my surprise there wasn't any bucket or bottles in the bathroom. *Am I off the hook?* I asked myself. This looked too easy. I timidly watched Mother as she turned the cold water tap in the bathtub fully open. I thought it was odd that she forgot to turn on the hot water as well. As the tub began to fill with cold water, Mother tore off my clothes and ordered me to get into the tub. I got into the tub and laid down. A cold fear raced throughout my body. 'Lower!' Mother yelled. 'Put your face in the water like this!' She then bent over, grabbed my neck with both hands and shoved my head under the water. Instinctively I thrashed and kicked, trying desperately to force my head above the water so I could breathe. Her grip was too strong. Under the water I opened my eyes. I could see bubbles escape from my mouth and float to the surface as I tried to shout. I tried to thrust my head from side to side as I saw the bubbles becoming smaller and smaller. I began to feel weak. In a frantic effort I reached up and grabbed her shoulders. My fingers must have dug into her because Mother let go. She looked down on me, trying to get her breath. 'Now keep your head below the water, or next time it will be longer!'

I submerged my head, keeping my nostrils barely above the surface of the water. I felt like an alligator in a swamp. When Mother left the bathroom, her plan became more clear to me. As I laid stretched out in the tub, the water became unbearably cold. It was as though I was in a refrigerator. I was too frightened of Mother to move, so I kept my head under the surface as ordered.

Hours passed and my skin began to wrinkle. I didn't dare touch any part of my body to try to warm it. I did raise my head out of the water, far enough to hear better. Whenever I heard somebody walk down the hall outside the bathroom, I quietly slid my head back into the coldness.

Usually the footsteps I heard were one of my brothers going to their bedroom. Sometimes one of them came into the bathroom to use the toilet. They just glared at me, shook their heads and turned away. I tried to imagine I was in some other place, but I could not relax enough to daydream.

Before the family sat down for dinner, Mother came into the bathroom and yelled at me, telling me to get out of the bathtub and put on my clothes. I responded immediately, grabbing a towel to dry myself. 'Oh, no!' she screamed. 'Put your clothes on the way you are!' Without hesitating, I obeyed her command. My clothes were soaked as I ran downstairs to sit in the backyard as instructed. The sun had begun to set, but half the yard was still in direct sunlight. I tried to sit in a sunny area, but Mother ordered me into the shade. In the corner of the backyard, while sitting in my 'prisoner of war' position, I shivered. I wanted only a few seconds of heat, but with every passing minute my chances of drying off were becoming less and less. From the upstairs window I could hear the sound of The Family passing dishes full of food to each other. Once in a while a burst of laughter would escape through the window. Since Father was home, I knew that whatever Mother had cooked was good. I wanted to turn my head and look up to see them eating, but I didn't dare. I lived in a different world. I didn't even deserve a glance at the good life.

The bathtub and the backyard treatment soon became routine. At times when I laid in the tub, my brothers brought their friends to the bathroom to look at their naked brother. Their friends often scoffed at me. 'What did *he* do *this* time?' they'd ask. Most of the time my brothers just shook their heads, saying, 'I don't know.'

With the start of school in the fall, came the hope of a temporary escape from my dreary life. Our fourth-grade homeroom class had a substitute teacher for the first two weeks. They told us that our regular teacher was ill. The substitute teacher was younger than most of the other staff, and she seemed more lenient. At the end of the first week she passed out ice cream to those students whose behavior had been good. I didn't get any the first week, but I tried harder and received my reward at the end of the second week. The new teacher played 'pop hits' on forty-five-rpm records, and sang to the class. We really liked her. When Friday afternoon came, I didn't want to leave. After all the other students had gone, she bent close to me and told me I would have to go home. She knew I was a problem child. I told her that I wanted to stay with her. She held me for a moment, then got up and played the song I liked best. After that I left. Since I was late, I ran to the house as fast as I could and raced through my chores. When I was finished, Mother sent me to the backyard to sit on the cold cement deck.

That Friday I looked up at the thick blanket of fog covering the sun, and cried inside. The substitute teacher had been so nice to me. She treated me like a real person, not like some piece of filth lying in the gutter. As I sat outside feeling sorry for myself, I wondered where she was and what she was doing. I didn't understand it at the time, but I had a crush on her.

I knew that I wasn't going to be fed that night, or the next. Since Father wasn't home, I would have a bad weekend. Sitting in the cool air in the backyard, on the steps, I could hear the sounds of Mother feeding my brothers. I didn't care. Closing my eyes, I could see the smiling face of my new teacher. That night, as I sat outside shivering, her beauty and kindness kept me warm.

By October my morbid life was in full swing. Food was scarce at school. I was easy prey for school bullies, who beat me up at will. After school I had to run to the house and spill the contents of my stomach for Mother's inspection. Sometimes she would have me start my chores right away. Sometimes she would fill the bathtub with water. If she was *really* in a good mood, she fixed up the gas mixture for me in the bathroom. If she got tired of having me around her house, she sent me out to find some mowing jobs, but not before beating me. A few times she whipped me with the dog's chain. It was very painful, but I just gritted my teeth and took it. The worst pain was a blow to the backs of my legs with the broom handle. Sometimes blows from the broom handle would leave me on the floor, barely able to move. More than once I hobbled down the street, pushing that old wooden lawn mower, trying to earn *her* some money.

There finally came a time when it didn't do me any good for Father to be home because Mother had forbidden him to see me. My hope deteriorated and I began to believe that my life would never change. I thought I would be Mother's slave for as long as I lived. With every passing day, my willpower became weaker. I no longer dreamed of Superman or some imaginary hero who would come and rescue me. I knew that Father's promise to take me away was a hoax. I gave up praying and thought only of living my life one day at a time.

One morning at school I was told to report to the school nurse. She questioned me about my clothes and the various bruises that spanned the length of both my arms. At first I told her what Mother had instructed me to tell her. But as my trust in her began to grow, I told her more and more about Mother. She took notes and told me I should come to see her anytime I wanted to talk to somebody. I learned later that the nurse became interested in me because of some reports she had received from the substitute teacher, earlier in the school year.

During the last week in October it was tradition at Mother's house for the boys to carve designs on pumpkins. I had been denied this privilege since I was seven or eight years old. When the night came to carve the pumpkins, Mother filled the tub just as soon as I had finished my chores. Again she warned me about keeping my head under the water. As a reminder she grabbed my neck and pushed my head under the water. Then she stormed out of the bathroom, turning the light out as she went. Looking to my left, I could see through the small bathroom window that night was beginning to fall. I passed the time by counting to myself. I started at one and stopped at one thousand. Then I started over. As the hours passed, I could feel the water slowly draining away. As the water drained, my body became colder and colder. I cupped my hands between my legs and laid the length of my body against the right side of the bathtub. I could hear the sounds of Stan's Halloween record that Mother had bought for him several years before. Ghosts and ghouls howled, and doors creaked open. After the boys had carved their pumpkins, I could hear Mother in her soothing voice telling them a scary story. The more I heard, the more I hated each and every one of them. It was bad enough waiting like a dog out in the backyard on the rocks while they enjoyed dinner, but having to lay in the cold bathtub, shivering to keep warm while they ate popcorn and listened to Mother's tales made me want to scream.

Mother's tone of voice that night reminded me of the kind of Mommy I had loved so many years ago. Now even the boys refused to acknowledge my presence in the house. I meant less to them than the spirits that howled from Stan's record. After the boys went to bed, Mother came into the bathroom. She appeared startled to see me still laying in the bathtub. 'Are you cold?' she sneered. I shivered and shook my head indicating that I was very cold. 'Well, why doesn't my precious little boy get his ass out of the bathtub and warm his hide in his father's bed?'

I stumbled out of the tub, put on my underwear and crawled into Father's bed, soaking the sheets with my wet body. For reasons I didn't understand Mother had decided to have me sleep in the master bedroom, whether Father was home or not. She slept in the upstairs bedroom with my brothers. I didn't really care as long as I didn't have to sleep on the army cot in the cold garage. That night Father came home, but before I could say anything to him, I fell asleep.

By Christmas my spirit was drained. I detested being home during the two-week vacation and impatiently awaited my return to school. On Christmas Day I received a pair of roller skates. I was surprised to get anything at all, but as it turned out, the skates were not a gift given in the spirit of Christmas. The skates proved to be just another tool for Mother to get me out of the house and make me suffer. On weekends Mother made me skate outside when the other children were inside because of the chilly weather. I skated up and down the block, without even a jacket to keep me warm. I was the only child outside in the neighborhood. More than once Tony, one of our neighbors, stepped outside to get his afternoon newspaper and saw me skating. He'd give me a cheerful smile before scurrying back inside to get away from the cold. In an effort to keep warm, I skated as fast as I could. I could see smoke rising from the chimneys of houses that had fireplaces. I wished that I could be inside, sitting by a fire. Mother had me skate for hours at a time. She called me in only when she wanted me to complete some chores for her.

At the end of March that year Mother went into labor while we were home from school on Easter vacation. As Father drove her to a hospital in San Francisco, I prayed that it was the real thing and not false labor. I wanted Mother out of the house so badly. I knew that with her gone, Father would feed me. I was also happy to be free from the beatings.

While Mother was in the hospital, Father let me play with my brothers. I was immediately accepted back into the fold. We played 'Star Trek', and Ron gave me the honor of playing the role of Captain Kirk. The first day Father served sandwiches for lunch and let me have seconds. When Father went to the hospital to see Mother, the four of us played across the street at the home of a neighbor named Shirley. Shirley was kind to us and treated us as though we were her own children. She kept us entertained with games like ping-pong, or just let us run wild outside. In some ways Shirley reminded me of Mom, in the early days before she started beating me.

In a few days Mother came home. She presented the family with a new baby brother named Kevin. After a few weeks had passed, things returned to normal. Father stayed away most of the time, and I continued to be the scapegoat upon which Mother vented her frustrations.

Mother rarely spent much time with neighbors, so it was not natural for her when she and Shirley became close friends. They visited each other daily. In Shirley's presence Mother played the role of the loving, caring parent – just as she had when she was a Cub Scout den mother. After several months, Shirley asked Mother why David was not allowed to play with the other children. She was also curious why David was punished so often. Mother had a variety of excuses. David either had a cold or he was working on a school project. Eventually, she told Shirley that David was a bad boy and deserved being grounded for a long, long time.

In time the relationship between Shirley and Mother became strained. One day, for no apparent reason, Mother broke all ties with Shirley. Shirley's son was not allowed to play with the boys, and Mother ran around the house calling her a bitch. Even though I wasn't allowed to play with the others, I felt a little safer when Shirley and Mother were friends.

One Sunday during the last month of summer Mother came into the master bedroom where I had been ordered to sit on my hands in my 'prisoner of war' position. She asked me to get up and sit on the corner of the bed. She then told me that she was tired of the life we were living. She told me she was sorry and that she wanted to make up for all the lost time. I smiled from ear to ear, as I jumped into her arms and held her tightly. As she ran her hand through my hair, I began to cry. Mother cried, too, and I began to feel that my bad times were finished. I let go of our hug and looked into Mother's eyes. I had to know for sure. I had to hear her say it again. 'Is it really over?' I asked timidly.

'It's over, sweetheart. After this moment, I want you to forget any of it happened at all. You will try to be a good boy, won't you?'

I nodded my head.

'Then I'll try to be a good mother.'

After making up, Mom let me take a warm bath and put on the new clothes I had received last Christmas. I had not been allowed to wear them before. Mom then took my brothers and I bowling while Father stayed home with Kevin. On the way home from the bowling alley, Mom stopped at a grocery store and bought each of us a toy top. When we got home, Mom said I could play outside with the other boys, but I took the top to the corner of the master bedroom and played by myself. For the first time in years, with the exception of holidays when we had guests in the house, I ate with my family at the dinner table. Things were happening too fast, and I felt that somehow it was too good to be true. As happy as I was, I felt as though I were walking on eggshells. I thought for sure Mother would wake up and change back to her old self. But she didn't. I ate all I wanted for dinner, and she let me watch television with my brothers before we went to bed. I thought it was strange that she wanted me to continue to sleep with Father, but she said she wanted to be near the baby.

The next day, while Father was at work, a lady from social services came to our house in the afternoon. Mom shooed me outside to play with my brothers, while she talked to the lady. They talked for more than an hour. Before the lady left, Mom called me into our house. The lady wanted to talk to me for a few minutes. She wanted to know if I was happy. I told her I was. She wanted to know if I got along all right with my mom. I told her I did. Finally, she asked me if Mom ever beat me. Before answering, I looked up at Mother, who smiled politely. I felt as though a bomb had exploded deep in the pit of my stomach. I thought I would throw up. It had suddenly occurred to me why Mother had changed the day before; why she had been so nice to me. I felt like a fool because I had fallen for it. I was so hungry for love that I had swallowed the whole charade.

Mother's hand on my shoulder brought me back to reality. 'Well, tell her, sweetheart,' Mother said, smiling again. 'Tell her that I starve you and beat you like a dog,' Mother snickered, trying to get the lady to laugh too.

I looked at the lady. My face felt flushed, and I could feel the beads of sweat forming on my forehead. I didn't have the guts to tell the lady the truth. 'No, it's not like that at all,' I said. 'Mom treats me pretty good.'

'And she never beats you?' the lady asked.

'No . . . uh . . . I mean, only when I get punished . . . when I'm a bad boy,' I said, trying to cover up the truth. I could tell by the look Mother gave me that I had said the wrong thing. She had brainwashed me for years, and I had said it badly. I could also tell that the lady had picked up on the communication between Mother and I.

'All right,' the lady said. 'I just wanted to stop in and say hello.' After saying goodbye, Mother walked her visitor to the door.

When the lady was clearly gone, Mother closed the door in a rage. 'You little shit!' she screamed. I instinctively covered my face as she began swinging. She hit me several times, then banished me to the garage. After she had fed her boys, she called me up to do my evening chores. As I washed the dishes, I didn't feel all that bad. Deep in my heart I had known Mother was being nice to me for some reason other than wanting to love me. I should have known she didn't mean it, because she acted the same way when somebody like Grandma came over for the holidays. At least I had enjoyed two good days. I hadn't had two good days for a long time, so in an odd way it was worth it. I settled back into my routine and relied on my solitude to keep me going. At least I didn't have to walk on eggshells anymore, wondering when the roof was going to cave in on me. Things were back to normal, and I was the servant for the family again.

Even though I had begun to accept my fate, I never felt as alone, as I did on the mornings that Father went to work. He got out of bed at about 5:00 A.M. on work days. He didn't know it, but I was always awake, too. I'd listen to him shaving in the bathroom, and I would hear him walking to the kitchen to get something to eat. I knew that when he put on his shoes, he was about ready to leave the house. Sometimes I turned over just in time to see him pick up his dark blue Pam Am overnight bag. He'd kiss me on the forehead and say, 'Try to make her happy and stay out of her way.'

I tried not to cry, but I always did. I didn't want him to leave. I never told him, but I am sure he knew. After he closed the front door, I counted the steps that it took him to get to the driveway. I heard him walking on the pathway from the house. In my mind, I could see him turning left down the block to catch the bus to San Francisco. Sometimes, when I felt brave, I hopped out of bed and ran to the window so I could catch a glimpse of Father. I usually stayed in bed and rolled over to the warm place where he had slept. I imagined that I could hear him long after he was gone. And when I accepted the fact that he was truly gone, I had a cold, hollow feeling deep in my soul. I loved my Father so much. I wanted to be with him forever, and I cried inside because I never knew when I was going to see Father again.

chapter 7

THE LORD'S PRAYER

About a month before I entered the fifth grade, I came to believe that for me, there was no God.

As I sat alone in the garage, or read to myself in the near darkness of my parents' bedroom, I came to realize that I would live like this for the remainder of my life. No *just* God would leave me like this. I believed that I was alone in my struggle and that my battle was one of survival.

By the time I had decided that there was no God, I had totally disconnected myself from all physical pain. Whenever Mother struck me, it was as if she were taking her aggressions out on a rag doll. Inside my emotions swirled back and forth between fear and intense anger. But outside I was a robot, rarely revealing my emotions; only when I thought it would please The Bitch and work to my advantage. I held in my tears, refusing to cry because I didn't want to give *her* the satisfaction of my defeat.

At night I no longer dreamed, nor did I let my imagination work during the day. The once vibrant escapes of watching myself fly through the clouds in bright blue costumes, were now a thing of the past. When I fell asleep, my soul became consumed in a black void. I no longer awoke in the mornings refreshed; I was tired and told myself that I had one day less to live in this world. I shuffled through my chores, dreading every moment of every day. With no dreams, I found that words like *hope* and *faith* were only letters, randomly put together into something meaningless – words only for fairy tales.

When I *was* given the luxury of food, I ate like a homeless dog; grunting like an animal at Mother's commands. I no longer cared when she made fun of me, as I hurried to devour even the smallest morsel. Nothing was below me. One Saturday while I was washing the morning dishes, Mother scraped some half-eaten pancakes from a plate into the dogs' dish. Her well-fed pets picked at the food until they wanted no more, then walked away to find a place to sleep. Later, as I put away some pots and pans in a lower cabinet, I crawled on my hands and knees to the dogs' dish and ate what was left of the pancakes. As I ate, I could smell traces of the dogs, but I ate anyway. It hardly bothered me. I fully realized that if The Bitch caught me eating what rightfully belonged to the dogs, I would pay dearly; but getting food any way I could was my only means of existing.

Inside my soul became so cold I hated everything. I even despised the sun, for I knew I would never be able to play in its warm presence. I cringed with hate whenever I heard other children laughing, as they played outside. My stomach coiled whenever I smelled food that was about to be served to somebody else, knowing it was not for me. I wanted so much to strike out at something every time I was called upstairs to play the role of the family slave, by picking up after those slobs.

I hated Mother most and wished that she were dead. But before she died, I wanted her to feel the magnitude of my pain and my loneliness for all these years. During all the years when I had prayed to God, He answered me only once. One day, when I was five or six years old, Mother had thrashed me from one end of the house to the other. That night before getting into bed, I got down on my knees and prayed to God. I asked Him to make Mother sick so she couldn't hit me any more. I prayed long and hard, concentrating so much that I went to bed with a headache. The next morning, much to my surprise, Mother was sick. She lay on the couch all day, barely moving. Since Father was at work, my brothers and I took care of her as though she were a patient of ours.

As the years passed and the beatings became more intense, I thought about Mother's age and tried to calculate when she might die. I longed for the day when *her* soul would be taken into the depths of hell; only then would I be free of her.

I also hated Father. He was fully aware of the hell I lived in, but he lacked the courage to rescue me as he had promised so many times in the past. But as I examined my relationship with Father, I realized that he considered me part of the problem. I believe he thought of me as a traitor. Many times when The Bitch and Father had heated arguments, Mother involved me. She would yank me from wherever I was and demand that I repeat every vile word Father might have used in their past arguments. I fully realized what her game was, but having to choose between them was not difficult. Mother's wrath was much worse for me. I always shook my head, timidly saying what she wanted to hear. She would then scream for me to repeat the words to her in Dad's presence. Much of the time she insisted that I make up the words if I couldn't remember. This bothered me a great deal because I knew that in an effort to avoid a beating, I was biting the hand that often fed me. In the beginning I tried to explain to Father why I had lied and turned against him. At first he told me that he understood, but eventually I knew he had lost faith in me. Instead of feeling sorry for him, I only hated him more.

The boys who lived upstairs were no longer my brothers. Sometimes in years past, they had managed to encourage me a little. But in the summer of 1972 they took turns hitting me and appeared to enjoy throwing their weight around. It was obvious that they felt superior to the family slave. When they approached me, my heart became hard as stone, and I am sure they saw the hate etched in my face. In a rare and empty victory, I'd sneer the word '*asshole*' under my breath as one of them strutted by me. I made sure they didn't hear me. I came to despise the neighbors, my relatives and anybody else who had ever known me and the conditions under which I lived. Hate was all I had left.

At the core of my soul I hated myself more than anybody or anything. I came to believe that everything that happened to me or around me was my own fault because I had let it go on for so long. I wanted what others had, but saw no way to get it, so I hated them for having it. I wanted to be strong, but inside I knew I was a wimp. I never had the courage to stand up to The Bitch, so I knew I deserved whatever happened to me. For years, Mother had brainwashed me by having me shout aloud, 'I hate myself! I hate myself!' Her efforts paid off. A few weeks before I started the fifth grade, I hated myself so much that I wished I were dead.

School no longer held the exciting appeal that it had years ago. I struggled to concentrate on my work while in class, but my bottled-up anger often flashed at the wrong times. One Friday afternoon in the winter of 1973, for no apparent reason, I stormed out of the classroom, screaming at everyone as I fled. I slammed the door so hard I thought the glass above the door would shatter. I ran to the bathroom, and with my tiny red fist I pounded the tiles until my strength drained away. Afterwards I collapsed on the floor praying for a miracle. It never came.

Time spent outside the classroom was only better than Mother's 'hell house'. Because I was an outcast of the entire school, my class-mates at times took over where Mother left off. One of them was Clifford, a school-yard bully who would periodically catch me when I ran to Mother's house after school. Beating me up was Clifford's way of showing off to his friends. All I could do was fall to the ground and cover my head, while Clifford and his gang took turns kicking me.

Aggie was a tormentor of a different sort. She never failed to come up with new and different ways of telling me how much she wished I would simply 'drop dead'. Her style was absolute snobbery. Aggie made sure she was always the one in charge of a small band of girls. In addition to tormenting me, showing off their fancy clothes seemed to be the main purpose in life for Aggie and her clique. I had always known Aggie didn't like me, but I really didn't learn how much until the last day of school in our fourth-grade year. Aggie's mother taught my fourth-grade homeroom, and on the last day of school Aggie came into our room acting as though she were throw-ing up and said, 'David Pelzer-Smellzer is going to be in my home-room next year.' Her day was not complete until she fired off a rude remark about me to her friends.

I didn't take Aggie very seriously; not until a fifth-grade field trip to one of San Francisco's Clipper Ships. As I stood alone on the bow of the ship, looking at the water, Aggie approached me with a vicious smile and said in a low voice, 'Jump!' She startled me, and I looked into her face, trying to understand what she meant. Again she spoke, quietly and calmly, 'I said you should go ahead and jump. I know all about you, Pelzer, and jumping is your only way out.'

Another voice came from behind her, 'She's right, you know.' The voice belonged to John, another classmate, one of Aggie's macho buddies. Looking back over the railing, I stared at the cold green water lapping against the wooden side of the ship. For a moment, I could visualize myself plunging into the water, knowing I would drown. It was a comforting thought that promised an escape from Aggie, her friends and all that I hated in the world. But my better senses returned, and I looked up and fixed my eyes directly on John's eyes and tried to hold my stare. After a few moments, he must have felt my anger because he turned away taking Aggie with him.

At the beginning of my fifth-grade year, Mr Ziegler, my homeroom teacher, had no idea why I was such a problem child. Later, after the school nurse had informed him why I had stolen food and why I dressed the way I did, Mr Ziegler made a special effort to treat me as if I were a normal kid. One of his jobs as sponsor of the school newspaper was to form a committee of kids to find a name for the paper. I came up with a catchy phrase, and a week later my entry was among others in a school-wide election to select the best name for the newspaper. My title won by a landslide. Later that day the voting took place, and Mr Ziegler took me aside and told me how proud he was that my title had won. I soaked it up like a sponge. I hadn't been told anything positive for so long that I nearly cried. At the end of the day, after assuring me that I wasn't in trouble, Mr Ziegler gave me a letter to take to Mother.

Elated, I ran to Mother's house faster than ever before. As I should have expected, my happiness was short-lived. The Bitch tore the letter open, read it quickly and scoffed, 'Well, Mr Ziegler says I should be so proud of you for naming the school newspaper. He also claims that you are one of the top pupils in his class. Well, aren't you special?' Suddenly, her voice turned ice cold and she jabbed her finger at my face and hissed, 'Get one thing straight, you little son of a bitch! There is nothing you can do to impress me! Do you understand me? You are a *nobody*! An *It*! You are nonexistent! You are a bastard child! I hate you and I wish you were dead! *Dead!* Do you hear me? *Dead!*'

After tearing the letter into tiny pieces, Mother turned away from me and returned to her television show. I stood motionless, gazing at the letter which lay like snowflakes at my feet. Even though I had heard the same words over and over again, this time the word '*It*' stunned me like never before. She had stripped me of my very existence. I gave all that I could to accomplish anything positive for *her* recognition. But again I failed. My heart sank lower than ever before. Mother's words were no longer coming from the booze; they were coming from her heart. I would have been relieved if she had returned with a knife and ended it all.

I knelt down, trying to put the many pieces of the letter back together again. It was impossible. I dumped the pieces of the letter in the trash, wishing my life would end. I truly believed, at that moment, that death would be better than my prospects for any kind of happiness. I was nothing but an '*It*'.

My morale had become so low that in some self-destructive way I hoped she would kill me, and I felt that eventually she would. In my mind it was just a matter of when she would do it. So I began to purposefully irritate her, hoping I could provoke her enough that she would end my misery. I began doing my chores in a careless manner. I made sure that I forgot to wipe the bathroom floor, hoping that Mother or one of her royal subjects might slip and fall, hurting themselves on the hard tile floor. When I washed the evening dishes, I left bits of food on the plates. I wanted The Bitch to know I didn't care anymore.

As my attitude began to change, I became more and more rebellious. A crisis erupted one day at the grocery store. Usually I stayed in the car, but for some reason Mother decided to take me inside. She ordered me to keep one hand clamped onto the cart and bend my head towards the floor. I deliberately disobeyed her every command. I knew she didn't want to make a scene in public, so I walked in front of the cart, making sure I was at least an arm's length away from her. If my brothers made any comments to me, I fired back at them. I simply told myself that I wasn't going to take anybody's crap anymore.

Mother knew that other shoppers were watching us and could hear us, so several times she gently took my arm and told me in a pleasant voice to settle down. I felt so alive knowing I had the upper hand in the store, but I also knew that once we were outside, I would pay the price. Just as I thought, Mother gave me a sound thrashing before we reached the station wagon. As soon as we were in the car, she ordered me to lie on the floor of the back seat, where her boys took turns stomping me with their feet for 'mouthing off' to them and Mother. Immediately after we entered the house, Mother made a special batch of ammonia and Clorox. She must have guessed I had been using the rag as a mask because she tossed the rag into the bucket. As soon as she slammed the bathroom door, I hurried to the heating vent. It didn't come on. No fresh air came through the vent. I must have been in the bathroom for over an hour because the gray fumes filled the small room all the way to the floor. My eyes filled with tears, which seemed to activate the poison even more. I spat mucus and heaved until I thought I would faint. When Mother finally opened the door, I bolted for the hallway, but her hand seized me by the neck. She tried to push my face into the bucket, but I fought back and she failed. My plan for rebellion also failed. After the longer gas chamber incident, I returned to my wimpy self, but deep inside I could still feel the pressure building like a volcano, waiting to erupt from deep inside my soul.

The only thing that kept me sane was my baby brother Kevin. He was a beautiful baby and I loved him. About three and a half months before he was born, Mother allowed me to watch a Christmas cartoon special. After the program, for reasons unclear to me, she ordered me to sit in my brothers' room. Minutes later she stormed into the room, wrapped her hands around my neck and began choking me. I twisted my head from side to side, trying to squirm away from her grip. As I began to feel faint, I instinctively kicked her legs, forcing her away from me. I soon regretted the incident.

About a month after Mother's attempt to choke me, she told me that I had kicked her so hard in the stomach that the baby would have a permanent birth defect. I felt like a murderer. Mother didn't stop with just telling me. She had several different versions of the incident for anybody who would listen. She said she had tried to hug me, and I had repeatedly either kicked or punched her in the stomach. She claimed that I had kicked her because I was jealous of the new baby. She said I was afraid the new baby would get more of her attention. I really loved Kevin, but since I was not allowed to even *look* at him or my brothers, I did not have a chance to show how I felt. I do remember one Saturday, when Mother took the other boys to a baseball game in Oakland, leaving Father to babysit with Kevin while I performed my chores. After I finished my work, Father let Kevin out of his crib. I enjoyed watching him crawl around in his cute outfit. I thought he was beautiful. When Kevin lifted his head and smiled at me, my heart melted. He made me forget my suffering for a while. His innocence was hypnotic as I followed him around the house; I wiped the drool from his mouth and stayed one step behind him so he wouldn't get hurt. Before Mother returned, I played a game of patty-cake with him. The sound of Kevin's laughter filled my heart with warmth, and later, whenever I felt depressed I thought of him. I smiled inside when I heard Kevin cry out in joy.

My brief encounter with Kevin quickly faded away and my hatred surfaced again. I fought to bury my feelings, but I couldn't. I knew I was never meant to be loved. I knew I would never live a life like my brothers. Worst of all, I knew that it was only a matter of time until Kevin would hate me, just like the others did.

Later that fall Mother began directing her frustrations in more directions. She despised me as much as ever, but she began to alienate her friends, husband, brother and even her own mother. Even as a small child, I knew that Mother didn't get along very well with her family. She felt that everybody was trying to tell her what to do. She never felt at ease, especially with her own mother who was also a strong-willed person. Grandmother usually offered to buy Mother a new dress or take her to the beauty parlor. Not only did Mother refuse the offers, but she also yelled and screamed until Grandmother left *her* house. Sometimes Grandmother tried to help me, but that only made things worse. Mother insisted that her appearance and the way she raised her family were 'nobody else's damn business'. After a few of these confrontations, Grandmother rarely visited Mother's house.

As the holiday season approached, Mother argued more and more with Grandmother on the telephone. She called her own mother every vicious name Mother could imagine. The trouble between Mother and Grandmother was bad for me because after their battle, I often became the object of Mother's anger. Once, from the basement, I heard Mother call my brothers into the kitchen and tell them that they no longer had a Grandmother or an Uncle Dan.

Mother was equally ruthless in her relationship with Father. When he did come home, either to visit or stay for a day, she started screaming at him the moment he walked through the door. As a result, he often came home drunk. In an effort to stay out of Mother's path, Father often spent his time doing odd jobs outside the house. He even caught her wrath at work. She often telephoned Father at the station and called him names. 'Worthless' and 'drunken loser' were two of her favorite names for him. After a few calls, the fireman who answered the phone would lay it down and not page Father. This made Mother furious, and again I became the object of her fury.

For a while Mother banned Father from the house, and the only time we saw him was when we drove to San Francisco to pick up his pay-check. One time, on our way to get the check, we drove through Golden Gate Park. Even though my anger was ever present, I flashed back to the good times when the park meant so much to the whole family. My brothers were also silent that day as we drove through the park. Everybody seemed to sense that somehow the park had lost its glamour, and that things would never be the same again. I think that perhaps my brothers felt the good times were over for them too.

For a short time Mother's attitude towards Father changed. One Sunday Mother piled everybody into the car, and shopped from store to store for a record of German songs. She wanted to create a special mood for Father when he came home. She spent most of that afternoon preparing a feast, with the same enthusiasm that had driven her years before. It took her hours to fix her hair and apply her makeup just right. Mother even put on a dress that brought back memories of the person she once was. I thought for sure that God had answered my prayers. As she paced around the house, straightening anything she thought was out of place, all I could think about was the food. I knew she would find it in her heart to let me eat with the family. It was an empty hope.

Time dragged on into the late afternoon. Father was expected to be home by about 1:00 P.M., and every time Mother heard an approaching car she dashed to the front door, waiting to greet him with open arms. Sometime after 4:00 P.M., Father came staggering in with a friend from work. The festive mood and setting were a surprise to him. From the bedroom I could hear Mother's strained voice as she tried to be extra patient with Father. A few minutes later Father stumbled into the bedroom. I looked up in wonder. I had never seen him so drunk. He didn't need to speak for me to smell the liquor on him. His eyes were beyond the bloodshot stage, and it appeared to be more of a problem than he could manage to stand upright and keep his eyes open. Even before he opened the closet door, I knew what he was going to do. I knew why he had come home. As he stuffed his blue overnight bag, I began to cry inside. I wanted to become small enough to jump into his bag and go with him.

When he finished packing, Father knelt down and mumbled something to me. The longer I looked at him, the weaker my legs felt. My mind was numb with questions. *Where's my hero? What happened to him?* As he opened the door to leave the bedroom, the drunk friend crashed into Father, nearly knocking him down. Father shook his head and said in a sad voice, 'I can't take it anymore. The whole thing. Your mother, this house, you. I just can't take it anymore.' Before he closed the bedroom door I could barely hear him mutter, 'I . . . I'm . . . I'm sorry.'

That year Thanksgiving dinner was a flop. In some kind of gesture of good faith, Mother allowed me to eat at the table with the family. I sat deep in my chair, quietly concentrating so I wouldn't say or do anything that might set Mother off. I could feel the tension between my parents. They hardly spoke at all, and my brothers chewed their food in silence. Dinner was hardly over when harsh words erupted. After the fight ended, Father left. Mother reached into one of the cabinets for her bottled prize and seated herself at the end of the sofa. She sat alone, pouring glass after glass of alcohol. As I cleared the table and washed the dishes, I could see that this time I wasn't the only one affected by Mother's behavior. My brothers seemed to be experiencing the same fear I had for so many years.

For a short time Mother and Father tried to be civil to one another. But by Christmas Day they had both become tired of their charade. The strain of trying to be so nice to each other was more than either could bear. As I sat at the top of the stairs, while my brothers finished opening their gifts, I could hear angry words being exchanged between them. I prayed that they could somehow make up, if only for that special day. While sitting on the basement stairs that Christmas morning, I knew that if God had wanted Mother and Father to be happy, then I would have to be dead.

A few days later Mother packed Father's clothes in boxes, and drove with my brothers and I to a place a few blocks from the fire station. There, in front of a dingy motel, Father waited. His face seemed to express relief. My heart sank. After years of my useless prayers, I knew it had finally happened – my parents were separating. I closed my fists so tightly I thought my fingers would tear into the palms of my hands. While Mother and the boys went into Father's motel room, I sat in the car, cursing his name over and over. I hated him so much for running out on his family. But perhaps even more, I was jealous of him, for he had escaped and I had not. I still had to live with Mother. Before Mother drove the car away, Father leaned down to the open window where I was sitting, and handed me a package. It was some information he had said he would get me, for a book report that I was doing at school. I knew he was relieved to get away from Mother, but I could also see sadness in his eyes as we pulled away into the downtown traffic.

The drive back to Daly City was solemn. When my brothers spoke, they did so in soft tones that wouldn't upset Mother. When we reached the city limits, Mother tried to humor her boys by treating them to McDonald's. As usual I sat in the car while they went inside. I looked out of the open car window at the sky. A dull gray blanket covered everything, and I could feel the cold droplets of fog on my face. As I stared into the fog, I became terrified. I knew nothing could stop Mother now. What little hope I had was gone. I no longer had the will to carry on. I felt as if I were a man on death row, not knowing when my time would come.

I wanted to bolt from the car, but I was too scared to even move an inch. For this weakness, I hated myself. Rather than running, I clutched the package Father had given me and smelled it, trying to pick up a scent of Father's cologne.

When I failed to pick up any odor at all, I let out a sobbing cry. At that instant, I hated God more than anything else in this or any other world. God had known of my struggles for years, but He had stood by watching as things went from bad to worse. He wouldn't even grant me a trace of Father's Old Spice after shave. God had completely taken away my greatest hope. Inside I cursed His name, wishing I had never been born.

Outside I could hear the sounds of Mother and the boys approaching the car. I quickly wiped my tears and returned to the inner safety of my hardened shell. As Mother drove out of the McDonald's parking lot, she glanced back at me and sneered, 'You are all mine now. Too bad your father's not here to protect you.' I knew all my defenses were useless. I wasn't going to survive. I knew she was going to kill me, if not today, tomorrow. That day I wished Mother would have mercy and kill me quickly.

As my brothers wolfed down their hamburgers, without them knowing I clasped my hands together, bent my head down, closed my eyes and prayed with all my heart. When the station wagon turned onto the driveway, I felt that my time had come. Before I opened the car door, I bowed my head and with peace in my heart, I whispered, '. . . and deliver me from evil. Amen.'

EPILOGUE
Sonoma County, California

I'm so alive.

As I stand facing the beauty of the never-ending Pacific Ocean, a late afternoon breeze blows down from the hills behind. As always, it is a beautiful day. The sun is making its final descent. The magic is about to begin. The skies are ready to burn with brilliance, as it turns from a soft blue to a bright orange. Looking towards the west, I stare in awe at the hypnotic power of the waves. A giant curl begins to take form, then breaks with a thundering clap as it crashes on the shore. An invisible mist hits my face, moments before the white foamy water nearly drowns my feet. The bubbling foam quickly recedes to the power of the surf. Suddenly a piece of driftwood washes onto the shore. It has an odd, twisted shape. The wood is pitted, yet smoothed and bleached from its time in the sun. I bend down to pick it up. As my fingers begin to reach out, the water catches hold dragging the wood back out to sea. For a moment it looks as if the wood is struggling to stay ashore. It leaves a trail behind before reaching the waters, where it bobs violently before giving in to the ocean.

I marvel at the wood, thinking how it reminds me of my former life. My beginning was extremely turbulent, being pushed and pulled in every direction. The more grisly my situation became, the more I felt as if some immense power were sucking me into some giant undertow. I fought as hard as I could, but the cycle never seemed to end. Until suddenly, without warning, I broke free.

I'm so lucky. My dark past is behind me now. As bad as it was, I knew even back then, in the final analysis, my way of life would be up to me. I made a promise to myself that if I came out of my situation alive, I had to make something of myself. I would be the best person that I could be. Today I am. I made sure I let go of my past, accepting the fact that that part of my life was only a small fraction of my life. I knew the black hole was out there, waiting to suck me in and forever control my destiny – but only if I let it. I took positive control over my life.

I'm so blessed. The challenges of my past have made me immensely strong inside. I adapted quickly, learning how to survive from a bad situation. I learned the secret of internal motivation. My experience gave me a different outlook on life, that others may never know. I have a vast appreciation for things that others may take for granted. Along the way I made a few mistakes, but I was fortunate enough to bounce back. Instead of dwelling on the past, I maintained the same focus that I had taught myself years ago in the garage, knowing the good Lord was always over my shoulder, giving me quiet encouragement and strength when I needed it most.

My blessings also mean having the opportunity to meet so many people who had a positive impact on my life. The endless sea of faces, prodding me, teaching me to make the right choices, and helping me in my quest for success. They encouraged my hunger to prevail. Branching out on a different level, I enlisted in the United States Air Force, discovering historical values and an instilled sense of pride and belonging that until then, I had never known. After years of struggle, my purpose became clear; for above all, I came to realize that America was truly the land where one could come from less than humble beginnings, to become a winner from within.

An explosive pounding of the surf brings me back to reality. The piece of wood I've been watching, disappears into the swirling waters. Without further hesitation, I quickly turn away and head back towards my truck. Moments later, I race my Toyota through the snake-like turns driving to my secret utopia. Years ago when I lived in the dark, I used to dream about my secret place. Now, whenever I can get away, I always return to the river. After stopping to pick up my precious cargo at the Rio Villa in nearby Monte Rio, I'm back on the single-lane black top. For me, it is a race against time, for the sun is about to set and one of my lifetime dreams is about to come true.

As I enter the serene city of Guerneville, the 4-Runner truck goes from a Mach-like speed to that of a snail. I tap on the brakes before turning right, onto Riverside Drive. With the windows rolled down, I fill my lungs full of sweet, purified air from the towering redwoods that gently sway back and forth.

I bring the white Toyota to a stop, in front of the same home where a lifetime ago my family and I stayed during our summer vacations.

17426 Riverside Drive. Like many things, the house too has changed. Years ago, two tiny bedrooms were added behind the fireplace. A vague attempt of expanding the tiny kitchen was made before the flood of 1986. Even the mighty tree stump, which years ago my brothers and I spent endless hours climbing on, is now in decay. Only the cabin's darkened cedar ceiling and the river-stone fireplace have been left unchanged.

I feel a little sad as I turn away, strolling across the small gravel road. Then, making sure not to disturb anyone, I lead my son, Stephen, through a tiny passage beside the same house that my parents led my brothers and I through, years ago. I know the owner and I am sure he wouldn't mind. Without saying a word, my son and I gaze westward. The Russian River is the same as it always was, dark green and as smooth as glass, as it flows ever so gently to the mighty Pacific. Bluejays call to each other as they glide through the air, before disappearing into the redwoods. The sky above is now bathed with streaks of orange and blue. I take another deep breath and close my eyes, savoring the moment like I did years ago.

As I open my eyes, a single tear rolls down the side of my cheek. I kneel down wrapping my arms around Stephen's shoulders. Without hesitation, he leans his head back and gives me a kiss. 'Love you, Dad.'

'Love you too,' I reply.

My son gazes up at the darkening sky. His eyes grow wide as he strains to capture the disappearing sun. 'This is my favorite place in the whole world!' Stephen announces.

My throat becomes tight. A small stream of tears begins to fall. 'Mine too,' I reply. 'Mine too.'

Stephen is at that magical age of innocence, but yet is wise beyond his years. Even now, as salty tears run down my face, Stephen smiles, letting me maintain my dignity. But he knows why I'm crying. Stephen knows my tears are tears of joy.

'Love you, Dad.'

'Love you, too, son.'

I'm free.

AFTERWORD
Dave Pelzer
Survivor

As a child living in a dark world, I feared for my life and thought I was alone. As an adult, I know now that I was not alone. There were thousands of other abused children.

Sources of information vary, but it is estimated that one in five children are physically, emotionally or sexually abused in the United States. Unfortunately there are those among the uninformed public who believe that most abuse is nothing more than parents exerting their 'right' to discipline their children and letting it get a little out of hand. These same people may believe that over-discipline is not likely to follow the child into adulthood. They are tragically misinformed.

On any given day some adult who is the victim of a dark past of child abuse may vent his or her pent-up frustrations on society or on those he or she may love. The public is well informed about the most uncommon cases. Unusual incidents attract the media and boost ratings. We heard about the lawyer father who struck out with his fist and left the child unconscious on the floor before retiring to bed. We heard about the father who dunked the small child in the toilet. Both children died. In a more bizarre case both a mother and a father each killed a child and hid their bodies for a period of four years. There are other high-profile stories, like the abused child who grew into the man who went on a killing spree at a McDonald's, gunning down helpless victims until the police took his life.

More common are the unknowns who disappear, like the homeless boy who sleeps under a freeway bridge and calls a cardboard box his home. Each year thousands of abused girls run away from home and sell their bodies in order to survive. Others strike out by joining gangs who are totally committed to violence and destruction.

Many child abuse victims hide their past deep inside, so deep that the possibility of becoming an abuser themselves is unthinkable. They live normal lives, becoming husbands and wives, raising families and building careers. But the ordinary problems of everyday life often force the former abuse victim to behave as they were taught as children. Spouses and children then become the object of their frustration, and they unknowingly come full circle, completing the never-ending cycle of rage.

Some child abuse victims stay quietly locked in their shells. They look the other way, believing that by not acknowledging their past it will go away. They seem to believe that above all Pandora's box must stay closed.

Each year millions of dollars are poured into child protection agencies in the United States and around the world. These dollars go to local facilities like foster homes and juvenile halls. There are dollar grants to thousands of private organizations whose mission includes basic child abuse prevention, the counseling of abusive parents and the victims. Every year the number grows larger.

Why? What causes the tragedy of child abuse? Is it really as bad as they say? Can it be stopped? And perhaps the most important of all questions, what is abuse like through the eyes of the child?

What you have just read is a story of an ordinary family that was devastated by their hidden secret. The story has two objectives: the first is to inform the reader how a loving, caring parent can change to a cold, abusive monster venting frustrations on a helpless child; the second is the eventual survival and triumph of the human spirit over seemingly insurmountable odds.

Some readers will find the story unreal and disturbing, but child abuse is a disturbing phenomenon that is a reality in our society. Child abuse has a domino effect that spreads to all who touch the family. It takes its greatest toll on the child and spreads into the immediate family to the spouse, who is often torn between the child and their mate. From there it goes to other children in the family who do not understand and also feel threatened. Also involved are neighbors who hear the screams but do not react, teachers who see the bruises and must deal with a child too distracted to learn, and relatives who want to intervene but do not want to risk relationships.

This is more than a story of survival. It is a story of victory and celebration. Even in its darkest passages, the heart is unconquerable.

It is important that the body survives, but it is more meaningful that the human spirit prevails.

This is my story and mine alone. For years I was confined to the darkness of my own mind and heart, being alone and a pitiful 'loser'. At first I wanted nothing more than to be like others, but that motivation grew. I wanted to become a 'winner'. For over thirteeen years I served my country in the military. I now serve my country giving seminars and workshops to others in need, helping them to break their chains. From one who has been there, I bring a message to abused children and those who work with them. I bring a perspective born in the brutal reality of child abuse and nurtured in hope for a better tomorrow. Most importantly, I broke the cycle and became a father whose only guilt is that of spoiling his son with love and encouragement.

Today there are millions around the world in desperate need of help. It is my mission to assist those in need of a helping hand. I believe it is important for people to know that no matter what lies in their past, they can overcome the dark side and press on to a brighter world. It is perhaps a paradox that without the abuse of my past, I might not be what I am today. Because of the darkness in my childhood, I have a deep appreciation for life. I was fortunate enough to turn tragedy into triumph. This is my story.

Perhaps at no time in history has the family been under more stress. Economic and social changes have pushed the family to its limit and made child abuse more likely. If society is to come to grips with the problem, it must be exposed. Once exposed, the causes of child abuse can be understood and support can truly begin. Childhood should be carefree, playing in the sun; not living a nightmare in the darkness of the soul.

Steven E. Ziegler
Teacher

September, 1992, began as a typical back-to-school month for me. In my twenty-second year of teaching, I found the usual hectic, nonstop confusion. There were close to two hundred new students who had names for me to learn and several new faculty members to welcome aboard. It was goodbye to summer vacation and hello to additional responsibilities, and the annual doom and gloom from Sacramento regarding money for schools. Nothing had seemingly changed about the beginning of school, until a telephone message arrived on the twenty-first that rather painfully jolted me back twenty years: 'A David Pelzer would like you to contact his agent, regarding some child abuse reports you were associated with twenty years ago.' The past came back all too quickly.

Oh, yes, how well I remember David Pelzer. I was a recent college graduate, a new teacher; and as I look back, I knew little about the real world of my chosen career. And the thing I knew least about was child abuse. In the early 1970s I didn't know if child abuse actually existed. If it did, it remained very much in the 'closet' as did so many unmentionable lifestyles and behaviors back then. We have learned so much; yet we have so far to go.

My mind returned to the Thomas Edison School in Daly City, California, September, 1972. Enter little David Pelzer as one of my fifth-grade students. I was naïve back then, but I was blessed with a sensitivity that told me there was something terribly wrong in David's life. Food missing from other students' lunches was traced to this thin, sad boy. Questionable bruises appeared on exposed parts of his body. Everything began to point to one thing: this kid was being beaten and punished in ways far beyond normal parental practise. It was several years later when I learned that what I was witnessing in my classroom was the third-worst case of child abuse on record in the entire state of California.

83

It is not for me to tell again all the graphic details my colleagues and I witnessed and reported to the authorities so many years ago. That account remains David's privilege and opportunity in this book. But what a wonderful opportunity it is for this young man to come forward and tell his story so that other children may not suffer. I deeply admire his courage in doing so.

My very best to you, David. There is absolutely no doubt in my mind how far you have truly come.

THE LOST BOY

To the teachers and staff who rescued me
Steven Ziegler, Athena Konstan, Joyce Woodworth, Janice Woods, Betty Howell, Peter Hansen, the school nurse of Thomas Edison Elementary School and the Daly City police officer

To the angel of social services
Ms Pamela Gold

To my foster parents
Aunt Mary, Rudy and Lilian Catanze, Michael and Joanne Nulls, Jody and Vera Jones, John and Linda Walsh

To those with a firm but gentle guiding hand
Gordon Hutchenson, Carl Miguel, Estelle O'Ryan, Dennis Tapley

To friends and mentors
David Howard, Paul Brazell, William D. Brazell, Sandy Marsh, Michael A. Marsh

In memory of Pamela Eby
who gave her life to saving the children of Florida

To my parents, *who always knew*
Harold and Alice Turnbough

And finally, to my son, *Stephen*
whose unconditional love for who I am and what I do keeps me going. I love you with all my heart and soul.

Bless you all, for,
'It takes a community to save a child.'

Contents

ACKNOWLEDGMENTS

This book would not have been possible without the tenacious devotion of Marsha Donohoe – editor extraordinaire – of Donohoe Publishing Projects. It was Marsha who not only edited the entire text from the original, dismayed *printed* version, but who also typeset, copyedited and proofread the tome to simplify the publication process. And, more important, she maintained the rigid, chronological perspective of the continuing journey through the eyes of a bewildered child. For Marsha, it was a matter of '. . . *If I Could*'.

Thank you to Christine Belleris, Matthew Diener and Allison Janse of the editorial department for their professionalism throughout the production of this book. And a special thank you to Matthew for handling all of our needs and last-minute requests with a smile, and expertly following through on everything.

To Irene Xanthos and Lori Golden of the sales department of Health Communications, Inc., for their undying genuine sincerity. And to Doreen Hess for all her kindness.

A gargantuan thank you to Laurel Howanitz and Susy Allen of Hot Guests, for their unyielding dedication and promotion. Thanks for believing.

To Cindy Edloff, for her efforts and time.

A special thank you to the owners and staff of Coffee Bazaar in Guerneville, California, for keeping the raspberry mochas coming, for allowing Marsha and me to plug in and camp out, and for providing us with 'The Big Table' – enabling us to spread out, take over and promote chaos within the quiet confines of this serene setting.

AUTHOR'S NOTE

Some of the names in this book have been changed in order to protect the dignity and privacy of others.

As in the first part of the trilogy, *A Child Called 'It'*, this second part depicts language that was developed from a child's viewpoint. The tone and vocabulary reflect the age and wisdom of the child at that particular time.

The perspective of *A Child Called 'It'* was based on the child's life from ages four to twelve; the perspective of *this* book is based on life from ages twelve to eighteen.

chapter 1

THE RUNAWAY

Winter 1970, Daly City, California – *I'm alone. I'm hungry and I'm shivering in the dark. I sit on top of my hands at the bottom of the stairs in the garage. My head is tilted backward. My hands became numb hours ago. My neck and shoulder muscles begin to throb. But that's nothing new – I've learned to turn off the pain.*

I'm Mother's prisoner.

I am nine years old, and I've been living like this for years. Every day it's the same thing. I wake up from sleeping on an old army cot in the garage, perform the morning chores, and if I'm lucky, eat leftover breakfast cereal from my brothers. I run to school, steal food, return to 'The House' and am forced to throw up in the toilet bowl to prove that I didn't commit the crime of stealing any food.

I receive beatings or play another one of her 'games', perform afternoon chores, then sit at the bottom of the stairs until I'm summoned to complete the evening chores. Then, and only if I have completed all of my chores on time, and if I have not committed any 'crimes', I may be fed a morsel of food.

My day ends only when Mother allows me to sleep on the army cot, where my body curls up in my meek effort to retain any body heat. The only pleasure in my life is when I sleep. That's the only time I can escape my life. I love to dream.

Weekends are worse. No school means no food and more time at 'The House'. All I can do is try to imagine myself away – somewhere, anywhere – from 'The House'. For years I have been the outcast of 'The Family'. As long as I can remember I have always been in trouble and have 'deserved' to be punished. At first I thought I was a bad boy. Then I thought Mother was sick because she only acted differently when my brothers were not around and my father was away at work. But somehow I always knew Mother and I had a private relationship. I also realized that for some reason I have been Mother's sole target for her unexplained rage and twisted pleasure.

I have no home. I am a member of no one's family. I know deep inside that I do not now, nor will I ever, deserve any love, attention or even recognition as a human being. I am a child called 'It'.

I'm all alone inside.

Upstairs the battle begins. Since it's after four in the afternoon, I know both of my parents are drunk. The yelling starts. First the name-calling, then the swearing. I count the seconds before the subject turns to me – it always does. The sound of Mother's voice makes my insides turn. 'What do you mean?' she shrieks at my father, Stephen. 'You think I treat The Boy bad? Do you?' Her voice then turns ice cold. I can imagine her pointing a finger at my father's face. 'You . . . listen . . . to . . . me. You . . . have no idea what It's like. If you think I treat It that bad . . . then . . . It can live somewhere else.'

I can picture my father – who, after all these years, still tries somewhat to stand up for me – swirling the liquor in his glass, making the ice from his drink rattle. 'Now calm down,' he begins. 'All I'm trying to say is . . . well . . . no child deserves to live like that. My God, Roerva, you treat . . . dogs better than . . . than you do The Boy.'

The argument builds to an ear-shattering climax. Mother slams her drink on the kitchen countertop. Father has crossed the line. No one ever tells Mother what to do. I know I will have to pay the price for her rage. I realize it's only a matter of time before she orders me upstairs. I prepare myself. Ever so slowly I slide my hands out from under my butt, but not too far – for I know sometimes she'll check on me. I know I am never to move a muscle without her permission.

I feel so small inside. I only wish I could somehow—

Without warning, Mother opens the door leading to the downstairs garage. 'You!' she screams. 'Get your ass up here! Now!'

In a flash I bolt up the stairs. I wait a moment for her command before I timidly open the door. Without a sound I approach Mother and await one of her 'games'.

It's the game of address, in which I have to stand exactly three feet in front of her, my hands glued to my side, my head tilted down at a forty-five-degree angle and my eyes locked onto her feet. Upon the first command I must look above her bust, but below her eyes. Upon the second command I must look into her eyes, but never, never may I speak, breathe or move a single muscle unless Mother gives me *permission to do so. Mother and I have been playing this game since I was seven years old, so today it's just another routine in my lifeless existence.*

Suddenly Mother reaches over and seizes my right ear. By accident, I flinch. With her free hand Mother punishes my movement with a solid slap to my face. Her hand becomes a blur, right up until the moment before it strikes my face. I cannot see very well without my glasses. Since it is not a school day, I am not allowed to wear them. The blow from her hand burns my skin. 'Who told you to move?' Mother sneers. I keep my eyes open, fixing them on a spot on the carpet. Mother checks for my reaction before again yanking my ear as she leads me to the front door.

'Turn around!' she yells. 'Look at me!' But I cheat. From the corner of my eye I steal a glance at Father. He gulps down another swallow from his drink. His once rigid shoulders are now slumped over. His job as a fireman in San Francisco, his years of drinking and the strained relationship with Mother have taken their toll on him. Once my super-hero and known for his courageous efforts in rescuing children from burning buildings, Father is now a beaten man. He takes another swallow before Mother begins, 'Your father here thinks I treat you bad. Well, do I? Do I?'

My lips tremble. For a second I'm unsure whether I am supposed to answer. Mother must know this and probably enjoys the 'game' all the more. Either way, I'm doomed. I feel like an insect about to be squashed. My dry mouth opens. I can feel a film of paste separate from my lips. I begin to stutter.

Before I can form a word, Mother again yanks on my right ear. My ear feels as if it were on fire. 'Shut that mouth of yours! No one told you to talk! Did they? Well, did they?' Mother bellows.

My eyes seek out Father. Seconds later he must have felt my need. 'Roerva,' he says, 'that's no way to treat The Boy.*'*

Again I tense my body and again Mother yanks on my ear, but this time she maintains the pressure, forcing me to stand on my toes. Mother's face turns dark red. 'So you think I treat him badly? I . . .' pointing her index finger at her chest, Mother continues, 'I don't need this, Stephen, if you think I'm treating It *badly . . . well,* It *can just get out of my house!'*

I strain my legs, trying to stand a little taller, and begin to tighten my upper body so that when Mother strikes I can be ready. Suddenly she lets go of my ear and opens the front door. 'Get out!' she screeches. 'Get out of my house! I don't like you! I don't want you! I never loved you! Get the hell out of my house!'

I freeze. I'm not sure of this game. My brain begins to spin with all the options of what Mother's real intentions may be. To survive, I have to think ahead. Father steps in front of me. 'No!' he cries out. 'That's enough. Stop it, Roerva. Stop the whole thing. Just let The Boy be.'

Mother now steps between Father and me. 'No?' Mother begins in a sarcastic voice. 'How many times have you told me that about The Boy? The Boy this. The Boy that. The Boy, The Boy, The Boy. How many times, Stephen?' She reaches out, touching Father's arm as if pleading with him; as if their lives would be so much better if I no longer lived with them – if I no longer existed.

Inside my head my brain screams, Oh my God! Now I know!

Without thinking, Father cuts her off. 'No,' he states in a low voice. 'This,' he says, spreading his hands, 'this is wrong.' I can tell by his trailing voice that Father has lost his steam. He appears to be on the verge of tears. He looks at me and shakes his head before looking at Mother. 'Where will he live? Who's going to take care of . . . ?'

'Stephen, don't you get it? Don't you understand? I don't give a damn what happens to him. I don't give a damn about The Boy.'

Suddenly, the front door flies open. Mother smiles as she holds the doorknob. 'Okay. All right. I'll leave it up to The Boy.' She bends down, just inches in front of my face. Mother's breath reeks of booze. Her eyes are ice cold and full of pure hatred. I wish I could turn away. I wish I were back in the garage. In a slow, raspy voice, Mother says, 'If you think I treat you so badly, you can leave.'

I snap out of my protective mold and take a chance by looking at Father. He misses my glance as he sips another drink. My mind begins to tumble. I don't understand the purpose of her new game. Suddenly I realize that this is no game. It takes a few seconds for me to understand that this is my chance – my chance to escape. I've wanted to run away for years, but some invisible fear kept me from doing it. But I tell myself that this is too easy. I so badly want to move my legs, but they remain rigid.

'Well?' Mother screams into my ear. 'It's your choice.' Time seems to stand still. As I stare down at the carpet, I can hear Mother begin to hiss. 'He won't leave. The Boy will never leave. It hasn't the guts to go.'

I can feel the inside of my body begin to shake. For a moment I close my eyes, wishing myself away. In my mind I can see myself walking through the door. I smile inside. I so badly want to leave. The more I envision myself walking through the door, the more I begin to feel a warmth spread through my soul. Suddenly, I can feel my body moving. My eyes pop open. I look down at my worn-out sneakers. My feet are stepping through the front door. Oh my God, I say to myself, I can't believe I'm doing this! Out of fear, I dare not stop.

'There,' Mother triumphantly states. 'The Boy *did* it. It's his decision. I didn't force him. Remember that, Stephen. I want you to know I didn't force him.'

I step through the front door, knowing full well that Mother will reach out and yank me back in. I can feel the hairs on the back of my neck stand up. I quicken my pace. After stepping past the door, I turn right and walk down the red steps. From behind me I can hear the sounds of Mother and Father straining themselves as they lean outside. 'Roerva,' Father says in a low voice, 'this is wrong.'

'No!' she replies in a flat voice. 'And remember, it was his decision. Besides, he'll be back.'

I'm so excited that I nearly trip over my own feet and stumble down the stairs. I grab onto the handrail to stabilize myself. I make it to the walkway, and I fight to control my breathing. I turn right and walk up the street until I'm sure no one can see me past The House, then I break into a run. I make it halfway up the street before stopping, only for a moment, to look back down at The House.

With my hands on my knees I bend down panting. I try to strain my ears for the sounds of Mother's station wagon. Somehow, Mother's letting me go seems all too easy. I know she'll be after me in a few moments. After catching my breath, I again quicken my pace. I reach the top of Crestline Avenue and stare down at the small green house. But there's no station wagon racing out of the garage. No one running after me. No yelling, screaming or hitting. I'm not sitting at the bottom of the stairs in the garage, not being beaten in the back of the knees with a broomstick and not getting locked in the bathroom with another concoction of ammonia and Clorox.

I spin around at the sound of a passing car. I wave.

Even though I'm wearing ragged pants, a torn, thin, long-sleeved shirt and a pair of worn-out tennis shoes, I feel happy inside. I'm warm. I tell myself I'm never going back. After years of living in fear, surviving torturous beatings and eating out of garbage cans, I now know I will somehow survive.

I have no friends, no place to hide, nothing to turn to. But I know exactly where I'm going – the river. Years ago, when I was a member of The Family, for every summer vacation we would drive up to the Russian River in Guerneville. The best times in my life were the days spent learning to swim at Johnson's Beach, riding down the super slide, going on hayrides at sunset and playing with my brothers on the old tree stump by our cabin. Remembering the smell of the giant redwood trees and the beauty of the dark green river makes me smile.

I'm not sure exactly where Guerneville is, but I do know it lies north of the Golden Gate Bridge. I'm sure it will take me a few days to get there, but I don't care. Once I'm there I can survive by stealing loaves of French bread and salami from the local Safeway supermarket, and sleep on Johnson's Beach while listening to the sounds of the cars rumbling across the old evergreen Parker truss bridge that leads into the city. Guerneville was the only place I ever felt safe. Ever since I was in kindergarten, I knew it was where I wanted to live. And once I make it there, I know I will live in Guerneville for the rest of my life.

I begin walking down Eastgate Avenue when a cold chill whistles through my body. The sun has set and the evening fog begins to roll in from the nearby ocean. I clamp my hands inside my armpits and make my way down the street. My teeth begin to chatter. The thrill of the great escape begins to wear off. I begin to think that maybe, maybe, Mother was right. As much as she beat me and yelled at me, at least the garage was warmer than out here. Besides, I tell myself, I do lie and steal food. Maybe I do deserve to be punished. I stop for a second to rethink my plan. If I turn back now, right now, she'll yell and beat me – but I'm used to that. If I'm lucky, tomorrow she may feed me some leftover scraps from dinner. Then I can steal food from school the next day. Really, all I have to do is go back. I smile to myself. I've survived worse from Mother before.

I stop midstride. The thought of returning to The House doesn't sound half bad. Besides, I tell myself, I could never find the river anyway. I turn around. She was right.

I picture myself sitting at the bottom of the stairs, shaking with fear, frightened of every sound I may hear from above. Counting the seconds and being terrified by every set of commercials; then waiting for the sound of the floor to creak upstairs when Mother gets up from the couch, strolls into the kitchen to pour herself a drink and then screeches for me to come upstairs – where she'll beat me until I can no longer stand. I may be unable to crawl away.

I hate commercials.

The sound of a nearby cricket rubbing its wings brings me back to reality. I try to find the insect and stop for a moment when I think I'm close. The chirping stops. I remain perfectly still. If I catch it, maybe I could put the cricket in my pocket and make it my pet. I hear the cricket again. As I bend over to reach out, I hear the rumbling sounds of Mother's car from behind me. I dive beside a nearby car the moment before the headlights spot me. The car creeps down the street. The sound of Mother's squeaky brakes pierces through my ears. She's searching for me. I begin to wheeze. I clamp my eyes closed as her headlights inch their way toward me. I wait for the sound of Mother's car to grind to a halt, followed by her leaping from the car, then throwing me back into her station wagon. I count the seconds. I open my eyes slowly, turning my head to the left just in time to see the rear brakes light up before the brakes squeal. It's over! She's found me! In a way, I'm relieved. I would have never made it to the river. The anticipation drained me. Come on, come on, I say to myself. Just do it. Come on.

The car cruises past me.

I don't believe it! I jump up from behind the car and stare at a shiny two-door sedan tapping its brakes every few seconds. Suddenly I feel light-headed. My stomach tightens up. A surge of fluid climbs up my throat. I stumble over to someone's grass and try to throw up. After a few seconds of dry heaves because of my empty stomach, I glance up at the stars. I can see patches of clear sky through the foggy mist. Bright silver stars twinkle above me. I try to remember how long it's been since I've been outside like this. I take a few deep breaths.

'No!' I yell. 'I'm not going back! I'm never going back!' I turn around and walk back down the street, north toward the Golden Gate Bridge. After a few seconds I walk past the car, which is now parked in someone's driveway. I can see a couple standing at the top of the steps being greeted by the host. The sound of laughter and music escape through the open door. I wonder what it would be like to be welcomed in a home. As I make my way past a house, my nose detects the smell of food, and the thought of wolfing down something to eat possesses me. It's Saturday night – that means I haven't eaten anything since

Friday morning at school. Food, *I think to myself.* I have to find some food.

Sometime later I make my way to my old church. Years ago Mother sent my two brothers, Ron and Stan, and me to afternoon catechism classes for a few weeks. I haven't been to the church since I was seven. I gently open the door. Immediately I can feel the heat seep through the holes in my pants and my paper-thin shirt. As quietly as I can, I close the door behind me. I can see the priest picking up books from the pews. I hide beside the door, hoping he won't see me. The priest makes his way to the back pews toward me. I so badly want to stay, but . . . I close my eyes, trying to absorb the heat for a moment, before my hand again reaches for the door.

Once outside I cross the street, where I can see a row of stores. I stop in front of a doughnut shop. One early morning, years ago, Father stopped to pick up some doughnuts before he drove the family to the Russian River. It was a magical time for me. Now I stare through the glass, then up at the fat, jolly, animated cartoon characters that were painted on the wall and going through the various stages of making doughnuts.

From my left the smell of pizza makes my head turn. I stumble past a few stores until I stop in front of a pizza bar. My mouth waters. Without thinking I open the door and make my way, in a daze, to the back of the room. My eyes take a few minutes to adjust. I can make out a pool table, the sounds of beer mugs clashing together and laughter. I can feel stares from above me, and I stop at the far corner of the bar. My eyes dart around in search of abandoned food. Finding none, I make my way to the pool table, where two men have just finished a game. I find a quarter on the table and slowly cover it with my fingers. I look around before dragging the quarter over the edge of the pool table and into my hand. The coin feels warm. As casually as possible I stroll back to the bar. A voice explodes above me. I try to ignore the sound. From behind, someone grabs my left shoulder. Instantly I tighten my upper body, waiting for a blow to my face or stomach. 'Hey, kid, what are you doing?'

I spin around toward the voice, but I refuse to look up.

'I said, what are you doing?' the voice again asks.

I look up at a man wearing a white apron covered with red pizza sauce. He places his hands on his hips, waiting for a reply. I try to answer, but I begin to stutter. 'Uhm. Noth . . . nothing . . . sir.'

The man places his hand on my shoulder and leads me to the end of the bar. He then stops and bends down. 'Hey, kid, you need to give me the quarter.'

I shake my head no. Before I can tell him a lie, the man says, 'Hey, man, I saw you do it. Now give it back. Those guys over there need it to play pool.' I clench my fist. That quarter can buy me some food, maybe even a piece of pizza. The man continues to stare at me. Slowly I uncurl my fingers and drop the coin into the man's hand. He flicks the quarter over to a pair of men holding pool sticks. 'Thanks, Mark,' one of them yells.

'Yeah, man, no problem.' I try to turn away, looking for the front door, when Mark grabs me. 'What are you doing here? Why'd you steal that quarter?'

I retreat inside my shell and stare at the floor.

'Hey, man,' Mark raises his voice. 'I asked you a question.'

'I didn't steal anything. I . . . I just thought that . . . I mean, I just saw the quarter and . . . I . . .'

'First off, I saw you steal the quarter, and secondly, the guys need it so they can play pool. Besides, man, what were you going to do with a quarter anyway?'

I could feel an eruption of anger surge through me. 'Food!' I blurt out. 'All I wanted was to buy a piece of pizza! Okay?'

'A piece of pizza?' Mark laughs. 'Man, where are you from . . . Mars?'

I try to think of an answer. I can feel myself lock up inside. I empty my lungs of breath and shrug my shoulders.

'Hey, man, calm down. Here, pull up a stool,' Mark says in a soft voice. 'Jerry, give me a Coke.' Mark now looks down at me. I try to pull my arms into my sleeves – to hide my slash marks and bruises. I try to turn away from him. 'Hey, kid, are you all right?' Mark asks.

I shake my head from side to side. No! I say to myself. I'm not all right. Nothing's right! I so badly want to tell him, but . . .

'Here, drink up,' Mark says as he slides over the glass of Coke. I grab the red plastic glass with both hands and suck on the paper straw until the soda is gone.

'Hey, kid,' Mark asks, 'what's your name? You got a home? Where do you live?'

I'm so ashamed. I know I can't answer. I act as if I did not hear him. Mark nods his head in approval. 'Don't move,' he states as he grabs my glass. From behind the bar I can see him fill up the glass as he grabs the phone. The phone cord stretches to its limit as Mark strains to give me another Coke. After he hangs up the phone, Mark sits back down. 'You want to tell me what's wrong?'

'Mother and I don't get along,' I mumble, hoping no one can hear me. 'She . . . ah . . . she . . . told me to leave.'

'Don't you think she's worried about you?' he asks.

'Right! Are you kidding?' I blurt out. Oops, I say to myself. Keep your mouth shut! I tap my finger on the bar, trying to turn away from Mark. I glance at the two men playing pool and the others beside them – laughing, eating, having a good time.

I wish I were a real person.

I suddenly feel sick again. As I slide down the stool, I turn back to Mark. 'I gotta go.'

'Where ya going?'

'Uhm, I just gotta go, sir.'

'Did your mother really tell you to leave?'

Without looking back at him, I nod my head yes.

Mark smiles. 'I bet she's really worried about you. What do you think? I tell you what. You give me her number, and I'll give her a call, okay?'

I can feel my blood race. The door, I tell myself. Just get to the door and run. My head frantically swivels from side to side in search of an exit.

'Come on now. Besides,' Mark says, raising his eyebrows, 'you can't leave now. I'm making you a pizza . . . with the works!'

My head snaps up. 'Really?' I shout. 'But . . . I don't have any . . .'

'Hey, man, don't worry about it. Just wait here.' Mark gets up and makes his way to the front. He smiles at me through an opening from the kitchen. My mouth begins to water. I can see myself eating a hot meal – not from a garbage can or a piece of stale bread, but a real meal.

Minutes pass. I sit upright waiting for another glance from Mark.

From the front door a policeman in a dark blue uniform enters the shop. I don't think anything of it until Mark walks toward the officer. The two men talk for a few moments, then Mark nods his head and points toward me. I spin around, searching for a door in the back of the room. Nothing. I turn back toward Mark. He's gone, and so is the police officer. I twist my head from side to side as I strain my eyes, hunting for the two men. They're both gone. False alarm. My heart begins to slow down. I begin to breathe again. I smile.

'Excuse me, young man.' I raise my head up to a police officer smiling down at me. 'I think you need to come with me.'

No! I say to myself. I refuse to move! The tips of my fingers dig into the bottom of the stool. I try to find Mark. I can't believe he called the police. He seemed so cool. He had given me a Coke and promised me some food. Why did he do this? As much as I hate Mark now, I hate myself more. I knew I should have just kept on walking down the street. I should have never, never come into the pizza bar. I knew I should have gotten out of town as soon as I could. How could I have been so stupid!

I know I've lost. I feel whatever strength I had now drain. I so badly want to find a hole to curl up into and fall asleep. I slide off the bar stool. The officer walks behind me. 'Don't worry,' he says. 'You're going to be all right.' I barely hear what he is saying. All I can think about is that somewhere out there, she is waiting for me. I'm going back to The House – back to The Mother. The police officer walks me to the front door. 'Thanks for giving us a call,' the officer says to Mark.

I stare down at the floor. I'm so angry. I refuse to look at Mark. I wish I were invisible.

'Hey, kid,' Mark smiles as he shoves a thin white box into my hands. 'I told you I'd give you a pizza.'

My heart sinks. I smile at him. I begin to shake my head no. I know I'm not worthy. I push the box back toward Mark. For a second, nothing else in my world exists. I look into his heart. I know he understands. Without a word, I know what he is telling me. I take the box. I look deeper into his eyes, 'Thank you, sir.' Mark runs his hand through my hair. I suck in the scent from the box.

'It's the works. And kid . . . hang tough. You'll be fine,' Mark says as I make my way out the door, holding my prize. The pizza box warms my hands. Outside a gray swirling fog covers the street where the police car is parked in the middle of the road. I hug the box close to my chest. I can feel the pizza slide down to the bottom of the box as the officer opens the front door of his car for me. I can hear a faint humming sound from the heat pump of the floorboard. I wiggle my toes to warm myself. I watch the officer as he makes his way to the driver's side. He slides into the car, then picks up a microphone. A soft, female voice answers his call. I turn away, looking back toward the pizza bar. Mark *and a group of adults shiver as they stand together outside. As the police car slowly rumbles away, Mark raises his hand, forms a peace sign, then waves goodbye. One by one, the others smile as they join him.*

My throat tightens. I can taste the salt as tears run down my face. Somehow I know I'll miss Mark. I stare down at my shoes and wiggle my toes. One of them pops through a hole.

'So,' the officer says, 'first time in a police car?'

'Yes, sir,' I reply. 'Am I . . . uhm . . . I mean, am I in trouble, sir?'

The officer smiles. 'No. We're just concerned. It's kinda late, and you're a little young to be out here alone. What's your name?'

I glance down at my dirty shoe.

'Come on, now. There's no harm in telling me your name.'

I clear my throat. I don't want to talk to the officer. I don't want to talk to anybody. I know every time I open my mouth, I'm one step closer to Mother's evil clutches. But, I tell myself, what can I do? I know whatever chances I had of escaping to the river are now gone. I don't care. As long as I don't have to return to her. After a few seconds I answer the officer; 'Da . . . Da . . . David, sir,' I stutter. 'My name is David.'

The officer chuckles. I smile back. He tells me I'm a good-looking boy. 'How old are you?'

'Nine, sir.'

'Nine? Kinda small, aren't you?'

We begin to talk back and forth. I can't believe how much the officer is interested in me. I feel he actually likes me. He parks the car in front of the police station and leads me downstairs to an empty room with a pool table in the middle. We sit beside the pool table, and the officer says, 'Hey, David, let's say we get to that pizza before it gets cold.'

My head bounces up and down. I rip open the box. I bend down and suck in the aroma. 'So, David,' the officer asks, 'where did you say you live?'

I freeze. The toppings from my piece of pizza slide off. I turn away. I was hoping he would somehow forget why he picked me up.

'Come on now, David. I'm really concerned about you.' His eyes lock onto mine. I can't turn away. I gently replace my piece of pizza in the box. The officer reaches out to touch my hand. By reflex, I flinch. Before the officer tries again, I stare him down. Inside my head I scream, Don't you understand? Mother doesn't want me, doesn't love me,

doesn't give a damn about me! All right? So . . . if you can just leave me alone, I can be on my way. Okay?!

The officer backs his chair away from the table before he begins in a soft voice, 'David, I'm here to help you. You have to know that, and I'm going to stay here with you as long as it takes.' He leans over and lifts my chin with his finger. Tears roll down my eyes. My nose is runny. I know now there is no escape for me. I don't have the guts to look the policeman in the eyes.

'Crestline Avenue, sir,' I say in a low voice.

'Crestline Avenue?' the officer asks.

'Yes, sir . . . 40 Crestline Avenue.'

'David, you did the right thing. Whatever the problem is, I'm sure we can work it out.'

I tell him the phone number and the officer disappears for a few moments. After he returns, he again attacks the pizza.

I pick up the same piece of pizza. It's cold and soggy. I so badly want to eat, but my mind is a million miles away. The policeman reassures me with a smile. 'Everything's going to be okay.'

Right! *I tell myself.* The only time I ever felt secure, safe and wanted was when I was a tiny child. *I was five that day when The Family waited for me as I raced up the small hill on the last day of kindergarten. I can still see Mommy's face glowing with love as she shouted, 'Come on, sweetheart. Come on now, David!' She opened the door for me after giving me a tight hug. Then she shut the door before Father sped away. Destination: the river. That summer Mommy taught me how to float on my back. I was scared, but Mommy stayed with me until I learned to float all by myself. I was so proud as I showed off to her, proving to Mommy I was a big boy, worthy of her attention and praise. That summer was the best time of my life. But now, as I sit in front of the policeman, I know nothing will ever be like it was back then. My good times are now only memories.*

The officer looks up. I turn my shoulders to find my father in one of his red cotton shirts standing behind me. Another police officer nods at the policeman sitting with me. 'Mr Pelzer?' the officer near me asks.

My father nods yes. The two of them disappear into an office. The policeman closes the door. I wish I could hear what they're saying. I'm sure it's about me and how I'm always in trouble with Mother. I'm only relieved that she didn't *come, but somehow I knew that she* would never dare risk exposing herself to anyone of authority. I know she always uses Father for her dirty work. She controls Father – the same as she tries to control everyone. Above all, I know she must hide the secret. No one must ever know about our private relationship. But I know she's slipping. She's losing control. I try to think what this means. To survive, I must think ahead.

Minutes later the door from the office creaks. Father steps out from the room, shaking the policeman's hand. The officer approaches me. He bends down. 'David, it was just a small misunderstanding. Your father here tells me that you became upset when your mother wouldn't let you ride your bike. You didn't need to run away for something like that. So, you go home with your father now, and you and your mother work this thing out. Your father here says she's worried sick over you.' He then changes the tone of his voice as he points a finger at me. 'And don't you ever put your parents through that again. I hope you've learned your lesson. It can be pretty scary out there, right?' the officer asks, while gesturing to the outside of the building.

I stand in front of the officer in total disbelief. I can't believe what I'm hearing. Ride my bike? I don't even have one! I've never even ridden on one before! I want to spin around to see if he is talking to some other kid. From behind, Father looks down at me. His eyes are blank. I realize this is just one of Mother's cover stories. It figures.

'And David,' the officer states, 'treat your parents with dignity and respect. You don't know how lucky you are.'

My mind becomes foggy. All I can hear inside my head is, 'how lucky you are . . . how lucky you are . . . ,' over and over and over again. I shudder when Father slams the door from the driver's side of the station wagon. He exhales deeply before leaning over to me. 'Jesus H. Christ, David!' he begins as he turns the ignition and pumps the gas pedal. 'What in the hell were you thinking? Do you have any idea what you did? Do you know what you put your mother through?'

My head snaps toward Father. Put *her* through? What about me? Doesn't anyone care about me? But . . . *I tell myself*, maybe she broke down. Maybe she's really concerned about me. Is it possible she knows she went too far? *For a moment I can imagine Mother sobbing in Father's arms, wondering where I am, whether I'm alive. Then I can see my mommy running up to me with tears in her eyes as she wraps me in love, showering me with kisses, tears rolling down her face. I can almost hear my mommy say the three most important words*

I long to hear. And I'll be ready to say the four most important words: I love you, too!

'David!' Father grabs my arm. I jump up, striking my head against the top of the car. 'Do you have any idea what your mother's been doing? I can't get a moment of peace in that house. For Christ's sake, it's been nothing but hell since you left. Jesus, can't you just stay out of trouble? Can't you just try and make her happy? Just stay out of her way and do whatever she wants. Can you do that? Can you do that for me? Well?' Father yells, raising his voice so loud I can feel my skin crawl.

Slowly I nod my head yes. I don't dare make a sound as I cry deep inside. I know I'm wrong. And, as always, it's all my fault. I turn to Father while shaking my head up and down. He reaches over to pat my head.

'All right,' he says in a softer tone, 'all right. That's my Tiger. Now let's go home.'

As Father drives the car up the same street I walked down hours ago, I sit at the far side of the car, resting the weight of my body on the door. I feel like a trapped animal who wants to claw its way through the glass. The closer we get to The House, the more I can feel myself quiver inside. I need to go to the bathroom. Home, *I say to myself. I stare down at my hands. My fingers tremble from fear. I know in a few moments I'll be back where it all started. In all, nothing's changed, and I know nothing will. I wish I were someone, anyone but who I am. I wish I had a life, a family, a home.*

Father drives into the garage. He turns to me before opening his door. 'Well, here we are,' he states with a false smile. 'We're home.'

I look right through him, hoping, praying he can feel my fear, my pain from inside of me. Home? *I say to myself.*

I have no home.

chapter 2

AN ANGEL NAMED MS GOLD

On March 5, 1973, I received the long-awaited answer to my prayers. I was rescued. My teachers and other staff members at Thomas Edison Elementary School intervened and notified the police.

Everything happened with lightning speed. I cried with all my heart as I said my final goodbyes to my teachers. I somehow knew I would never see them again. By the tears in their eyes I realized they understood the truth about me – the *real* truth. Why I was so different from the other children; why I smelled and dressed in rags; why I climbed into garbage cans to hunt for a morsel of food.

Before I left, my homeroom teacher, Mr Ziegler, bent down to say goodbye. He shook my hand and told me to be a good boy. He then whispered to me that he would tell my homeroom class the truth about me. Mr Ziegler's statement meant the world to me. I so badly wanted to be liked, to be accepted by my class, my school – by everyone.

The police officer had to nudge me through the door of the school office. 'Come on, David, we gotta go.' I wiped my nose before I stepped through the door. A million thoughts raced through my mind, all of them bad. I was terrified of what the consequences would be when Mother found out. No one had ever crossed The Mother like this before. When she found out, I knew there would be hell to pay.

As the police officer led me to his car, I could hear the sounds of all the schoolchildren playing in the yard during their lunch break. As we drove off, I twisted around in my seat to catch a glimpse of the schoolyard one last time. I left Thomas Edison Elementary School without having a single friend. But my only regret was that I did not have a chance to say goodbye to my English teacher, Mrs Woodworth, who was ill that day. During the time I was Mother's prisoner, Mrs Woodworth, without knowing, helped me escape my loneliness through the use of books. I had spent hundreds of hours in the dark, reading books of high adventure. This somehow eased my pain.

After filling out some forms at the police station, the officer called Mother to inform her that I was not coming home that afternoon, and that she could call the county's juvenile authorities if she had any questions. I sat like a statue, feeling both horror and excitement as the officer spoke on the phone. I could only imagine what was going through Mother's head. As the policeman spoke with a dry voice on the phone, I could see beads of sweat cover his forehead. After he hung up the phone, I wondered for a moment if anyone else had ever had the same experience after talking to Mother. It seemed to be very important to the officer that we leave the station right away. I didn't help matters by pestering him over and over again as I jumped up and down and asked, 'What'd she say? What'd she say?' The officer refused to answer. He seemed to breathe easier once we drove past the city limits. He then bent down and said, 'David, you're free. Your mother is never going to hurt you again.'

I didn't fully understand the weight of his statement. I had hoped that he was taking me to some kind of jail, with all the other bad children – as Mother had programmed into me for so many years. I had decided long ago that I'd rather live in jail than live one more minute with *her*. I turned away from the sun. A single tear rolled down my face.

As long as I could remember, I had always wiped my tears and retreated inside my shell. This time I refused to wipe the tear away. I could feel the tear reach my lips, tasted the salt and let the tear dry on my skin as the rays from the sun baked through the windshield. I wanted to remember that tear not as a tear of fear, anger or sorrow, but as one of joy and freedom. I knew that from that moment on, everything in my life was new.

The officer drove me to the county hospital. Immediately, I was taken into an examination room. The nurse seemed shocked by my appearance. As gently as possible, she bathed my entire body from head to toe with a sponge before the doctor examined me. I couldn't look at her. I felt so ashamed as I sat on top of the cold metal examination table, wearing only my soiled underwear briefs filled with holes. As she washed my face, I turned away and kept my eyelids closed as tightly as I could. When the nurse finished, I gazed at the yellow-colored room filled with Snoopy cartoon characters. I looked down at different parts of my body. My legs and arms were a combination of yellow and brown. Dark circles of purple bruises faded on top of fresh rings of blue bruises – where I was either grabbed, punched or slammed down on the kitchen floor. When the doctor came into the room he seemed very concerned about my hands and arms. My fingers were dry, raw and red from all the years of using the combinations of cleaning chemicals used to complete my household chores. The doctor pinched the tips of my fingers, asking me if I could feel the pressure. I shook my head no. I hadn't been able to feel the tips of my fingers for some time now. He shook his head, claiming it was nothing to worry about, so I didn't think anything more of it.

Afterward, the police officer kindly led me through the maze of corridors as we made our way from room to room for lots of examinations, tests, blood samples and X-rays. I found myself moving in a daze. I felt as if I were watching someone else's life through my own eyes. I became so scared that I first asked, then begged the policeman to check around every corner and enter every room before I did. I knew that somewhere out there Mother was poised, ready to snatch me away. At first the officer refused, and only after I became so petrified that I couldn't breathe or move did the policeman humor me and follow my requests. I knew deep inside my heart that things were happening too fast – it was too easy for me to escape Mother.

Hours later we ended up with the same nurse who bathed me. She bent down to say something. I waited. She stared into my eyes, then after a few moments, she turned away. I could hear her sniffle. The doctor walked up behind me, patted my shoulder and gave me a bag containing cream for my hands. He then instructed me to keep my arms as clean as possible and said that it was too late to cover them. I looked at the officer, then down at my arms. I didn't understand. To me, my arms seemed the same as they always did – dark red with little skin. Both arms itched quite a bit, but that was normal for me. Before the policeman and I left, the doctor reached over and said to the officer, 'Make sure David gets plenty of food. And make sure he gets lots of time in the sun.' Then the doctor bent a little closer to him and asked, 'Where is she? You're not sending him back to his . . . ?'

The policeman locked eyes with the doctor. 'Not to worry, Doc. I gave this kid my word. His mother is *never* going to hurt him again.'

From that moment on, I knew I was safe. Standing near the officer, I wanted to hug his leg, but I knew I shouldn't. My eyes gleamed with joy. The police officer became my hero.

A few minutes after we left the hospital, he slowed his car as he drove through the hills on the narrow one-lane roads. I rolled down my window and stared in amazement at the sloping brown hills and tall redwood trees. Moments later the officer parked the car. 'Well, David, here we are.' I gazed down below me at the prettiest home I had ever seen. The officer explained that I would live here for a while and that this would be my new foster home. I had never heard the words *foster home* before, but I knew I would love the home. To me it seemed like a giant log cabin with lots of open windows. I could see that behind the home was a huge backyard, where sounds of screeching and laughter echoed by the tiny creek.

The elderly woman who ran the temporary foster home introduced herself as 'Aunt Mary' and greeted me at the kitchen door. I thanked the police officer with the strongest handshake I could. I felt bad that he had worked overtime for me. He knelt down and said in a deep voice, 'David, it's kids like you that made me want to become a policeman.' Without thinking, I grabbed his neck. The moment I did, my arms felt as if they were on fire. I didn't care. 'Thank you, sir.'

'Hey, kid, not a problem,' he replied. He then strolled up the curved walkway and saluted me from his car before driving off. I didn't even know his name.

After Aunt Mary fed me a delicious dinner of filet of sole, she introduced me to the seven other children who, like myself, for one reason or another no longer lived with their parents. I stared into every one of their faces. Some eyes were hollow, some full of worry, others full of confusion. I had no idea there were other unwanted children, too; for years I had felt I was all alone. At first I acted shy, but after a few questions from the other children, I opened up. 'What are you in for?' they asked. 'What happened to you?'

I bent my head down before replying that my mother didn't like me because I was always in trouble. I felt ashamed. I didn't want to tell them the secret about Mother and me. But none of that mattered to any of them, for I was just another face in the crowd. I was instantly accepted. I felt a surge of energy erupt from inside. From that moment on, I became a wild child. I blitzed through the home as if my pants were on fire. I joked, laughed and screamed with joy, releasing years of solitude and silence.

I was uncontrollable. I ran from room to room, jumping on every mattress in the home. I bounced so high my head banged again and again against the ceiling. I didn't stop until I saw stars. I didn't care. The other children clapped their hands, egging me on. Their laughs were not cold, like the snide remarks reserved for me back at school, but were full of delight and approval.

My frolicking ended suddenly when I ran through the living-room, nearly knocking over a lamp. By reflex, Aunt Mary grabbed my arm. She was about to scold me until she looked down at me. I covered my face, and my knees began to shake. Aunt Mary was a strict, elderly woman who stood her ground, but she didn't yell as she was known to do. For that evening my hyperactivity ended as quickly as air could escape a balloon. Aunt Mary released her grip and knelt down, asking, 'What did she do to you?'

'I'm sorry,' I stuttered in a low voice. I was still unsure of Aunt Mary's intentions. I retreated into my protective position. 'I was a bad boy, and I deserved what I got!'

Later that evening Aunt Mary tucked me into bed. I began to cry, explaining to her that I was afraid Mother would come and take me away. She assured me I was safe and stayed with me until I felt secure. I stared up at the dark cedar ceiling. It reminded me of the old cabin in Guerneville. I fell asleep knowing that Mother was out there, somewhere, waiting to get me.

Alone in my dreams I found myself standing at the end of a long, dark hallway. A shadowy figure emerged at the opposite end. The figure transformed into *The Mother*. She began to march toward me. For some reason, I stood still. I couldn't move; I didn't even try. The closer The Mother came, the more her red face, filled with hatred, came into focus. The Mother held a shiny knife above her, poised and ready to strike me down. I turned and ran down the endless hallway. With all my strength I pumped my legs as fast as I could, searching for a light. I ran forever. The hallway twisted and turned as I hunted for an escape. I could feel The Mother's rancid breath on my neck and hear her cold voice chanting that there was no escape and that she would never let me go.

I snapped out of my dream. My face and chest were covered with a cold, sticky sweat. Not knowing if I was still dreaming, I covered my face. After my breathing began to slow down, I frantically looked all around. I was still in the cedar room. I still had on a pair of pajamas that Aunt Mary had loaned me. I patted myself, feeling for any wounds. *A dream*, I told myself. *A bad dream, that's all.* I tried to control my breathing but couldn't shake the vision. The Mother's words echoed in my mind: '*I will never let you go. Never!*'

I jumped out of bed and scrambled around in the darkness to throw on my clothes. I returned to the head of the bed and held my knees close to my chest. I couldn't go back to sleep. That's where The Mother now lived – in my dreams. I felt it was a mistake that I was taken away, and I knew I would soon be returned to her. That night, and those to follow, while everyone slept, I held on to my knees as I rocked backed and forth, humming to myself. I would stare through the window and listen to the trees sway in the evening breeze. I told myself that I would never fall into the nightmare again.

My first encounter with the county's Child Protective Service agency came in the form of an angel named Ms Gold. Her long, shiny blonde hair and bright face matched her name. 'Hi,' she smiled. 'I'm your social worker.' And so began the long and drawn-out sessions in which I had to explain things I did not totally understand. In the beginning of our first session, I huddled at the far end of the couch while Ms Gold sat at the other end. Without my knowing, she slowly inched her way toward me until she was close enough to hold my hand. At first I was too scared to have her touch me. I did not deserve her kindness. But Ms Gold held on to my hand, caressing my palm, assuring me that she was there to help me. That day she stayed with me for over five hours.

The other visits were just as long. At times I was too scared to talk and long moments of silence followed. Other times, for no apparent reason and not understanding why, I'd burst into tears. Ms Gold didn't care. She simply held me tight and rocked me back and forth, whispering in my ear that everything was going to be all right. Sometimes we would lie at the end of the couch, and I would talk about things that were of no relation to my bad past. During those times I would play with the long strands of Ms Gold's shiny hair. I'd lie in her arms and breathe in the fragrance of her flowery perfume. I soon began to trust Ms Gold.

She became my best friend. After school, whenever I saw her car, I'd spring down the walkway and burst into Aunt Mary's home, knowing Ms Gold had come to see me. We always ended our sessions with a long hug. She would then bend down and assure me that I did not deserve to be treated the way I was and that what my mother did to me was not my fault. I had heard Ms Gold's words before, but after years of brainwashing I wasn't so sure. So much had happened so fast. One time I asked Ms Gold why she needed all of this information on Mother and me. To my horror, she told me that the county was going to use it against my mother. 'No!' I pleaded. 'She must never know I told you! *Never!*'

Ms Gold assured me that I was doing the right thing, but when she left me alone to think, I came to a different conclusion. As long as I could remember, I had always been in trouble. I was always being punished for one thing or another. Whenever my parents had fought, my name was always thrown into the ring. Was it really Mother's fault? Maybe I deserved everything I got over the years. I did lie and steal food. And I knew I was the reason why Mother and Father no longer lived together. Would the county throw Mother in jail? Then what would happen to my brothers? That day after Ms Gold left, I sat alone on the couch. My mind raced with questions. I felt my insides turn to jelly. *My God! What have I done?*

Days later, on a Sunday afternoon, while I was outside learning to play basketball, I heard the old familiar sound of Mother's station wagon. My heart felt as though it had stopped beating. I closed my eyes, thinking I was daydreaming. When my brain responded, I turned and ran inside Aunt Mary's home and smashed into her. 'It's . . . it's my . . .' I stuttered.

'Yes, I know,' Aunt Mary gently spoke as she held me. 'You're going to be all right.'

'No! You don't under . . . she's going to take me away! She found me!' I yelled. I tried to squirm myself away from Aunt Mary's grip so I could run outside and find a safe place to hide.

Aunt Mary's grip didn't budge. 'I didn't want to upset you,' Aunt Mary said. 'She's just going to drop off some clothes. You're going to court this Wednesday, and your mother wants you to look nice.'

'No!' I cried. 'She's going to take me! She's going to take me back!'

'David, be still! I'll be right here if you need me. Now, please, be still young man!' Aunt Mary did her best to calm me down. But my eyes nearly popped out as I watched The Mother stroll down the walkway with *her* four boys in tow.

I sat by Aunt Mary's side. Greetings were exchanged, and like a trained dog I became my old self – the child called 'It'. In an instant I went from an enthusiastic boy to Mother's invisible house slave.

Mother didn't even acknowledge my presence. Instead, she turned to Aunt Mary. 'So, tell me, how is *The Boy*?'

I looked up at Aunt Mary's face. She seemed startled. Her eyes flickered for just a second. '*David*? David is quite fine, thank you. He's here, you know,' Aunt Mary responded, holding me a little tighter.

'Yes,' Mother said in a dry voice, 'I can see that.' I could feel Mother's hate burn through me. 'And how does he get along with the other children?'

Aunt Mary cocked her head to one side. 'Quite fine. *David* is very polite and extremely helpful around the home. He's always looking to help out,' she answered, knowing that Mother had no intention of talking to me directly.

'Well . . . you should be careful,' Mother warned. 'He's tried to hurt other children. He does not get along well with others. *The Boy* is violent. He needs special attention, discipline that only I know how to instill. You don't know *The Boy*.'

I could feel the muscles on Aunt Mary's arm become tight as a drum. She leaned forward, giving Mother her best smile – the kind of smile that Aunt Mary would like to slap Mother silly with. '*David* is a fine young man. *David* may be a bit rambunctious . . . but that's to be expected considering what *David*'s been put through!'

Suddenly I realized what was happening. Mother was trying to gain control of Aunt Mary, and Mother was losing. On the outside my shoulders slumped forward, and I gave Mother my timid puppy dog look as I stared down at the carpet. But on the inside my ears became like radars, picking up every phrase, every syllable of the conversation. *Finally*, I said to myself. *Someone had finally put Mother in* her *place. Yes!*

The more I heard Aunt Mary's tone change toward Mother, the more my face lit up. I was enjoying this. I slowly lifted my head up. I looked right into Mother's eyes. Inside I smiled. *Well, isn't this nice. It's about time*, I said to myself. As I listened to them, my head began to weave from left to right, then back again, as if I were watching a tennis match. Aunt Mary tried again to have Mother acknowledge me. I nodded my head at Mother as I openly agreed with Aunt Mary.

I began to feel extremely confident. *I am someone. I am somebody*,

I told myself. I could feel parts of my body begin to relax. I was no longer scared. For once, everything was fine – right up until the moment I heard the phone ring. My head snapped to the right as the kitchen phone shrilled. I counted the rings, hoping someone would hang up. I became tense after the twelfth ring. Aunt Mary turned toward the kitchen. I grabbed her arm. *Come on,* I said to myself. *No one's home. Just hang up.* But the phone kept ringing – sixteen, seventeen, eighteen times. *Just hang up! Just hang up!* I could feel Aunt Mary lean forward to get up. I kept my hand on her arm, trying to force her to stay. When she stood up, I followed. My right hand clamped onto her left arm. She stopped midstride and pried my hand off, finger by finger. 'David, please. It's just the phone. For goodness' sake, don't be rude. Now go back in there.' I stood still. I locked onto Aunt Mary's eyes for a brief moment. Aunt Mary understood. She nodded her head. 'Okay,' she said in a low voice. 'Come on, you can stay with me.'

I let out a sigh of relief as I followed her feet to the kitchen. Suddenly, I felt my left arm being yanked backwards. I nearly lost my footing. I fought to regain my balance. I closed my eyes as I bit my lip. My legs began to shake. Inches in front of me sat Mother. Her heavy, raspy breathing made me quiver. Mother's face was dark red. I could tell that from behind her glasses her eyes were on fire. I tried to search for my savior, but Aunt Mary had already turned into the kitchen.

I stared down at the carpet, wishing her away. Mother squeezed my arm tighter. 'Look at me!' she hissed. I became frozen. I wanted to yell, but my voice became mute. Her evil eyes locked onto mine. I closed my eyes as I felt Mother's head inch its way toward my face. Mother's monotone voice became vicious. 'Cocky little bastard, aren't you? Well, you don't look so tall now. Do you? What's the matter? Has your little Aunt Mary left you?' she said in a sarcastic, whining voice. Mother then yanked me so close to her face that I could smell her breath and feel droplets of saliva spray on my face. Mother's voice turned ice cold. 'Do you know what in the hell you've done? Do you?! The questions they've asked me? Do you realize the embarrassment you've cost *This Family*?' Mother asked, as she spread her left hand at my brothers sitting beside her.

My knees began to buckle. I wanted to go to the bathroom and throw up. Mother smiled, showing me her dark yellow teeth. 'They think I tried to hurt you. Now why would I do that?'

I tried to turn my head toward the kitchen. I could barely make out Aunt Mary's voice on the phone.

'Child!' Mother hissed. 'Boy . . . get this straight! I don't care what they say! I don't care what they do! You're not out of this yet! I'll get you back! You hear me? *I'll get you back!*'

When she heard Aunt Mary hang up the phone, Mother released my arm and pushed me away. I sat back in the wide chair and watched my savior stroll back into the living-room and sit down beside me. 'I'm sorry about that,' Aunt Mary said.

Mother batted her eyes and waved her hand. Suddenly she became regal. The act was on. 'That? Oh, the phone? No problem. I have to . . . I mean, we have to get going anyway.'

I stole a glance at my brothers. Their eyes were hard and fixed. I gazed at them, wondering what they thought of me. Except for Kevin, who was still a toddler, the three of them seemed as if they wanted to throw me outside and stomp on me. I knew they hated me, and I felt I deserved it. For I had exposed the family secret.

I tried to imagine what it must be like for them to live with Mother now. I prayed that somehow my brothers would forgive me. I felt like a deserter. I also prayed that the cycle of hate had not moved on to one of them. I felt sorry for them. They had to live in total hell.

After another round of pleasantries and final warnings from Mother to Aunt Mary, The Family departed. As I heard the sound of Mother's tires from her station wagon mash down on the rocks as she drove away, I remained glued to the chair. I sat in the living-room for the rest of the afternoon, rocking back and forth, repeating Mother's pledge over and over again, *I'll get you back. I'll get you back.*

That evening I couldn't eat. In bed I rolled back and forth until I sat up clutching my knees. The Mother was right. I knew in my heart she would get me back. I stared out the window of my room. I could hear the wind howl through the tops of trees and the branches rub against each other. My chest began to tighten. I cried. I knew at that moment there was no escape for me.

At school the next day I couldn't concentrate on my work. I strolled around the schoolyard like a zombie. Later that afternoon I met Ms Gold at Aunt Mary's home. 'David, we're going to court in two days. I need to ask you just a few questions to clarify our case. Okay, honey?' she asked with a bright smile.

I refused to speak and sat rigidly at the far end of the couch. I couldn't look at Ms Gold. To her dismay I muttered, 'I don't think I should say anything.'

Ms Gold's mouth nearly fell to the carpet. She began to speak, but I raised my hand, cutting her off. I then retracted as many statements as I could, claiming that I had lied about everything. I had caused all of the household problems. I told her that I had fallen down the stairs. I had run into doorknobs. I had beaten myself. I had stabbed myself. I then cried to Ms Gold that my mommy was a beautiful, kind woman, with the perfect flower garden, the perfect home, the perfect family, and that I craved her attention because of my other brothers. And everything was all my fault.

Ms Gold became speechless. She scooted over to where I sat. She tried several times to reach out and hold my hand. I brushed her delicate fingers away. She became so frustrated that she began to cry. After several hours and many attempts, Ms Gold looked at me with dried streaks of tears and blotches of black eyeliner running down her face. 'David, honey,' she sniffled. 'I don't understand. Why won't you talk to me? Please, honey.'

Then she tried to switch tactics. She stood up and pointed her finger at me. 'Don't you know how important this case is? Don't you know that all I talk about in my office is a cute little boy who is brave enough to tell me his secret?'

I looked through Ms Gold and tuned her out. 'I don't think I should say anything else,' I coldly replied.

Ms Gold bent over, trying to force me to look into her face. 'David, please . . .' she begged.

But to me, she just wasn't there. I knew that my social worker was trying everything in her power to help me, but I feared Mother's wrath more than Ms Gold's. From the moment Mother stated, 'I'll get you back,' I knew everything in my new world was lost.

Ms Gold reached out to hold my hand. I slapped her fingers away. I turned my back to her. 'David James Pelzer!' she barked, 'do you have any idea what you're saying? Do you understand what you're doing? You had better get your story straight! You're going to have to make a major decision pretty soon, and you better be ready for it!'

Ms Gold sat back down, wedging me between her knees and the end of the couch. 'David, you have to understand that in a person's life there are a few precious moments in which decisions, choices that you make now, will affect you for the rest of your life. I can help you, but only if you let me. Do you understand?'

I again turned away. Suddenly Ms Gold sprang up from the couch. Her face became bright red and her hands were shaking. I tried to hold back my feelings, but a surge of anger erupted. 'No!' I cried out. 'Don't you get it? Don't you understand? She'll get me back. She'll win. She always wins. No one can stop The Mother. Not you, not anyone! She'll get me back!'

Her face went blank. 'Oh my God!' Ms Gold exclaimed as she bent down to hold me. 'Is that what she said to you? David, honey . . .' Her arms stretched out to embrace me.

'No!' I yelled. 'Won't you just leave me alone? Just . . . go . . . away!'

Ms Gold stood over me for a few moments, then turned on her heels and stormed out of the room. A few seconds later I could hear the sound of the screen door slamming in the kitchen. Without thinking, I ran into the kitchen, but I stood frozen behind the door. Through the screen I could see Ms Gold stumbling up the steep walkway. She lost her grip on her papers and tried to catch some of them in midair. 'Shit!' she cried out. The papers scattered as she desperately tried to gather them into one pile. As soon as she stood up, she fell down, scraping her right knee. I could see the frustration on her face as she clamped her hand over her mouth. Ms Gold tried again to stand up, but this time with more caution as she made her way to the county car. She slammed the car door shut and bent her head against the steering-wheel. As I stood behind the screen door, I could hear Ms Gold – my angel – sobbing uncontrollably. After several minutes she finally started her car and sped off.

I stayed behind the kitchen screen and cried inside. I knew I could never forgive myself, but lying to Ms Gold was the lesser of two evils. I stood alone, confused, behind the screen door. I felt that by lying, I had protected Mother, that I had done the right thing. I knew Mother was going to get me back and no one could stop her. But then when I thought of how kind Ms Gold had been throughout everything, I suddenly realized the terrible position I had just put her in. I never meant to hurt anybody, especially Ms Gold. I became a statue as I stood behind the screen door. I only wished that I could crawl under a rock and hide, forever.

chapter 3

THE TRIAL

Two days later Ms Gold drove me to the county courthouse. The ride began in total silence. I sat on the far side by the door, staring at the scenery. We drove north on Highway 280 beside the aqueduct, the same water reserve the family used to drive by on our way to Memorial Park years ago. Ms Gold finally broke the ice, explaining in a soft voice that today the judge would decide whether I was to become 'a permanent ward of the court' or be returned to my mother's custody. I didn't understand the 'ward of court' part, but I knew what returning to my mother's custody meant. I shivered at this last part of Ms Gold's sentence. I looked up at her, wondering whether I would be riding back with Ms Gold after court or in the back of Mother's station wagon. I asked Ms Gold whether there was a possibility of Mother taking me back with her today. Ms Gold reached out, patted my hand and nodded yes. My head slumped forward. I didn't have the energy to resist anymore. I hadn't been able to sleep since our last meeting. The closer Ms Gold drove to the courthouse, the more I could feel myself slipping from her safety and back into Mother's clutches.

My hands formed into a tight fist. The countdown now began.

I felt a soft caress on my left hand. My arms flew up to protect my face. It took a moment for me to realize that I was only daydreaming. I took a deep breath and nodded to myself, trying to calm myself down. 'David,' Ms Gold began, 'listen to me very carefully. This is Pam talking, not Ms Gold, your social worker. Do you understand?'

I let out a deep sigh. I knew we were only a few miles away from the courthouse. 'Yes, ma'am, I understand.'

'David, what your mother did to you was wrong. Very wrong. No child deserves to be treated like that. She's sick.' Pam's voice was soft, and calm. She seemed on the verge of tears. 'Remember Monday afternoon when I told you that one day you'd have to make a decision? Well, today is that day. The decision you make today will affect you for the rest of your life. Only *you* can decide your fate. I've done all that I can do. Everyone's done what they can do – your teachers, the school nurse, Aunt Mary, everyone. Now it's up to you.

'David, I see so much in you. You're a very brave young man. Not many children can tell their secret. Someday this whole experience will be behind you.' Ms Gold stopped for a moment. 'David, you're a very brave young man.'

'Well, I don't feel very brave, Ms Gold. I feel . . . like . . . like a traitor.'

'David,' Pam smiled, 'you're not a traitor! And don't you forget it.'

'If she's sick,' I asked, 'then what about my other brothers? Are you going to help them, too? What if she goes after one of them?'

'Well, right now my only concern is you. I don't have any information that your mother was or is abusing your brothers. We have to start somewhere. Let's take this one step at a time. All right? And David . . .' Ms Gold switched off the ignition. We had reached the courthouse.

'Yes, ma'am?'

'I want you to know that I love you.'

I looked deep into Ms Gold's eyes. They were so pure. 'I really do,' she said, stroking the side of my cheek.

I cried as I nodded my head. Ms Gold lifted my chin with her fingers. I pressed my head against her hand. I cried because I knew that in a few minutes I would betray Pam's love.

Minutes later we walked into the waiting room of the county courthouse, and Ms Gold grabbed my hand. Mother and the boys were waiting on one of the benches. Ms Gold nodded at Mother as the two of us walked by. I stole a glance. Mother was wearing a nice dress and had fixed up her hair.

Ron had a cast on his leg.

No one acknowledged my presence, but I could feel Mother's hate. Ms Gold and I sat down, waiting our turn. The delay was unbearable. Burying my head under my right arm, I mumbled to Ms Gold, asking her for a pen and paper. I proceeded to scribble a small note.

To Mother:
I'm so sorry. I didn't mean for it to come to this. I didn't mean to tell the secret. I didn't mean to hurt the family. Can you ever forgive me?
                                                                    Your son, David

Ms Gold read the note and nodded, giving me permission to give the note to Mother. I shuffled over to Mother, becoming a child called '*It*' once again – with my hands stuck to my sides and my head cocked down toward the floor. I waited for Mother to say something, to yell at me, snap her fingers, anything. She didn't even acknowledge my presence. I inched my head upward, moving my eyes up her body, and stuck my hand out, holding my note. Mother snatched the paper, read it, then tore it in half. I bowed my head before returning to Ms Gold, who put her arm around my shoulder.

Minutes later Ms Gold, Mother, my four brothers and I filed into the courtroom. I sat behind a dark table, gazing in awe at the man above me dressed in a black robe. 'Don't be afraid,' Ms Gold whispered. 'The judge may ask you a few questions. It's important, very important that you tell him the truth,' she said, stressing the last part of her sentence.

Knowing that my final outcome would be decided in the next few minutes, I reached over and nervously tapped Ms Gold's hand. 'I'm sorry for all the trouble I caused you . . .' I wanted to tell her the truth – the real truth – but I didn't have the guts. The lack of sleep had drained all of my inner strength. Ms Gold smiled at me reassuringly, revealing her pearly white teeth. A subtle yet familiar fragrance filled my head. I closed my eyes, taking in a deep breath . . .

Before I knew it, the clerk began to read off a number and stated my name. At the mention of my name my head snapped up at the judge, who adjusted his glasses and glanced down at me. 'Yes, the . . . uhh . . . Pelzer case. Yes. I presume the representative from the county is present?' the judge asked.

Ms Gold cleared her throat and winked at me. 'Here we go. Wish me luck.'

The judge nodded at Ms Gold. 'Recommendations?'

'Thank you, Your Honor. As the court is well aware through the extensive briefs from the pediatrician's examinations, interviews with the minor's former teachers, other interviews and my reports, the county recommends that David Pelzer become a permanent ward of the court.'

I stared up at Ms Gold. I could barely make out her voice. I knew it was she who was talking, but her voice cracked. I glanced down at her skirt. Her knees were shaking. I clamped my eyes shut. *Oh my*

God, I said to myself. As I opened my eyes, Ms Gold returned to her seat, covering her trembling hands.

'Mrs Pelzer? Is there anything you wish to state?' the judge asked.

Every head swung to the right, stopping at Mother. At first I thought Mother did not hear the judge. She simply stared up at his bench with a blank expression. After a few seconds, I realized what Mother was trying to do. She was trying to stare the judge down.

'Uhh . . . Mrs Pelzer? Do you wish to make a statement in regard to your son, David?'

'I have nothing to say,' Mother said in a flat tone.

The judge rubbed his forehead then shook his head. 'Fine. Thank you, Mrs Pelzer. Duly noted.'

The judge then turned to Ms Gold. 'This is a very disturbing, very unusual case. I have read thoroughly all of the statements, and I have been troubled with the . . .'

I lost track of time as the judge began to ramble. I felt myself shrinking inside. I knew in a matter of minutes the proceedings would be over and I would be back with Mother. I glanced over to the right to look at her. Mother's face was stone cold. I closed my eyes, visualizing myself back at the bottom of the stairs and sitting on top of my hands, hungry – like a starving animal. I didn't know whether I could go back to that life again. I only wanted to be free of the pain and the indignity.

'David?' Ms Gold whispered as she poked me. 'David, the judge wants you to stand up.'

I shook my thoughts clear. I had fallen asleep, again. 'What? I don't under . . .'

Ms Gold grabbed my elbow. 'Come on, David. The judge is waiting.'

I stared up at the judge, who nodded for me to stand. My throat felt as if an apple were stuck in it. As I pushed my chair behind me, Ms Gold tapped my left hand. 'It's all right. Just tell the judge the truth.'

'Well, young man,' the judge began. 'What it boils down to is this: If the court so desires and if you believe that your home setting is undesirable . . . you may become a permanent ward of the court, or you may return and reside with your mother at your home residence.'

My eyes grew wide. I couldn't believe that this moment had finally come. In unison, every person in the small room turned toward me. A lady with grayish white hair held her fingers just above a strange-looking typewriter. Every time someone spoke, the lady tapped keys that looked like tongue depressors. I swallowed hard and clenched my hands. From the right I could feel Mother's radar of hate turn on.

I tried to look at the judge. I swallowed hard once more before I started to deliver my rehearsed line about how I had lied and that I had indeed caused all the problems at home and that Mother had never abused me. From the corner of my right eye I could see Mother's eyes locked on to me.

Time stood still. I closed my eyes and imagined myself being driven back to The House with The Mother, where she would beat me and I would be forced to live at the bottom of the stairs, dreading the second set of commercials, wishing I could someday escape and become a normal kid who was allowed to be free of fear, to play outside . . .

Without Ms Gold knowing, I turned to her and inhaled again. Suddenly it hit me – Ms Gold's perfume. It was the same perfume she wore whenever she gave me a hug or held me as we lay at the end of the couch. I saw myself playing with her hair.

My mind switched to seeing myself outside, laughing with the other children, playing basketball, searching for each other in a game of tag and running at hypersonic speeds through Aunt Mary's home; then at the end of the day being dragged in from outside after hunting for snakes or playing by the creek. I opened my eyes and peeked at my hands. They were no longer red. In fact, my skin had a light tan.

I could feel Mother's radar drill through me. I felt myself leaning to the right, a surge of fear creeping up my back. I took in another whiff of Ms Gold's perfume.

I held my breath for a fleeting second, then before my courage disappeared I blurted out, 'You, sir! I want to live with you! I'm sorry! I'm so sorry! I didn't mean to tell! I didn't mean to cause any trouble!'

Mother's radar of hate intensified. I tried to remain standing, but my knees began to buckle.

'So be it,' the judge quickly announced. 'It is the recommendation of this court that the minor, David James Pelzer, shall become a ward of the court and remain so until his eighteenth birthday. This case is closed!' the judge quickly concluded, as he slammed his gavel on a piece of wood.

I felt paralyzed. I wasn't sure what had just happened. Ms Gold sprang up and hugged me so tightly that I thought she'd crush my ribs. All I could see was a forest of blonde strands, and I gagged as I almost swallowed clumps of Ms Gold's hair. After a few moments, Ms Gold regained her composure. I wiped my tears and my runny nose. I looked up at the bench. The judge smiled at me. I returned the gesture. Then, for a brief moment, I thought His Honor winked at me.

I felt Mother's radar of hate flicker, then turn off.

Ms Gold held my shoulders. 'David, I'm so proud of you!' Before she could say anything else, I whimpered, 'I'm so sorry. I didn't mean to lie to you the other day. I'm sorry I made you cry. Can you ever forgive me? I just wanted to . . .'

Ms Gold parted my hair from my eyes. 'Shh. It's all right. I knew what you were doing. But now, your mother wants to . . .'

'No!' I cried. 'She'll take me away!'

'She only wants to say goodbye,' Ms Gold assured me.

As Ms Gold and I slowly made our way out of the courtroom, I could see ahead of us that Mother was crying, too. Ms Gold nudged me forward. I hesitated until I felt sure that Ms Gold would stay nearby. The closer I walked to Mother, the more I cried. Part of me didn't want to leave her. Mother's arms opened wide. I ran into them. Mother hugged me as if I were a baby. Her feelings were sincere.

Mother let go, took my hand and led me to her car. I felt no fear. At the station wagon Mother loaded me up with new clothes and lots of toys. I was astounded. My mouth hung open as Mother continued to fill my arms.

My voice cracked as I said goodbye to my brothers, who shook their heads in response. I felt like a traitor, and I thought they hated me for exposing the family secret.

'I'm going to miss you,' Mother cried.

Before I could think, I replied, 'I'll miss you, too.'

As happy as I was for the judge's decision, I became filled with sadness. I felt torn between my freedom and being separated from Mother and the family. Everything was too good to be true – my freedom, the new clothes, the toys. But the thing I cherished most was the warmth of Mother's hug.

'I'm so sorry about everything,' I sobbed. 'I really am. I didn't mean to tell.'

'It's not your . . .' Mother began. Her eyes changed. 'It's all right.' Mother's voice became firm. 'Now listen to me. You have another chance. This is a new beginning for you. I want you to be a good boy.'

'I will,' I said, as I wiped away my tears.

'No!' she stated in a cold voice. 'I mean it! You have got to be a good boy! A better boy!'

I looked into her swollen eyes. I felt that Mother wanted the best for me. I realized that before Mother went into the courtroom, she had already predicted the outcome.

'I'll be good. I'll try real hard,' I said, as I squared my shoulders like I did back in the basement years ago. 'I'll make you proud of me. I'll try my best to make you proud.'

'That's not important,' Mother stated. Before she sent me away, she gave me a final hug. 'Have a happy life.'

I turned away sniffling. I didn't look back. I thought about what Mother had last said. *Have a happy life.* I felt as if she were giving me away. I almost collapsed when I reached Ms Gold, who helped me load her car with my prized possessions. We stood together as Mother drove off. I waved to everyone, but only Mother returned my gesture. Her window was rolled up, but I watched Mother's lips as she repeated, 'Have a happy life.'

'How about an ice cream?' Ms Gold asked, breaking the tension.

I stood up straight and smiled. 'Yes, ma'am!'

Pam gently took my hand, wrapping her long fingers around mine, and led me to the cafeteria. We strolled past the other cars and a few scattered trees. I caught a whiff of the trees' scent. Then I stopped to gaze at the sun. I stood still for a moment, taking in my surroundings. A soft wind blew through my hair. I didn't shiver. The grass was a bright yellow-green. I knew that my world was different now.

Ms Gold stopped to look at the sun, too. 'David, are you going to be all right?'

'Yes!' I smiled. 'I just don't want to forget this first day of the rest of my life!'

chapter 4

NEW BEGINNINGS

After the effects of the trial had worn off, my insides became numb.

I fully realized that Mother could not physically harm me. But I still felt an eerie sensation that told me Mother was somewhere out there, coiled like a rattlesnake, waiting to reach out and strike with a vengeance.

But another part of me felt that I would never see Mother or my brothers again. I became confused, sensing that I didn't deserve to live with them, that I was unworthy and that Mother had thrown me away. I tried my best to tell myself that through the wonder of the county's social services and the court system, I had a new lease on my life. I tried my best to isolate my past, to bury my dark experiences deep inside my heart. Like a light switch, I imagined myself flicking off my entire past.

I quickly became accustomed to the routine at Aunt Mary's home, as well as to my new school. Even though I was spontaneous and free at Aunt Mary's, I still became lifeless and shy around my classmates. It seemed difficult for me to make friends. I stood out, especially whenever children asked why I didn't live with my parents. And whenever some of my classmates persisted, I stuttered and turned away. I couldn't look into their eyes.

Other times I'd happily state, 'I'm a foster child!' I was proud to be a member of my new family. I began to repeat this saying until one day one of the older foster children pulled me aside at school, warning me not to tell anyone 'what' I was because '. . . a lot of folks don't like our kind.'

' "Our kind?" What are you taking about?' I asked. 'We didn't do anything wrong.'

'Don't worry, little brother. You'll find out soon enough. Just be cool and keep your mouth shut.' I obeyed the command, realizing I now lived in another world of prejudice.

During recess, I watched the other kids laugh as they played tag and handball, while I kept to myself and wandered around the school in a daze. No matter how hard I tried, my mind kept flashing back to my other school in Daly City. I thought of Mr Ziegler and his animated 'happy face' suns, which he would draw on my papers, Mrs Woodworth's dreaded spelling tests or running to the library, where Ms Howell played 'Octopus's Garden', by The Beatles, on her record player.

In my new school I had completely lost interest. I no longer absorbed my subjects as I had just a few weeks ago. I sat behind the gray steel desk half-dazed, scribbling on my papers, counting down the minutes until the end of the school day. What was once my sanctuary soon became a prison that kept me from my playtime at my foster home. As my attention span drifted, my handwriting, once cursive and graceful, became chicken scratch.

At Aunt Mary's my awkward sense of humor and naïve excitability made me popular with the older foster children. Whenever some of them were granted permission to leave Mary's home for the afternoon, I was allowed to tag along. Sometimes they stole candy bars from the local grocery stores. Wanting total acceptance and having already stolen food for years, I immediately followed their lead. If someone stole two candy bars, I stole four. It seemed so easy to me that after a few afternoon trips, I became a legend within the group. I was fully aware that what I was doing was wrong. I also knew that some of the bigger boys were using me, but I didn't care. After years of isolation, I was finally accepted within a group.

My stealing was done within the foster home as well. Waiting until everyone was outside, I'd sneak into the kitchen and take slices of bread and stash them under my pillow. Then late at night I'd sit up on my bed and nibble on my prize, like a mouse nibbling on a piece of cheese. One Sunday afternoon I grew tired of bread and decided to steal Dolly Madison cupcakes from the freezer. In the early morning hours I awoke to find an army of ants leading to the head of my bed. As quickly and quietly as I could, I tiptoed to the bathroom and flushed my goodies, along with the ants, down the toilet. The next day, as Aunt Mary prepared our lunches for school, she discovered the missing desserts and blamed Teresa, one of the other foster children.

Even though Teresa was severely scolded and grounded to her

room after school that day, I remained silent. I didn't steal from Aunt Mary's home for the thrill of it, but only to have a ready-made storage of food in case I ever became hungry.

It didn't take long for Aunt Mary to discover that I was the one responsible for the missing food. From that moment on, Aunt Mary eyed me carefully around her home and did her best to restrict my afternoon adventures. At first I felt ashamed because I had betrayed her trust and kindness. But on the other hand, I simply didn't care what 'Old Maid' Aunt Mary thought of me. My only concern was total acceptance by the older foster children.

My welcome at Aunt Mary's was probably worn out even before the first week of July, when I was placed in my first permanent foster home. Just as before, when the police officer had driven me to Aunt Mary's for the first time, I couldn't wait to see the new home. My new foster mother, Lilian Catanze, greeted Ms Gold and me at the door. As I followed Mrs Catanze and Ms Gold up the wide, open stairs that led into the living-room, I tightly clutched a brown grocery bag containing all my worldly possessions. The night before, I made sure to pack my bag and keep it close to my side.

I knew from experience that if I left anything behind, I would never see it again. I was shocked when I first witnessed the foster children who transformed into frenzied piranhas whenever a child left Aunt Mary's home. Within seconds of the child's departure, the others would swarm through the room, checking under the bed, in the closets and through the clothes hamper – everywhere – searching for clothes, toys or other valuables. The ultimate prize was to find a stash of money. I quickly discovered that it didn't matter whether the thieves needed or even desired the items. Possession of an article, any article, meant trading power for other things – household chores, late-night desserts or an exchange for money. As usual, I adapted quickly, and joined in the hunt whenever a child left. I learned that rather than walking a child to the car and wishing him or her good luck, I would instead say my goodbyes in Aunt Mary's home . . . and then stay close to the departing child's room so I could have a head start on the other kids. But as a sign of respect, we all knew to never enter a room until the child had left. I also learned that deals were usually made the night before, and as a courtesy the roommate would get first dibs. So I, too, would give away a few shirts and a couple of toys.

As I began to imagine the other foster children ransacking my old room, I heard Mrs Catanze ask, 'Well, David, what do you think?'

Still holding my bag, I nodded my head up and down before saying, 'It's a very nice house, ma'am.'

Mrs Catanze waved a finger in my face. 'Now, we'll have none of that. Everyone here calls me either "Lilian" or "Mom". You may call me "Mom"'.

I again nodded, but this time at both women. I didn't feel comfortable calling Mrs Catanze, some lady I just met a few moments ago, Mom.

As the two ladies chatted for several minutes, Lilian leaned close to Ms Gold, hanging on her every word and shaking her head from side to side. 'No contact? None at all?' she asked.

'Correct,' Ms Gold replied. 'David is to have no contact with his mother or his brothers, unless Mrs Pelzer makes the arrangements.'

'And the father?' Lilian asked.

'Not a problem. He has your number and should be calling you soon. David's father did not make it to the court proceedings, but I've kept him informed of David's status.'

Mrs Catanze leaned a little closer to Ms Gold. 'Anything special I need to know?'

'Well,' Ms Gold began, 'David is still in the adjustment phase. He's a bit hyper and into everything – and I mean everything. He's a bit light-fingered, if you know what I mean.'

Sitting on the couch, I acted as if I were not paying attention, but I could hear every word.

'David,' Mrs Catanze said, 'why don't you wait in the kitchen, and I'll be with you in just a few moments.'

As I followed Mrs Catanze into the kitchen, I still held on to my grocery bag. I sat by the table and drank a glass of water as Lilian closed the sliding door, separating the two rooms. I could hear Mrs Catanze sit back down, but the two women started whispering. I watched the numbers of a clock radio flip over every time a minute passed. Before I knew it, the sliding door opened.

Ms Gold smiled at me before giving me a hug. 'I really think you're going to like it here,' she said. 'There's a play park nearby, and you'll have lots of other foster children to play with. I'll check in on you as soon as I can, so be extra good.'

I gave Ms Gold another quick hug, thinking I'd see her in a few days, and waved goodbye to her from the upstairs window. Before Ms Gold drove down the street, she waved a final goodbye, then blew me a kiss. I stared through the window, not knowing what to do next.

'Well,' Mrs Catanze asked, 'would you like to see your room?'

My eyes lit up as she took my hand. 'Yes, ma'am.'

'Remember what I told you,' Lilian warned.

I nodded my head. 'I'm sorry. I forget things sometimes.'

Mrs Catanze led me into the first room down the hall. After putting my clothes away I joined her on the twin-sized bed. 'I need to explain a few things to you – the home rules. You are responsible for keeping your room clean and helping out with the chores. You do not enter someone else's room without their permission first. There is no lying or stealing in this home. If you want to go somewhere, you first ask me and tell me where and how long you'll be away . . .'

'You mean I get to go anywhere I want to?' I asked, amazed that I suddenly had all of this unexpected freedom.

'Within reason, of course,' Lilian responded. 'This home is not a prison. As long as you act responsible, you'll be treated as such. Do I make myself clear?'

'Yes, Mrs Catanze,' I said in a soft, slow voice, still feeling awkward calling her Mom.

Mrs Catanze patted my leg before leaving the room and closing the door. I leaned back on the bed, smelling the fresh-scented pillowcase. I tried to focus on the sounds of cars rushing up and down the steep street, until I finally gave in to sleep. As my mind began to drift off, I began to feel safe and secure in my new setting.

Sometime later I awoke to the sounds of voices, coming from the kitchen. After I cleared my eyes, I walked out of the bedroom and into the kitchen.

'Is this him?' someone with long blond hair chided. 'This ain't no kid. He's a runt.'

Lilian leaned over and smacked the tall, blond teenager in the arm. 'Larry, now watch your mouth! David, please excuse him. This,' she said, still staring at Larry, 'is Larry Junior. You'll meet Big Larry in a few minutes.'

'C'mon Larry, he's small, but kinda cute. Hi, I'm Connie. And I don't want you going through my things in my room. You got that?' As Connie leaned over, I nearly choked on her perfume. She had shiny black hair and long eyelashes, and wore a minidress. I couldn't help myself as I stared up at her legs. Connie stepped back, and her face turned red. 'Mom, he's a little pervert!'

I turned to Mrs Catanze. 'What's a "pree-vert"?'

Lilian laughed. 'Someone who shouldn't look up young ladies' dresses!'

I didn't understand. I wanted to know what it meant. I began to ask the same question when Mrs Catanze cut me off. 'And this is Big Larry.'

I looked as far up as I could, to see a huge man with dark curly hair and black-framed glasses. He had a kind, gentle face. Big Larry smiled as he shook my hand. 'Mom,' he said, 'I'm gonna go to the show tonight. Mind if I take Dave with me?'

Lilian smiled. 'I don't mind, but you make sure you take care of him.'

'Yeah,' Larry Jr chimed, 'make sure he doesn't get scared or see anything that's . . . nasty!'

About an hour later Big Larry and I began our journey to the movie theater. I could tell that he was childlike and shy. I liked him immediately. As we walked up and down the endless streets of Daly City, we both talked about things of no importance. Somehow we each knew not to ask why the other was in foster care. It was a sort of code that was explained to me while I stayed in Aunt Mary's home. The closer we strolled to the theater, the more Big Larry became my friend.

Larry claimed to have seen the movie *Live and Let Die* a dozen times, so I couldn't understand why he so badly wanted to see it again. But after the first ten minutes of the show, I, too, sat paralyzed. I became mesmerized by the action scenes and the fast-paced music that carried the film. After years of living in the dark, craving adventure, I finally saw it on film. While Larry gazed at the girls in bikinis, I fidgeted in my seat, waiting impatiently for James Bond to make his next narrow escape from death while at the same time saving the world from doom. After seeing this movie, the character of James Bond became etched in my mind, much in the same way as Superman had years earlier.

The next day was just as special. Rudy, Lilian's husband, loaded their two cars full of foster children and mountains of food for their annual Fourth of July family get-together picnic at Junipero Serra Park – the same park I went to as a small boy when I was considered a member of Mother's Family. When we arrived at the park, I helped carry containers and bags full of goodies, not knowing where to place them. 'What do I do with these?' I asked no one in particular.

'David, just place it anywhere,' Rudy replied.

'But all of the tables are already full of stuff from other people,' I whined.

Lilian stepped beside Rudy. They joined hands. 'Yes, David, we know,' she said. 'These people are our family.'

I looked at the scores of adults drinking soda and beer. Kids ran in every direction as they played tag. 'Wow, all these people are your kids?'

Suddenly a woman screamed. I nearly recoiled into my protective shell as the woman frantically ran toward me in thick, funny-looking wooden shoes. 'Mom! Dad!' the woman howled. She then tried to wrap her arms around both Lilian and Rudy. I stared at her face. She didn't look anything like Mr or Mrs Catanze.

Lilian cried as she blew her nose, then gave her handkerchief to the woman and closed her eyes for a brief moment to recompose herself. 'David, this is one of our first foster children, Kathy.'

Now I understood. I turned my head from side to side, straining my eyes as streams of people flocked over to Rudy and Lilian.

'And Mom, Dad, I got a job. I'm married. I'm going to night school and this . . . is my new baby!' Kathy announced, as a man with a beard handed over a baby wrapped in a yellow blanket into Rudy's open arms. 'Oh, Mom, Dad, it's so good to see you!' Kathy cried.

A small mob of adults crowded around the Catanzes. Swarms of children jumped up and down, screaming for attention, as babies and hugs were exchanged. After a few minutes, I excused myself from the crowd and made my way to the edge of the hill. I sat down, staring at the planes lifting off from the nearby airport.

'Pretty cool, isn't it?' a familiar voice said.

I turned to look at Big Larry.

'Every year it's the same thing, but more people. I guess you can say they love kids. So what do you think?' Larry asked.

'Wow! There must be hundreds of folks here!' I exclaimed. 'Have you ever been here before?'

'Yeah, last year. How about you?'

I stopped for a moment to study a jumbo jet dipping its wing to the west. 'When I was a kid . . .' I caught myself, not sure if I really wanted to say anything. I had held back so much for so long. I cleared my throat before continuing. 'My parents – my real mom and dad – would always take my two brothers and me to this park when we were just kids.' I smiled. 'We'd spend the entire day just down the hill, playing on the swing set . . .' I closed my eyes, seeing Ron, Stan and me as happy, bright-faced kids. I wondered what they were doing now . . .

'Dave! Hey, David! Earth to Dave, come in!' Larry blared as he cupped his hands together, acting as if they formed into a blow-horn.

'Sorry,' I automatically replied. 'I think . . . I think I'll take a walk.'

After asking permission from Lilian, I strolled down the paved hill. A few minutes later I found myself standing on the same grassy area as I did a lifetime ago. Back then, I was a member of the perfect family. Now I was still a child, searching for my past. I walked toward the swing set and sat on one of the black swings. I kicked the sand, filling the heels of my shoes with some of it. My mind began to drift off again.

'Hey, mister? Are you going to play or what?' a small child asked.

I slid off the swing and walked away. My insides felt hollow. In front of me, beneath a shade of trees, a young couple sat on the same table as Mother and Father did years ago. The woman got up and called out to her children with her hands on her hips – just as Mother had done when she had called to her children. For a second our eyes met. The lady smiled at me as she bowed her head. As I heard the sounds of children running from the swing set, I closed my eyes, wishing I had the answers to why everything had gone so wrong with Mother and me.

The two questions that tumbled over and over in my mind were whether Mother ever loved me and why she treated me the way she did.

Later that evening I wanted so badly to talk to Mrs Catanze, but I couldn't work up the nerve. The next morning I woke up late and shuffled into the kitchen. 'She ain't here, runt,' Larry Jr hissed. 'You'll have to feed yourself.'

I didn't know what to do. I didn't know how to cook, and I didn't know where cereal bowls were, or even where the cereal was.

'So,' Larry Jr began, 'I hear your mother used to kick the crap outta you. Tell me, what's it like? I mean, to have someone use your face for a mop?'

I couldn't believe this creep. Every time I was with Larry Jr, he was always trying to put me down. I bit my lip, trying to think of something to say. I failed to think of anything smooth. A surge of anger began to race through me.

'So tell me, man, what's it like? I mean, I'm curious. Seriously, what's it like to have the crap kicked out of you? Why didn't you fight back? What are you, some sort of wimp?'

I turned away from him and ran to my room. I could hear him laughing behind me as I slammed the door shut. I burrowed into my bed and cried without knowing why. I stayed in the room all day.

'Mrs Catanze, am I a wimp?' I asked her the next day as she drove me to the shopping mall.

'A wimp? David, where did you hear that?'

I did not want to rat on Larry Jr. But he was a turd, and I didn't like him anyway. I still felt upset about how he and the other big kids thought of me. I swallowed hard before I answered Lilian.

'Pay Larry no mind,' Mrs Catanze said afterward. 'He's a very upset young man. David, we have quite an array of . . .'

I gave her a puzzled look.

'. . . quite a mixture of young folks who have different . . . special needs. Larry is just at that age when he's rebellious. He wants to fight everything and everyone. Give him a wide berth – lots of room. He's just feeling you out. Give it some time. Okay?'

'Yes, ma'am. I understand, but am I a wimp 'cause I didn't fight back? I mean, is it right to fight your own mother?'

Mrs Catanze shoved the gear shift into park as she stopped in front of Tanforan Park. She turned to the right as she took off her glasses. 'No, David,' she stated matter-of-factly. 'You are not a wimp for not fighting back. I don't know all that happened, but I do know you're not a wimp. Now come on. I've got a check here for $127 from the county to buy you some clothes. And,' Lilian smiled, 'I'm not afraid to spend it. Lesson number one: Let's go shopping!'

As Lilian took my hand, I screeched, 'Wow, $127! That's a lot of money!'

'Not for a growing boy. And you do plan on growing, don't you? That's all the money they gave us for this year. Wait until you have kids of your own,' Lilian stated, as she opened the door into Sears.

A couple of hours and three shopping bags later, Lilian and I returned to her home. I smiled from ear to ear as I closed the door to my room, then laid out all of my clothes as neatly as I could. Next, I arranged the shirts by their colors and folded my underwear briefs and socks just right before putting them away. I sat by the foot of the bed for a few seconds before I ripped open the drawers and rearranged my clothes again. After the fourth time, I slowly opened the drawers. As gently as I could, I removed a dark blue shirt. My hands trembled. I breathed in the smell of cotton. *Yes!* I told myself. *These are* my *clothes!* Clothes that no one had ever touched or worn before. Not rags that Mother had made me wear or clothes she had given me out of pity, that she had stored since last Christmas, or clothes from Aunt Mary that other foster children had worn before.

'Yes!' I squealed out loud. Then without thinking, I flung open the drawers and threw everything back on the bed. It took me forever to repack my clothes. But I didn't care – I was having fun.

A few days later, before lunch, Lilian hung up the phone in the kitchen before calling me away from the television. 'So,' she asked, 'how are you feeling today?'

I shrugged my shoulders. 'Fine, I guess.' My eyes grew wide. 'Did I do something wrong? Am I in trouble?'

'No, no,' she said in a calm voice. 'Now stop that. Why do you always say that whenever someone asks you a simple question?'

I shook my head. I understood what she said, but I did not know why I always felt on edge whenever someone asked me a question. 'I dunno.'

Lilian nodded. 'Hey, let's say we have some lunch. I'll kick Larry Junior out, and it will just be the two of us, all right?'

My face lit up. 'Sure!' I liked it whenever Mrs Catanze and I were alone. I felt special.

Lilian made a couple of bologna sandwiches as I grabbed a bag of chips. She first warned, then ordered me to slow down my eating

and to use better table manners. I obeyed her by not seizing everything in sight or shoving food into my mouth. I smiled at her,
proving to her that I could indeed chew with my mouth closed.

Mrs Catanze seemed to take her time as she delicately ate her
sandwich. I almost asked her why she chewed so slow, when I heard
a loud banging on the door. Without thinking, I blurted, 'I'll get it!'
Still chomping on my food I bolted down the stairs and opened the
door. A split second later I nearly coughed up my food. My brain
locked up. I couldn't break away from looking at *her*.

'Well, aren't you going to invite us in?' Mother asked in a kind
voice.

From behind me, I could hear Lilian rush down the staircase.
'Hello . . . I'm Lilian Catanze. We spoke on the phone today. We
were just finishing lunch.'

'You did say one P.M., didn't you?' Mother asked in a demanding
tone.

'Uhh . . . yes, I did. Please come in,' Lilian said.

Mother marched in, followed by the boys. Stan came in last, with
a grin on his face as he pushed in my bike, which Grandmother
had purchased for me last Christmas. I remembered that day when
Mother had allowed me to ride the bike, twice. I had never ridden
before, and I fell several times before I got the hang of it. And at the
end of the day I ran over a nail, and the front tire went flat. Now as
Stan shoved the bike into Lilian's house, I could immediately see
that both tires were flat and parts were missing from the bike.

But I didn't care. The yellow and candy-apple-red Murray bicycle
with its metallic-red banana seat was my prized possession. I was
shocked that Mother decided to give it to me.

Mother and the boys only visited for a few minutes, but Lilian
made it a point to stay by my side. Even though Mother's attitude
seemed more relaxed – not cold and demeaning, as when she had
come to see me at Aunt Mary's – she still wouldn't talk to me. I had
so much to tell her. I wanted to show her my room, my new clothes
and the artwork that I did in school. Above all, I wanted so badly to
prove to Mother that I was indeed worthy of her acceptance.

'Well,' Mother said as she got up from the couch, 'I just wanted
to drop by. Remember, David, I *will* be checking in on you from
time to time, so . . . *you be good*,' Mother stated in a sly voice.

Lilian raised her hand, stopping me before I could say anything.

'Thank you for stopping by, Mrs Pelzer. And remember, do call *if* you drop by again,' Lilian replied, as Mother stepped through the door.

I raced up the stairs. I stopped in front of a tall window and remained perched behind the glass as I watched Mother and the boys pile into her faded gray station wagon. As she drove off, I waved frantically, but no one saw me. In my heart I knew my effort was in vain. I wished that just once – just once – someone would smile and wave back.

Lilian let out a deep sigh, then placed her hands on my shoulders. 'So, that's your mother? Are you all right?'

I nodded my head yes. I looked up at Lilian. Tears rolled down my face. 'She doesn't love me, does she? I mean . . . I just don't understand. Why? Why won't she even talk to me? Am I that bad? Why didn't you tell me she was coming over? Why?

'I'm tired of her treating me like . . . like I'm nothing. I'm tired of her, my brothers, that creep Larry . . .' I pointed my finger at the window. 'She didn't even talk to me. She never talks to me. Never!' I spun around to Lilian. 'Am I that bad? I try to be nice. I try to be good. I didn't tell her to come over, did I?' I began to rant and rave, throwing my hands into the air as I paced the living-room. 'Did I tell her to beat me . . . to . . . to not feed me for days or . . . or have me live and sleep in the garage like . . . like . . . *an animal*?

'At night she wouldn't even give me a blanket. Sometimes I got so cold . . . I tried to stay warm. I really did,' I cried as I nodded my head.

I wiped my runny nose with my finger and closed my eyes. For a brief moment, I saw myself standing in front of the kitchen sink – back at The House. Beside me I could see a smelly, pink paper napkin. I took a deep breath before I opened my eyes. 'I . . . I . . . remember one Saturday afternoon . . . she had me pick up some dog poop . . . and . . . I was in the kitchen; she was in the living-room lying down on the couch watching her shows. That's all she does, all day, every day, is watch her shows. Anyway . . . all I had to do was throw the poop in the garbage disposal, and she'd never know. I knew if she found out, it'd be too late. I mean, by the time she heard me turn on the disposal, it would be too late . . . but I ate it 'cause she told me to. As I did, I cried inside, not because of . . .

but . . . because I had *let* her do that to me. For all those years I had let her treat me like she did. For years I was so ashamed.'

I began to whimper. 'I never told. I never told . . . Maybe Larry's right. Maybe I am a wimp.'

'Oh, David! Oh my God!' Lilian cried. 'We didn't know . . .'

'Look at this . . .' I yanked up my shirt. 'This . . . this is where she stabbed me. She didn't mean to. It was an accident. But you know why?'

The blood drained from Lilian's face. She closed her eyes before she covered her mouth with her hand. 'No, David, I don't know. Why did she?'

'She said she'd kill me if I didn't "do the damn dishes in twenty minutes". Ain't that a kick? The funny thing is that ever since the accident, I just wanted to tell her I knew she didn't mean to kill me, that I knew it was an accident. I actually prayed that the accident would bring us together – that somehow she knew she'd gone too far, that she couldn't hide the secret anymore. I wanted her to know that I forgave her.

'But no! I'm the bad guy. She won't even talk to me. Like . . . like I'm the one who's the bad guy!' I could feel my arms tighten up and my hands form into fists. I stared through Mrs Catanze as I slowly turned my head from side to side. 'Damn it! She won't even talk to me! Why? Why? Why?!'

Lilian knelt down in front of me. She was sobbing, too. 'David, I don't know. We need to have you talk to someone, someone who can help you. This is something you need to get out of your system. You need someone who's more qualified . . . who knows what to do. Ms Gold and I will arrange for you to talk to someone who will help you find some answers. All right?'

I felt myself drifting away. I focused on Lilian's mouth moving, but I couldn't make out what she was saying. She took my hand and led me into my room. As I lay in bed, she stroked my hair, whispering, 'It's all right. I'm right here. Everything's going to be all right.'

Hours later I woke up refreshed and followed Mrs Catanze as she bounced down the staircase to examine my bike. Moments later I shook my head in disgust. 'Stan did this,' I said. 'Mister Fix-It. It's his way of getting back at me.'

'Well, David,' Lilian said in a firm tone, 'the question is: Are you going to sit here and sulk about it, or are you going to do something about it?' She stopped for a moment as if to ponder an idea. 'You know, if you wanted to . . . you could probably earn some extra money and fix up your bike. That is, if you wanted to.'

A few minutes later I walked back up the stairs and plopped myself on the couch. I now became consumed with fixing my bike. When Big Larry came home from work, I ran to his room to seek his advice. Throughout the evening, Larry and I schemed on the quickest way to achieve my goal. After ten o'clock, we came up with the perfect plan, a plan so flawless that Larry guaranteed I would have my bike up and running in thirty days or less. Larry, who claimed to be a 'master strategist' – I had no idea what his statement meant – went on to boast that when Mom and Dad saw me coming, they would willingly throw money at me.

'Wow!' I gasped. 'This is just too cool!'

Before quitting for the day, Big Larry and I dubbed our plan 'Operation: Bug the Parent'.

The following morning I stayed glued to Lilian's side, begging her for extra work. An hour later she threw her arms in the air. 'All right! I give up! Here, take these rags and clean the bathroom. You do know how to clean a bathroom, don't you?'

I smiled and said to myself, *Like you wouldn't believe!* As I gazed up at her, I cocked my neck to one side. 'How much?'

Lilian blinked her eyes. 'What?'

'How much to clean the bathroom?' I stated in my most serious voice.

Mrs Catanze nodded her head. 'Oh, I understand. Okay, little big man, I'll tell you what: I'll pay you a quarter . . .'

Before Lilian could complete her sentence, I replied, 'No! Not enough.'

'Aren't you the greedy one. Okay, how much?'

I could feel myself retreat inside. Big Larry hadn't taught me what to do in this case. 'I dunno,' I said, as I felt all my confidence shrinking away.

'I'll tell you what,' she said, hovering over me. 'I'll give you thirty cents. Take it or leave it.'

I knew from what Big Larry had instructed me to do that whenever someone said 'take it or leave it', it meant I should take the deal and run. I nodded my head triumphantly. 'It's a deal. Let's shake on it.'

Looking at Lilian, I could tell she wasn't ready for all my high-powered art of deal making. I felt I had tricked her into not only paying me, but giving me more money than she had originally offered.

It took me nearly two hours to clean the bathroom – as Mrs Catanze put it, 'by the employer's standards'. I felt that she had somehow taken advantage of me. As I scrubbed the tile floor for the third time, I knew that evening I would need to talk to Big Larry and complain about our fool-proof plan.

My mixed feelings suddenly disappeared when Lilian dropped a nickel and a quarter into my eager palm. Forgetting to thank her, I raced into my room, found a jar I had saved and dropped the change into the jar. I stared into the jar every day. In less than a month I had earned over four dollars – more than enough, I figured, to fix my bike. Finally, after the right amount of pestering again, Tony, Lilian's son, drove me in the back of his beat-up orange Chevy pickup truck to the bicycle shop. Tony knew, without my bugging him, all the parts I needed. I didn't seem to notice how when the bill arrived, Tony came up with more cash than I had.

That day, without permission, I borrowed some tools I had found and began to piece my bike together. After dozens of attempts at forcing the inner tubes into both tires I wiped off my bloody knuckles, jumped on my bike and, for the first time in my life, let out a howl of victory as I breezed down the street without a care in the world.

I remember August 21, 1973, as *my* day on *my* bike. That day was the first time I felt that I was a *normal* kid, caught up in the splendor of a never-ending day. For years I had heard the sounds of kids zooming down the street, screaming with joy as they flew by on their bikes. That day I must have ridden up and down the street a thousand times. Mrs Catanze had to drag me inside. 'David Pelzer, it's been dark for over an hour now! Get your little butt in here, now!' she barked, as I sailed past her in defiance.

Even though my legs ached from the strain of pumping my bike up the street, I didn't want my special day to end. As Lilian stood with her hands on her hips, I jumped off my bike and puffed all the way as I walked my bike up to her home. I could tell by the look on her face that she was about to yell at me. But I beat her to the punch by giving her my best smile.

'All right,' she said as she threw her arm around me. 'Get in here. Don't worry; tomorrow's another day. After you're done with your chores, you can take your bike to the park.'

I clenched my fist in victory. 'Yes!' I cried.

Early the next morning, as I stepped out of bed, I discovered that I could barely bend my legs. I looked into the mirror and smiled. 'Yes!'

chapter 5

ADRIFT

After my initial taste of freedom, I spent as much time as I could riding my Murray bicycle. As soon as I rolled out of bed, I'd scramble to the open window (I never slept with the blinds down) and check the weather. Then I'd gulp down breakfast, blitz through my chores, race down the stairs and slam the front door shut, after yelling to Mrs Catanze that I was leaving.

Mrs Catanze usually watched my departure through her kitchen window. Never missing an opportunity to show off, I'd wave to her behind my back. At times I'd pedal down the street so fast that I thought I was flying. Minutes later I'd prop my feet on the center bar and coast through the freshly cut grass of the play park. After parking my bike, I'd scramble through the immense tri-layered wooden fort. I'd climb all the ropes, and run and jump on the chained drawbridge. After exhausting myself, I'd lie down to catch my breath. I always stretched out on the highest level so I could feel the warmth of the sun's rays as they inched their way across the park.

Whenever I heard laughter, I'd peek over the ledge of the fort and stare with fascination as other children, mostly younger than I, played with their friends or parents. I wanted to join in, but I always chickened out before I approached them. Somehow I knew I did not fit in.

I always stayed at the park until I could no longer suppress my growling stomach. Then I'd hop on my bike and casually pedal up the street to Lilian's home. As a habit, whenever I'd burst through the front door, I'd suck in my breath and then scream, 'I'm back!' Lilian always answered my call, but one day she did not reply. I skipped up the stairs and ran into the kitchen.

I whirled around when I heard someone behind me. 'She ain't here, runt,' Larry Jr was in one of his usual moods.

I wanted so badly to tell him off, but I bit my lip and stared down at the floor, acting timid, and nodded my head without looking up, indicating he had won. As I tried to scoot past him so I could go to my room and wait for Lilian, he blocked my path. Without warning he seized my arm.

'Where's Momma's little boy going?' he whined, as he tightened his grasp.

I shot a look of hate into his eyes as I tried to squirm out of his grasp. 'Hey, man . . . let go!' I exclaimed.

'Yeah, Larr . . . Larry, jus . . . just let . . . ah . . . let the kid . . . go,' Chris stuttered. I turned my head upward to Chris, one of my other foster brothers. I was surprised to see him because he usually stayed downstairs in his room.

Larry Jr maintained his grip on my arm, but I could tell by his snide expression that he was going to turn his attention toward Chris. He gave me a final squeeze before shoving me aside. 'Da . . . da . . . what does the retard want? Shouldn't the retard be hiding in his little room?' Larry said mockingly.

Chris was the first person I had known who had cerebral palsy. I could see the pain in his eyes. I knew what it was like to be ridiculed, and I hated it. I also knew Larry's sole pleasure was to hurt Chris's feelings. Chris inched his way toward Larry until he stood toe to toe in front of Larry's face. Larry fluttered his eyebrows as he cocked his right arm up and back. I could almost imagine Larry striking Chris and smashing his teeth. Without thinking I yelled, 'No! Stop it! Just stop it!'

Larry Jr swung his arm toward Chris, but at the last moment he brushed his hand through his hair. 'Psych!' Larry sneered. 'Hah! It doesn't take much to fool a couple of morons, does it?'

I could feel my body temperature rise. 'Go to hell!' I yelled.

Larry's eyes grew wide. 'Oh, so Momma's little boy has a mouth. I'm *sooo* scared. I tell you what, runt,' Larry snarled, as he pushed me against the kitchen countertop, 'why don't you make me?'

I knew by the size of him that he could snap me like a twig. I didn't care. 'Back off, man,' I blurted. 'I'm tired of you. Just because you're older and bigger . . . that doesn't give you the right to treat us that way, does it? How would you like it if someone picked on you?'

For a moment Larry seemed to be in a daze. Then he shook his head clear. 'And who do you think you are – Dr Spock?' I stopped for a second, thinking of what Larry had just said. *Spock? Did he mean the Vulcan dude from* Star Trek? I asked myself.

'If I were you,' Larry continued, 'I'd stick to my own business and ride my little bicycle. Otherwise,' he added with a wide grin, 'I might use your little face to mop the floor.'

I lost control. I wanted to climb up his legs and beat his face. I ran up to Larry. 'I'm tired of taking crap from guys like you. You . . . you . . . butt head! You think you're *so* big. You're a creep . . . a bully. You ain't . . . you ain't shit. You're *so* tough, aren't you? Like it really takes a tough guy to pick on someone like Chris. You wanna take a punch? Okay, come on, do it! Show me what you got. Come on tough guy! Well . . . ?'

I could feel my fingers coil. I knew that what I was doing was wrong, but after all the years of being put down by others who *felt* they were so superior, I had had it. And seeing how Larry Jr treated Chris made my blood boil. I had to do something.

As I felt my breathing become heavier, I could tell I was getting to Larry. His face became tight as I badgered him relentlessly. For once, I was on the giving end. I liked the feeling. Larry's face twisted from side to side until he elbowed me against the kitchen countertop. I felt my head strike something hard, but my anger kept the pain away.

Before Larry stormed out of the kitchen, he raised his fist at Chris. 'Hey, man, you better watch yourself, or one of these days you may find yourself getting tripped down the stairs and breaking that retard neck of yours. And know this: it's going to take someone more than this excuse of a wimp to fight your battles!

'And you!' Larry stopped as he looked at me. 'You better watch that mouth of yours. If I wanted to . . . I could clean your clock . . . just like that!' he boasted, as he snapped his fingers. 'Both of you, stay the hell outta my way. You got me? You pair of freaks!'

I clamped my hands on the countertop until I heard Larry slam the door to his bedroom so hard that the windows upstairs rattled. After a few seconds, I finally released my grip. I closed my eyes as I tried to control my breathing. It seemed to take me forever to breathe normally again.

I opened my eyes and searched for Chris. He had disappeared. As I ran out of the kitchen and into the living-room, I heard the door to Chris's room slam shut, too. I raced downstairs and quickly knocked on Chris's door before I burst in. He sat on the foot of his bed, staring at the floor. Tears rolled down his face. I tilted my head to one side. 'Did Larry hit you?'

'Na . . . ah . . . no! I ca . . . can take ah . . . care of myself, you know! I don't need a li . . . little runt to . . .' Chris stuttered.

'Man, what are you talking about?' I asked. 'Larry is the biggest creep on the planet. I'm tired of him picking on me and you all the time.'

Chris's head shot up. 'You ah . . . just bet . . . better take care of yourself. Ah . . . you can get into a lot . . . of . . . of trouble. If Mom . . . ah ever heard you ah . . . swear . . . swearing . . . she'd . . .'

I brushed Chris's statement away with my hands as I watched him limp his way to his stereo. He grabbed a thick, red cartridge, then shoved it into a tape machine he called an eight-track player. I had never seen one before. After a couple of clicking sounds, a singing group called Three Dog Night began to wail 'Joy to the World'. As Chris's worn-out speakers vibrated, I sat next to him on his bed. I realized that what I had done upstairs was wrong. 'Hey man,' I told Chris, 'I'm sorry. I was just ticked off.' Chris indicated that he forgave me. I smiled back. 'Hey, Chris, what does Larry mean when he says he'd "clean my clock"?'

Chris laughed as drool escaped from the side of his mouth. 'Ee . . . ah . . . means he'll kick your butt!'

'But why does he pick on you? You never do anything to him. I don't understand.'

Chris's eyes shone. 'Ah man, you are ah . . . fun . . . funny. Look at me. He don't need a reason. People like Larry pick on me 'cause I'm . . . I'm ah diff . . . different. You're . . . ah different, too. You's small and gots a big mouth.'

I leaned back on Chris's bed as he went on to explain that his real parents had abandoned him as a small child and he had lived in foster care ever since. He told me that he had been in over a dozen foster homes until he moved in with Rudy and Lilian. The Catanzes were the closest thing to a real home for him. I listened carefully as Chris talked. In a way, his stuttering reminded me of myself just a few months ago. But Chris seemed scared. Behind his eyes he looked frightened. Chris informed me that this was his last year in foster care.

'What does that mean?' I asked, as the tape cartridge changed tracks.

Chris swallowed hard, trying his best to concentrate before he answered. 'Uhm . . . it . . . ah means that when you turn uh . . .

eighteen, you . . . move out and have to ah . . . to take care of yourself.'

'And you're seventeen?' I asked.

Chris nodded.

'Then who's going to take care of you?'

Chris glanced down at the floor. He rubbed his hands together for several seconds. At first I thought that maybe he had not heard me, but when he looked back up at me, I realized why he was so scared and why he had been crying.

I nodded in return. Now I understood.

After my argument with Larry Jr, I kept to myself and tried to stay as far away from him as I could. But whenever no one was around and I found myself running into him, for no reason I'd blurt out feelings of hatred at him. Sometimes he'd simply swear, while other times he'd chase me around the home. Larry would always catch me and tackle me to the floor. Once, after punching me a few times in the arm, he yelled, 'Say "uncle"!'

I didn't understand. I twisted from side to side, trying to squirm myself out from under Larry as he sat on top of my chest and continued to hit me. 'No way!' I yelled back.

After a few minutes I could see the sweat pour from his forehead. 'Say uncle! Say it!' Larry panted. 'Give up, man!'

Even though I was exhausted from struggling to get away, I felt that I was wearing Larry down. 'No way! You ain't my uncle. Now get off!'

Larry let out a laugh as he rolled off me. Without thinking, I laughed, too. He patted me on the back. 'You okay, kid?' I nodded. 'I'll say one thing for you, runt: you got a lot of nerve. You never give up,' he said, still panting. 'But you are the most craziest son of a—'

Suddenly I sprang up and shoved Larry on the floor with all my might. I pointed my finger at him, and he seemed dazed by my actions. 'I'm not crazy! And don't you ever, *ever*, say that to me again!' I screamed, as I burst into tears.

From below I could hear Mrs Catanze close the front door. I fixed my eyes on Larry as long as I dared, before hiding in my bedroom.

'What's going on now?' Lilian asked with a huff. 'Are you two fighting again? I tell you, I've about had it with the both of you.'

'Mrs C, it ain't me, but the runt,' Larry said in a low voice. 'He ain't right. I mean, he's loony toons, man. I was just playing with him, and he went off on me.'

I turned away from the door and cried.

I didn't know why I was so stupid. I had tried so hard to understand what the other foster kids were saying so I could learn – so I could be accepted within the group of the older kids. I wanted so badly to be liked. But I still couldn't comprehend. *Maybe*, I told myself, *I* am *a moron. Maybe, I* am *crazy.*

I turned when I heard a faint tapping on the door. I quickly wiped my nose with the sleeve of my shirt before opening the door. 'Can I come in?' Mrs Catanze said with a bright smile. I nodded my head yes.

'So, you and Larry were at it again?' she asked.

I nodded my head again, but more slowly.

'Well, what do you think we ought to do?'

I closed my eyes as tears rolled down my face. 'I just don't know why I feel so bad,' I cried.

Mrs Catanze wrapped her arms around my shoulders. 'Not to worry. This is something we'll just have to work through.'

A few days later Rudy and Lilian drove me to a doctor's office. Rudy stayed in the blue Chrysler as Lilian walked me to the office. She and I waited for several minutes until an elderly woman directed Lilian into another room. After a few minutes Lilian returned. She knelt down and told me I was going to see a special doctor who was going to make me feel better 'up here,' Lilian said, as she pointed to my head.

Moments later, I followed the same lady who had escorted Lilian. She opened a wide door and waved her hand as if telling me to enter. As carefully as I could, I walked into the room. The lady closed the door behind me. I stood alone in a dark room. I searched for an open window, but I could tell that the shades were drawn. The room had an eerie feeling. I remained standing in the middle of the room for several seconds until a man, whom I hadn't seen when I came in, told me to sit down. I jumped when I heard the stranger's voice. The man flicked on the light on his desk. 'Come on now, sit; sit down.' I obeyed, finding an oversized chair. I sat and stared at the man. I waited for him to say something, anything. *Am I in the right room, the right office? Is he the doctor? Surely he can't be a psychiatrist!*

Seconds turned into minutes. Though I tried, I could barely make out the outline of the man's face. He rubbed his two hands together as he appeared to study me. My eyes darted from side to side. I could see there was a long couch against the wall behind me. The other walls of the room were covered with shelves filled with books.

As the man continued to stare at me from behind the desk, I began to fumble with my hands. I couldn't take it any longer. 'Excuse me, sir, are you the psychiatrist? Do you want me to lay down on the couch, or is it okay to sit here?' I asked in a broken voice.

I could feel my words trailing off as I waited for some sort of response from him. He folded his hands. 'Why did you ask that question?' the man asked in a flat voice.

I bent my head down so I could hear better. 'Sir?' I asked.

The man cleared his throat. 'I said, why did you ask that question?' he said, emphasizing every word.

I felt about ten inches tall. I didn't know what to say. It seemed to take forever before I replied, 'I dunno.'

In a flash, the man picked up a pencil and began to scribble on a piece of paper. A moment later the pencil disappeared. He smiled. I smiled back. I knew my last statement was a dumb one, so I tried to think of something clever to say. I wanted the man to like me. I didn't want him to think I was a complete idiot, I nodded my head with confidence. 'Kinda dark in here, huh?'

'Really?' the doctor immediately began to write again, at a frantic pace. I then realized that whenever I said anything, the man – the doctor, I assumed – would record everything.

'And why did you ask that question?' the doctor asked.

I thought very carefully before I answered. ''Cause . . . it's dark,' I said, searching for approval.

'And you are afraid of the dark – yes?' the doctor said, as if finding his own answer.

Crazy, I said to myself. *He thinks I'm crazy*. I squirmed in my seat, not knowing how to reply. I began to rub my hands. I wished Mrs Catanze would burst through the door and take me away.

A long stretch of silence followed. I felt I'd be better off not digging my grave any deeper. I looked down at my moving fingers. The doctor cleared his throat. 'So, your name is Daniel?'

'David, sir. My name is David,' I proudly stated, as my head snapped forward. At least I knew my name.

'And you are in foster care, is that correct?'

'Yes . . . sir,' I answered slowly, as I began to think about where his questions were leading.

'Tell me, why is that?' the doctor asked, as he folded his hands behind his head and looked up at the ceiling.

I was not sure of the question. 'Sir?' I asked, sounding hollow.

The doctor tilted his head toward mine. 'Tell me, young David, why is it that you are in foster care?' he asked with irritation in his voice.

The doctor's question was like a punch in the face. I felt creepy all over. I did not mean to make him mad, but I just did not understand his questioning. 'I . . . uh . . . I dunno, sir.'

He picked up his pencil and began to tap the eraser on top of his desk. 'Are you telling me that you have no idea why you are in foster care? Is that what you are telling me?' he asked as he made more notes.

I closed my eyes, trying to think of an answer. I could not think of the right response, so I leaned close to the doctor's desk instead. 'Whatcha writing, sir?'

The doctor flung his arm on his desk, covering his notes. I could tell I had upset him. I sat rigid in the back of the seat. He fixed his eyes on mine. 'Perhaps I should set the ground rules. *I* ask the questions. *I* am the psychiatrist. And *you*,' he said, pointing his pencil at me, 'are the patient. *Now*, do *we* understand each other?' He nodded his head as if telling me I should agree and smiled when I returned his nod. 'So,' he said in a kinder voice, 'tell me about your mother.'

As I cleared my thoughts, my mouth seemed to hang open. I felt so frustrated. Maybe I wasn't so smart, but I didn't think that I deserved to be treated like an idiot. The doctor studied my every expression as he took more notes. 'Well,' I began, as I fumbled for words, 'my mother . . . I really don't think . . . she was—'

He cut me off with a wave of his hand. 'No! In here *I* perform the analyses, *you* answer the questions. Now tell me, why did your mother abuse *you*?'

I let out a deep sigh. My eyes scanned behind his desk. I tried to imagine what was behind the window blinds. I could hear the sounds of cars rushing past the building. I imagined Rudy, sitting in his Queen Mary-sized car, listening to the radio station that played oldies . . .

'Young man? Daniel! Are you with me today?' the doctor asked in a bellowing voice.

I lurched deeper into the back of the chair, ashamed that I was caught daydreaming in the presence of a doctor. I felt ashamed for acting like a little kid.

'I asked you, *why* did your mother abuse *you?*'

Without thinking, I snapped back. 'How do I know? *You're* the doctor. You figure it out. I don't understand you . . . your questions . . . and every time I try to answer them, *you* cut me off. Why should I tell you about me when you don't even know *my name?*'

I stopped to catch my breath, when I heard a buzzing sound. The doctor pushed a button, picked up the phone, nodded, then put the phone back down. He waved his hand in front of me as he jotted down another note before saying, 'Would you hold that thought for me? That's all the time we have for this week, and I'll . . . let me see . . . I'll pencil you in for next week. How's that sound? I think we have a real good start here, Daniel, okay? So I'll see you next week. Goodbye now,' he said, with his head bent over his desk.

I gazed at him in total disbelief. My mind was so jumbled that I didn't know how to react. *Is this the way a session normally goes with a psychiatrist?* I asked myself. Something was wrong, and I felt that that something was me. I sat motionless for a few moments, then slid out of the chair and walked to the door. As I opened it, the doctor muttered for me to have a nice day. I turned around and smiled. 'Thank you, sir,' I said in a cheerful voice.

'Well,' Mrs Catanze said, 'how did it go in there?'

'I dunno. I don't think I did too well. I think he thinks I'm dumb,' I said, as Lilian led me back to the car. 'He wants to see me next week.'

'Well then, you must have made a good impression. Relax; you worry too much. Come on now, let's go home.'

I slid into the backseat of Rudy's car. I became lost as the street signs streaked by. I felt more upset than I had before. I wanted to tell Lilian how I felt, but I knew if I did, my words would come out wrong and I would make a fool of myself in front of her and Rudy.

Lilian broke my concentration. 'So, how do you feel?'

I crossed my arms tightly across my chest. 'Confused,' I announced in a firm tone.

'Well,' she said, as she tried to find the right words to make me feel better, 'these things take time.'

My next session was just as bizarre.

'Today, let's begin our session by telling me . . . Daniel, how did you feel when your mother abused you? I understand that at one time she . . .' The doctor flipped through an open file that I had figured was on me. He began to mumble to himself until he closed the folder. 'Yes,' he stated to himself. 'You were eight years old when your mother . . .' – he put on his glasses as he began to read a paper from the file – '. . . held your arm, your right arm . . .' he nodded again, but at me, '. . . over a gas stove. Is that correct?'

A bomb exploded inside my stomach. My hands began to twitch. Suddenly my entire body felt like rubber.

I stared at his facial movements as he casually replaced the sheet of paper on his desk – a paper that contained the most horrible parts of my life. *Scribbled on that sheet is my life – my life, which the great* doctor *holds in his hands – and he still doesn't even know my name! My God!* I yelled to myself. *This is nuts!*

'Daniel, why do you think your mother burned you that day? You do remember that incident, don't you . . . Daniel?' he paused for a moment.

I stroked my right forearm as I felt myself hovering in time.

'Tell me,' he added, 'how do you feel toward your mother?'

'David,' I said in an ice-cold voice. 'My name is *David*!' I shouted. 'I think she's sick and so are you!'

He didn't even blink an eye. 'You hate your mother, don't you? That's perfectly understandable. Express yourself. Go on, tell me. We have to begin somewhere so we can work through these things, problems, in order to . . .'

I lost track of the doctor's voice. My right arm began to itch. I scratched it before I glanced down. When I did, I saw that my right forearm was engulfed in flames. I nearly jumped out of my seat as I shook my arm, trying to put out the fire. I clenched my fist as I blew on the flames. *Oh my God, no!* I screamed to myself. *This can't be happening! Please help me! Please!* I tried to cry out to the psychiatrist. My lips parted, but nothing came out. I could feel the sides of my face flooding with tears as flames of orange and blue danced on my arm . . .

'Yes! That's it!' the doctor yelled. 'Good! Let it out! That's fine,

Daniel. Now, Daniel, tell me, how do you feel right now? Are you . . . upset? Do you feel violent? Do you want to take out your aggression on someone or something?'

I looked at my arm. The fire was gone. As much as I tried, I could not control myself from shaking. I cupped my arm and gently blew on it as if to make myself feel better. I leaned forward to get up, still clutching my right arm. I wiped my face as best I could before I opened the door to leave.

The doctor sprang up from behind his desk. 'All right, you can leave early. We've made progress today. Don't let this upset you. I'll pencil you in for next . . .'

Slam! I closed the door with all my might.

In the outer office, the elderly receptionist jumped from her seat. I stopped by her desk for a moment. The woman seemed as if she were about to scold me, until she took a long look at my face. She stopped mid-sentence and turned away as she seized the phone. The next patient turned his head, too, as I marched out of the office.

By accident I slammed the door to Lilian's car. She flung her paperback book into the air. 'David! What . . . ? You're early. Is everything all right?'

I clenched my two hands together. 'No! No! No!' I yelled. 'That man,' I pointed my finger at the building across the street, 'is sick! He asked me the weirdest questions. Today he asked me how I felt when . . .'

'Well, David,' she said in a firm voice, 'that's his job. He's the doctor. I'm sure he's only trying to help . . .'

'No!' I blurted, as I shook my head. 'He doesn't ask questions like you or Ms Gold, but sick ones. Like, *what did it feel like to be burned on a gas stove?* And that *it was all right to hate my mother,*' I said, imitating the doctor's tone of voice. 'I don't know what to say or do around him. He's weird. He's the one who needs help, not me. He's the sick one.'

'Is that the reason why you were so upset last week? Did he treat you like that last time?' Lilian asked.

I nodded. 'I just don't know. I feel so dumb, so small. I mean, I know what happened with Mother and I was wrong and I'm really trying to forget all about it. I mean, maybe my mom's sick. I know it's the booze, but I have to know: am I sick, too? Am I going to end up like her? I just want to know. I just want to know why it all happened the way it did. We were the perfect family. What happened?'

After I blew off my steam, I stretched out in the passenger seat. Lilian leaned over, 'All better now?'

'Yes, ma'am,' I answered. She started the car. I could feel myself drifting off to sleep. I held my right arm just above my wrist. I strained myself to stay awake a little bit longer. 'Mrs C, I don't ever want to go back there – ever,' I said. And then my world went black.

I stayed by myself in my room for the next few days. Then Big Larry asked if I wanted to watch him bowl. I happily accepted, and once again my big foster brother and I set out for another adventure. I found out our destination as we rode our bikes through nearby Daly City. Larry and I rode down the small street that led into the parking lot of Thomas Edison Elementary School. Slowing my bike, I watched as the children played on the swing sets. I skidded to a stop, breathing in the smell of fresh tanbark. It seemed like a lifetime ago that I was a child who happily played in the same play yard during recess.

A heavy fog seemed to hover over the school before it lowered itself. The outline of the children became lost as the gray mist seemed to swallow them, too. After a few minutes, only their sounds of laughter told me that the children were even there.

I shook off the thoughts of my past as I pumped my bike up another hill and away from my old school. About ten minutes later, Larry and I stopped at the Sky Line grocery store – the same store I had stolen from when I ran from the school during my lunch recess. I stayed close to Larry's side. I thought for sure someone would recognize me. 'Are you okay?' Larry asked as we strolled down the aisles.

'Yeah,' I answered in a low voice. My eyes darted around every corner. I walked in slow motion and grabbed Larry's belt to tell him to slow down. I was on Mother's turf now.

'Hey, man, what's your problem?' he asked after my last tug.

'Ssh. I used to live here,' I whispered.

'Really? Cool,' Larry said, as he chomped on a fruit pie as we were walking outside the store. 'Is that why you acted funny at that school?'

'I . . . I guess so,' I answered.

After Big Larry finished two more cream pies, a few candy bars and two sodas, we set off to the bowling alley. The ride up Eastgate Avenue became too much for me. I hopped off my bike and stared down the street as I walked past. 'Stop!' I barked without warning.

From behind me Larry was panting like a dog. 'What's up?'

'Do me a favor,' I said. 'Let's take a break and ride down this street.'

A cloud of mist escaped his mouth. 'Yeah, okay. What gives?' he asked.

'You promise not to tell?'

'Yeah, man, what's up?'

'Don't tell . . . but I used to live on this street.'

Larry's head swiveled to the street sign. 'Cool! Which house?'

'The dark green one. On the left side, in the middle of the block,' I said, as I pointed down the street.

'Hey, man, I don't know about this,' he said, shaking his head. 'Mom would definitely say no. So, no it's not a good idea! What if your mother or your brothers are outside?'

I parked my bike behind a clump of bushes, staying close as I peered down the street. I could hear Larry stumbling behind me. My heart raced. I knew that what I was doing was wrong and dangerous. 'If you decide to accept this mission . . .' Larry whispered, as if we were both working on an assignment from *Mission: Impossible*.

'Come on. The coast is clear,' I said, giving Larry the high sign.

Larry shook his head. 'I don't know about this.'

'Come on,' I begged. 'I've never asked you for anything. Mrs C will never find out. Besides, I'll . . . I'll do your chores for a whole week. Okay? Please?'

'Okay, kid. It's your neck.'

I jumped back on my bike and kept the pressure on my brake as I slowly rode. No one seemed to be outside. I could see that the garage door to Mother's house was closed. As we approached the green and black house, I let out a shriek of joy. *This is so cool*, I told myself. Suddenly a pair of heads popped up from my brothers' bedroom window. 'Shit!' I muttered.

'What's wrong?' Larry asked.

'Just go!' I snapped.

'What?'

'I said, let's go!'

'Hey, man, what's the problem?'

'Not now!' I yelled. 'Come on! Go! Go! Go!'

I leaned forward on my handle bars and pedaled so hard that I thought my chain would fly off. I skidded to a stop at the bottom of the street. My heart seemed as if it were stuck in my throat. I waited for the garage door to swing open, followed by Mother racing out in her station wagon or my brothers flying off on their bikes and chasing after me down the street. I had already calculated several escape routes.

'Did you see that?' I asked.

'See what? Man, what's wrong with you?' Larry asked.

'The window!' I said, still panting as I pointed up the street. 'My brothers . . . they saw me!' My eyes stayed fixed on every sound, every movement, from The House.

Nothing happened.

'Man,' Big Larry whined, 'you got too much of that James Bond stuff in your head. I didn't see nothing. You're just seeing things. Come on, let's go. And remember,' Larry said, as he pedaled off, 'A deal's a deal.'

'Just as long as Mrs C don't find out!' I replied, as I tried to catch up.

Hours later I felt a cold chill as Larry and I returned to Lilian's home. 'What's up?' I whispered to Larry. He gave me one of his 'I dunno' looks.

'Hey,' he said, 'I'll go upstairs, get a bite to eat and check things out for you, okay?'

I eagerly agreed as I watched Larry from the bottom of the stairs. Suddenly Mrs Catanze came into view. By instinct I hid in the shadows. 'Larry!' she barked. 'Get that overstuffed face up here this moment! And you,' she pointed her finger down at me, 'I can see you! You can wait for me in your room. Now move it! The both of you.'

My eyes became the size of silver dollars. I smiled wide, showing my teeth as I pointed at my chest. 'Me?' I asked. She returned my smile. I could see that her hands were on her hips. That was the moment I knew I was in serious trouble. I waited in my room and wondered what I may have done. I hadn't stolen any candy from the local stores in the last several days. And Larry Jr and I were staying out of each other's way. I had no idea what I did wrong.

I didn't have to strain my ears to listen. '. . . you're supposed to be responsible when David's with you. He's just a baby. You've seen what he's like.'

'Come on now, Mom. He's twelve years old. He does okay for himself. Besides, we didn't do nothin',' Larry shot back. I still had no idea what Larry and I did wrong.

'No? Then why has David's mother, the Mother Superior, been on the phone with me all afternoon?'

Uh oh, I said to myself as I swallowed hard. From outside I heard the sound of a car door slam shut. I jumped to the window to see Rudy wave at me. I slumped back on my bed, waiting my turn.

'*Mister* Pelzer . . . get your little butt in here, now!' Lilian yelled.

In an instant I sprang up and ran into the kitchen. I knew I was in an interesting position. Even though I was in trouble, it wasn't as though Mrs Catanze was going to beat me. As I entered the kitchen, I became anxious to see what exactly Lilian had in store for me. This was the first time that I was in what Big Larry had called 'The Dog House'.

'Tell me,' Lilian began, with her hands glued on her hips, 'tell me that you didn't convince this walking paramecium over here to drive by your mother's house.'

I swallowed hard and again attempted to turn on my charm, flashing Mrs C my best smile. 'Para . . . ?'

'An insect with no brains! And that's what you're going to be if I don't get any answers!' Lilian spouted.

'What in the Sam Hill is going on here?' Rudy shouted as he entered the kitchen.

'Freeze! Don't either one of you move!' Lilian warned, as she turned to her husband.

Without her knowing, I cupped my hand to my mouth and let out a giggle. I thought her remark about Big Larry was hilarious. I could imagine him with big bug eyes and oversized wings, flying around, trying to find something to eat. I had never seen Lilian get that upset before. And I knew that all I had to do was ride out the storm. *What's the big deal?* I said to myself.

On the other hand, Big Larry looked as if he had just weathered some pretty rough seas.

Lilian marched right up to Rudy, whose eyes darted between Larry and me. 'The moron twins – Doofus and Wonder Boy here – took a little ride by his mother's house.'

'Jesus!' Rudy exhaled.

I stood in front of the three of them, not understanding the consequences of my actions. *What's the big deal?* I asked myself again.

'I'm sorry,' I blurted. 'It's all my fault. I asked Larry to do it. All we did was ride down the street. What's the problem?' I asked innocently.

'Well, your mother has been on the phone all afternoon, ranting and raving about you,' Lilian said, pointing a finger at me, 'terrorizing the streets.'

'No!' I shook my head. 'She's lying! All we did was ride down the street. We didn't do anything, honest,' I said, doing my best to sound calm.

'David,' Lilian said as she let out a deep sigh, 'don't you understand? *You* are not *allowed* to go anywhere near her house, her boys or her.'

My hands shot up in the air. 'Wait! Slow down. What do you mean, *I'm not allowed?*' I shouted, as I tried to get Lilian's attention. But I couldn't stop her; she was on a roll.

'That's only the half of it. Your mother, the sainted Mother Teresa, tells me that if *I* cannot *manage The Boy, she'll* find someone who can!'

My mind fought to sort out the words *allowed* and *manage.*

Lilian bent down. 'Don't you ever, ever do that again! You're grounded!'

'Grounded?'

'That's right, you're grounded until . . . until I decide to un-ground you!' Lilian finished with a huff before I could ask her what she meant.

Larry stood in disbelief. 'Man, I told you that was a bad idea.'

'So . . . ? That's it?' I asked. I knew Lilian was mad, but I expected . . . well, I didn't know what to expect. *This I can handle,* I told myself.

As Big Larry wiped his forehead, Lilian marched back in the kitchen. 'Wipe that smirk of your face, Wonder Boy,' she said as she looked at me. 'I forgot – your father's coming over tomorrow morning at 7:00, so you'll have to get up early. You can *manage* that, can't you?' Lilian asked with a sly smile.

'Yes, ma'am. I can *manage*,' I replied in a sheepish tone.

'And you!' she yelled as she turned her attention to Larry. 'Go to your room!'

Larry shrugged his shoulders. 'Oh, Mom, do I have to?'

'Move it!' Lilian barked.

Once Larry left the kitchen, Lilian wiped her eyes. 'Come here and sit down. Now listen very carefully. Your mother . . .' She stopped to clear her throat. 'David, I've been taking care of kids since I don't know when. I have never, ever met anyone as cold as your mother.'

'You're telling me!' I interrupted.

'David, this is not the time to act funny. You have to understand something: You're a foster child. *A foster child.* And because of that, you've got two strikes against you. You have to be careful of everything you say and everything you do. If you get into trouble, we . . . we could lose you.'

I knew by the seriousness of her tone that what she was telling me was important. But I simply could not understand the message.

Lilian nodded, indicating she was again talking over my head. 'David, if you get into trouble, you could end up in the hall – juvenile hall. That's where they send foster children who end up in trouble. It's a place you never want to end up. I don't know what your mother's up to, but *you*, young man, better learn how to *manage* yourself a little better. Otherwise you'll be grounded – for a year.' Lilian patted my knees and then walked out of the kitchen.

I knew that she was using Mother to scare me. I also knew that Mother could never get to me, now that I was in foster care . . . *could she?*

'Hey, Mrs C,' I shouted, 'what's *grounded*?'

'Oh, don't you worry. You'll soon find out,' Lilian laughed, as she strolled down the hall and into her bedroom. '*You'll manage!*'

That evening I thought long and hard about what Lilian had told me. After Rudy and Lilian left for dinner, I had an overwhelming urge to call Mother. Strangely, I just wanted to talk to her, to hear her voice. I picked up the phone several times, but I couldn't bring myself to dial her number.

I wiped away my tears as Connie bounced into the kitchen. 'Hey, what's up?'

I broke down and told her what I was trying to do. Without a word, Connie took the phone and dialed my mother's number. Moments later I nearly choked as I heard the recording that

Mother's number was '. . . no longer in service.' Connie persisted and called the operator, who confirmed the number was now unlisted.

I stood in front of Connie not knowing what to say or do. I didn't know how I should feel. I knew that Mother had changed her telephone number as a form of another 'game' – I was not *allowed* the privilege of *her* number.

After Connie's date came to pick her up, I sat down and stared at the television. I had never been alone in the house before. I counted the hours until Father would pick me up the next morning. I drifted off to sleep as I watched the black-and-white snowflakes dance across the TV screen.

The next morning I stumbled out of bed as I rubbed my eyes, then made my way over to the bedroom window. I turned and looked behind me. I didn't remember how I got to bed. After I put on my best clothes and washed my face, twice, I ran to the living-room window. I stood tall as I waited for Father.

After a few minutes my shoulders became sore, but I remained rigid as the clock in the living-room struck 7:00. At 7:35 I heard the distinctive sounds of Father's borrowed VW. I allowed myself a smile after making sure my hair was just right. I could see an off-brown VW struggle as it made its way up the street. But the car continued to drive by. *Well, maybe he doesn't have the right address*, I told myself. *He'll be back in a few seconds.*

At 7:55 I heard the sound of another VW Bug go past Lilian's house.

I then convinced myself that I had heard the wrong time – that Father would pick me up at 8:00, not 7:00; that I had made another mistake. *Whoops, stupid me!* I said to myself.

8:00 came and went, as did more than a dozen cars that cruised by. As every car drove up the street, I knew in my heart that the next car had to be the one with Father in it.

Around 9:00 Lilian yawned as she stumbled into the kitchen. 'David, are you still here?' I merely nodded. 'Well, let me check the calendar. I know your father said 7:00 A.M. sharp. For goodness' sake, I wrote it down.'

'I know, Mrs C,' I said, trying not to show my feelings. 'He'll be here any . . .' My head spun to the window when I heard the rumblings of another VW lurch its way up the steep street. 'See?

Here he is!' I cried out, as I pointed at the window. I grabbed Lilian's hand. I wanted to show her off as Dad pulled into the driveway. 'Yes!' I shouted.

The car slowed for a moment, but only to shift into a lower gear before chugging its way past. My hand fell from Lilian's grip. She looked at me as if she wanted to say something to make me feel better.

My insides felt tight. A solid lump was caught in my throat. 'Don't say it!' I yelled. 'He'll be here! I know he will! You'll see! My dad will be pulling up here any second! You watch! My father loves me! And one of these days we're going to live together and . . . and we'll be happy for the rest of our lives. I know *she* doesn't love me, but my dad does. *She's* the one who needs a psychiatrist, not me. *She's* the sick one . . .'

My chest seemed to shrink as I continued to ramble on. I felt a firm grip on my shoulder. I clenched my right fist, spun round and swung wildly. As my eyes focused on my target, I tried to stop. But I couldn't. A moment later I struck Rudy, square in the forearm.

I looked up with tears in my eyes. Rudy had never seen me act like that before. In an instant I wanted to apologize, but I couldn't. I was tired of being sorry for everything – for not understanding words or phrases; for feeling so humiliated by Larry Jr, and the crazy psychiatrist; for riding my bike down a street; or for just trying to hear my mother's voice. And then I was telling myself that *I* was the one who got the time wrong for when Father would drop by!

I had known all along that Father wasn't coming; that he was probably lost in some bar. He never made it for a visit. But I had always told myself that this time was going to be different, that today Father was going to make it and we would have such a good time.

I just could not accept the realities of my life. *How in God's name did I let it come to this?* I asked myself. I knew, as I stood staring out the living-room window, that I would spend another day hiding in the only place I felt safe and warm – the covers of my bed.

I looked up at Rudy and then at Lilian. I wanted to tell them both how sorry I was, how bad I felt inside. I opened my mouth. Before I could say the words, I turned away. As I marched into my room, I could hear Rudy whisper to Lilian, 'I think we have a serious problem.'

chapter 6

THE DEFIANT ONE

A few weeks before I started the sixth grade, I began to turn off my feelings. By then I was completely drained of emotion. I had become fed up with the teeter-totter effect of my new life. On the up side, I was elated to play in the bright rays of the summer sun. On the down side, I dreaded being teased by other children or having to wait like a trained dog for the remote possibility of a visit from Father. I was fully aware that a cold change was taking place inside of me. I did not care. I told myself that in order to survive, *I* had to become so hard so that *I* would never allow anyone to hurt *me* again.

At times, instead of riding to the park, I would journey to the local grocery store and stuff my pockets full of candy that I would steal. I didn't even want the sweets; I knew I could never eat all those candy bars. I stole to discover if I could get away with it. I felt a gut-wrenching thrill of calculating my next move, followed by the spine-tingling sensation of strolling out of the store uncaught. Sometimes I'd steal from the same store two or three times a day. Whatever I did not smuggle into Mrs Catanze's home, I'd give away to kids in the park, or I would leave the candy in small piles just outside the store's entrance.

When swiping candy became too boring, I raised the stakes by stealing larger objects – toy models. I became so arrogant that several times I would simply strut into the store, snatch an over-sized model and stroll right out – all in less than a minute. Some of the kids from the neighborhood who had heard of my candy giveaways would follow me to the stores and watch me. I loved the attention. It got to the point where the kids would dare me to steal things for them. My only concern was for acceptance. It was almost like the days when I would play with the younger foster children at Aunt Mary's home. I felt so good inside whenever the kids would call my name or greet me as I rode into the play park. Now I was receiving the same kind of attention again.

Whenever I decided to steal a serious item, I became extremely focused inside. Before making my move I would imagine every aisle and the entire layout of the toy shelves. I plotted my primary and alternate routes of escape. In the event that I was caught, plan number one called for an 'off-the-cuff' lie, while plan number two meant that I would simply run like hell.

One time, as a group of kids waited outside the store, I turned myself off, once again becoming a cyborg – half human, half machine. My mission: grab and go. Johnny Jones wanted a B-17 Flying Fortress model airplane. I accepted the challenge, taking three deep breaths before grabbing the glass door and pulling it toward my chest. I could hear the boys cheering me on, but I shut them out as the door closed behind me. I knew that somewhere in the store Johnny was watching. He wanted to see my bravery in person. I didn't care. I had an objective to accomplish.

In order not to be noticed by the string of checkout clerks, I walked down the first aisle leading to the back of the store. I then swiveled right and slowed my pace. By then my ears had become like radar, distinguishing between the sounds of the shoppers and the store employees. I slowed my pace before I turned right again and bent my head down to see if anyone was behind me. The coast was clear. My heart was racing as my objective came into view on the top shelf of aisle four. I knew this job was going to be a challenge. For a split second something didn't feel right. I thought of aborting. *Negative*, I told myself a second later. As I reached up with both hands, I could hear, then feel someone walking up the aisle. I shook the thought clear as I strained my legs to reach a little higher. A moment later I plucked my prize from the shelf. I showed no emotion as I marched down the aisle, passing Johnny, who was grinning from ear to ear.

My chest was beating like a drum. *Now the hard part.* Just in front of me was the door to victory. Ever so slightly, I dipped my head and listened for anyone behind me or someone shouting for me to stop. The delicate moment had arrived. My face became tight as I reached out to push that door open, just enough to allow me to slide out, so in case someone had followed me, that person would have to spend the extra time and effort of pushing the door open –

providing me an additional chance of sprinting away. I smiled to myself, knowing that I had thought of everything.

Behind the glass door, I could hear the group of boys clapping and shouting for me. Johnny was already outside, his eyes as big as pancakes. I broke my concentration for a moment – but only for a moment – thinking what my latest risk would do for my acceptance among the group. At times in the past, the boys had teased me and played tricks on me in the park. I knew all along that they were taunting me, but I went along with the gags anyway. Any attention was better than none.

I held my head high, smiling as I slid out of the door. By then the boys were laughing, and they began to attract attention. I thought I heard the sound of the door swish open from behind me. I started to reach over with my right hand and toss my prize to Johnny, when screams of laughter erupted. Johnny laughed so hard that he had tears in his eyes. I snapped out of my concentration and laughed, too. 'David,' Johnny howled, 'I'd like you . . . oh man, this is just too much!' he giggled. 'I'd like you to meet my dad.' In an instant my feet transformed into solid blocks of ice. I turned to see a man in a red Walgreens vest with a name tag that read 'Mr Jones – Store Manager'.

Mr Jones snatched the model, then grabbed my shirt. I walked in front of him as he opened the door to the store. As the glass door closed behind me, I turned my head. The group of boys leaned on their bikes and yelled, 'Busted!' at the top of their lungs.

'We've had our eye on you for quite a while. My son told me all about you . . . David.'

I closed my eyes, thinking what a complete fool I was. I wasn't sorry for stealing. I knew that what I was doing was wrong and I had accepted that fact. I even knew that my luck would eventually run out. But to be set up by the kid's father! I knew that Johnny himself was swiping candy at the store next to Walgreens. *I should have known better*, I told myself. *I knew they couldn't have liked me for just being another kid.*

About an hour later I returned to Lilian's home. I opened the door and could hear her run from the couch. As I dragged myself up the stairs, she stood with her hands glued to her hips. Her face was cherry red.

I slid into the kitchen chair before Lilian began her fury of questions, statements and past observations on my past behavior. I simply stared through her, nodding when I felt a response was necessary. I tried to convince her that I was indeed sorry. As the words spilled out, they seemed too easy. I knew my heart wasn't in it. Afterward, I plodded off to my room where I lay on my bed, staring at the ceiling. I was grounded for a week. *Big deal*, I told myself.

A few moments after Rudy came home, I stood in front of him. I silently let out a sigh. *Round two*, I told myself.

'I don't know what it is with you,' Rudy began to rave, 'but I'll tell you this. I'm not putting up with a thief! I know I've let some things slide by, and I know that Lil's a bit easy on you. I can accept that. I also know you've had some hard times . . . but I'm not going to stand for this anymore – that potty mouth of yours, the fighting, the hitting, the yelling, calls from your mother, slamming my doors around this home. Do you know how much doors cost? Well, do you?'

I shook my head no.

'Well, it's more than you'll ever make. I work hard, and I love you kids. But I don't need your crap. You hear me?' Rudy yelled.

I nodded again, knowing that Rudy knew I didn't care.

'Are you the one who's been stealing my cigarettes?'

My head swung upward. 'No, sir!'

'And you expect me to believe you!' Rudy shot back. 'If I hear you've caused any more problems . . . I'll send your little butt to The Hill.'

My face lit up. '*The Hill?*'

'Oh! Now I have your attention. Ask around,' Rudy twirled around. 'Ask Larry Junior here. I've driven him to The Hill a time or two, haven't I, Larry?'

Larry Jr, who had been chuckling behind Rudy's back, now put on a serious, frightened face. 'Right, Dad,' he said in a fearful tone, as he bowed his head.

'I don't want to – you're a bit young – but I'll load that butt of yours in the car and haul you myself. If there's one thing I will not tolerate, it's a liar and a thief!' Rudy huffed, as Lilian approached his side. 'And Lil can cry her eyes out, but that's the way it's going to be in this house. Am I clear, young man?'

I nodded.

'Are you too big in the britches that you can't say yes or no?' Rudy barked.

'Yes, sir,' I said in a defiant tone. 'I understand.'

'Then go to your room. You're grounded.'

I sat in my room and stewed. *Yeah*, I said to myself, *grounded. Big deal*. I wasn't mad at Rudy or Lilian for yelling at me, or even for being set up by Johnny and the other kids. I was furious for allowing myself to let down my guard. *David!* I yelled at myself. *How could you have been so stupid?* I then jumped off the bed and began pacing the floor, becoming more upset at everything in my life.

That Saturday I put little effort into my chores. I carelessly vacuumed the home and barely removed the dust from the furniture. When the chores were completed, Rudy took Lilian shopping for groceries. All alone, I rocked on Rudy's recliner chair and flipped through the TV channels. I soon lost interest when I realized that the morning cartoons had already been on.

I rolled out of the chair and strolled over to the living-room window, staring outside. I thought that maybe Dad would visit me tomorrow. After a few seconds I chuckled to myself, knowing how foolish I was being. Suddenly the blur of a kid whizzing down the street on his bike caught my eye.

Without thinking I ran into my bedroom, emptied my money jar into my hand and grabbed my jacket before trotting down the stairs. I proudly wheeled out my bike and made it a point to slam the door extra hard. I had decided that I was going to run away.

I felt a rush of excitement as the howling wind struck my face, and I pedaled up and down the slopes leading into Daly City and the Serramonte-6 movie theater. Once there I parked my bike and watched James Bond three times in a row before sneaking into the other shows. Later that evening the theater attendant kicked me out so he could close for the day. The reality of my decision began to sink in. As I unlocked my bike, I shivered from the chilling fog that seeped through my clothes. After my stomach growled, I dug into my pocket to count my savings – $2.30. I pocketed the change and turned my hunger off, focusing on shelter instead. To help stay warm I pedaled my bike. Only after I rode past the darkened homes in the neighborhoods did I realize that it was after 11:30 P.M.

Sometime later I rode down the street leading to my old elementary school. I coasted past the play yard, listening to the sounds of the swings sway from the breeze. Afterward, I walked my bike up the seemingly endless hill of Eastgate Avenue. When I reached the top of Crestline Avenue, just as I had a few weeks before, I hid beside a clump of bushes as I peered down the foggy street.

I couldn't resist riding down the street. I stopped a few houses above Mother's house. A soft yellow light shone through her draped bedroom windows. I wondered whether Mother ever thought about me as I did her. I began to think of how my brothers spent their time at Mother's house. A howling wind blew through my hair. I rolled up the collar of my shirt. I realized that the house I was spying on was not the same home that had entertained an army of children when Mother was a Cub Scout leader, or the same home that had been the most popular home on the block during Christmas season, so many years ago. After Mother turned off her bedroom light, I said a prayer before I coasted down the street to return to the area by the movie theater. That night I fell asleep curled up, shivering underneath an air-conditioning unit.

The next day I spent the entire day in the movie theater and fell asleep to Bruce Lee's *Enter the Dragon*. That evening after the theater closed, I rode up to the local Denny's restaurant, where I salivated as plates of food whizzed by the counter. The manager, who had eyed me for two days now, sat down and talked to me. After a few minutes of prodding, I gave him the Catanzes' phone number. I gulped down a burger before Rudy picked me up in his blue Chrysler.

'David,' Rudy began, 'I'm not going to badger you. All I can say is, you can't keep acting like this. This is no way to live – for you or for us. You've got to shape up.'

Once we arrived at their home, I took a quick bath, then drifted off to sleep as Rudy and Lilian discussed how to handle me.

The next day Ms Gold made a rare appearance. She didn't seem to be her bouncy self, and I noticed she forgot to give me a hug. 'David, what seems to be the problem here?' she asked in a firm voice.

I played with my hands as I tried to avoid looking at Ms Gold. 'How come you never come to visit?'

'David? Now, you know there are lots of other children who, like you, need my help. You understand that, don't you?'

'Yes, ma'am,' I said in agreement. I felt guilty taking Ms Gold's time away from the other children, but I missed seeing her as much as I had before the trial.

'David, Mrs Catanze tells me that you're having a very hard time adjusting here. Is it that you don't like the home? What's going on inside of you? Where's that cute little boy I knew a few weeks ago, huh?'

I stared at my hands. I was too embarrassed to answer.

After a minute of silence she said, 'Don't worry, I know all about the psychiatrist. It's not your fault. We'll find you one who's used to relating with kids . . .'

'I'm not a kid. I'm twelve years old, and I'm tired of being picked on!' I stated in a cold tone. I had to catch myself before I revealed another side of my personality that, until recently, had never existed.

'David, why are you so upset?'

'I dunno, Ms G. Sometimes I just . . .'

Ms Gold scooted closer to me from the other side of the couch. She lifted my chin with her fingers as I sniffled and wiped my nose. 'Are you getting enough sleep? You don't look so good. Do you not like it here?'

'Yes, ma'am,' I nodded. 'I like it here a lot. Mrs Catanze is real nice. It's just that sometimes . . . I get scared. I try to tell her, but I can't. There's just so much I don't understand, and I wanna know why.'

'David, I know this may be hard for you to swallow, but what you're feeling right now, right this moment, is perfectly normal. If you weren't a little confused or worried, then I'd be concerned. You're perfectly fine.

'*But* what I *am* concerned about right now is your behavior. I know you're a better boy than you've been acting here recently. Am I right? And Mr Catanze is not very happy with you right at this moment, is he?'

'So I'm okay?'

Ms Gold smiled. 'Yeah, for the most part, I'd say so. We've still got to iron out a few wrinkles, but if I could only get you to modify your behavior, you'd be fine. Now, do you have any questions for me?'

'Yes, ma'am . . . Have you heard anything from my dad?'

Ms Gold raised her eyebrows. 'Hasn't he been by to visit? He was supposed to have seen you weeks ago,' she said, as she flipped through her notebook.

I shook my head no. 'I've wrote him some letters, but I don't think I have the right address. I don't get any letters back . . . and I don't have his phone number. Do you know if my dad's okay?'

She swallowed hard. 'Well . . . I . . . do know your father's moved into another apartment . . . and he's transferred to a different fire station.'

Tears dribbled down my face. 'Can I call him? I just want to hear his voice.'

'Honey, I don't have his number. But I promise I'll try to call your father as soon as I can. I'll try to call him today. Is that why you drove by your mother's house and tried to call her a few weeks ago?'

'I dunno,' I answered. I didn't dare tell Ms Gold about cruising by Mother's house the other Saturday night. 'How come I'm not allowed to call her?'

'David, what is it you're expecting? What are you looking for?' she asked in a soft tone, as she, too, seemed to search for answers.

'I don't understand why I'm not allowed to see or talk to her or the boys. What did I do? I just want to know . . . why things happened like they did. I don't want to turn into the kind of person she is now. The psychiatrist says I should hate my mom. You tell me what I'm supposed to do.'

'Well, I don't believe you should hate your mother, or anyone else for that matter. How could I put this . . . ?' Ms Gold put a finger to her mouth and gazed at the ceiling. 'David, your mother's a wounded animal. I have no logical answer why she changed her telephone number or why she acts the way she does.' She drew me to her side. 'David, you're a little boy – excuse me, a twelve-year-young man – who's a little confused, thinks too much about some things and not enough about other things. I know you must have had to think ahead a great deal in order to survive, but you need to turn that off. You may never find your answers, and I don't want your past to tear you up. *I* don't even know why these things happen to children, and *I* may never know. But I do know that you need to be very careful of what you're doing right now, today, rather than trying to find the answers to your past. I'll help you as much as I can, but you have to really make a better effort to maintain yourself.'

Ms Gold held me for a long time. I heard her sniffle and felt her body shudder. I turned to look up at her – my loving social worker. 'Why are you crying?'

'Honey, I just don't want to lose you,' she said, smiling.

I smiled back. 'I won't run away again.'

'Honey, I can only tell you one more time. You need to be very, very good. I don't want to lose you.'

'I'll be good, I promise,' I said, trying to reassure my angel.

After Ms Gold's visit, I returned to my usual joyful self. I felt good inside again. I didn't think about the nutty psychiatrist, I made an extra effort to get along with Larry Jr and I performed my chores with pride. I did not even mind being grounded. I simply snuck downstairs, borrowed some old car wax and polished my bike from end to end. I kept my room spotless, and waited impatiently for a change of pace and for the start of the school year.

Once school started I kept to myself, as I watched other kids from my class show off their fancy clothes and their colored markers. During recess I strolled out to the grass and watched some of the boys play football. I turned my head for a moment and a second later a football struck the side of my face. As I rubbed the sting on my right cheek, I could hear laughter. 'Hey, man,' the biggest kid shouted, 'throw us the ball.' I became nervous as I bent down to pick up the ball. I had never thrown a football before. I knew I couldn't throw a smooth spiral. I tried to imitate the other boys as I sucked in my breath, then flung the ball. The football wobbled end over end before it dived a few feet in front of me.

'What's the matter, man?' a kid said as he picked up the ball. 'Haven't you ever thrown a football before?'

Before I could reply, a boy from my class strolled over. 'Yeah . . . he's the one I was telling you guys about. Check out the clothes and the shoes, too. He looks like his mother dresses him or something. The kid's a walking dork!'

Without thinking, I spread my arms and examined my outfit. I felt proud of my blue shirt. My pants had a patch on each knee and my Keds sneakers were a little scuffed, but they were still new as far as I was concerned. After inspecting myself I studied the other boys, who all seemed to have better clothes and fancier shoes. Some of them were wearing thick, black turtleneck sweaters. I stared at myself again, feeling ashamed. But I wasn't sure why.

In class I became a nervous wreck whenever I was called on by the teacher. Sometimes I'd stutter in front of everyone. Afterward, the football boys would imitate me as I slid down into my seat, trying to hide from their remarks. During English I'd always write a story about how my brothers and I had become separated and struggled to find each other. I always drew pictures of my brothers and me being separated by either a body of dark water or black jagged cliffs. In every drawing I'd borrow my teacher's crayons and draw a big smile on every face, and a giant happy-face sun that shone above my four brothers and me.

Once while walking home from school, a couple of the football boys teased me about using crayons. I wanted so badly to tell them off, but I knew I'd probably screw that up, too. I ran off, my feelings hurt. Soon I met up with another kid from my class named John. Like me, John stuck out. He had scraggly, long black hair and thin, worn-out clothes. John had a very distinctive walk, and I suddenly realized that no one seemed to pick on him. As I ran up to John, I noticed a cigarette in his hand.

'Hey,' John said, 'you that new kid in school?'

'Yeah,' I replied, feeling proud as we began to stroll along.

'Don't worry about those guys,' John said, pointing behind him. 'I know what it's like to be picked on. My dad used to beat up on my mother and me. He don't live with us anymore.' I quickly zeroed in on his rough attitude. John went on to explain that his parents had just divorced and his mother had to work full-time in order to feed his other brothers and him. I felt bad. At the end of the corner we said goodbye. As I made my way up to Lilian's home, a cold feeling reminded me of how much I had dreaded returning home from school.

I met John the next day in the schoolyard during recess. He seemed extremely upset because our teacher had scolded him in front of the class about not turning in his homework. John boasted to his two other friends and me that he was going to get even with the teacher. He seemed to guard his words as I leaned in closer to hear his plan.

'Hey, man, you're not going to fink on me, are you?'

'No way!' I assured him.

'All right. You see, you have to be a member of my gang to hang around me. I tell you what. You meet us at the parking lot after school. I'll tell you the plan then.'

I accepted John's challenge, knowing I was getting into trouble. In class he would always act tough; even the rich football boys stayed away from him. As I daydreamed in class that day, I thought a thousand times about chickening out. I told myself that when the bell rang at the end of the day, I'd stay behind and be the last person to leave. Then I'd sneak around the parking lot, missing the boys. The next day I'd simply tell John that I had forgotten.

When the bell rang that afternoon, I flung the lid to my desk open as if I were frantically searching for something. I heard the kids' feet shuffle as they flocked out of the class. When I felt I was safe, I slowly closed the lid to my desk . . . and saw John standing in front of me. I let out a sigh, accepting the fact that I had to go with him. John flipped up the collar of his black vinyl jacket. At the parking lot, John's two friends fidgeted as they, too, tried to look cool.

'This is it,' John bragged. 'I've decided the new kid here is good enough to join our gang. He's going to flatten the tires of Mr Smith's new car. And I mean *tires*, as in two or more,' he stated as he stared into my eyes. 'That way Smith won't be able to use his spare tire. Pretty smart, eh?' John laughed.

I turned away from him. I knew that when I stole candy and toys from the stores, I was wrong. But I had never hurt anyone's personal property before, and I didn't want to now. I could feel the stares around me. I swallowed hard. 'Gosh, John . . . I really don't think we oughta . . .'

As John's face turned red, he punched me in the arm. 'Hey, man, you said you wanted to be *my* friend and join *my* gang, didn't you?'

Some of them began to close in around me. The two other boys nodded in approval.

'Yeah, man, all right. I'll do it. *But*, after that, I'm in the gang, and I don't have to do anything like this again, *right*?' I said in a broken voice, as fear overtook my weak efforts to sound tough.

John slapped the back of my shoulder. 'See, I told ya! The kid's all right!'

I narrowed my eyes and tightened my face. I became cold inside. 'Let's do it!' I said in my new macho voice.

John led me to a brand new, light yellow sedan. He nodded at me as he eased himself away from the scene of the crime. The two other boys giggled as they followed their leader.

I let out a deep breath and knelt down, not believing what I was about to do. I could feel my heart race. I wanted to stand up and run away, but I shook it off. *Come on!* I yelled at myself. *Just do it! Come on!*

I scanned the area before I tried to unscrew the cap to the tire stem. After a few seconds my fingers began to tremble, and I still had not removed the rubber cap. I felt as if every eye were on me, as the sounds of other people slamming their car doors echoed above my head.

Finally, the black cap fell onto the ground. Immediately I snatched a pencil from my back pocket. I turned behind me and met John's eyes. His face was tight, and he raised his eyebrows telling me how disappointed he was with my performance. John then mouthed, 'Come on, move it!'

I took a quick breath before I jammed the end of the pencil into the stem of the tire. The air seemed to explode as it howled out of the tiny opening. I knew that everyone could hear what I was doing. I hesitated for a second as I searched for John, who nodded for me to continue. A blanket of fear seemed to cover me. *No!* I yelled at myself. *This is totally wrong!* On purpose I snapped the end of my pencil, stood up and walked past John, who dared me to finish the job. I brushed past him as I made my way out of the parking lot. John and the *gang* taunted me all the way down the street, until they turned the corner to John's house.

The next day, John's razzing continued. In the schoolyard, without warning, he shoved me to the ground. As I got up, a small circle formed. 'Fight! Fight!' they chanted. I kept my head down as I tried to break through the crowd. A round of insults flew above me.

Within minutes, the entire school seemed to know that I had betrayed John and his gang. I felt a coldness that was worse than the one at Thomas Edison Elementary School.

The next morning, I made a string of excuses to Lilian about how I felt too sick to go to school. I never told her about John or my social problems at school. If I did, I knew Rudy and Ms Gold would be furious.

After a few weeks of the cold shoulder, I apologized to John *and* his gang. As a way of showing my friendship, I presented John with a carton of Marlboro cigarettes I had stolen the day before. 'All right, kid,' John smiled. 'The boys and I forgive your weakness, *but* you still have to be initiated into our group.'

I nodded to myself as my mind replayed all the stories I had heard about John punching and kicking the two other boys of his gang until they fell to the ground. I saw myself with a bloody face, broken glasses and smashed-in teeth. I stared into his eyes, giving him my tough-guy look. 'Okay, man, I can handle it!' I said smoothly.

'No, man,' John said as he showed off his unlit cigarette. 'I've got something special for you. Listen carefully. I'm tired of Mr Smith. He thinks he's so tough 'cause he's the teacher. He wrote a letter to my mother, and because of him she's on my ass. So . . . I say . . . let's burn down his class!'

My mouth fell open. 'Nah, man, you, ah . . . can't be serious?'

'Hey, I'm not saying you got to do it. I'm just saying I need you to be the lookout for me, that's all. I can't count on those two wusses. They're wimps. But you . . . you've got guts.' Suddenly John's voice changed. 'And if you ever fink on me, I will stomp all over you.' A split second later he changed his tone back again. 'Hey, man, don't sweat it. I'm not talking about doing it today. Just be there when I need ya. All right?'

'Yeah, man,' I nodded. 'I'll help you out. I'm cool.' I walked away, telling myself that he was just acting tough. *Nobody ever burns down a school*, I assured myself. *But what if he's serious? What should I do?* I couldn't tell Mrs Catanze and especially not the teachers. But no matter what, I would never turn John in. Not because I wanted to be nice, but because of the fear of being brutalized and living through the humiliation afterward.

I dreaded running into John over the next few days, as he continually renewed his vow that one day soon, *he* was going to teach the teacher a lesson. As the weeks dragged by, I began to think that he was simply showing off to receive attention from anyone who'd listen. At times, whenever a large crowd gathered, I'd brag, too, stating that John and *I* had developed 'The Plan' that would show everyone in the school just how tough we were. The more I boasted, the larger the crowds grew. I was amazed at how the kids who had ridiculed me before were now hanging on my every word. After a few days of spinning tales, John's involvement disappeared, as I found myself stating that *I* would be the person who would do the deed.

Weeks passed, and soon I had forgotten about 'The Plan' – until one day after school, John had a deep, cold look in his eyes as he ordered me to be back at the school in an hour. I felt a lump creep up my throat. 'Okay, man, I'll be back,' I said, before I could think of an excuse. About an hour later, as I walked back on the school grounds, I prayed that he had chickened out.

The smell of papers burning filled the hallway. I broke into a run as I followed the smoke and made my way to the classroom module. Seconds later I found John bent over a small hole, as black smoke poured out of a kicked-in air vent. I stood in total disbelief. I never thought he'd actually do it.

'John!' I yelled.

John's head shot up. 'Jesus, man. Where ya been? Come on . . . help me!' I stood behind him, still unsure of myself. 'Come on, man, help me! Help me put out the fire!' he cried.

My brain locked up until I shook my head clear, as smoke continued to escape the open vent. John's face was seized with terror. After a few seconds, he fell backward. 'No way, man! It's out of control! I'm outta here! Come on, let's go!' Before I could reply, I saw his shadow disappear down the hall.

I bent down in front of the vent and turned my head, coughing from the dark smoke. A small, red-orange fire began to take form. In a flash I grabbed the can of lighter fluid that John had left and pulled it out from the vent. As I withdrew the can, I squeezed it so hard that a stream of fluid ignited, racing from the can and toward my hand, soaking it with the clear fluid. For a moment I thought the tin can would explode – and my right hand with it.

I hurled the can behind me and searched for help. Time seemed to stand still until I finally heard the sound of small shoes skipping across the hallway. A little girl stopped a few feet beside me then gawked. 'Get help!' I yelled. 'Pull the alarm! Pull the alarm!' The girl threw both hands on her tiny mouth. 'Come on!' I ordered. 'Move your ass!'

The girl blinked her eyes. 'Oh . . . I'm telling,' the girl cooed before she broke into a run. A few moments later I heard the clanging sound of the alarm. Using both hands, I scooped up pebbles of gravel and tossed them into the flames. Knowing that fire needed oxygen to grow stronger, I intended to shovel enough gravel to snuff it out.

When I saw that the mountain-sized pile of gravel smothered the flames, I fell backward to watch the wisps of gray smoke that rose. I wiped the sweat from my face with my blackened hands. My head snapped to the right when I heard someone scream, 'Over here! The fire's over here!' A feeling of fear crept up my spine. A moment later I sprinted down the street as the screeching sounds of fire trucks pierced my ears and a small fleet of trucks raced by. Out of habit, I waved. A fireman strapped to the end of one of the trucks smiled as he waved back.

The next morning I met John on the corner by his house. We both agreed to deny any involvement in yesterday's fire, and he again stressed his threat to me. 'Besides,' John said with a wide smile, 'you're a member of the gang now. You're vice president.'

I felt on top of the world, until I strolled into the classroom. Every head turned my way as my sixth-grade teacher, Mr Smith, sprang up from his desk, grabbed my arm and led me into the principal's office. 'How could you have done it?' my teacher asked. 'I would have never expected something like that from you.'

Later I sat in front of the principal, who informed me he was going to call the police, the fire chief and my foster parents. I shuddered at the last part of his statement. All I could think of was Rudy's face. 'Before you say anything,' the principal stated, 'you've already been identified as starting the fire—'

'No!' I blurted. 'I didn't do it! Honest, sir.'

'Really?' the principal smiled. 'Fine. I believe you. Show me your hands.'

I stuck out my two arms, unsure of the principal's intentions. He leaned over and grabbed my hands. Then he rubbed the stubble from my burned hairs. 'I think I've seen enough,' he said as he flung my arms back at me.

'But I didn't do it!' I began to cry.

'Look at yourself. I can still smell the smoke on you. I have statements from teachers claiming that you were the child who's been bragging about this same thing. For goodness' sake, your father's a fireman. You don't need to say another thing. The police will be here soon, and you can tell your story to them. You're excused to wait in the other room. *I* have phone calls to make,' the principal said, with a wave of his hand.

I closed the door behind me and began to sit down. I could feel the resentment from the elderly secretary. I nodded at her as I took my seat. She gave me an evil glance before she huffed in my direction and turned away. 'Foster child! We don't need *your* kind!'

I gripped the arms of the chair and leaped out of the seat. 'I know what you think of me! All of you! But know this. *I* didn't do it!' I yelled, as I slammed the door behind me. A moment later I could see the principal fly out of his office, waving his fist at me. Without thinking I ran from the school and didn't stop until I reached the bottom of the hill by John's house. I hopped the fence, hid in his play fort and waited for him.

'Man, this is too cool! You escaped!' John panted, when he discovered me knocking on his back door hours later.

'What?' I exclaimed.

'Man, the kids in school think the police came to arrest you and you beat 'em up and ran off. Man, this is just too much!' he said, unable to control himself. 'Everyone thinks you're so cool!'

'Wait a minute, man! Stop it! Wait up!' I yelled, cutting him off. 'The principal thinks I did it. He thinks I started the fire and that I've already been identified. You gotta help me, man. You gotta tell them the truth!'

'Hey, man, no way,' John said, backing away from me with his hands in the air. 'You're on your own.'

I shook my head from side to side. Tears were starting to swell in my eyes, but I held them back. 'Man, this is serious. You gotta help me. What am I going to do?'

'Yeah, man, all right. You can't go home . . . Tell you what. I'll hide you here until we figure out what to do.'

'Okay,' I said, trying to relax my heaving chest. 'But you gotta tell them what really happened at school.' John's mouth quivered. He began to mutter something. In a flash I grabbed his shirt. 'Shut up and listen! *You* did it! I didn't! I saved your ass! I put out the fire! You tell 'em the truth! I mean it!' I yelled.

John's tough-guy act melted away. 'Yeah . . . all right. Tomorrow, man, okay? Just relax.'

That night I shivered on a makeshift wooden bed in John's clubhouse outside. Earlier I had picked up the phone to call Lilian, but I slammed it down when I heard Rudy's stern voice on the other end. 'David!' he had said after a long pause, 'I know it's you! If you know what's good for you, you'll . . .'

The next day the hours seemed to drag on as I waited for John's return. When he finally came home, he flung the sliding door open. I ran inside to warm myself. 'Okay?' I asked, rubbing my hands. 'Everything's all right. You told 'em, right? You told them the truth?' I asked, feeling relieved that the incident was over and I could go back to the Catanzes.

John slumped his shoulders and stared at the floor. I knew even before he spoke that I was doomed. 'Man, you promised!' I whimpered.

'Well . . . the principal pulled me from class,' he said in a soft voice, as he continued to stare at the floor. He stopped for a moment. I thought he was about to give me another excuse when he looked up and into my eyes and smiled. 'I told him . . . you did it. That it was your idea.'

My hands began to shake. 'You *what*? *What* did you do?'

John grinned. 'What did *I* do? *I* didn't do a thing. Man, you gotta go. You can't stay here,' he said in a dry voice.

I was dumbstruck. 'Where do I go? What do I do?'

'You should have thought about that before *you* burned the room, man.'

My mind tumbled in confusion. 'I thought you were my friend,' I pleaded, as John turned away.

Moments later I quietly closed the door to his house, then made my way to the local shopping center in hopes of finding food to steal. I jumped in a clump of bushes whenever I heard a car coming. *This is stupid*, I yelled at myself. *I can't live like this.* I turned around and made my way to Rudy and Lilian's home. Taking a deep breath, I opened the door and crept up the stairs, hearing the television set blare above me. As I shuffled into the living-room, I was greeted by Larry Jr's alligator smile. 'He's . . . here!'

Lilian dropped the blanket she was crocheting. 'My God, David, where have you been? Are you all right?'

Before I could reply, I could feel the floor vibrate from Rudy storming down the hallway. 'Where is he?' he bellowed.

I swallowed hard before I gave my prepared speech, that everything was a simple misunderstanding. That I, in fact, was the one who *put out* the fire, and not the person who started it. I knew Rudy would yell at me for a few minutes and he'd probably ground me for another week for not coming home, but I knew once they understood the truth, everything would go back to normal. I smiled at Rudy, who breathed above me like a dragon. 'You're not going to believe this, but—'

'You're damn right I'm not!' Rudy roared. 'I don't believe anything anymore. In the last two days I've had calls from the school, the police, juvenile probation, your father and that mother of yours. Ever since he stepped foot in this house . . .' Rudy pointed at Lilian before focusing again on me. 'I told you to keep your nose clean, and now you go off and do something like this! What in the hell were you thinking about? I can't believe it! Stealing isn't good enough for you? No, you've got to prove yourself, is that it? You say you feel lost, that you don't fit in – well, I know who you are. You're an arsonist! That's what you are! Were you the one who's been setting all those grass fires around here—?'

'My God, Rudy, settle down,' Lilian broke in. 'He wasn't even here back then.'

'Well, I've seen enough. I've heard enough. That's it – he's out of here!' Rudy yelled. Then he shook his head and let out a deep sigh, indicating he was finished.

A long silence followed. He breathed over me while Lilian stayed glued by his side. Up until a few moments ago, I felt I could have cleared up the confusion with a few words, but I suddenly realized it was my past actions that had led Rudy to his conclusion. To him I was guilty, and I knew that nothing I could say would change his mind. I gazed up at Rudy with tears in my eyes. I wanted so much for him to believe in me.

'Those crocodile tears might work on Lil, but they won't do a bit of good with me,' he stated.

I cleared my throat before whimpering, 'My dad called?'

Lilian indicated yes by nodding her head before tugging on Rudy's sleeve. 'Let's put it to bed for now, hmm?'

Rudy turned his frustration on Lilian. 'Wake up, Lil. For God's sake, we're not talking about snatching another candy bar. He burned a school—'

'No!' Lilian said, cutting him off. 'The principal believes there was another boy involved!'

Rudy seemed tired. I could see the dark circles under his eyes. 'Come on, Lil, does it matter? He's a foster child. He's been picked up for shoplifting, and his mother's filed bogus police reports against him. Who do you think they're going to believe? That's the bottom line.'

Lilian broke out in tears. 'Rudy, I know. *I know* he's not a bad child. He's just . . .'

I wanted to hug her and take away all the pain I had caused her.

'Well,' Rudy replied in a calmer voice, 'Lil, I know he's not half bad . . . but he's got one foot in the grave and the other on a banana peel. He's dug himself a deep grave this time and . . . well . . .' he said, rubbing his forehead. 'David,' Rudy continued in a reassuring voice as he held my shoulders, 'I know I bark at you quite a bit, and you may think I'm an ogre. But I do care about you; otherwise I would have shipped you out of here a long time ago. You're in some mighty hot water, and there's not a thing I can do. That's why I'm so upset. But no matter what happens, I want you to know that we care for you.' He stopped for a moment to rub his eye. He stared down at me and massaged the tops of my shoulders. 'I'm sorry, son, but it's out of my hands. Tomorrow I have to take you to Hillcrest.' Tears began to trickle down Rudy's face.

chapter 7

MOTHER'S LOVE

As Rudy Catanze drove me to San Mateo County Juvenile Hall, I nearly blacked out from hyperventilation. The upper part of my chest felt as if a giant rubber band were tied around it. Even as Rudy gave me his last-minute advice, I couldn't concentrate because I was so terrified of what would happen to me next. The night before, Larry Jr had been very descriptive about what the bigger, older boys did to the young, soft, puny kids – the 'fresh meat'. I felt so degraded as I stripped in front of the counselor during my in-processing, spread my butt cheeks before I showered, then put on the stale-smelling 'county clothes'.

I shuddered when the thick oak door to my cell slammed shut behind me. It took me less than a minute to examine my new environment. The walls were composed of dirty white cinder blocks. The cell had a faded, waxed cement floor. I stuffed my wet towel, change of underwear and socks in the tiny shelf. I sat on the foot of the wall-mounted bed and felt an urgent need to go to the bathroom – when I noticed there was no toilet in the cell. After I covered my head with the black wool blanket, the invisible bands around my chest began to loosen. Moments later I drifted off to sleep.

The first time the door to my cell opened for afternoon recreation time, I walked down the hall as if I were walking on eggshells. The other kids seemed more like giant, walking tree stumps than they did teenagers. In my first few days I developed a plan for survival. I would fade into the background so as not to draw attention and, for once, keep my alligator-sized mouth clamped shut. During my initial week at Hillcrest, six frenzied fights broke out in front of me, three of them over whose turn it was to play pool. I bumped into a few walls as I spent a lot of time with my head bent down for fear of making eye contact, and I stayed the farthest away from the pool table.

I breathed a little easier when I was transferred from the new-detainee section, the A-Wing, to the upstairs C-Wing section that housed the smaller, more hyperactive kids. I learned that the new wing's set of directives were less strict. I didn't feel the need to scurry to my cell, the way I had whenever the staff from the A-Wing turned their backs as the kids were sent to their rooms. The counselors in C-Wing seemed more open, more out-going when dealing with the kids. I felt safe.

One afternoon I was unexpectedly called from the recreation room. Moments later I discovered I had a visitor. As the counselor instructed me on the visiting procedures, my stomach tightened from excitement. Up until that moment, I did not know I could be seen by anyone, so I wondered who had come all the way to Hillcrest to visit me.

As I burst through the small door, visions of Ms Gold and Lilian filled my head. A second later my body became limp. Behind the tiny desk, Father sat with his chair against the wall. Besides Mother, Father was the last person I wanted to see while I stayed at juvenile hall.

My hands trembled as I reached for a chair.

'So, David,' Father said in an emotionless tone. 'How are you?'

'Fine, sir,' I replied, as I tried to avoid Father's gaze.

'Well . . . you've grown some. How long has it been?'

'About a year, sir.'

My eyes inched up Father's body. I tried to remember the last time I truly looked at him. *Was it when I lived at The House?* I asked myself. Leaning on the small table in front of me, Father seemed so thin. His face and neck were dark red and leathered. His once finely combed hair was now an oily gray. He coughed every few seconds. His hand disappeared into his jacket pocket and fumbled for a pack of cigarettes. He pulled one out and tapped it on the table before lighting it. After a few drags, his hands quit shaking.

I felt too ashamed to look into his eyes. 'Uhm . . . Dad, before you say anything . . . I just want you to know—'

'Shut up!' Father's voice suddenly cracked like thunder. 'Don't even begin to tell me your lies!' He inhaled deeply before smashing his cigarette and lighting another. 'For Christ's sake, if they ever find out about this at the station . . . do you know what this could do to me? It's not like I don't have enough problems to deal with there!'

I bowed my head, wanting to disappear.

'Well?' Father's voice rumbled. 'And if that weren't enough, you've given that crazy mother of yours all the ammunition she's ever needed!' He stopped to take another drag. 'Jesus H. Christ! You had it made! Then, out of nowhere, I get call after call from that social worker lady . . .'

'Ms Gold?' I muttered.

'I finally make time to give her a call, and she tells me you've run away and have been stealing and landing yourself into all kinds of—'

'But Dad, I really didn't—'

'You had better shut that mouth of yours before I shut it for you!' Father roared. He stopped for a moment and blew out a cloud of smoke. 'You couldn't let it go, could you? It wasn't enough for you to involve the police and have them take you away from school, then drag your mother and brothers into court. Jesus! You're really a work of art, aren't you? You had everything. A new life, a new start. All you had to do was keep your nose clean. And you couldn't do that, could you?

'Do you have any idea what your mother wants to do with you? Do you?' Father demanded, raising his voice. 'She wants me to sign some papers. She's been after me to sign them for . . . how long . . . do you know?' he asked, more to himself than to me. 'Do you have any idea how fuckin' long she's been after me to sign those papers?'

I shook my head no, tears rolling down my face.

'Years! Ever since she threw you out that one day. Hell, maybe she was right all along. Maybe you do need . . . You think it's easy on me? How do you think it makes me feel to have a son of mine at a place like that . . . or a place like this?' Father's eyes seemed so cold as they pierced through me. 'Arson. They're charging you with arson! Do you know how many firemen die because of arsonists? Hell, maybe she's right. Maybe you are incorrigible.'

I watched the orange ring of the cigarette creep its way toward Father's fingers.

'Well,' he said, after several minutes of silence, 'I've got to get the car back. I'll, ah, see . . .' Father stopped mid-sentence as he pushed himself away from the table.

My eyes scanned his body. His eyes looked so tired and empty. 'Thanks . . . for coming to see me,' I said, trying to sound cheerful.

'For Christ's sake, boy, keep your nose clean!' Father snapped back. He began to push the door open when he stopped and looked deep into my eyes. 'I've given up a lot for you. I've tried; God knows I've tried. I'm sorry for a lot of things in my life. I can forgive you for a lot of things – for all the trouble you've caused, for what you did to the family – but I can never, *never* forgive you for this.' The door shut behind him, and he was gone.

'I love you, Dad,' I said, looking across the empty table.

That evening at dinner, while a sea of hands fought for any portion of every container of food, I nibbled away at my salad. I felt so sick and hollow inside. I knew I was the reason why my parents were so unhappy, why they had separated, why they both drank so much and why my father – a man who had fought to save so many people's lives – now lived in a crummy apartment. *I* had knowingly, willingly, exposed the family secret. I suddenly realized that Father was right. Father had been right all along.

After dinner, as I performed my work assignment, mopping the dining-room floor, one of the counselors peeked around the corner. 'Pelzer. Visitor at the front desk.' Minutes later I sucked in a deep breath and closed my eyes before I again opened the door to the visitor's room. I prayed deep inside that Mother had not come.

It took several blinks of my eyes for me to comprehend that it was Lilian's face, and not Mother's, that I was gawking at.

Lilian leaped up and hugged me from the other side of the desk. 'So, how are you?' she asked.

'Fine! I'm great now!' I exclaimed, 'Wow, I can't tell you how . . . it's so good to see *you*!'

Lilian sandwiched my hands between hers. 'Sit down now and listen. We have a lot to talk about, so pay attention. David, has your father come to see you yet?'

'Yes, ma'am,' I replied.

'If you don't mind my asking, what did you two talk about?'

I leaned back in my seat, trying to visualize the entire scene so that I could repeat word for word my visit with Father.

'Did your father mention anything about a paper . . . ? Anything at all?' Lilian gently prodded.

'Uhm . . . no. No, ma'am, not that I remember,' I said, scratching my head.

Lilian tightened her grip on my hands until it was so hard they hurt. 'David, please,' she begged, 'this is important.'

In a flash I recalled Father's frustration about a set of papers Mother wanted him to sign. I carefully attempted to reconstruct Father's words. 'He said something about Mother being right and that he was thinking of signing papers saying that I was . . . *in-carriage-able*?'

'But he didn't sign them?!' Lilian burst.

'I don't . . . I don't know . . .' I stuttered.

'Damn it!' she barked. I lowered my head, thinking I did something wrong – again. Lilian looked away from the gray table, then at me. 'No! No! It's not you, David. It's just . . . have you heard from your mother? Has she come to see you?'

'No, ma'am!' I stated, shaking my head.

'Listen carefully, David. You do not have to receive a visit from anybody you do not want to see. Do you understand? This is important. When you're told you have a visitor, ask who that person is.' Lilian stopped to collect herself. She seemed on the verge of tears. 'Honey, I'm not supposed to tell you this, but . . . don't accept a visit from your mother. She's fighting the county to have you put away.'

'You mean like to stay here? An institution, right? Oh, I know all about that. It's okay!'

Lilian's face turned snow white. 'Where did you hear that?'

'A lady from mental health. She says she works with all the young kids who come here to The Hill. She kept asking me about consent . . . Yes!' I shrieked. 'That's it! The lady said it would be a lot easier for me if I gave my consent for the institution.' I knew by Lilian's expression that something was horribly wrong. 'Doesn't it mean that by me signing the paper, that I promise, I *consent*, to be on my best behavior while I'm here? Does it, Mrs C?'

'David, it's a trap! She's trying to trick you!' Lilian said with panic in her voice. 'Listen to me! I'm going to spell it out for you: Your mother is claiming that your past behavior at her house *warranted* her to *discipline* you because you were so incorrigible. She's trying to have you put away in a mental institution!' Lilian exhaled.

I leaned back in my steel chair and stared at her. 'You . . . ah . . . mean . . . a crazy home . . . don't you?' I stuttered as my breathing accelerated.

Lilian plucked a tissue from her purse. 'I could lose my license as a foster parent, but I don't give . . . I don't care anymore. You can never, ever, repeat this to anyone. I've spoken with Ms Gold, and we think your mother has somehow cooked up this plan – this institution thing – to somehow validate everything she's ever done to you. Do you understand?'

I nodded yes.

'David, your mother has contacted this lady from mental health and has told her all sorts of things. David, I'm going to ask you a question and I need the absolute truth, okay? Did you ever start a fire at your mother's house, *in the garage of her house*?' Lilian carefully asked.

'No!' I exclaimed. I then curled my fingers into the palms of my hands. 'Once . . .'

Lilian gritted her teeth as I continued.

'. . . once, when I was four or five, I set the napkins by the candles before dinner . . . and they caught on fire! I swear, cross my heart, I didn't mean to, Mrs Catanze! It was an accident!'

'Okay, all right,' Lilian said, as she waved her hands. 'I believe you. But David, she knows. Your mother knows everything. From Walgreens, to running away – even the problem you had with the psychiatrist. Ms Gold thinks she may have slipped up and told your mother more than she needed to know, but Ms Gold is required to keep your mother informed about you. Damn it all! I've never seen anyone fight so hard to have their own flesh and blood—'

My body temperature shot up. 'What do you mean, the problem with the doctor? I didn't do anything!'

'Now, I'm getting this secondhand from Ms Gold—'

'How come I'm not allowed to see Ms Gold anymore?' I interrupted.

'Because you have a probation officer now: Gordon Hutchenson,' Lilian replied, as she shook her head, trying to remain on track. 'Now please, listen. I'm not even supposed to know this, but from what I understand, the psychiatrist wrote a report claiming that you have violent behavior tendencies. He's claiming something about you jumping from your seat, waving your arms and nearly attacking him?' she said, looking more confused than her question sounded.

My head swiveled from side to side. 'No, ma'am! He told me I should hate my mother, remember?' I cried as I flung my head backward, hitting the wall. 'What's happening? I don't understand! I didn't do it! I didn't do anything!'

'Listen! Listen to me!' Lilian cried. 'Ms Gold thinks your mother's been waiting for you to screw up – and now she has you.'

'How can she? I live with you!' I said pleadingly, as I fought to understand how my world could suddenly crumble.

'David,' Lilian said with a huff, 'Rudy and I are just your legal guardians, that's all. A piece of paper states that we maintain your well-being. We foster you. Legally, your mother has quite a bit of latitude. This is her way of striking back. Your mother has probably been fighting to put you away ever since you were placed in foster care, and this school incident makes her case.'

'So now what?' I whimpered.

'Understand this. You're in for the fight of your life. If your mother can convince the county that it's in their best interest, she'll have them put you in a mental institution. If that ever happens . . .' Lilian's face suddenly erupted in a fury of tears. 'I want you to know this. I don't care what anybody, *anybody*, tells you. Rudy and I are fighting for you, and we'll do whatever it takes. If we have to hire a lawyer, we'll do it. If we have to go to hell and back, we're prepared to do that, too. We're here to fight for you. *That's why we're foster parents!*'

Lilian stopped for a moment to collect her thoughts. She then began in a low, calm voice. 'David, I don't know why it is, but for some reason a great deal of individuals look down on foster care. And these people believe that you children are all bad, otherwise you wouldn't be in foster care. And if they can keep *you* out of *their* society, well, the better for them. You understand, don't you?'

I shook my head no.

Lilian raised a finger to her lips while rethinking her statement. 'You know what the word *prejudice* means, don't you?'

'Yes, ma'am.'

'It's the same thing. You see, if these same people acknowledge – admit – a need for foster care, that means they are admitting to a bigger problem of what got you kids into foster care in the first place. And that means admitting to things like alcoholism, child abuse, children who run away or get into drugs . . . You get it? We've made a lot of changes in the last few years, but we still live in a closed society. A lot of folks were raised to keep things to themselves, hoping no one ever finds out about their *family secret.*

Some of them are prejudiced, and that's why whenever a foster child gets in trouble . . .'

Her statement hit me like a ton of bricks. Now I understood. The bands around my chest seemed to come alive as I began to wheeze. 'Uhm . . . before . . . when I first came to your house . . . and I got into trouble . . .'

'Yes?' Lilian whispered.

'I heard what you said back then . . . but I just didn't listen.'

Lilian cupped my hands in hers. 'Well, all that's in the past. I know that being here at The Hill isn't easy, especially for you, but you have to be on your absolute best behavior. I mean that,' she emphasized. 'The counselors write behavior reports on you that are turned in to your probation officer. You've met Gordon Hutchenson, haven't you?'

'Yes, ma'am,' I replied.

'Those reports will have a strong impact against your mother trying to place you in an institution. All she has right now is a pack of lies she's been feeding everyone. Your mother has made you out to be some crazed child – which you are, of course!' Lilian joked. 'So if we can prove to the court that you did not set the fire and that you've been a model child, this blows your mother out of the water – once and for all.'

'So what do I do?' I asked.

Lilian smiled. 'David, just be yourself. That's all you have to do. Don't ever try to be someone you're not. The staff here will see through that in a heartbeat. Just be the boy who first came into my house – before you landed in all this hot water. But,' she warned, 'no mistakes. Don't you fly off the handle when you get upset. You put a lid on that potty mouth of yours. You got me?'

I nodded again.

'David, you've got your head in a noose. Lord knows, one more incident, and you're hung for sure. You've overcome more in twelve years than most folks will ever accomplish in a lifetime. If you can do that . . . you can do this too. But you have to fight a good fight! You do whatever Mr Hutchenson or the staff here tells you. I don't care how off-the-wall it sounds. I've known Gordon for years, and he's the best. You just think long and hard before you do something you're gonna regret. All right?'

As Mrs Catanze held my hands, I wanted to explain how sorry I was for all the trouble I had caused her and her family. But I knew I had told her that so many times in the past – when I really didn't care. *So*, I asked myself, *why would she believe me now?* I peered into her gentle eyes, knowing that I was the cause of her sleepless nights and hours of frustration.

Lilian did her best to give me a wide smile. 'Oh, before I forget, I have something for you,' she said, as her hand disappeared inside her purse. A second later she pulled out a small, chocolate-coated cherries box. Her face lit up as she pushed the box over to me.

'Candy?' I asked.

'Just open it,' Lilian said, beaming.

I carefully opened the tiny lid and let out a shriek as I gazed at my tiny red-ear turtle, twisting its neck up at me. Gently I plucked my pet from the box and placed him on my hand. The reptile quickly retreated into his shell. 'Is he okay? Is he eating?'

'Yes, yes,' Lilian replied in her motherly voice. 'I'm taking care of him. I'm changing his water . . .'

'Every other day?' I said, with concern for my pet.

'Every other day, yes, I know, I know. Of all things, I never thought I'd ever be taking care of an ol' turtle.'

'He's not an old turtle. He's just a baby . . . see?' I cooed. 'I think he likes you.' Lilian gave me a stern look as I thrust my turtle towards her face.

'David,' she said lovingly, as she leaned over to stroke my hair, 'looking at you with that turtle . . . If only they saw you the way I do.'

I carefully replaced my turtle in the candy box. Then I reached out to Lilian's hands. 'I know I've been bad and that I deserved to be punished for what I did, but I promise – cross my heart and hope to die – I'll be good. Real good. I promise . . . Mom.'

That evening, while I stared out of the window of my cell, a warm feeling from deep inside my soul began to take form. *I'm going to do it!* I vowed. *I'm going to prove to Mrs C, Mr Hutchenson and to Mother that I am a good kid!* I knew that my court date was only a few weeks away. *So*, I told myself, *I'll have to work a little harder.* I fell asleep, no longer feeling afraid.

Within days, my daily behavior scores nearly doubled. I had thought I was doing rather well before, but when Carl Miguel, the C-Wing superintendent, told me in front of everyone what a great week I was having, I wanted to prove myself even more. By the end of that week, I had achieved the highest status that the wing held: gold. Mr Hutchenson informed me that it normally took a pretty good kid three or four weeks to make gold. I smiled inside, knowing that I had made it in under two weeks. During that visit, Gordon informed me that my court date had been moved up a few days. 'So, when do we go to court?' I asked.

'The day after tomorrow,' he answered. 'You gonna be okay?'

'Yes, sir,' I said, trying to sound sure of myself, when inside I was terrified.

'David, I'm not going to confuse you on what can or cannot happen when we get in the courtroom. I've seen enough to know that some cases can go either way, and you have one of those cases. I can only tell you to keep your cool, and if you believe in God, I recommend you pray.'

Alone in my cell, I could feel myself become lightheaded. I closed my eyes, turned off my anxiety, and prayed.

Two endless days later, I sat perfectly upright as I strained to remember everything Lilian and Gordon had fed me. I nodded to Lilian, who sat behind me, and I smiled to her. As I turned away from her, I saw Mother sitting to the right of me in one of the front-row seats. I closed my eyes for a moment to make sure they weren't playing tricks on me. But when I opened them, I could see Mother cradling Kevin in her arms.

My feelings of confidence evaporated. 'She's here!' I whispered to Gordon.

'Yeah, and remember, keep your cool,' he warned.

Moments later my case number was announced. I squirmed in my seat before stealing a glance at Mother. My lawyer, whom I had met only a few minutes earlier in the outer chamber, stood up, rattling off dates and other official-sounding numbers and statements so fast that I wasn't sure whether everything he stated was about my case or someone else's.

The judge acknowledged my lawyer after he returned to his seat. From my right, another man in a dark suit cleared his throat before he spoke. Gordon leaned over and tapped me on the knee. 'No matter what he says, keep your cool. Don't smile, don't move and don't show any emotion.'

'Your Honor, on or about the week of January 10, the minor,

David Pelzer, after extensive premeditation, did knowingly commit arson and attempted to burn a classroom at the Monte Cristo Elementary School . . .'

A slow panic began to consume my body.

'The minor, Your Honor, has an extensive history of extreme rebellious behaviour. You have the brief from the minor's psychiatrist, as well as statements from the minor's teacher and staff members of Monte Cristo Elementary. I have statements from the minor's former social worker, who also claims that "while David's naïveté can be rather enchanting, he does, at times, require close supervision. While residing under the most liberal foster conditions, David has displayed *aggressive behavior toward others* and *has*, on occasion, *been argumentative and disruptive* while in foster care."'

I sank into my seat. The same building that had granted me freedom would now be my doom. After an eternity the other lawyer thanked the judge before taking his seat, then nodded to Mother.

'Did you see that?' I asked, nudging Gordon.

'Ssh,' he warned, 'don't blow it!'

'Rebuttal?' the judge, sounding bored, asked in my direction.

'Your Honor,' my lawyer chuckled as he stood up, 'Ms Gold's statement is taken totally out of context. I submit that his Honor take the time to read the entire text. As for the charge of arson, the case has been founded on purely circumstantial evidence. While David was initially the suspect for the charge, I have in my possession statements attesting to the fact that David *stopped the spread of the fire set by another minor*. As for behavior reports while under detention, David has been, and I quote, "exceptional". As for David's foster placement, the Catanzes eagerly await David's return. Thank you, Your Honor.'

The judge scribbled down some notes before nodding at the other lawyer, who sprang from his seat. 'Your Honor, while no direct corroboration has *yet* been made, the minor *has* an established pattern of *extreme* dysfunctional behavior. In addition, I have a signed affidavit, from the minor's biological mother, Mrs Pelzer, stating that the minor *has* set several fires in the basement of his former residence. Mrs Pelzer regrettably confesses that she could not control the minor under any normal conditions, and that the minor *is* extremely manipulative and harbors violent tendencies. Please review the order transferring custody, dated last March.

'Your Honor, it has become dramatically apparent, for whatever reason, that the minor cannot be managed in his former home setting or in foster care. The county believes that the minor is an extreme burden to society. The county hereby recommends the minor to be immediately admitted to psychiatric evaluation for possible admission into a facility that can best support his needs.'

'What does all that mean?' I asked Gordon, after the lawyer was through. Before Gordon could even hush me, the judge rubbed his temples and asked, 'Juvenile probation?'

Mr Hutchenson buttoned his coat as he stood. 'Probation recommends continued monitoring and consultation from a different psychiatrist. I have seen nothing to make me believe that David is a threat to himself or to others. I recommend replacement with David's foster guardians.'

'Gluttons for punishment, are they?' the judge chuckled before continuing. 'Prior convictions?' he asked, as he turned to my lawyer.

'None, Your Honor,' the lawyer stated, as he leaned forward.

The judge leaned back into his chair. As his eyes looked down on me, I could feel the hairs on the back of my neck begin to rise. I moved my left hand to scratch my right arm. I held my breath, waiting for the judge's answer. The judge fingered his mustache. With a sudden nod of his head he turned to the court reporter. 'Pending no further verification on the charge of arson . . . the court recommends sentencing of . . . one hundred days in juvenile detention, honoring time already served.

'And off the record,' the judge stated, 'young man, the charge of arson is a most serious one. The only reason I am not sentencing you for that is I have no direct proof. While it appears you *may not* have committed this crime, you have in fact been skating on thin ice for quite some time. You appear to have some good qualities and ample guidance,' the judge said, nodding to Mrs Catanze, 'but . . . be wise enough to employ them both.'

Immediately after the judge struck his gavel, Gordon whispered, 'You'll be out in thirty, thirty-four days.'

'But I didn't do it!' I whined.

'Doesn't matter,' Gordon stated matter-of-factly. 'That's rarely the issue. Believe me, kid,' he said, pointing to the judge, 'that guy's a Santa Claus. If the prosecution had any hard evidence, I'd be fitting you for a straitjacket for the funny farm right about now.

Besides, the ol' man has a soft spot for scrawny little wimps like you. Come on, back to your cell, you animal,' Gordon joked, as we stood up.

Without warning, Mother stepped in front of Gordon and me. 'You're wrong! You're all wrong! You'll see! I warned that social worker broad, and now I'm warning you!' Mother screeched, as she thrust her finger at Mr Hutchenson. 'He's bad! He's evil! You'll see. And next time he'll hurt somebody! The sooner *that boy* is dealt with, the sooner you'll see that I was right and I didn't do a damn thing wrong! You're fooling yourself if you think this is the end of it! You watch! There's only one place for *that boy*. You'll see!' Then she stormed out of the room, yanking Kevin behind her.

I inched my way to Gordon, whose face was chalk white. 'Where does your mother live?'

'At home,' I replied.

'Oh?' Gordon asked, as he raised his eyebrows. 'The home you *burned*? I mean, if you burned the basement . . . you must have gutted the house, too.'

'Yeah!' I laughed, after I realized he was only joking.

Thirty-four days later, I cried as I stuffed my collection of arts-and-crafts projects and the folders of schoolwork I had acquired into a small cardboard box. In an awkward sense, I didn't want to leave. In 'the outs' – the outside world – it was too easy for me to get into trouble. While at Hillcrest, I had grown used to my surroundings. I knew exactly what was expected of me. I felt safe and secure. As Carl Miguel escorted me to the front desk, he explained that the outside world would indeed be the real test of my survival. 'Pelz,' Carl said, as he took my hand, 'hope I never see you again.'

I returned Carl's handshake before I gleamed at Mrs Catanze, who seemed shocked at the sight of my pants, which I had grown out of. 'Well?' she asked.

'How's my turtle?' I inquired.

'Right about now, I'd say he's soup.'

'Mom!' I whined, knowing Lilian was only teasing me. 'Come on,' I said, as I spread my fingers, 'let's go home!'

Lilian's face lit up like a Christmas tree when she realized that this was the first time I had called her house my home. She took my open hand. 'Home it is!'

chapter 8

ESTRANGED

Things were never the same after I was released from juvenile hall and returned to the Catanzes. The other foster kids seemed to eye me with suspicion. Whenever I walked into a room, they would suddenly quit talking and flash me fake smiles. Whenever I'd try to join in on a conversation, I'd find myself standing in front of everyone with my hands buried in my pant pockets. Then after an eternity of silence I'd leave the living-room, feeling stares on the back of my neck. Even Big Larry, whom I once considered my 'big brother', brushed me off before he moved out. After a few days of the cold shoulder, I found myself spending all of my time fiddling in my room. I didn't even care that my Murray bike began to rust.

One Friday afternoon, in July 1974, Gordon Hutchenson dropped by. I felt a surge of excitement as he marched up the stairs and to my room. I couldn't wait for someone to talk to. But I knew by his grim look that something was horribly wrong. 'What is it?' I asked in a low voice.

Gordon placed a hand on my shoulder. 'You need to pack a bag,' he said with pity.

I brushed his hand away. Visions of Hillcrest filled my head. 'Why?' I exclaimed. 'What'd I do?'

Gordon gently explained that I was not in any trouble and that he knew about the struggle I was having at the Catanzes' home since I had moved back. He also stated that he had been trying to move me into another foster home with fewer kids. 'Besides,' he confessed, 'I'm in a jam. I got a bigger kid being released next Monday from The Hill and, well, he's been assigned to live here. So come on now, move it.'

I wanted to cry, but instead I ran to my room. My heart raced from a combination of excitement and fear of not knowing what was going to happen to me next. With the speed of lightning I flung drawers open, yanked clothes from hangers and stuffed everything I could into a large brown grocery bag. Minutes later, I stole a moment of time to take a final look at the room I had slept, cried, played and spent so much time thinking in for just over a year. Even when I had thought that my world was crumbling around me, I always felt safe and secure in *my* room. As I gently closed the door, I closed my eyes and yelled at myself for again being so stupid. The first two ultimate rules of being a foster child that I had learned while at Aunt Mary's were never to become too attached to anyone and never to take someone's home for granted. And I had foolishly broken both rules. I had been so naïve as to convince myself that I would live with Rudy and Lilian for the rest of my life. I closed my eyes as I fought back the tears.

After Gordon placed a phone call to another foster home, he had to separate Lilian and me as we sobbed in each other's arms. I looked into Lilian's eyes, promising her that I would be a good boy and that I'd stay in touch. Outside, Gordon swung open the door to his brown Chevy Nova, then hurled my belongings in the backseat before allowing me to slide into his car. As he backed out of the driveway, I could clearly see the streaks of black mascara run down Lilian's face. She stood in front of the same living-room window where I had spent so many endless hours – waiting for the remote possibility of a visit from my father. As I waved goodbye to Lilian for the last time, I suddenly realized that she and Rudy had cared for me and treated me better than my own parents.

Neither Gordon nor I spoke a single word for several minutes. He finally cleared his throat. 'Hey, Dave, I know this is all coming at you pretty fast, but, ah . . .'

'But why?' I whined.

Gordon's face tightened with frustration. 'Listen!' he barked. 'It's rare, damn rare, that a kid stays in a home for as long as you did. You know that, don't you? And you were there for how long? Over a year? Hell, that's a record.'

I sank in the seat, knowing that everything he was saying was true. I had taken so much for granted for so long. I turned my head to the window, watching familiar parts of the city zoom past.

Gordon broke my concentration. 'Hey, David, I'm sorry. I shouldn't have dumped on you like that. It's just that sometimes I forget what it's like to be a kid in your position. You see, I had assigned you to another home yesterday, but I got stuck in court before I could pick you up. And, well, now that home has another kid and . . . hell, I don't know what to do with you.'

'You could take me back to the Catanzes,' I suggested in a soft voice.

'Can't do that. Like I already said, I had signed you out of the Catanzes' yesterday, which means they are no longer your legal guardians. It's, well, very complicated to explain. The bottom line is, I've got to find you a home.'

As Gordon stumbled for words, my heart seized with fear. I suddenly realized that I had forgotten my bike and, more important, my pet turtle. Gordon laughed when I told him, so I playfully tugged his arm. He knew how much my things meant to me, but we both knew finding me a place to stay was far more important.

Gordon stopped off at his home. Soon the phone became glued to his ear as he pleaded, then begged, foster parents on the other end of the line to take me in, if only for a few days. After several hours, he slammed down the phone in frustration. 'Damn it!' he said. 'There are never enough homes! And all the homes we have are full!' I watched him as he again attacked the phone. Seconds later his tone changed. Even though he turned his back to me, I could still hear him quietly ask, 'What's the count on A-Wing? Yeah? Okay, put a bed on hold for Pelzer. No, no, he's clean; no charges. I'm just trying to *place* him, and I'm running out of homes. Okay, thanks. I'll give you a call before we come in.'

As Gordon spun around to look at me, he realized I knew what was about to happen. 'Sorry, David, I just don't know what else to do.'

I was so mentally exhausted, I no longer cared. In a strange way I actually looked forward to the routine at The Hill and seeing counselors like Carl Miguel again. Before I could tell Gordon to drive me to The Hill, he snapped his fingers and grabbed his jacket, streaking out the front door and ordering me to follow him to the car. Inside the Chevy Nova he gave me a sly smile. 'I should have thought of this earlier. It's impossible for some of these parents to say no, once they've had a good look at you kids. I know it's a raw deal, but desperate times call for desperate measures.'

I squinted my eyes as I tried to understand what Gordon's words meant. Before I could ask, my chest jerked forward as he jammed the gear shift into park. 'Well,' he proudly announced, 'this is it. Put on your best face.' Gordon surged with pride as he rapped his knuckles on the screen door, a split second before he marched in.

I felt like a burglar as I tiptoed into someone else's home without permission. A pair of heads popped out from a nearby kitchen. 'Just be cool and have a seat.' Gordon gestured to a couch before giving me a wink. He spun on his heels and opened his arms. 'Harold! Alice! Good to see ya! How have you been?' He strolled into the kitchen.

I shook my head and chuckled to myself at Gordon's chameleon-like personality. I knew if he wanted to, he could charm anyone into anything. He reminded me of those crazy guys on TV who desperately tried to con people into buying cars.

Before Gordon pulled up a chair at the kitchen table, I knew we were in trouble. The man, Harold, who was wearing a straw hat, shook his head. 'Nope, can't take any more. Got no room,' he grumbled as he took a drag from a thin cigarette.

I clutched my already crumpled bag and was about to stand up to leave when the lady, Alice, said, 'Now, Leo, settle down. He looks like a good kid.' Alice leaned over and gave me a smile. I raised my eyebrows and smiled back.

'We're not licensed for boys. You know that,' Harold stated.

Gordon butted in. 'It'd only be for a few days, just until I can find him another home. I should have a place for him by, let's say, Monday . . . Wednesday by the latest. You'd really be doing me, and David, a big favor.'

'And the papers?' Alice asked.

Gordon raised a finger. 'Uhm . . . I don't have them with me, but . . . I'll bring them by next week and . . . we'll just . . . we'll just backlog the dates . . . Hey, look at the time! I gotta run! Thanks again. I'll see you next week,' he said, and fled from the house before Harold and Alice could change their minds.

I sat glued to the couch, hugging my bag to my chest. I kept my head bent down while Alice and Harold eyed me with caution and crept into the living-room. 'Well, where's he going to sleep?' Harold asked in a stern tone. After a small squabble, Alice decided I would share a room with Michelle, a seventeen-year-old foster child who worked at night. Harold continued to protest, claiming that sharing a room with a young lady was not proper. Trying to make a good first impression, I marched up to him, looked him straight in the eye and shrieked, 'Oh, it's okay! I don't mind!'

As the words spilled out, I knew I was in trouble. For the next four nights, I curled up beneath a set of old wool blankets on the living-room couch. I didn't know why I had made Harold so upset, but at least I had a place to stay. For that, I was thankful.

The next week, after taking a quick survey of my contents in my grocery bag and waving goodbye to Alice – Mrs Turnbough – I climbed into Gordon's car as we set out for another foster home. He assured me that he had discovered the perfect home, even though my new parents had never had any foster children before and only received their license yesterday. My head began to swim with emotions. The more Gordon tried to convince me about my new foster parents, the more I knew how desperate he was to place me.

A half mile later, Gordon parked his car in front of a small brown house. Stepping out of the car, I exhaled and gave the woman who stood on the porch a false smile. Before Gordon could introduce us, the woman flew down the stairs and smothered me against her chest. My arms hung from my side as the woman's sandpaper-like hands scoured my face. I wasn't sure what to do. I thought the woman mistook me for another child. After an eternity of cheek pinching and another round of bone-crushing hugs, the lady held me at arm's length. 'Oh, just look at you!' the woman cooed, as she shook my shoulders so fast that my head bounced up and down. 'Oh, I could just eat you alive! Gordon, he's *sooo* cute! David,' the woman shrieked, as she jerked me up the stairs and into the house, 'I've waited so long for a boy like you!'

I stumbled into the small living-room, fighting hard not to lose my balance. The moment my head cleared, the crazy woman shoved me onto her couch. Gordon tried his best to calm the woman down by forcing her to read endless stacks of papers before assuming custody of me. Finally, he sat her down and explained everything he could about my character, over and over again, emphasizing the fact that if she had any questions, to give him a call. 'Oh, not to worry,' the lady said, as she smiled at me and seized my hand. 'A little boy like this should be no problem at all.'

Gordon and I blinked at each other at the same moment. 'Well then,' he chuckled, 'I'll be on my way and let you two get to know each other.'

I walked Gordon to the door. Without the lady knowing, he bent down and whispered, 'Now be a good *little* boy.' I cringed, as he knew I would.

After Gordon drove away, the woman flopped onto the couch. She batted her eyes and shook her head from side to side for several minutes. I thought she was going to cry. 'Well . . . just look at you!'

I returned her smile, and without thinking, I stuck out my hand. 'I'm David Pelzer.'

The woman covered her mouth with her hand. 'Oh, how silly of me. I'm Joanne Nulls, and you may call me Mrs Nulls. How's that sound?'

I nodded my head, knowing full well that Joanne thought of me as a kid rather than the thirteen-year-old teenager that I wanted to be recognized as. 'That's very kind of you . . . Mrs Nulls,' I replied.

In a flash, Mrs Nulls sprang up from the couch and proudly showed me a framed picture of her husband. 'This is Michael,' she cooed. '*Mr Nulls*. He works at the post office,' she stated, as she cradled the photograph to her chest and patted it as if she were holding a child. But I felt better after finally meeting Mr Nulls, who insisted that I openly address him as '*Michael*'. I knew by the look on Joanne's face that she didn't like Michael's easygoing nature or having her rules challenged.

She would always seem to bite her lip in front of Michael, but the moment he left for work, she would return to treating me as if I were a toy doll. Joanne insisted on washing my hair, prohibited me to ride my bike past the corner of the block and instead of the $2.50 allowance I had received from the Catanzes, she proudly dropped two quarters into the palm of my hand. 'Now, don't spend this all in one place,' she warned.

'Oh, don't worry. I won't,' I assured her, wondering what to do with two measly quarters.

Because of Joanne's restrictions, I spent most of my time wandering through her home. The living-room was smothered with every item from the Avon catalog. I'd spend hours gazing at the thousands of articles. By early afternoon I became so bored that I'd plop down in front of the television and watch Speed Racer cartoons. When I could not stand another animated episode, I'd drag myself to my room and kill time by coloring in a coloring book she had given me.

Just as when I lived with Mother, I seemed to know when something was wrong. Even with my bedroom door closed, I could hear hushed disagreements turn into raging battles. Several times I heard Michael yelling about my presence in *his* home. I knew that having me as a foster child had been Joanne's idea because, as she had told me, she was lonely and could not have any children. Whenever Joanne and Michael fought, thoughts of Mother and Father raced through my head. I fully realized I was not in any physical danger, but I stayed huddled against the far corner of my room with a blanket over my head. Once, a few days before school started, their yelling became so extreme that the windows to my bedroom would shake.

The next morning I tried to talk to Joanne, who seemed to be on the verge of a collapse. I stayed by the side of the couch the entire day, watching her clutch her wedding picture to her chest as she slowly rocked back and forth in the chair. As quietly as I could, I tiptoed to my room and packed my clothes into my weathered brown paper bag. At that moment I knew it was only a matter of time before I would be moving on.

My problems with the Nullses evaporated on my first day at Parkside Junior High School. I sat tall and proud at the big round table in my homeroom class. I smiled at the other boys who openly joked with me. One of them, Stephen, nudged me, claiming that a girl from the other table kept looking at me. 'So?' I asked. 'What's the big deal?'

'If you like a girl, you call 'em a *horror*,' Stephen explained.

I tilted my head to one side. While I thought about the word Stephen wanted me to say, the other boys nodded with approval. After extensive coaching from my new friends, I tried to be cool as I bent over to the girl and whispered, 'You're the best-looking *horror* I've ever seen.'

The entire room, which had been rumbling with noise, suddenly became quiet as a church. Every head swung toward me. The girls at the table clamped their hands to their mouths. I swallowed hard, knowing I had screwed up – again.

When class ended, the entire room full of kids fought for the door. The moment I stepped outside, the sun seemed to disappear. I gazed straight up and stared into the face of the most gigantic eighth-grader I had ever seen. 'What'd you call my sister?' he sneered.

I swallowed hard again. I tried to think of something clever to say. Instead I told him the truth. 'A *horror*,' I whimpered. A second later warm blood gushed from my nose. The eighth-grader's fist was so fast that I didn't see it coming.

'*What* did you call her?' he repeated.

I closed my eyes before giving him the same answer.

Smash.

After six blows to my face, I realized I shouldn't say the word *horror* because it meant something very bad. I apologized to the gorilla-sized kid, who struck me again and bellowed, 'Don't you ever, ever, call my sister a *whore* again!'

That afternoon at Joanne's home, I stayed in my room as I tried to fix the frames of my bent glasses. I didn't seem to notice that Joanne stayed inside her room as well. As the days passed, I so desperately wanted to ask her and Michael what a 'whore' was, but I knew by the way they acted toward each other that I'd be better off keeping my problems to myself.

A couple of weeks later, returning from school, I found Joanne with her head buried in her hands. I rushed up to her. She whimpered that she and Michael were getting a divorce. My head began to throb. I sat by her feet as she informed me that Michael had been having an *affair* with another woman. I nodded as Joanne wept, but I didn't know what she really meant. I knew better than to ask.

I held her until she cried herself to sleep. I felt proud. For the first time in my life, *I* had been there for someone. I turned off the living-room lamp and covered Joanne with a blanket before I checked my belongings in my grocery bag one last time. I lay on my bed, knowing deep in my heart that I had somehow been one of the reasons for the Nullses' divorce. Two days later I turned my head away from Joanne, who wept from her porch as Gordon eased his Chevy Nova down the street.

I dug into my pant pocket and pulled out a crumbled piece of paper containing the addresses and phone numbers of all my former foster homes. Borrowing one of Gordon's pens, I drew a line through Joanne and Michael Nulls. I didn't feel any remorse. I knew that if I thought about my feelings toward Joanne Nulls, Alice Turnbough or Lilian Catanze, I would break down and cry. I felt I was beyond that. Carefully I folded my address sheet and stuffed the paper back into my pocket.

I cleared my head of any feelings I had about the Nullses – or anyone else – as I glanced out of the car window. My eyes blinked. For a moment I thought Gordon was driving me to Daly City. 'Are you going in the right direction?' I asked in a squeaky voice.

Gordon let out a breath. 'David, ah . . . we've run out of foster homes. The only one left is a home by your mother's.'

I felt a lump creep up my throat. 'How close?' I whimpered.

'Less than a mile,' Gordon replied in a dry voice.

I nodded my head as Thomas Edison Elementary School came into view. I calculated the distance from my old school to Mother's house to be under a mile. I could feel my chest begin to tighten. The thought of living so close to Mother made my heart skip a beat. But something seemed out of place. I nearly pressed my face to the side of the window. The school looked radically different. 'What happened?' I asked, shaking my head from side to side.

'Oh it's a junior high school now. That's where you'll be going.'

I let out a sigh. *Doesn't* anything *stay the same anymore?* I asked myself in a sarcastic voice. A flicker of excitement over seeing my teachers that had rescued me soon vanished. Only when Gordon wheeled his car away from the school, in the opposite direction to Mother's house, did I breathe a little easier. I felt as if I had stepped into a time warp as the Chevy Nova chugged up streets that were lined with houses of the same style as Mother's on Crestline Avenue. I couldn't believe how small they seemed. Strangely, though, I felt secure. I let out a smile as I marveled at the tall palm trees in the front yards of the single-storey homes that seemed so tiny now. I couldn't believe it had been nearly two years since my rescue. I rolled down the window, closed my eyes and breathed in the moist, chilly air.

Gordon parked his car at the top of a steep hill. I followed him up a set of red-colored stairs to a house that looked identical to Mother's. When the front door opened, my eyes nearly popped out of my head. Gordon leaned over to my side. 'You going to be all right? You're not prejudiced, are you?'

I shook my head as my mouth hung open. 'Prejudiced?' I asked. I had never had black foster parents before. A tall lady shook my hand and introduced herself as Vera. I automatically took my position on the living-room couch as Gordon and Vera talked in the kitchen. My eyes darted in every direction, searching every corner, every beam of Vera's home. The entire floor plan seemed the same. I remembered that the walls of Mother's house usually reeked from the thick, choking smell of cigarette smoke and the heavy stench of animal urine. But Vera's home had an open, clean feeling to it. The more I gazed at Vera's home, the more I smiled.

Minutes later Gordon sat down by me on the couch. With his hand on my knee, he warned me that Mother's house was off limits, with a radius of one mile. I nodded my head, understanding the meaning of Gordon's order. But I was frightened of Mother finding me. 'Are you going to tell her where I'm at?'

'Well,' Gordon began, as he fought to say the right words, 'by law I am only required to inform your mother that you are residing in the city limits. Other than that, I really don't see a need to tell her anything else. As you can tell, I'm not a big fan of hers.' Then his facial expression changed. 'And for God's sake, you make damn sure you stay the hell away from her! Am I clear on this?'

'Like crystal,' I replied, giving him a salute.

Gordon playfully slapped my knee as he got up from the couch. I walked him to the door and shook his hand. Having Gordon leave me in a strange home was the hardest, but most familiar, part of our relationship. I always felt a little scared. He seemed to always sense it. 'You'll be fine. The Joneses are good people. I'll check in on you in a few weeks.'

Vera gently closed the door behind Gordon, then led me down a narrow hallway. 'I'm sorry, but we weren't expecting you,' she explained in a kind voice, as she opened the bedroom door at the end of the hallway. I stepped into a vacant, white-walled room containing a twin-sized mattress on one side of the wall and a box-spring on the other. Vera reluctantly explained that I would be sharing the room with her younger son. I gave Vera a false smile as she left me alone in the room. Very slowly I plucked my rumpled clothes from my grocery bag and stacked them in neat little piles by the head of my box-spring bed. I killed time by rearranging my clothes as if they were in a dresser drawer. Suddenly I closed my eyes and cried inside at the thought of never being with the Catanzes again.

Later that afternoon I was introduced to the seven other foster teenagers who lived in a makeshift room in the garage. Mattresses were crammed into every corner and any other open space available.

A pair of old lamps gave the room a soft glow, and makeshift bookcases were used to store whatever belongings the teenagers possessed. I shrugged off whatever anxiety I had after meeting Jody, Vera's husband, who chuckled like Santa Claus as he hoisted me so high that my head almost struck the ceiling. I quickly learned that no matter what was going on, whenever Jody came home, every-thing and everyone came to a halt and competed for his attention. As cramped as things were, there was a genuine family bond. I only hoped I would stay long enough to memorize their phone number.

My first day at Fernando Riviera Junior High was a huge im-provement over the one at Parkside Junior High in San Bruno. I kept my mouth shut and my head down. At recess I desperately tried to find out what happened to my former teachers, only to discover that they had been transferred to other schools across the district. I felt empty and sorry for myself, until one day I made friends with Carlos, a shy Hispanic boy. We shared most of the same classes, and at recess we'd stroll throughout the school. We seemed to have a lot in common, but unlike my 'friend' John at Monte Cristo Elementary, Carlos didn't have a mean bone in his body. Because Carlos could not speak English very well, we did not feel a need to talk to each other that much. In an odd sense Carlos and I had a way of knowing what the other was thinking, just by our expressions. We soon became inseparable. At the end of the school day, we always met by our adjoining lockers so we could walk home together.

One day, out of boredom I convinced Carlos to walk across the street to the new Thomas Edison Elementary School. As Carlos and I strolled down the corridors, I couldn't believe how puny the other kids looked. Loads of children bubbled with laughter as they raced to the play yard or for their rides home. With my head bent to the side, I turned a corner and bumped into a big kid. I muttered an instant apology before I realized the kid was my brother Russell. His head reeled back for a second. My eyes examined his every feature. I knew in a flash that Russell would let out a blood-curdling scream, but I couldn't break away from staring at him. His eyes flickered. I felt my body tense the way it always did the moment before I sprinted away. My head leaned forward when Russell's lips began to quiver. I sucked in a deep breath and told myself, *Okay, David, here it comes.*

'Holy cow! Oh my God! David! Where did you . . . how the hell are you?' Russell asked with a choking voice.

My mind raced with all my options. Was Russell for real? Would he strike out and hit me or run and tell Mother that he saw me? I turned to Carlos, who raised his shoulders. I wanted so badly to hug Russell. My mouth suddenly went dry. 'I'm, ah . . . I'm fine,' I stuttered, shaking my head. 'You okay? I mean . . . how are you? How's things at home? How's Mom?'

Russell's head dipped to his worn-out sneakers. I realized how withdrawn he looked. His shirt was paper-thin and his arms were spotted with small, dark purple marks. My head snapped up to his face. I knew. I shook my head, not knowing what to say. I felt so sorry for him. For years I had been the sole target of Mother's rage. Now in front of me stood my replacement.

'Do you have any idea of what she'd do if she ever found out I talked to you?' Russell said, his voice trailing off. 'Things are bad. I mean *real* bad. All she does is rant and rave. She drinks more than ever. She does *everything* more than ever,' Russell said, again looking at his shoes.

'I can help!' I stated with sincerity. 'Really, I can!'

'I . . . ah, I gotta go.' Russell spun away, then stopped and turned around. 'Meet me here tomorrow after school.' Then he flashed me a wide smile. 'Hey, man . . . it's really good to see you.'

I walked forward. I felt an overwhelming urge to be close to him. I stuck out my hands. 'Thanks, man. I'll see ya.'

Afterward I smiled at Carlos. 'That's my brother.'

Carlos nodded. '*Si, hermano! Si!*'

I thought about Russell the rest of the afternoon. I couldn't wait to see him the next day. *But what can I do?* I asked myself. Would Russell come to Jody and Vera's home with me so Jody could call the police and maybe rescue him as I had been? Or did I imagine the marks on Russell's arms to be abuse rather than battle wounds from playing hard? Maybe, I thought, Russell was trying to set me up like he did years ago when he planted candy bars in my rag box, then ran off to inform Mother that he had caught me stealing. He then had the privilege of watching me receive my punishment for my *crime*. Mother had trained Russell to be her spy, but then again, he was only a small child back then.

That night I tossed and turned in my bed, wondering what to do.

Sometime in the early morning hours I finally drifted off to sleep. In my dream, I found myself waiting for *her*. My head tilted to one side when I heard Mother's forced breathing. Our eyes locked for a moment. I saw myself walking toward her. I wanted to talk to her, to ask her – to plead with her – why me, why Russell? My mouth moved, but the words didn't come. In a flash Mother's face turned cherry red. *No!* I yelled at myself. *You can't keep doing this! It's over!* The shiny razor-edged knife suddenly appeared above Mother's head. I tried to twist my body and run away, but my feet failed to respond. I tried to yell her away. My eyes followed the knife as it flew out of her hands. I knew I was dead. I screamed for my life, but I couldn't hear my terror.

My head bounced off the floor. I found myself scrabbling to stand up. I stood alone in a dark room, unsure whether I was awake or still in my dream. I strained my eyes, searching through the darkness. My heart seemed stuck in my throat. *My God!* I said to myself. *What if I'm still* there *with her?* I emptied my lungs when I recognized the sound of Jody's son snoring in his bed. Grabbing a piece of my clothing, I held it to my chest as I waited for the sun to come up.

The next day after school, I physically dragged Carlos to Thomas Edison Elementary. 'This no good idea,' Carlos stated. 'Your *mamasita*, she *loca!*' he said, twirling a finger to the side of his head. I nodded in agreement. I had decided after my nightmare that nothing would keep me from seeing Russell. Carlos and I stopped in the same hallway as the day before. A group of children screamed and yelled as they seemed to run through our legs. As the kids grew bigger in size, I twisted my neck in search of Russell. My eyes found him at the far end of the hall with his head bent down. 'Russell!' I shouted. 'Over here!' Russell's head bobbed, but he didn't make eye contact as he had the day before.

I felt something tug on my arm. I smirked at Carlos, whose eyes darted in every direction. 'This no good. Your mama, she *loca!*' he warned.

'Not now!' I said, still keeping my eyes fixed on the top of Russell's head. 'My brother . . . ah, *si, hermano! Si?* He needs help, like me, remember?' I said, pointing toward Russell, who slowed his pace.

I leaned forward when Carlos grabbed my arm. 'No!' Carlos shouted. 'You wait here!'

I brushed Carlos's hand away. Fighting my way against the tide of children, I made my way to Russell. Still walking, I extended my hand. Russell saw me, but for some reason he kept his head down. I stopped mid-stride.

My legs buckled. My arm seemed to just hang in front of me. Even before Carlos yelled, I knew something was horribly wrong. 'Run, David!' Carlos shrieked. 'Run!'

I looked just above Russell's hair and saw Mother walking behind him with her head bent down. Mother's ice-cold, evil eyes locked onto mine as her face came into full view. Kids seemed to dance around her as they scattered in every direction. Inches in front of me Russell stopped, then turned toward Mother, who smiled. Her hand disappeared into her purse as she came closer still. For a split second Mother's face seemed to hesitate, as she withdrew a shiny piece of metal . . .

I lost my balance when my arm jerked backward. I fell on my back; my eyes still fixated on Mother. Above me Carlos began to drag me backward. I knew this had to be a dream, but Carlos's badgering made everything real. I struggled to stand up, feeling Carlos's hands lift me to my feet.

I blinked my eyes and saw Mother's bony fingers stretch out toward my neck. She was so close I caught a whiff of her putrid body odor. In a flash Carlos and I weaved our way through the mass of smaller children. As we fled, I looked behind me. Mother seized Russell's arm as she quickened her pace. Carlos grabbed my hand, leading me to the parking lot. My chest heaved from absolute terror and lack of oxygen. My arms swung wildly. I ran into the parking lot and again searched behind me. My eyes sought out any sign of Mother and Russell. Without warning, I tripped off the curb. As my body flew through the air, I tried to swing my head forward in an effort to regain my balance. A second later my chest collided against the hood of a moving car. Behind the windshield, a woman's eyes grew wide. I felt myself rolling off the hood as I tried to grab anything that would keep me from falling. My hands slapped the far end of the hood, fingers flailing, as I tried to latch onto the wiper blades. I closed my eyes and felt my body sink in front of the car. My ears burned from the sound of my own scream.

A moment later my head struck the pavement. I heard a screeching sound. I tried to cover my head with my hands. Somewhere in the crowd I heard someone else scream. I closed my eyes and emptied my lungs. Seconds later I uncovered my face and peeked through my fingers. Inches in front of my nose were the grooves of a front left tire.

Carlos plucked me from the pavement. I drooped an arm across his shoulder as he led me to the sidewalk. I looked back at the car. A young woman flung open the car door, and stood and shook.

Without skipping a beat, Mother marched at full speed to her station wagon.

Without my saying a word, Carlos understood my fear. My legs felt rubbery, and he had to practically drag me up the same small hill that I had, years ago, raced from into Mother's waiting arms before we left for the river. Now that same hill seemed to be my doom. My legs became tangled, my knee scraped the sidewalk and my teeth were clenched from the jolt of pain.

From the top of the hill Carlos and I could see small clusters of children and adults pointing in our direction. My eyes scanned the stream of cars as they emptied from the parking lot. I would not know in which direction to flee until I spotted Mother. After a few sweeps I shook my head. 'She's gone! She's not there!'

Carlos jabbed my sore arm. 'There!' he pointed. Mother's station wagon had climbed the hill in no time flat. I could see the rage on her face as she pounded wildly on her horn. Because of the traffic, she could not make her left turn. Carlos and I nodded to each other before running across the street and up another hill to his house. My energy seemed to come from nowhere, and my ears picked up the distinctive rumbling sounds of the worn-out muffler on Mother's ancient station wagon.

Carlos and I bolted up the stairs to his house. He dug into his pockets and fumbled with the keys to the door. 'Come on!' I pleaded. Carlos's twitching fingers dropped the keys. Even though I could hear the sound of Mother's car chugging up the hill, I stood and watched the shiny reflection from the keys that tumbled down the stairs. *Keys!* I yelled at myself. *Mother wasn't taking a knife out of her purse! It was a set of keys!*

Carlos's shouting woke me from my spell. I raced down the stairs and tossed the keys to Carlos, who jammed a key in the lock before flinging the door open. On my hands and knees, I scrambled up the stairs, rolled into Carlos's house and slammed the door shut. No one was home. Creeping to the front window, we stayed glued to the floor and peeled back the drapes as much as we dared, just as Mother's station wagon rocketed up the street. Carlos and I began to let out a laugh – until I heard the familiar sound of Mother's car creep down the street, as she tapped the brakes every few feet, her eyes piercing into every house. 'She's searching for us,' I whispered.

'*Si*,' Carlos replied. 'Your mama, she *loca!*'

After hiding behind the living-room curtain for over an hour, Carlos and I walked to the halfway mark to Jody's home. We grinned at each other. His brown eyes smiled. 'Just like, eh, James Bondo!'

'Yeah,' I laughed. 'James Bondo!' I shook his hand and nodded to him that I'd see him tomorrow. I watched Carlos stroll down the street, then disappear as he rounded the corner. I never saw him again.

I jogged up the set of hills and didn't stop until I slammed the front door to Jody's home. I huffed behind the door for several seconds until I realized that Vera and Jody were screaming at each other in the kitchen. I cursed to myself, knowing that Mother must have just called. I sailed past the kitchen and into my room, knowing that Jody would soon yell for me. As I sat on my box-spring bed, I knew I had broken one of the most important rules Gordon Hutchenson had pounded into me – stay the heck away from Mother. Thoughts of Gordon driving me to juvenile hall filled my head.

After a few minutes I leaned against the bedroom door to better hear what the commotion was all about. I discovered that Jody and Vera were not yelling about me, but about some girl. I opened the door and sneaked down the stairs to the older boys' room. All at once every head snapped up in my direction. Their faces were long and withdrawn. They all seemed busy, their bodies bent over as they stuffed their clothes and other belongings into brown bags and pillowcases. I knew, but I had to ask. 'What's wrong? What's going on?'

The oldest kid, Bobby, stated, 'They're shutting down the house. You better pack whatever you got 'cause tomorrow we're outta here.'

My mouth hung open. 'Why? What's wrong?'

No one answered. I ran to the bottom of the stairs and tugged on

Bobby's shirt. As he looked down at me, I could tell by his eyes that he had been crying. I didn't know that older kids did that. Bobby shook his head. 'Jody's been accused of statutory rape.'

'Statue . . . what?' I asked.

'Hey little dude, the word is that the Joneses took in this girl a few months back, and this chick now says she was raped, even though Jody was never alone in the house with her. If you ask me, I know it's all a lie. That chick was crazy,' Bobby said. 'Just go pack your stuff and don't forget to check the laundry basket. Now scram!'

It only took me a minute to repack my things. As I stuffed my grocery bag, I turned off any feelings of sorrow I had for the Joneses. They were nice people, and I felt sorry for Jody and Vera, but my worldly possessions came first. To me it was a matter of survival.

The next morning a fleet of cars arrived, and one by one the other foster children and I said our goodbyes. I kissed Vera on the cheek and hugged Jody's jolly tummy. As the social worker drove me down the hills, then past my school, I took out my sheet of addresses and scratched the Joneses from my list. I had stayed at their home for just over two months – my third foster home in half a year.

The social worker informed me that some of the other foster kids I had lived with would end up in juvenile hall because there were no homes available. He went on to explain that Gordon couldn't pick me up because he had called in sick. But, the social worker smiled, Gordon had given him a lead to a foster home that might take me in for a few days.

I slumped in my seat and nodded my head. *Yeah, yeah,* I said to myself. *How many times have I heard that before?*

A couple of hours later I burst from the county car and into Alice Turnbough's living-room. I hugged Alice with all my heart. Moments later the social worker knocked on the screen door before entering. 'You two know each other?' he asked in a weary tone. My head rattled up and down like a puppy dog. 'Mrs Turnbough, I, ah . . . I know it's kind of short notice, but we had a situation . . . Can we place David here . . . for a while?' he pleaded.

'Well, I really don't have the room, and I can't have him sharing a room with the girls. Is there any other . . . ?'

My heart ached. I wanted to stay with Alice so badly. My eyes began to water as I looked up at the social worker, who hesitated for a moment. I then turned to Alice, who seemed to act the same.

Alice shook her head. 'I don't think it's right, for David, I mean . . .'

A long stretch of silence followed. I let go of Alice and gazed at the carpet. 'Well,' Alice said in a defeated tone, 'can you at least tell me how long you expect him to stay? I guess I can put him back on the couch. That is, if you don't mind too much, David.'

I clamped my eyes shut for the longest time. My head swam with a stream of endless thoughts. I didn't care. I didn't care whether I slept on a couch or a bed of nails. I just wanted to stay at a place that I could call *home*.

chapter 9

COMING AROUND

My stay with the Turnboughs was day by day. The days turned into weeks, with still no word of where I would end up. Out of frustration, Alice re-enrolled me into Parkside Junior High. As happy as I was to return to school to see my teachers again, I still felt a dark cloud over me. I dreaded walking to Alice's home after school. I'd peek around the corner looking for a county car, knowing I'd soon be driven off. Every day, out of fear, I'd bug Alice in my desperate effort to find out any news from Gordon Hutchenson. I just wanted to know.

As the weeks turned into months, I found myself still sleeping on the couch and living out of a grocery bag. My clothes became weathered and moldly because I only washed them on Saturday afternoon after 3:00 P.M. or on Sunday – I knew that those were the only times I was safe from being moved. After forgetting my pet turtle at the Catanzes, I didn't want to take the chance of losing anything else again. Every night after everyone had gone to bed, I would pray on the couch that tomorrow Gordon would decide my fate.

One day, when I returned to Alice's home after school, she sat me down. I swallowed hard as I braced myself for the bad news. But no word had come. Alice informed me of something else: I would be seeing a psychiatrist tomorrow. I shook my head no. Alice went on to explain that she understood the problems about my former doctor. I was surprised that she knew so much about my past, when I hadn't told her anything. 'So, you've been talking to my probation officer, and he still hasn't seen me?' I asked, feeling exposed and ashamed.

Alice explained that she was working on a plan to have me placed with her, but it would take time to receive a license to have boys in her home. 'But not to worry,' she stated. 'Harold and I have decided that we'd like you to stay with us for a while.'

Without hesitating I gave Alice a kiss. Then I thought about her last statement and gave her a frown. 'You mean Harold wants me to stay, too?'

Alice laughed. 'Just because Harold doesn't talk that much to you doesn't mean he doesn't like you. He just has a hard time understanding you. Frankly, I'm sure a lot of people would. But take my word, if Harold didn't want you, you wouldn't be here.' Her big hands wrapped around my skinny fingers. 'Ol' Leo likes you more than you know.'

Alice's explanation of Harold meant the world to me. Ever since I had blurted out to him about sharing a room with a girl, I felt Harold thought of me as a weird kid. He never seemed to talk to me. Whenever he did utter a few words in my direction, he'd try to get me to read rather than watch television. Every night after dinner, like clockwork, Harold would always pull out an old Western paperback and smoke his Camel cigarettes before going to bed precisely at 9:00 P.M.

I respected Harold so much, although he never knew. As a carpenter, he had a passion for his craft. I hoped I could stay with the Turnboughs long enough for Harold to teach me a few things. Ever since I was a small child I had fantasized about building a log cabin at the Russian River, so at times I'd imagine Harold and me working on a project together, in hopes of bringing us closer. *Maybe*, I thought, by then *I could prove myself to him.*

The next day, after much prodding from Alice, I hopped on a bus and went to meet my new psychiatrist, Dr Robertson, who turned out to be the complete opposite of 'The Great Doctor' I had before. He greeted me with a handshake and told me to call him by his first name, Donald. His entire office was bathed in bright warm sunlight, but the thing that meant the most to me was that Dr Robertson treated me like a person.

On my weekly visits to Dr Robertson, I never felt forced to talk about anything, but soon found myself initiating the conversation about my past. *I* questioned *Dr Robertson* about everything, including whether I was doomed to follow in my mother's footsteps. Dr Robertson always tried to steer me in another direction, but I fought to maintain my lifelong course of finding my answers. I learned to trust him as he gently led me through the maze of the sensitive parts of my past.

Because of my persistence, Dr Robertson suggested some books for me to study on basic psychology. Soon afterward, Harold and I seemed to bicker about who was hogging the lamp by the end of the couch, as I tried to read books on self-esteem by Norman Vincent Peale or others on the stranger side, such as *Your Erroneous Zones*. I found myself intrigued with the basic theories of survival traits, as written by Dr Abraham Maslow. At times I'd become frustrated with the big words, but I hung tough and soon discovered it had taken a lot just for me to make it as far as I had. Although on the inside, parts of me still felt awkward and hollow, I realized *I* was stronger than most of the kids at school who seemed to live in a 'normal' world.

At Alice's home I found myself opening up to her about everything, all the time. Sometimes she and I would gab far into the early morning hours. I never worried about how I talked or what I said. Whenever I became nervous and began to stutter, Alice would teach me how to slow down my train of thought, and have me picture myself saying the words before I spoke them. Within a few weeks my speech problem disappeared.

Every Saturday afternoon, after Alice danced her usual jig to *American Bandstand*, she and I would venture past the railroad tracks on our way to the same mall where Mrs Catanze had taken me shopping for my clothes. We always saw a movie, and that was the only way Alice could get me to sit still for any length of time. As I sat quietly beside her, I'd wring my hands as I scrutinized every scene. My mind raced to stay one step ahead of the sometimes mindless plot. I became fascinated by complicated screenplays and how the director pieced everything together. After every show, Alice and I went back and forth with our own critiques.

Other times, for no special reason, she would buy me toys 'just because'. At first I felt awkward and unworthy, partly because I was not used to receiving presents, and also because I knew how hard Harold worked and how he saved every penny. In time I learned to accept presents. For me that was a very hard lesson to swallow.

The most important gift the Turnboughs gave me was my one last chance at being a kid, while preparing me for my life as an adult. In an effort to show Alice and Harold how much they meant to me, one afternoon at the kitchen table – the famed 'Table of Talk' – I plucked a soiled piece of torn paper from my pant pocket and ripped it into tiny fragments. 'Now, what's that all about?' Harold scowled, as tears rolled down Alice's cheeks.

'I don't need it anymore,' I boasted. 'And I know your phone number, too. Wanna hear?' Alice nodded her head yes. 'It's 555–2647,' I proudly stated, as I looked straight into Harold's blue eyes.

'Well, maybe now's the time to get that unlisted phone number,' he grumbled, before winking at me.

Whenever Alice and I talked for any great length of time, the subject of my future always came up. Even the simple question 'What do you want to do when you grow up, David?' caused me to become scared from the bottom of my soul. I always seemed to picture Chris, the foster kid from the Catanzes' home, and how frightened he was to turn eighteen. I had never thought that far ahead. In order to survive against Mother's torture, I only had to plan hour by hour, or day by day at the most. Being alone in the wide open world was the most frightening thing I could ever possibly imagine. I'd become so scared and tense that I'd begin to stutter again. Alice always seemed to calm me down, but at night, when I finally had a room of my own to sleep in, I'd shiver with fear at the thought of how I was going to buy food or where I would live. I would think so hard that I'd fall asleep with an enormous head-ache. For me, at age fifteen, the countdown began.

Soon after the initial shock wore off, I decided to find ways to make money. I started out by shining shoes, and my first day out I earned $21.00 polishing dozens of shoes in just under six hours. I felt so proud as I juggled my shoe-shine kit and a box of doughnuts in one hand, and a bouquet of flowers for Alice and a couple of paperback books for Harold in the other. I soon added a job at a watch repair shop, where I worked about twenty hours a week for $10.25 take-home pay. The amount of money wasn't important to me. At the end of the work week, I'd fall asleep feeling that I had accomplished something – and that was what was important. While other kids played street ball or hung around the mall, *I* was becoming self-sufficient.

It was very difficult for me to find anything I had in common with the other kids at school. Most of them fought to impress others by acting cool. I knew that on the outside I didn't fit in, so I simply gave up trying. At times I played the role of class clown, but for the most part I didn't care what my classmates thought of me. Whenever they bragged about their weekend ski trips, I'd think about how I could squeeze in an extra hour of work.

One Friday, a few weeks before I graduated from Parkside Junior High, a group of rich kids were bragging about their upcoming graduation and plans of going to Disneyland or traveling to Hawaii first-class. Instead of feeling sorry for myself, I ran from the bus stop that afternoon and nearly knocked down the screen door to Alice's home. 'What is it?' she shrieked.

I gulped down a glass of water before answering. I was pushing sixteen and did not know how to cook for myself. Alice assured me that she would teach me when the time came. I persisted. I wanted to learn how to cook *now*. I gave her one of my serious looks, the kind I had learned from Mrs Catanze, who always placed her hands on her hips. It worked. Even though Alice had just cleaned her home for their bridge party, which would be held in just a couple of hours, she decided to teach me how to make pancakes.

Alice's decision was her undoing. In a matter of minutes I went through two boxes of Bisquick pancake mix, four dozen eggs and two gallons of milk. Every square inch of the gas stove was covered with the thick, white, gooey mix, and the ceiling was splattered with a few well-intended tossed pancakes. The floor looked as if a blizzard had blown through, and every time Alice or I shuffled across it, we nearly suffocated from the clouds of white powder. The strain on her face was quite visible, but she laughed with me – and I didn't quit until I made the perfect pancake.

Every day seemed to hold a new adventure. Sometimes after school, I'd play on the living-room floor with my Legos or my Erector set, while other times I was the little big man, returning to Alice's home after school just long enough to change clothes before zipping off to work at one of my jobs. For the first time, I had a real life.

By July 1976 my life took another turn. I grew tired of riding my bike to work every morning, while everyone else was still fast asleep. Then one afternoon, after a frustrating day on the job, I returned from work to find that not one, but two older foster boys had moved in. I took an instant dislike to one of the boys, Bruce, partly because I had to share a room with him and partly because I knew he got away with conning Alice blind. Even though both boys were seventeen, they didn't seem too concerned about supporting themselves. I began to resent them both. Whenever I pedaled off to work, they spent the day at the mall with Alice. In an odd sense I felt threatened and violated by their presence. I knew my childlike times with Alice were over, but I just wanted to hang on a little bit longer before I had to grow up.

After a few weeks, I discovered that my stash of money and some of the things I had bought through my earnings were missing. At first I thought I had misplaced my items, but one day, for no special reason, I had had enough. I marched up to Alice and demanded that either they leave or I would. I knew I sounded like a spoiled brat, but I could no longer tolerate trying to hide my things all the time, wondering at work how to make up for the stolen money. Everything I had worked so hard for slowly disappeared. I hoped Alice would give in, but I soon found myself packing. I felt like a complete fool leaving the Turnboughs. To me it was a matter of honor – if I said something, I had to be responsible for my word.

I stayed at juvenile hall for a few weeks until my new probation officer, Mrs O'Ryan, placed me with John and Linda Walsh, a young couple in their twenties who had three kids. John had long black hair and played piano in a rock-and-roll band, while Linda was a beauty consultant at the local Walgreens drugstore. They were both very nice, and I was extremely surprised by their carefree attitude. They pretty much allowed me to do as I pleased. When I wanted to buy a minibike, John said yes. One day when I timidly asked John if he could drive me to the local sport shop so I could buy a BB gun, he replied, 'Let's go.' I was stunned. I would have never even thought of asking Mr or Mrs Turnbough, but John didn't even blink. His only condition was that he had to teach me gun safety, and I could only shoot against paper targets under his supervision. I soon forgot about looking for another job and developed the Walshes' laid-back attitude.

A few weeks into my freshman year in high school, John and Linda told me that they were moving. Without thinking, I huffed into the room I shared with their two-year-old boy and crammed everything I owned into a pillowcase. I was livid. It seemed that every time, *every time*, I adjusted to a new environment, something happened. I realized that John and Linda seemed to fight all the time, but I got used to that as well as having to babysit their bratty kids. With my belongings slung over my shoulder, I marched back into the living-room. 'All right,' I demanded, 'let's go! Take me to The Hill!'

John and Linda both looked at each other and laughed. 'No, man,' John said, as he waved his hand in front of his face. 'I said we're moving, and *you're coming with us*; that is, if you don't have a problem with that?'

I became so upset at myself. So I stood in front of them and stewed for several minutes, until I smiled and said, 'I don't know what you two are laughing at, but I'm already packed! What about you?'

Linda jabbed John in the gut. 'Smart kid.'

The next day I stood in the back of an oversized U-Haul while John drove to the edge of the county. When he finally stopped, I leaped from the trailer. I couldn't believe what I saw. It was as if the Walshes and I had moved into the *Leave It to Beaver* neighborhood. I stepped around the U-Haul and gawked at the entire block. Every lawn was perfectly manicured. The immaculate houses looked more like miniature mansions than ordinary homes, and every car in its driveway had a blinding shine, as if it had just been waxed. As I strolled down the middle of Duinsmoore Drive, I breathed in the sweet smell of flowers, and I could hear the sound of the wind fluttering through a giant weeping willow.

I shook my head and smiled inside. 'Yes!' I shouted. 'I could live here!'

In no time at all I made friends with Paul Brazell and Dave Howard, two neighborhood teenagers who seemed fascinated by my dark, rusty-red minibike and my Daisy BB gun. Their eyes seemed hungry for adventure. I was more than happy to feed them. I discovered Paul had a minibike, too, and soon the three of us held drag races in the middle of the lifeless street. Paul always won, for three reasons: his minibike had more horsepower than mine, he weighed less than I did, and he had brakes – allowing him to slow down long after I did.

Out of the hundreds of races, I won only one. That day my throttle became stuck. I wasn't worried since I had a cutoff switch – which I immediately discovered would not shut off the engine. Since I didn't have any brakes, I tried to slow down by dragging my feet. As I did, my shoes slipped and the bottom of my shirt became caught in the rear sprocket. For a moment I had one hand on the throttle while the rest of my body flailed, before being dragged down the middle of the street. I was too scared to let go. I finally released my grip, and a split second later my minibike jumped the sidewalk, flying up and over a bush.

Just in front of me, Dave hit the ground, rolling with laughter. Seconds later Paul pulled up. His eyes were as big as silver dollars. 'Man, that was too cool! Can you do that again?' As I struggled to stand up, I could see some of the adults from the neighborhood staring in our direction. They seemed more concerned over the damage to the bush than my medical condition. Trying to forget the unfriendly looks, I blocked out the pain and gave Paul my widest smile. From that moment on I was dubbed 'The Stuntmaster of Duinsmoore'.

That evening the three of us plotted our next adventure. Paul's parents had a 16mm camera, so Paul decided to make a James Bond-style movie, casting me as the lead actor. The climax of the film was to have Dr Strange, played by Dave, drag Bond up and down the street while Paul filmed from all angles. I told Paul I wasn't so sure about the stunt, while Dave panted like a dog, claiming he wouldn't mind watching my knees turn into hamburger. Dave doubled as my stunt coordinator, which entailed keeping the street clear of all traffic under the age of ten and having a set of Band-Aids at the ready whenever my gag was completed. I was thankful the next day when Paul's camera ran out of film – before my death-defying climax.

One day Paul helped me prepare to meet a girl from around the block. I had never talked to a girl before, but Paul loaned me his best shirt and coached me on what to say. At that time in my life I was barely looking at myself in the mirror, let alone having the confidence to talk to a girl. After combing my hair, hearing more coaching and having no more excuses, I let Paul kick me out of his house, and I strolled down Duinsmoore. As I turned the corner, I felt like a normal person. I lived in a perfect neighborhood, my foster parents let me do as I wished, I didn't have to work, and most important, my life was centered around the best friends in the entire world.

Minutes later I rapped on the front door and waited. My hands shook, and I felt lightheaded, as sweat seemed to escape from every pore of my body. I was actually excited to be a little frightened. This was a good scare. I began to rub my hands when the door opened. I thought my mouth would fall to the floor. I felt tingly all over as I stared into the face of the prettiest girl I had ever seen. Without the girl knowing, I regained my composure as she began to talk. The more she spoke, the better I felt about myself. I couldn't believe how easy it was to make the girl laugh. I was enjoying myself – right up until the moment when the girl's mother pushed her aside.

It took a moment for my eyes to adjust. When they did, I looked up at a woman who looked more like the lady from *The Brady Bunch* than someone's mother. The woman quickly jabbed a finger in front of my face. 'You're that little . . . that little *F-child*, aren't you?' she sneered, with a tight smirk on her face.

I was too stunned to speak.

'Have you no respect for elders? Answer me, boy!'

'Ma'am?' I said, shaking my head.

'Listen to me,' the woman raved, 'I know all about you and . . . those motorcycles, making all that reverberating noise and the willful destruction of private property. How did *the association* ever approve of . . . *your kind* of people residing in *our* neighborhood. I know all about *your kind*. You're a filthy little hooligan! Just look at your attire – you reek of street trash. I don't know what you children do to become . . . *fostered children*,' she said, covering her mouth as if she had just spoken a swear word, 'but I'm sure *you* did something hideous, didn't you?' The woman's face turned so red that I thought she was going to explode. 'Don't you dare approach *my household* or converse with *my children*, ever!'

I stood mesmerized by the woman's perfectly manicured red fingernail in my face.

'And just a piece of advice,' the woman went on. 'Don't waste your time trying. *You* don't have what it takes to make it. *I* know! Believe me, *I'm* actually doing you a favor!' She smiled as she tossed her hair to the other side of her face. 'You'll see! *I'm* a very open-minded person who knows a thing or two. So the sooner you learn that you're only an *F-child*, the better off you'll be! So stick with your own kind!'

Before I could respond, the front door slammed shut with such a fury that I felt a rush of air hit my face. I stood by the door dumbstruck. I didn't know what to do. I felt as if I were an inch tall. I gazed at the sleeves of Paul's red-and-black flannel shirt. They were a little short, but I thought the shirt looked nice. I ran my hand through my oily hair. *I guess I could use a bath,* I muttered to myself. I knew that on the outside I was a walking geek, but on the inside I felt better about myself than ever before. I tried so hard to do things that normal kids took for granted. I just wanted to fit in. I wanted to be like a normal kid.

Minutes later, with my head hung low, I passed Paul, who danced around me as he pestered me with questions about meeting the girl. I waved off my best friend and hid in my room for the rest of the day.

The next afternoon, while I was tinkering with my minibike, a tall man walked up to me with a beer can in one hand and a baby stroller in the other. 'So, you're the neighborhood threat?' he said with a sly grin. I kept my head down as I felt my body temperature begin to rise. Before I could mouth off, the man breezed on by.

About half an hour later, the man reappeared in the opposite direction. I waited for another put-down, but this time I was ready to fire off an insult. He gave me a wide smile before saying, 'Good on you, boy! Get some!'

I shook my head, thinking my ears were clogged. *Good on me? Get some? Get some what?* I asked myself.

I stood up, wiped a spot of black oil onto my dirty white tank top and watched the man as he bobbed past me to the driveway next door. He gave me another nod before disappearing into the garage. I was so stunned that I sat down on the grass and thought about what the crazy man meant. As demented as he seemed, he did have a way with words.

The next afternoon, at the same time, the man reappeared in the same outfit: a pair of white shorts that showed off his ash-white, bony knees, an undersized T-shirt that read 'Fudpuckers – We've Been Flying Since the World's Been Square', a baseball cap with silver-winged feathers pinned in the middle and a cigarette that seemed to dangle from his bottom lip. Again, with a beer in one hand and a baby stroller in the other, he stopped in front of me and winked. 'Airborne material you're not, but don't worry, Slim; every dog has his day.' And he pushed on.

I repeated his message over and over again as I tried to find a meaning to the phrase 'every dog has his day'. Just like clockwork, the man returned thirty minutes later. I jumped up and waited for his eloquent words of wisdom. 'Know this,' the man said with a bow, 'there's always profit in mass confusion.'

'Hey, mister . . .' I said before I could think.

The man's head spun around like a top. 'You inquired?'

My mouth hung open. I didn't know how to respond. I could feel myself choke up. He bowed his head. 'If you can wash your hands and change your attire, you may join me at my humble abode.'

In a flash, I raced through the Walshes' house, scrubbed my arms and hands, dirtying their bathroom sink, and changed my shirt before bursting through the man's front door. Before I could yell my presence, a giant hand slapped me in the center of my chest. I lost my breath and thought my chest would cave in. The man looked down and smiled, 'Let's try that again, shall we?' he said, as he led me out the front door and closed it in my face.

I frowned to myself. 'How rude!' I said out loud. For a moment I thought I was being put down the way *The Brady Bunch* lady had done. I was about to leave when I heard a muffled voice from behind the door state, 'Knock on the door.'

I rolled my eyes as my knuckles rapped on the front door. A moment later, the door flung open, and the man bowed at the waist as he waved his arm, permitting me to enter. He smiled as he introduced himself. 'Michael Marsh: keeper of the faith, soldier of fortune and the Doc Savage of Duinsmoore Drive.'

And so began my first of many visits to 'Marsh Manor'. Days later I met Mr Marsh's wife, Sandra, who was quiet and shy compared with her peculiar husband. I was instantly taken with their two boys, William and Eric. Watching their toddler, Eric, dribble as he crawled around the house reminded me of my brother Kevin when he was that age.

The Marshes treated me like a real person. While the Walshes argued more than ever, the Marshes' home became my safe haven. Whenever I was not promoting chaos with Paul and Dave, I spent hundreds of hours sitting in a corner of Michael's famed 'Hall of Knowledge', reading books about movies, race cars and airplanes. Ever since I was a prisoner in Mother's house, I developed a fascination for aircraft. The many times I would sit on top of my hands in the bottom of the cold garage, I'd escape by fantasizing I was Superman. I always wanted to fly.

Although I was never allowed to take any of Mr Marsh's books to the Walshes' home, I'd sometimes sneak off with a book and stay up all night, reading about the real-life adventures of World War II fighter pilots or the development of specialized aircraft like the Lockheed SR-71 Blackbird. Michael's library opened up a whole new world to me. For the first time in my life, I began to wonder what it would be like to fly aboard a real airplane. Maybe, I thought, one of these days . . .

Paul's father, Dan Brazell, was the Mr Goodwrench of the neighborhood, and he had the same effect on me as Mr Marsh. At first Mr Brazell was wary of me, but eventually he grew to tolerate my standing over his shoulder, quizzing his every movement. Sometimes Paul, Dave and I would peek into Mr Brazell's garage and stare in awe at whatever projects he was building from scratch. Whenever he left the garage for a few minutes, Paul would strut in, while Dave and I followed in Paul's footsteps for fear of disturbing a piece of metal or a placed tool. However, as soon as the door opened, the three of us would scurry out of the garage before Dan caught us. We knew that the garage was a special domain where Dan, Michael and a host of other men from the neighborhood gathered for their daily meetings.

Sometimes during the daily gatherings, a few of the men from the neighborhood frowned at me, as they complained about the fear of 'plummeting real estate values in the local area'. Mr Marsh always came to my rescue. 'Back off, boys,' Michael once warned. 'I have plans for my young ward. I predict that Mr Pelzer here will become the next Chuck Yeager or Charles Manson. As you can see, I'm still working on the details.'

I smiled at the compliment. 'Yeah,' I nodded in defiance, 'Charles Manson!' I did feel a little foolish that I did not recall Charles Manson as an Ace fighter pilot.

My times at Duinsmoore were the best in my teenage life. At night, after reading one of Mr Marsh's 'borrowed books', I'd fall asleep to the scent of flowers from a soft outside breeze. Every day after school carried a new adventure, waiting for *my* two friends and me to discover.

My stay at the Walshes was not so good. Raging arguments were a daily occurrence, and at times both of them would storm out of the house, leaving me to watch their children. Sometimes I'd try to time the fights, so that before John and Linda began to hit each other, I could grab the youngest child and order the other two children to follow me outside until things calmed down.

As much as I loved Duinsmoore, I knew I couldn't keep living like I did. I felt that *I had to do something*. Finally, after an explosive argument, I called Mrs O'Ryan, my probation officer, and begged her to move me, even if it meant returning to The Hill. Mrs O'Ryan seemed pleased with my decision and thought she could convince the Turnboughs to take me back.

Leaving Duinsmoore was one of the hardest decisions I had to make. In a matter of months, in the tiniest fraction of my life, Duinsmoore had given me so much.

I made it a point not to say goodbye. Paul, Dave and I seemed choked up, but we hid our feelings behind our age. At the last moment Dave gave me a hug. Mr Brazell saluted me while holding a wrench, while Mr Marsh presented me with a book on airplanes – the same book I had sneaked out of his house dozens of times. 'This way you won't have to break in my house . . . you hooligan.' He also gave me an autographed Delta Airline postcard. On it he scrawled his address and phone number. 'Stay in touch, Slim,' Michael said, as I felt myself beginning to get emotional. 'Day or night, Sandra and I are here for you. Hang tough, Airborne! Get some!'

Before climbing into Harold Turnbough's ancient, blue-and-white Chevy pickup, I cleared my throat, then announced in my Michael Marsh-like voice, 'Shed no tears. Have no fear . . . for . . . I shall return!'

As Mr Turnbough and I motored away from Duinsmoore Drive, I saw *The Brady Bunch* woman, who stood on her immaculate front porch with her arms tightly across her chest. She gave me a sneering smile. I smiled back before shouting, 'Love you, too!'

Almost an hour later I burst through Alice Turnbough's screen door. After a quick hug she pushed me away. 'This is the last time,' she warned. 'Speak now or forever hold your peace.'

I nodded before replying, 'I know where I belong: 555–2647!'

chapter 10

BREAK AWAY

During the middle of my sophomore year in high school, I grew frustrated and bored. Because I had moved so much and never stayed in one school for more than a few months at a time, I was placed in a class for slow learners. I fought the idea at first, until I discovered that very little was expected of me. By then I abandoned all of my academic studies, for *I* knew my future lay outside the school walls. I was putting in over forty-eight hours of work a week through a string of jobs, and I believed that nothing I learned from high school could be used in the real world.

My hunger for work was fueled by the fact that I was seventeen and had less than a year to go in foster care. During sixth period, I'd race from school to Alice's home, change clothes, then speed off again to one of my jobs at a fast-food restaurant or the plastic factory, where I worked until one or two in the morning. I knew that the odd hours and lack of sleep were taking their toll on me. In school, teachers had to prod me awake as I snored in their classes. I resented the kids who laughed at me. Some of these same kids acted high and mighty whenever they saw me labor at the restaurants, strutting in to show off their dates or flashy clothes, knowing they would never have to work like I did in order to survive.

Sometimes during my free period, I'd stroll over to visit my English teacher, Mr Tapley. Since he didn't have class that period, Mr Tapley used his time to correct papers. I'd plant my elbows on his desk and bug him with an endless stream of questions about my future. He knew how hard I struggled, but I was too embarrassed to tell him why I would always fall asleep. Mr Tapley would look up from his pile of work, run a hand through his thinning hair and feed me just enough advice to get me through the weekend – to bury myself in my homework assignments.

As much as I labored through the week, I tried to schedule every other weekend off, on the off chance of visiting Father in San Francisco. Over the years, I had left hundreds of messages to all the fire stations throughout the city. Father never called back. One afternoon I lost it when a hesitant fireman tried to put me off. 'Is this the right station?' I pleaded. 'Just tell me, what shift does he work?' I begged, raising my voice.

'Uhh . . . Stephen works at different stations at different times. We'll get the message to him,' the fireman said before the line went dead.

I knew something was horribly wrong. Alice tried to stop me from fleeing her home. 'My dad's in trouble,' I shouted, my chest heaving.

'David, you don't know that!' Alice blasted back.

'That's exactly what I mean,' I said, pointing a finger at her. 'I'm tired of living in the dark . . . of hiding secrets . . . of living a lie. What can be so bad? If my dad's in trouble . . .' I stopped for a moment as my imagination began to take hold. 'I just have to know,' I said, kissing Alice on the forehead.

I hopped on my motorcycle and sped off to the heart of San Francisco. On the freeway I dodged and swerved through the traffic, and I didn't slow down until my motorcycle rumbled into the alley next to 1067 Post Street – the same fire station Father had been assigned to since I was a baby.

I parked my motorcycle by the back entrance of the station. As I walked up the steep incline, I noticed an old familiar face. At first I thought the face belonged to Father, but I knew it wasn't him when the face smiled. Father never smiled. 'My Lord, son! How long has it been? I haven't seen you boys in . . . I don't know how long.'

I shook hands with Uncle Lee, my father's long-time partner and best friend. 'Where's Dad?' I asked in a stern voice.

Uncle Lee turned away. 'Well . . . he just left. He just went off shift.'

'No, sir!' I demanded. I knew Uncle Lee was lying – firemen changed shifts in the morning, not in the middle of the afternoon. I lowered my defenses. 'Uncle Lee, I haven't seen Dad in years. I have to know.'

Lee seemed choked up. He rubbed a tear from the corner of his eye. 'Your father and I started out together, ya know. I got to tell ya, your old man was one hell of a fireman . . . There were times when I thought we wouldn't make it . . .'

I could feel it coming. My insides became unglued. My eyes searched for something to grab onto, to keep me from falling. I bit my lip. I nodded my head as if telling Uncle Lee to just let it out and tell me.

Lee's eyes blinked, showing that he understood. 'Your father . . . doesn't work for the department anymore. Stephen . . . your father . . . was . . . asked to retire early.'

I let out a sigh of relief as I fought to control my feelings. 'So he's alive! He's okay! Where is he?' I shrieked.

Uncle Lee laid it all down, telling me that Father had not had work for over a year. So when his money ran out, he moved from place to place, and at times Lee feared that Father slept on the street. 'David, it's the booze. It's killing him,' he said in a soft but firm tone.

'So where is he now?' I begged.

'I don't know, son. I only see him when he needs a few bucks.' Uncle Lee stopped for a moment to clear his throat. He looked at me in a way he never had before. 'David, don't be too hard on your old man. He never really had a family. He was a young man when he first came here to the city. He loved you kids, but the marriage destroyed him. His job wasn't easy on him, either. It's all that kept him going. He lived for the station. But his drinking . . . it's all that he knows.'

'Thanks, Uncle Lee,' I said, as I shook his hand. 'Thanks for not putting me off. At least now I know.'

Uncle Lee walked me down to my motorcycle. 'I should see your dad in a few days. Hell, maybe you can help him out of this mess.'

'Yeah,' I replied, 'maybe.'

Two weekends later, I rode on a Greyhound bus to the Mission district of San Francisco. At the bus station I waited for Father for over an hour. From outside I spotted a rundown bar. I took a chance, walked across the street and found Father slumped over on top of a table. My head swiveled around, searching for help. I couldn't believe how people strolled by Father's table without the slightest concern, or sat by the bar nursing their drinks as if my father were invisible.

I gently shook my childhood superhero from his slumber.

Father's coughing seemed to awaken him. His stench was so bad that I held my breath until I could help him stumble from the bar. The outside air seemed to clear his head. In the sunlight Father looked worse than I ever imagined. I deliberately did not look at his face. I wanted to remember my father for the man he once was – the tall, rugged, strong firefighter with gleaming white teeth, who placed himself in danger to help a fellow fireman or rescue a child from a burning building.

Father and I walked for several blocks without saying a word. I knew better than to question him on his drinking or his lifestyle. But Uncle Lee's warning about doing something, anything, to help Father echoed in my mind. Without thinking, I closed my eyes, spun around and held out my hand, stopping him. 'What happened, Dad?'

Father stopped and let out a hacking cough. His hands trembled as he struggled to light a cigarette. 'You'd be better off forgetting all about it, the whole thing – your mother, the house, everything. It never happened.' Father took a deep drag. I tried to look into his eyes, but he kept dodging my glance. 'It's your mother. She's crazy . . . You'd be better off forgetting the whole thing,' he ordered with a wave of his hand, as if sweeping the *family secret* under the carpet for the final time.

'No, Dad, it's you! I'm worried about you!' A chill blew across my face. My body shuddered, and I clamped my eyes shut. I wanted to cry out to Father, and yet I didn't have the guts to tell him how much I was scared for him. My brain struggled with what was right and what was proper. I knew by Father's look that his life was his business and that no one ever questioned a father's authority, but he was a walking death. His hands rattled every few seconds and his eyelids were drooped so low that he could barely see. I felt so awkward. I didn't want to make Father mad, but I soon found myself becoming upset. *Why weren't you there for me? Couldn't you have at least called me? Can't you be like a regular dad, with a job and a family, so I could be with you and play catch or go fishing? Why can't you be normal?* my brain screamed.

I sucked in a deep breath before I opened my eyes. 'I'm sorry. It's just that you're my dad . . . and I love you.'

Father wheezed as he turned away. I knew he had heard me but he couldn't bring himself to reply. The river of alcohol and the destroyed family life had stripped him of his innermost feelings. I realized that inside, my father was truly dead. Moments later he and I continued our journey to nowhere, with our heads bent down, looking at no one – especially not ourselves.

Hours later, before Father loaded me onto the bus, he pulled me aside. 'I want to show you something,' he said with pride, as he reached behind him and plucked out a black leather covering with the emblem of the fireman's shield on it. Father smiled as he opened the casing, revealing a bright, shiny silver fireman's badge. 'Here, hold it,' he said, as he gently placed the badge in my open palms.

'R-1522,' I read aloud, knowing that the R signified that Father was indeed retired and not fired as I had feared, while the numbers were those assigned to Father when he first joined.

'That's all I have now. That's one of the only things in my life that I didn't screw up too badly. No one can ever take that away from me,' he stated with conviction, pointing to his prize. 'Someday you'll understand.'

I nodded my head. I understood. I always had. In the past I had imagined Father dressed in his crisp, dark-blue fireman's uniform, as he strolled to a podium to receive his badge of honor in front of a frenzied crowd shouting his name, with his beautiful wife and family standing by his side. As a child, I had dreamed of Father's big day.

I now looked into his eyes as I gave him his lifetime achievement. 'I'm really proud of you, Dad,' I said, gazing down at the badge. 'I truly am.' For a split second Father's eyes gleamed. And for a moment in time his pain disappeared.

A few minutes later Father stopped me on the steps of the bus. He hesitated. His eyes looked down. 'Get out of here,' he mumbled. 'David, get as far away from here as you can. Your brother Ronald joined the service, and you're almost at that age. Get out,' Father said as he patted my shoulder. As he turned away, his final words were, 'Do what you have to. Don't end up like me.'

I pressed my face to the window of the bus and strained my eyes as I watched Father disappear into the crowd. I wanted to jump off and hug him, to hold his hand or sit by his side the way I did as a child whenever he read his evening paper – like the dad I knew so many years ago. I wanted him to be a part of my life. I wanted a dad. As the bus lumbered out of San Francisco, I lost control of my emotions and cried inside. I clenched my fist, as the tremendous pressure I had stored for years burst inside my soul. I realized the horribly lonely life that Father lived. I prayed with all my heart that God would watch over him and keep him warm at night and free from any harm. A mountain of guilt weighed on my shoulders. I felt so bad for everything in my father's life.

After visiting Uncle Lee, I had fantasized that maybe I could buy a home in Guerneville and have Father move in. Only then could I help ease his pain or could we spend some time together as father and son. But I knew, as always, that fantasies were dreams and reality was life. I cried throughout the bus ride to Alice's home. I knew that Father was dying, and I became terrified that I would never see him again.

Months afterward, during the summer of 1978, after dozens of interviews, I landed a job selling cars. Selling cars was mentally exhausting. The upper managers would threaten the sales staff one day, then bait us with money incentives the next. The competition was fierce, but I somehow managed to keep my head above water. If I had a weekend off, I'd race off to Duinsmoore and forget about having to be an adult, as Paul, Dave and I searched for new adventure on four wheels – loaned to me by the car dealer. Once, after seeing a movie on Hollywood stuntmen, the three of us sat facing forward as I drove backward in a perfectly straight line, without looking behind my back. Our stunt caused a few wrecks with confused drivers, and the three of us had a few minor scrapes with the law. But I knew my adventurous times would be coming to an end when Paul and Dave matured and began to look for jobs, too.

More than ever, I sought guidance from Duinsmoore Drive. One time Dan drove to Alice's home so he could talk me out of my pipe dream of becoming a Hollywood stuntman. With his son Paul by his side, Mr Brazell spent hours of his time telling me how foolish I was. I had always been fond of Dan, and as I walked him and Paul outside after abandoning my lame idea. I realized that I was closer to Dan than to my own father.

The Marshes were just as caring. Many times I'd help Sandra with her housework, as I learned other ways to become self-sufficient. Mr Marsh recommended that I join the service. Immediately I'd think of the Air Force, but as a freshman in high school I had taken the aptitude test and failed miserably. I had convinced myself that I could make it in the outside world without any schooling.

Summer passed, and I decided – because I was almost eighteen and had to make money in order to survive – to drop out of high school. Alice was livid, but my career as a salesman was on the rise. Out of a sales staff of over forty, I was consistently one of the top five salesmen. But months after my eighteenth birthday, the recession hit, gas prices shot up, my savings withered and the reality of going nowhere fast hit me in the face.

To escape my troubles, one Sunday I rode off in my beat-up, orange '65 Mustang and headed north to find the Russian River. I didn't know exactly how to get there, but I drove by instinct, relying on my memories as a child. When I sensed the correct exit, I turned off. I knew I was close when the towering redwood trees filled my windshield. My heart seemed to skip a beat when I parked my car at the old Safeway supermarket. My eyes gaped at the same aisles I had strolled through as a child. At the checkout counter, I dug through my pant pockets and spent the last of my splurge money on a stick of salami and a loaf of French bread. I sat on a deserted sandbar of Johnson's Beach and slowly gnawed on my lunch, listening to the rippling sounds of the Russian River and the scraping metal of an oversized motor home that rumbled its way across the narrow evergreen bridge. I found myself at peace.

In order to fulfill my vow of living at the Russian River, I knew I had to first find myself. I couldn't do it living so close to my past. I had to break away. As I collected my trash and walked away from the beach, the sun shone on my shoulders. I felt warm inside. I had made *my* decision. Turning to face the river one last time, I felt like crying. If I wanted to, I could move to the river, but I knew it wouldn't be right. I took in a deep breath and spoke in a slow voice, renewing my lifelong promise. *I will be back.*

Months later, after obtaining my high school G.E.D. and completing a series of tests and background checks, I proudly enlisted into the United States Air Force. Somehow word got to Mother, and she called me a day before I reported for basic training. Her voice wasn't that of the *evil mother*, but *my mommy* from years ago. I could almost see Mommy's face on the other end of the phone as she cried. She claimed that she thought of me all the time and that she had always wanted nothing but the best for me. We talked for over an hour, and I strained my ears in hopes of hearing the three most important words I had wanted Mom to say all my life.

Alice stood beside me as I cried into the telephone. I wanted to be with my mom. I wanted to see her face in hopes of hearing those three words. I realized that I was being foolish, but I felt I should at least try. It took all of Alice's persuasive powers to keep me from visiting Mom. But in my heart I knew that *Mother* was just toying with my emotions. For over eighteen years, I wanted something I knew I would never receive – Mom's love. Without a word, Alice opened her arms. And as she held me, I suddenly realized that my lifelong search for love and acceptance had finally ended in the arms of a foster parent.

The next day I stood tall as I looked into Harold's blue eyes. 'Be good now, son,' he said.

'I will, sir. You watch. I'll make you proud.'

Alice stood beside her husband. 'You know who you are. You've always known,' she said, as she held out her hand and gave me a shiny yellow key. 'This is your home. It always has been and always will be your home.'

I pocketed the key to my home. After kissing Alice, *my mother*, and shaking Harold's, *my father's*, hand, I opened my mouth to say something appropriate. But this moment in time needed no words, for we knew what we all felt – the love of a family.

Hours later, as the Boeing 727 banked its way from California, I closed my eyes for a final time as *a lost boy*. I pictured 'The Sarge', Michael Marsh, in all his glory, with his eyes pierced toward the sky when he had said, 'Well, Airman Pelzer, any thoughts?'

'Well,' I had replied, 'I'm a little scared, but I could use that to my advantage. I have a master plan. I'm focused, and I know I'm going to make it.'

Then my mentor had glanced down on me and smiled. 'Good on you, Pelz-man. Get some.'

Aboard my first plane ride, I opened my eyes for the first time *as a man named Dave*. I chuckled to myself. '*Now* the adventure begins!'

EPILOGUE
December 1993,
Sonoma County, California

I'm alone. On the outside I'm so cold that my entire body shivers. The tips of my fingers have been numb for some time. As I exhale, a frosty mist escapes through my nose. In the distance I can hear the rumbling sounds of dark gray clouds colliding against each other. A few seconds later, thunder echoes from the nearby hills. I can see a cloudburst approaching.

I don't mind. I'm sitting on top of an old rotted log in front of a long stretch of empty beach. I love gazing at the splendor of the powerful dark green waves that form into a curl before pounding the beach. A coat of salty spray covers my glasses.

On the inside I'm warm. I'm no longer afraid of being alone. I love spending time by myself.

From above, a flock of seagulls squawks at each other as the birds comb the beach in search of any morsel of food. Moments later a single gull struggles to maintain flight. As much as the bird pounds its wings, it cannot keep up with the flock, let alone maintain altitude. Without warning, the gull crashes beak first into the sand. The bird flops up and hobbles on a single, webbed orange leg. After a short search, the seagull finds a fragment of food. Suddenly, out of nowhere, the flock of seagulls returns, hovers above the beach, then dives to pick on the weaker gull for its meal. The gull seems to know it cannot flee, so it stands its ground and pecks at the other birds with furious intensity. Within a blink of an eye the struggle is over, and the flock of birds flies off in search of an easier victim.

The seagull screeches at the flock as if telling them that it was victorious, then turns toward me and squawks a warning. As I study

233

the gull's movements, I recall how its battle mirrored my own challenges while in foster care. Back then nothing was more important than wanting to be accepted and finding the answers to my past. But the more I matured on the inside, the more I realized I had to carve my own path. I also learned to be content in not finding all the answers of my quest. But like most things in my life, my answers seemed to come without effort after I joined the United States Air Force, where I achieved my lifelong dream of flying. As an adult I came full circle. One of the things I accomplished was visiting my mother and asking her the most important question of my life: Why?

Mother's own secret made me cherish the life that I lead even more.

The screeching sound of the seagull breaks my trance. In front of me my hands quiver, but it's not from the cold. I wipe a stream of tears from my cheeks. I don't cry for myself as much as I do for my mother. I begin to cry so hard that my body shakes. I can't stop. I cry for the mother and father I never had and the shame of the family secret. I become unglued because at times I have doubts about making a difference in the lives of others, and I feel unworthy for the recognition I've received.

I cry to let everything out.

I close my eyes and say a quick prayer. I pray for the wisdom to become a better, stronger person. As I stand up, facing the dark green ocean, I feel cleansed inside. It's time to move on.

After a relaxing drive with the windows rolled down and listening to Pat Metheny's Secret Story, I park my 4-Runner in front of my second home – the Rio Villa in Monte Rio. The owners, Ric and Don, wave as they scurry about to prepare for incoming guests. The serene beauty of the Rio Villa still takes my breath away. For years now Ric and Don have gone out of their way to make my son, Stephen, and me feel a part of their family. To be welcome means so much to me.

After I wrestle him to the floor, Stephen wraps his arms around my neck. 'You okay?' he asks. Even though he is only a child, in so many ways Stephen's sensitivity is beyond his years. I'm amazed that at times he can feel my innermost feelings. As much as he is my son, Stephen is also one of my closest friends.

The two of us spend the remainder of the day designing multicolored Creepy Crawlers plastic toys, and playing Sorry and Monopoly over and over and over again. I quickly discover that my years of training in military strategy are no match for the mind of a ruthless seven-year-old, who acquires both Park Place and Boardwalk, with hotels. (I still owe Stephen back rent.)

After several annihilating lessons of Sorry, Stephen and I make our way down to the deck by the Russian River. A thick odor of burning wood mixes in with the sweet aroma of redwood trees. The shallow green river becomes transparent, with only a soft trickling sound that makes the water real. As the sun disappears behind a hill, the reflection of a Christmas tree shimmers from across the river. A blanket of fog seeps down from the hills. Without a word, Stephen and I join hands. I can feel a lump creep up my throat as we tighten our grip.

Stephen clamps onto my leg. 'Love you, Dad. Happy birthday.'

Years ago, I truly doubted whether I'd make it out alive. In my former life I had very little. Today, as I stand in my utopia, I have what any person could wish for – a life and the love of my son. Stephen and I are a family.

PERSPECTIVES ON FOSTER CARE
David Pelzer
Foster child

There is not a doubt in my mind that had I stayed with my biological mother much longer, I would have definitely been killed. Foster care was not only an escape, but literally a whole new world. At times it was extremely difficult to adjust, for I never quite knew what to expect.

As an adult survivor, I am forever grateful to 'The System' that so many in society ridicule without mercy. It would have been easy for me to exploit the weakness of social services and foster care and all that they entail. That was *never* the premise of the story, but rather to take the reader into a world rarely seen by the general public – through the eyes of a tortured, programmed-to-fail child who is 'placed' into the care of others.

My social worker, Ms Gold, stays etched in my mind simply because of her genuine concern for *my* safety and security. Though I thought retracting my statements within days of my disposition was unique to my case, this is an everyday occurrence for most of those who work in her field. Very few people truly know what Child Protective Service workers go through.

There are many who believe that social workers are nothing more than homewreckers who barge into a private residence and pluck a child from the arms of a loving parent. Or that **they** *never* respond to a *real* case involving child abuse. The reality of the situation is far more horrifying. In 1973, in California, I was among several thousand cases reported. Twenty years later the same state reported more than 616,000 cases.

There are too few social workers available to respond to the never-ending siege of 'youth at risk'. For them, it is a matter of triage – a minor who is in harm's way the most receives immediate attention first. Then, once a report is under investigation, *no* information can be given to the general public on the status of the case, which causes stress to those who dared to file the report in the first place and who in turn may surmise that social services never follows through. Again, the operating principle of social services is to preserve the privacy, safety and security of the *minor*. Needless to say, burnout plays a major role for these angels – whose *sole* purpose is that of saving the life of a child.

As for my foster parents, **they** made me the person I am today. **They** took in a heap of hideous mass and transformed a terrified child into a functional, responsible human being. I owe each of them so much. Unfortunately for them, I put my foster parents through absolute hell – especially the Catanzes, during my critical 'adjustment phase'. They saved me from almost certain doom. The Turnboughs were a godsend, with something so simple as teaching me how to walk, talk and act like a *normal* child, while assuring me that I was worthy and could overcome any challenge that life had to offer.

This is the work that **foster parents** do!

As an adult I will never understand why **these** people put up with so much. One can barely fathom what it is like to deal with a child who came from a past like mine, let alone the half a dozen other foster children residing in the average foster home.

And yet the general public rarely, if ever, hears of the love and compassion for what some folks dub *F-parents* – as if the words *foster parent* belonged to a deadly epidemic. These same individuals may assume that foster parents 'are only doing it for the money', that foster parents are nothing more than parental mercenaries, making a profit off of society's ills. If this is true, then why is it that over 65 percent of the foster parents in Iowa end up adopting their foster children, thus making the foster parents ineligible for financial assistance? Like most foster parents, they fall victim to the emotion of love. To be adopted is the highest honor bestowed on a child who longs to become a member of a family.

But society is never made aware of those stories. It appears that foster parents only receive attention when a child is hurt while under the guardianship of foster care. The press clamors to 'inform' the public of a child victim becoming victimized again. Investigations are made, and it is most likely that the foster parents in question may not have been suited as foster parents. An obvious answer! Because of such publicity, the question brought up by many is, has 'The System' failed the child again? Hardly!

Don't get me wrong; harming a child is absolutely wrong and should never be tolerated! However, those cases are rare, and they undermine the incredible work that foster care performs. The *real* question is, how did those adults receive a license as foster parents in the first place? The answer may be for the simple reason that so many children need to be placed into homes – yesterday. Again, society's ills tax 'The System' to overwhelming proportions. There are literally millions of children in need and only several thousand homes available. Alleviating this situation may lie with a thorough screening process for those who apply for foster licenses, including background checks – much like those used for any county or government job. Perhaps training programs on how to deal with the endless and various needs of the foster children could help as well.

On the other hand, the press was kind enough to pay homage to Charlotte Lopez, a foster child for fifteen of her seventeen years, who won the title of Miss Teen USA in 1993. I was extremely intrigued by Charlotte's confidence and inner beauty. I wonder where Miss Lopez received her esteem and poise from? Could it have been from her foster parent, Janet Henry? One can only imagine the endless hours that Janet and Charlotte spent together. I can only assume that Charlotte's main concern was not so much for her smile or her technique for strolling down the runway, as it was for her inner fear, which most foster children possess – seeking answers to their condition, while struggling to fit into an ordinary world.

There are other dedicated foster parents, like Debbe Magnusen, who takes in babies, in the middle of the night, that were born addicted to crack cocaine. Like so many others, Debbe, too, has adopted her former foster children. Legends in the field of foster care include Nina Coake, Judy Fields and Lennie Hart, who have each been in service to children at risk for over thirty-five years, fighting for the care and rights of foster children. Another is Pamela Eby, who literally dedicated her life to saving children until losing her final battle to cancer.

I cannot begin to state how much I cringe when I hear the term 'cop' or 'pig'. Again, one can only imagine what type of world we would live in if it were not for our police officers, who rescue children from abusive situations and wear bulletproof vests for fear of being killed in a domestic dispute. When folks gripe about our educational system, they may fail to realize that the teachers and staff see victims of child abuse firsthand and are the ones who are overburdened. If this statement sounds doubtful, step into a classroom holding seventy-five students. I don't call that teaching as much as I do crowd control. Besides parents and legal guardians, who has the most influence over our children's lives but teachers? As for those who work in social services – from counselors at juvenile halls, Child Protective Service members, juvenile probation officers and Court Appointed Special Advocate (CASA) volunteers to foster parents – I can never admire and respect **their** efforts enough.

There are organizations that play a priceless role for 'youth at risk' in our communities, such as the members of the United States Junior Chamber of Commerce, better known as the Jaycees. The main purpose of the Jaycees, who are volunteers, is the service of humanity. For instance, every year the state of Nebraska raises several thousand dollars for its Aid to Foster Children program. During the Christmas season, Jaycee chapters from across the nation donate Christmas trees to children who have never seen, let alone smelled, a Douglas fir. Their dedication doesn't stop there. Jaycees invade stores with hundreds of children in tow – children who have never shopped for toys for themselves. These children never crave such niceties as Game Boys or Nike Air Jordan shoes. Instead, these children wish for clothes that are a size too big – so as to get more wear out of them.

Another organization is The Arrow Project, a nonprofit organization that addresses the needs of children and families in several states by providing foster care, diagnostic and educational services and other interventions.

In March 1994 I was in Ohio presenting a keynote address to local law enforcement officers, teachers and social service workers. The lady who preceded me made a statement that made everything crystal clear: 'It takes a community to save a child!'

All too often, as a result of dissolving families and values, a lack of concern for minors and a lack of proper guidance, children grow up to become 'killing machines'. By investing in our 'youth at risk' today, does society not stand a better chance of a 'higher yield' tomorrow – an adult serving our community rather than rotting away in some jail?

While 'The System' is not perfect, it does in fact work. In my estimation 'The System' will never be perfected – the demands from society are just too much. Many of us look toward 'The System' and demand that 'they' solve our problems, to our satisfaction, right now.

Like the Jaycees and The Arrow Project, maybe society can ease some of the frustrations of those in their chosen field. Maybe **we** can mail a card to a teacher for no special reason and just say thanks, or give a small bunch of flowers to a social worker. Perhaps the next time **we** see a police officer, **we** can smile and wave hello; or present a foster family with a pizza. If **we** can treat those in entertainment and sports like gifts from the gods, why can't **we** show a little bit of gratitude to those who play such a priceless role in **our** community?

As much as this book takes the reader behind the scenes, its main theme is always that of the child who seemingly comes from another planet. Some people may believe that once a child is removed from a threatening environment, the minor's problems instantly disappear. The actuality is, that is when the troubles begin. Like so many other children who enter 'The System', I was brought up in a violent, controlled environment. My problem was twofold: first, the need to deprogram my hideous past; and second, the need to be guided into mainstream society.

In so many ways I was so lucky. I was able to use my dark past to propel me to a brighter future. But like so many other lost children, in the beginning I failed to realize that I could take the same techniques I had used to survive my abusive past and apply them to the real world. In general, foster children are far more mature, resilient and focused on their futures than mainstream children because foster children have had to adapt at an earlier age. (The key word is adapt, not give up!) Foster children, for the most part, do not sit around waiting for the silver spoon – they rely on themselves. I could have fallen through the cracks and then blamed my failed future on my past, had it not been for proper guidance and a little bit of love. However, the single biggest mistake I've ever made was dropping out of high school. But like most foster children, I simply had to adapt and overcome. After being exposed to a different world, in order to make it, I knew *I had to want it more.*

While at times foster care was frustrating, it did give me the chance to see how other families lived. Like a great deal of those in foster care, I didn't know how good I had it until I moved out on my own. Foster children *never* forget their foster parents. I am the same. Like others, I have many regrets. One of them is that Harold Turnbough passed away before I had my son, Stephen. Another regret was not being able to present Harold with my first book, which was nominated for a Pulitzer Prize. However, today Alice Turnbough lives hours from my home. The highest compliment I can pay to my foster mother is this: Alice is my son's grandmother. That's how much foster care means to me.

In January 1994 I had the privilege of presenting a training program in Ottumwa, Iowa, for a group of foster parents who had traveled from throughout the region during the middle of a snowstorm that closed down that part of the state. I presented a program on working with children who come from abusive backgrounds and how to better deal with them. During the course, I gave an illustration of how I used to escape my pain by dreaming of a hero. On the outside my hero did not fit into mainstream society, yet on the inside my hero knew who he was and wanted to do good for others in need. In my dreams I saw myself as my hero. I flew through the air, I wore a cape of red and I had an 'S' on my chest. I *was* Superman. When I stated this, the foster parents erupted with applause. As tears rolled down some of their faces, they held up a bumper sticker that read, **SUPERMAN HAD FOSTER PARENTS.**

To all of you who work with *The Lost Boys and Girls*, God bless **YOU!**

Alice Turnbough

Foster mother

Dave came to us when he was thirteen years old. I guess I'm still his foster mom. At first I think he was a combination of scared and defensive. He was a little wild and extremely frustrated, but for the most part did what he was told.

At the time Dave came to us we had all teenage girls. He drove them a little crazy, following them and tattling on them all the time. Plus, Dave was a neat freak, and the girls weren't. He didn't have much, but what he did have he treated like gold. And everything needed to be in the right place. A lot of foster children are like that.

Dave never acted his age, period. He always tried to act older, staying busy and finding work. He was thirteen going on twenty and was always thinking ahead.

I have been a foster parent for thirty years, fostering approximately seventy-five children. It all started when a gentleman introduced me to two children who needed help.

We never got into morals. These children were just like other children – except for the treatment they received from others. For the most part, foster children need someone to talk to. As a foster parent, I would like to see improved screening processes in order to better place children in the right homes, rather than dropping them off and hoping for the best.

One of the rewards of being a foster parent is seeing the kids turn out the way you had always hoped they would.

I always knew that David would make it. One of the most memorable moments was when David joined the Air Force. He had a devil of a time enlisting. I had to get used to him always flying away. Harold and I were very surprised and proud that he took it upon himself to carve out his future. Many foster children don't have the motivation.

Although I always knew that Dave would do all right, I never thought he'd go as far as he has. The day I found out that he had received the Ten Outstanding Young Americans (TOYA) award was one of my proudest days as a foster parent. Foster children hardly ever achieve that kind of status because they allow the prejudices of our society to hold them back.

Dave was the last foster child to leave my home. I'm proud to be Dave's mother.

Dennis Tapley
Teacher

I have been teaching for more than twenty years. When I was a freshman teacher at San Bruno, 'special education', as we now know it, had just received major support from the federal government. The special education program recognized that some children with minor learning disabilities had not been receiving an appropriate education. Children who had difficulty in learning basic skills were to be given special instruction to remedy those weak or unlearned skills.

There was talk about teachers being aware of some negative emotional concerns among these students. Some families produced schoolchildren who brought their family confusion with them to school. The confusion was evidenced in schoolyard social difficulties or classroom learning problems.

Teachers were as aware as we could be in working with the parents of these children. But this was two decades before Dave Pelzer published his book, *A Child Called 'It'* (and Jane Smiley her *1000 Acres*, and Susan Griffin her *Chorus of Stones*). We did not know – and were cautioned not to know – too much, for fear of being accused of interference.

From the 1970s point of view, foster care was not accepted. For a child to go to foster care meant there was something wrong – a complete failure in parenting. This was a failure that society did not want to face, even when given details of some drastic home situations. Because of this, foster care was twisted into something very negative. Individuals involved in foster care – both parents and children – were seen as second-class. The viewpoint even went so far as to believe that foster children had done something bad – unlike an orphan who was an innocent victim, for example. It has taken, and still takes, a long time to come to grips with what foster care, and the parents involved, can accomplish.

Today, child-rearing dynamics, awareness of the dysfunctional family, and direct evidence of the product of loveless or abusive parenting are matters of public record and psychological and educational research. Teachers and counselors are being trained to manage, test, evaluate and intervene.

I have been teaching special education now for twelve years. I have seen learning disabilities and delays in learning in specific areas. But family dysfunction and abuse cause emotional disturbances and learning delays that can be horrendous. I have seen students steal to gain attention, or carve the life out of shop and cooking equipment for the complex pleasure of artistic revenge. Such students are incapable of social self-restraint, and press their peers and teachers to react.

The disability of poor parenting is more likely to cause disruption in a child's intellectual and social growth than a physical disability. A child who has supportive parents and a reading disability may be delayed in reading, but in my mind has a better chance of general life success than an abused child without a disability.

David Pelzer is an exception. Although all I knew about him was that his home life had been incredibly bad, I was very aware that he was an extreme individual. In class he wasn't as 'shifty' as the others, but very restricted in movement. I knew him because he was a demanding student who pressed his questions and pressed for answers. No other high school kid would stay after class, actually sitting on my desk to gain attention. He made sure he was noticed. Students would often visit their teachers with the simple intent of being friendly, but David was more purposeful and demanded consideration through his attitude and posture.

David is – even now, after twenty years – a rare student in his forcefulness and his directness. He is to be congratulated on his success.

Carl Miguel

Chief probation officer

Dave Pelzer, a seriously abused child, was booked into the San Mateo County Juvenile Hall in 1974. As a result of Dave's background, his case was immediately reviewed by a team of juvenile hall staff that included a doctor, psychologist and detention supervisor. It was decided to house Dave on C-Wing – a living unit for children that were suffering from physical, psychological or sexual abuse. This was a special unit with an excellent staff-to-child ratio and a program designed to have a high degree of one-to-one, staff-to-child counseling.

Dave's case was reviewed by C-Wing staff, and he was assigned to me during his stay at juvenile hall. Dave thrived on the individual attention and the behavior modification program. He established a bond with all the staff and demonstrated phenomenal growth both socially and emotionally. Dave entered the juvenile justice system at a time when resources were available to focus on the individual.

Dave left San Mateo Juvenile Hall in a much healthier state than when he arrived. In 1989, fifteen years later, Dave and I met again in the most unusual manner. I was the superintendent of the Yuba/Sutter Juvenile Hall, and Dave was stationed at Beale Air Force Base in Yuba County. Dave came to the juvenile hall to volunteer his services to the youths detained there. Dave worked as a very effective volunteer and was eventually hired as a part-time staff person until being transferred by the Air Force.

It is with great pleasure and deep personal and emotional satisfaction that I have had the opportunity to see Dave rise above his excruciating childhood. He is a living example and a model to others who have suffered under similar circumstances. As Dave walked out of juvenile hall in 1974, as a child, I bade him good luck. And as he walked back into juvenile hall in 1989, as a counselor, I felt a tear in my eye and simply said, 'Bravo.'

Michael Marsh

Mentor

One day in 1976, in the quiet, blue-collar Californian neighborhood of Menlo Park, I walked out of my garage and was disheartened to view the driveway scene next door. For almost a year now, houses in the neighborhood that came on the market were being snapped up by opportunistic Realtors and turned into rental properties. The house next door was such a house, and its tenants were scruffy-looking people who derived a significant amount of their income from the state of California by being foster parents.

What I was viewing on this day was their latest 'acquisition' – a tall string bean of a kid in a filthy, sleeveless, ribbed T-shirt. He was working on a miniscooter engine, had a sort of leering grin – as a natural part of his facial features – and had intense eyes that darted about from behind a thick pair of glasses.

Initially I resented him, feeling that my hard work and that of my wife toward purchasing our first home in a decent neighborhood was being defeated by real estate speculators who were making a buck off importing families into *my* neighborhood. But David Pelzer wasn't shy – in fact, he was persistent in his friendliness. As I got to know David a little, I began to see he was bright and had a keen sense of humor, in spite of the fact that he had been kicked around in a dismal childhood and what was looking to be an even drearier adolescence.

At first it was somewhat like housebreaking a pet. As we got more familiar, he was at our house more and more, asking about my Vietnam experiences, pursuing my aviation library and wanting to talk about almost anything. My wife and I began to require things from him – small, essential things like courtesy and consideration. He was to knock before entering the house. Some of his conversational manners were horrid, and his telephone and table manners were nonexistent.

The day came when David left the neighborhood. His 'foster parents' simply weren't acceptable to him, and I still don't blame him one iota for having the courage to pull up stakes and seek something better. But he stayed in touch and started showing up on weekends, wanting to be with friends he had made in the neighborhood and wanting to stay at our house. We finally told him that he would be welcome under most circumstances on most weekends but that he must call in advance, ask and make 'reservations'. This he began to do, and some time passed before there was trouble. Trouble in a nearby park. Trouble with a pellet pistol. Trouble with neighbors who felt David was a bad influence on their children. These things were discussed, and I made it very clear to David that any more trouble, and it was bye-bye to the neighborhood that he loved to come and visit.

When pressed about his past or his school, he was always purposefully vague, so we never really knew what was going on in his life. A couple of years went by with intermittent trouble and calls from the Menlo Park police. David was never an angry, rebellious individual – he was just thick-headed and had a penchant for finding trouble or letting it find him. Maybe it was from some sort of misguided sense of adventure; I don't know. But there came the day when I asked him how his school was doing, and he said, 'Oh, I quit.' I hit the ceiling and chewed his butt out for an hour. When I asked him what he was going to do, he mentioned he was going to sell cars. I went ballistic again. A skinny, wimpy, pimply-faced kid was selling cars in the Bay Area? Get real, kid. A week or so later he called to say he had the job and was looking forward to being 'Salesman of the Month', which bore the distinctive honor of driving a Corvette for a thirty-day period. Right, Dave . . . something to shoot for, all right.

A couple of months later I received a telephone call from David, who said he wanted to visit. I said, 'No, I have to go up to San Francisco International to pick up my paycheck.' 'Great,' he says, 'I'll drive you up there. I want to show you something.' What he wanted to show me was, of course, a black Corvette that he was the owner/operator of for the next month. A few months later David arrives in an El Camino – his company car – with a motorcycle strapped to the back. Dave mentioned that he might try a new job. I asked what he was planning, and he replied, 'Well, I'm going to

Hollywood to become a stuntman.' There was what a writer would describe as a pregnant pause, as the impact of his words crashed into my unbelieving psyche. I chastised him, focusing on his lack of athletics and experience, his clumsiness and, of course, the absence of other contacts in L.A. I then ripped into him for another half hour with heavy emphasis on the importance of a high school diploma.

Months later, although wounded, David was considering another plan. He wanted to go into the military. So we went to the recruiters and began watching videos of paratroopers and rangers. They, of course, looked good. To the United States Army, however, David didn't. No diploma? Sorry. Perhaps it took that letdown for the importance of a high school diploma to sink into David's concrete-thick head. He called me a few weeks after and said, 'I'm in! The Air Force will take me and get me a G.E.D.' He had pursued it *on his own* and was finally going out into the world. I was gratified, hopeful and proud of him for getting down to personal pragmatics, so to speak.

Shortly after David joined the Air Force, we moved to Denver, Colorado. David had stayed in touch and ended up training at Lowry Air Force Base in Denver. He was there to visit the first week we were in our new home. He subsequently went to Florida and was unhappy with his assignment – which was cooking. I counseled patience, and he ultimately made the best of an unhappy assignment by finessing his way into cooking for the Ranger School candidates stationed in the jungle/swamp phase of the Army Ranger program in Florida. *Then* he finagled a slot in the Army Parachute School, known as the Airborne Course, and on receiving his silver jump wings, became a member of an extraordinarily proud fraternity.

Then once again David persisted and ultimately found a niche: boom operator on an aerial tanker! He landed an assignment 'booming' on the supersecret Mach 3 spy plane – the SR-71 Black-bird. He was hooked for years. During this period he became involved in the community around him, on and off base. His awareness of what he had and who he was brought to the surface a drive within him to diminish other people's hurts, to wade in and solve problems, and to contribute some positive payback.

In January 1993 I sat in the Center for the Performing Arts in Tulsa, Oklahoma, as David received an honor. He was out of the Air

Force and had not just moved on, but moved forward. On this evening, which was actually the culmination of a week's festivities, David was being honored as one of the Ten Outstanding Young Americans in the United States by the National Junior Chamber of Commerce organization. The list of previous recipients reads like a *Who's Who* of American industry, politics and society. And there he was, David, the wannabe stuntman, who had pulled off the Big One, and had done it with determination, guts and resolve, and maybe a little luck. I'm proud of who you were, David – that hurt person who refused to 'die'. And I'm more proud of who you've become – a caring, giving, fixing person, the guy with the same sense of humor and that deft, sensitive touch. Good on you, David. I love you.

To the lady who gave her all to make me the man I am today, my lovely bride, my best friend, Mrs Marsha Pelzer. You make me whole and will forever be my Princess.

To my son, Stephen, I can never tell you how precious you are and how much you have changed my life for the better. Everything I do, I do for you.

Contents

ACKNOWLEDGMENTS

Since this has been my most arduous project, it is only prudent I pay respect to those who made this book possible:

With all respect, I bid adieu to my former publisher. I wish to convey my deepest thanks to Irene Xanthos, Lori Golden, Ronnie O'Brien, Jane Barone, Joy Fauver, Doreen Hess, and the small band of others who truly believed in my works before their commercial success.

Also, to Peter, Terri, Kim, and Bob: against all odds, thank you for allowing me to become a *New York Times* best-selling author.

To my dear friend Youngsuk Chi, 'The Book Expert', for his excitability, mentoring, and for believing, just as I do, in maintaining the uncompromising standard of excellence. With dignity and honor!

A special thankyou to the owners and staff of Sonoma County's finest coffee establishment, Coffee Bazaar, for again allowing me and Marsha to plug in, take over, and wreak havoc at all hours, while maintaining the maximum level of mocha-ness that is still keeping us up at nights.

To Cathy Lewis and Nancy Graves of Carmel's Carriage House Inn – my home away from home – taking me in from the cold and putting me up in 'my room'.

A special thankyou to the institution formerly known as the Hogs Breath Inn of Carmel, where Law, Order, and Ice Cream still prevail. My gratitude to Tim, Joyce, Lana, and the entire crew for granting me space so to slave away at all hours among the beauty of your serene town.

To the musician Pat Metheny, who unknowingly provided haunting yet soul-stirring theme music to all three tomes. With *A Child Called 'It'* it was 'Farmer's Trust', for *The Lost Boy*, 'If I Could', and now with *A Man Named Dave*, the incredibly moving music of 'The

Bat, Part II'. Spending endless hours listening to these tracks made me draw from the recesses of my soul.

To Marsha, editor extraordinaire, of Donohoe Publishing Projects for her absolute devotion to every word of every page. This is only one of the many reasons why I love you. For Marsha, it was a matter of . . . 'The Bat, Part II'.

To the staff of Dutton Plume for their overwhelming professionalism and sincere kindness, as well as believing that I was indeed worthy of being a hardcover author. To Brian Tart, editor-in-chief, for his trust, genuine sincerity, and meticulous attention to detail as well as for his patience when it counted the most. I also wish to thank Mary Ellen O'Boyle for an inspiring and majestic cover to the book. To everyone at Dutton Plume, thank you for making me a member of your family.

Finally, to the millions of readers who took *A Child Called 'It'* and *The Lost Boy* into their hearts: I am forever grateful. You may not realize, but your actions have made the world a better place.

AUTHOR'S NOTE

Some of the names in this book have been changed in order to protect the dignity and privacy of others.

As with the first two installments of the trilogy, this third part depicts the language and wisdom that was solely developed from my viewpoint as well as that particular time period.

This book is not under any circumstances meant to be used as a reprisal or an opportunity to be vindictive, but rather to serve a purpose of what transpires in my life and the valuable lessons learned.

chapter 1

THE END

March 4, 1973, Daly City, California – I'm scared. My feet are cold and my stomach cries for food. From the darkness of the garage I strain my ears to pick up the slightest sound of Mother's bed creaking as she rolls over in the bedroom upstairs. I can also tell by the range of Mother's hacking cough if she's still asleep or about to get up. I pray Mother doesn't cough herself awake. I pray I still have more time. Just a few more minutes before another day in hell begins. I close my eyes as tightly as I can and mumble a quick prayer, even though I know God hates me.

Because I am not worthy enough to be a member of 'The Family', I lie on top of an old, worn-out army cot without a blanket. I curl up into a tight ball to keep as warm as possible. I use the top of my shirt as a tent to cover my head, imagining my exhaled air will somehow keep my face and ears warm. I bury my hands either between my legs or into my armpits. Whenever I feel brave enough, and only after I'm certain that Mother has passed out, I steal a rag from the top of a dirty pile and wrap it tightly around my feet. I'll do anything to stay warm.

To stay warm is to stay alive.

I'm mentally and physically exhausted. It's been months since I've been able to escape through my dreams. As hard as I try, I cannot go back to sleep. I'm too cold. I cannot stop my knees from shaking. I cautiously rub my feet together because I somehow feel if I make any quick movements, 'The Mother' will hear me. I am not allowed to do anything without The Mother's direct authority. Even though I know she has returned to sleep in the bottom bunk bed of my brother's bedroom, I sense that she still has control over me.

The Mother always has.

My mind begins to spin as I fight to remember my past. I know that to survive somehow my answers are in my past. Besides food, heat, and staying alive, learning why Mother treats me the way she does dominates my life.

My first memories of Mother were caution and fear. As a four-year-old child, I knew by the sound of Mother's voice what type of day was in store for me. Whenever Mother was patient and kind, she was my 'Mommy'. But whenever Mother became cross and snapped at everything, 'Mommy' transformed into 'The Mother' – a cold, evil person capable of unexpected violent attacks. I soon became so scared of setting The Mother off, I didn't even go to the bathroom without first asking permission.

As a small child, I also realized that the more she drank, the more my mommy slipped away, and the more The Mother's personality took over. One Sunday afternoon before I was five years old, during one of The Mother's drunken attacks, she accidentally pulled my arm out of its socket. The moment it happened, Mother's eyes became as big as silver dollars. Mother knew she had crossed the line. She knew she was out of control. This went far beyond her usual treatment of face slapping, body punching, or being thrown down the stairs.

But even back then Mother developed a plan to cover her tracks. The next morning, after driving me to the hospital, she cried to the doctor that I had fallen out of my bunk bed during the night. Mother went on to say how she had desperately tried to catch me as I fell, and how she could never forgive herself for reacting so slowly. The doctor didn't even bat an eye. Back at home, Father, a fireman with medical training, didn't question Mother's strange tale.

Afterward, as Mother cuddled me to her chest, I knew never, ever to expose the secret. Even then I somehow thought that things would return to the good times I had with Mommy. I truly believed that she would somehow wake up from her drunken slumber and banish The Mother forever. As a four-year-old child, rocking in Mother's arms, I thought the worst was over and that Mother would change.

The only thing that had changed was the intensity of Mother's rage and the privacy of my secret relationship with her. By the time I was eight, my name was no longer allowed to be spoken. She had replaced 'David' with 'The Boy'. Soon The Boy seemed too personal, so she decided to call me 'It'. Because I was no longer a member of 'The Family', I was banished to live and sleep in the garage. When not sitting on top of my hands at the bottom of the staircase, my function was to perform slave-like chores. If I did not meet one of Mother's time requirements for my task, not only was I beaten, but I was not allowed to receive any food. More than once Mother refused to feed me for over a week. Of all of Mother's 'games' of control, she enjoyed using food as her ultimate weapon.

The more bizarre things The Mother did to me, the more she seemed to know she could get away with any of her games. When she held my arm over a gas stove, she told horrified teachers that I had played with a match and burned myself. And when Mother stabbed me in the chest, she told my frightened brothers that I had attacked her.

For years I did all that I could do to think ahead, to somehow outwit her. Before Mother hit me, I would tighten up parts of my body. If Mother didn't feed me, I would steal scraps of food anywhere I could. When she filled my mouth with pink dishwashing soap, I'd hold the liquid in my mouth until I could spit it in the garage garbage can when she wasn't looking. Defeating The Mother in any way meant the world to me. Small victories kept me alive.

My only form of escape had been my dreams. As I sat at the bottom of the staircase with my head tilted backward, I saw myself flying through the air like my hero, Superman. Like Superman, I believed I had two identities. My Clark Kent personality was the child called 'It' – an outcast who ate out of garbage cans, was ridiculed, and did not fit in. At times as I lay sprawled out on the kitchen floor unable to crawl away, I *knew* I was Superman. I knew I had an inner strength, a secret identity that no one else realized. I came to believe if Mother shot me, the bullets would bounce off my chest. No matter what 'game' Mother invented, no matter how badly she attacked me, I was going to win; I was going to live. At times when I couldn't block out the pain or the loneliness, all I had to do was close my eyes and fly away.

Just weeks after my twelfth birthday, Mother and Father separated. Superman disappeared. All my inner strength shriveled up. That day I knew Mother was going to kill me – if not that Saturday, then someday soon. With Father out of the way, nothing could stop The Mother. Even though for years Father had at times watched in dismay while he sipped his evening drink when Mother had me swallow teaspoons of ammonia or shrug his shoulders while she'd beat me senseless, I had always felt safer whenever he was in the house. But after Mother dropped off Father's meager belongings and drove away, I clasped my hands together as tightly as I could and whispered, '. . . and may He deliver me from evil. Amen.'

That was almost two months ago, and God never answered my prayers. Now, as I continue to shiver in the darkness of the garage, I know the end is near. I cry for not having the courage or the strength to fight back. I'm too tired. The eight years of constant torture have sucked my life force out of me. I clasp my hands together and pray that when The Mother kills me, she will have the mercy to kill me quickly.

I begin to feel light-headed. The harder I pray, the more I feel myself drift off to sleep. My knees stop quivering. My fingers loosen from digging into my bony knuckles. Before I pass out, I say to myself, *God . . . if You can hear me, can You somehow take me away? Please take me. Take me today.*

My upper body snaps upright. I can hear the floorboards strain upstairs from Mother's weight. Her gagging cough follows a moment later. I can almost visualize her bent over as she nearly coughs up her lungs from the years of heavy smoking and her destructive lifestyle. *God, how I hate her cough.*

The darkness of my sleep quickly fades away. A chill fills my body. I so badly want to remain asleep, forever. The more I wake from my slumber, the more I curse God for not taking me in my sleep. He never answers my prayers. I so badly wish I were dead. I don't have the energy to live another day in 'The House'. I can't imagine another day with The Mother and her sinister games. I break down and cry. A waterfall of tears runs down my face. I used to be so strong. I just can't take it anymore.

Mother's stumbling brings me back to my dismal reality. I wipe my runny nose and my tears away. I must never, *ever* expose a sign of weakness. I take a deep breath and gaze upward. I lock my hands together before retreating inside my shell that will protect me for another day. *Why?* I sigh. *If You are God, what is Your reason? I just . . . I so badly want to know, why? Why am I still alive?*

Mother staggers out of her bedroom. *Move!* my brain screams. *Move it!* I only have a few seconds before . . . I was supposed to be up an hour ago to begin my chores.

I stand up and fumble through the darkness, trying to find the light switch to the garage. I trip over one of the legs to the army cot. By reflex, I reach out to the floor to soften the impact, but I'm too slow. A moment later the side of my face smashes against the cold cement. Bright silver dots fill my view. I smack the palms of my hands on the floor. I so badly want to pass out. I never want to regain consciousness ever again.

I push myself up off the cement as I hear Mother's footsteps leading to the bathroom. After flicking on the light switch, I snatch the broom before racing up the staircase. If I can finish sweeping the stairs before Mother catches me, she will never know I'm behind. *I can win.* I smile as I tell myself, *Come on, man, go! Move it!* I seem so out of breath. My mind races at supersonic speed, but my body responds in slow motion. My feet feel like blocks of cement. The tips of my fingers are so cold. I don't understand why I'm so slow. I used to be lightning fast.

Without thinking, I reach my left hand out to the wooden rail that I use to pull myself up the stairs. *I'm going to win,* I say to myself, *I'm actually going to make it!* I can hear the gurgling sound of the toilet flushing from above. I quicken my pace. I extend my arm toward the rail. I smile inside. *I'm going to beat her.* A split second later my heart skips a beat as my hand misses the rail and grabs air. My body begins to wobble. *The rail! Grab the stupid rail!* As hard as I fight to concentrate, my fingers refuse to obey.

My world turns black.

A blinding glare pierces my eyes. My head seems as if it is stuck in a fog. I can make out a figure standing above me in front of a bright white light. '. . . aht ime is it?'

I try to shake my head clear. For a moment I thought I was staring at an angel sent to take me to heaven.

But Mother's sickening cough soon erases my fantasy. '*I* said, "What time is it?" ' The sound of her voice nearly makes me pee my pants. Mother uses a soft, evil tone so as not to wake up her precious babies. 'Let's see how fast . . . you can move that sorry little behind of yours up here . . . now!' Mother demands with a snap of her fingers. My body shudders as I place the broom against the base of the stairs.

'Oh, no!' Mother beams. 'Bring your friend with you.' I'm not sure what she means. I spin around, then look back up at Mother. 'The broom, you moron. Bring it with you.'

With every step I take, my mind begins to plot a defense for whatever game Mother has in store for the crime of not completing my chores on time. I warn myself to stay focused. I know she plans on using the broom as a weapon, against either my chest or face. Sometimes when we're alone, Mother likes to smash the end of the broom directly behind my knees. If she has me follow her into the kitchen, I'm dead. I won't be able to walk to school, let alone run. But if Mother keeps me on the stairs, I know she'll only hit me in my upper body.

Upon reaching the top of the stairs, I automatically assume 'the position of address': my body stands perfectly straight, with my head bent down and my hands glued to my sides. I am not allowed to move a muscle, blink, look at her or even breathe without Mother's direct permission.

'Tell me, tell me *I'm stupid*,' Mother whispers as she leans over. I cringe as I imagine her taking a bite from my ear. It's part of the game. She's testing me to see if I'll flinch. I dare not look up or back away. My heels hang over the edge of the stair. I pray Mother doesn't push me . . . today.

'Go ahead, tell me. Please,' Mother begs. The tone of her voice changes. Mother's voice seems calm, nonthreatening. My mind spins. I don't understand. Did Mother just give me permission to speak? I have no idea what she expects of me. Either way, I'm trapped. I focus my energy on the front of my shoes. The more I stare, the more my body begins to sway.

Without warning Mother thrusts a finger under my chin, lifting my face to hers. Her rancid breath makes my stomach coil. I fight not to pass out from her stench. Even though she does not allow me to wear my glasses at home, I glance at Mother's puffy, reddened face. Her once gleaming hair is now oily and matted against the sides of her face. 'Just how stupid do you think I am? Tell me, exactly: How stupid am I?'

I sheepishly look up and reply, 'Ma'am?'

A raging fire stings the side of my face. 'Just who in the hell gave you permission to speak, let alone look!' Mother hisses.

I snap my head back down as I quickly bury the pain inside. *My God*, I say to myself, *I didn't see it coming. What's happening to me?*

I'm always able to see her arm swing back before she strikes me. I cannot figure out why I am so slow. *Dammit, David, stay focused! Think!*

'When is *It* going to begin *Its* chores?' Mother bellows. 'What is it with you? I bet you think I'm stupid! You think you can get away with whatever you damn well please! Don't you?' Mother shakes her head. 'I'm not the one hurting you. You are. You choose your actions. You know who – what – you are and what your purpose is in this household.

'If *It* wants to be fed, then it's simple: *It* does exactly as *It's* told. If It doesn't want to be punished, then It stays out of trouble. It knows the rules. I don't treat you any different from anybody else. It simply refuses to obey.' Mother stops to take a deep breath. Her chest begins to wheeze. It's time for her fix. I know what's coming next. I wish she'd go ahead and hit me. 'And what about me?' Her voice rises. 'I should be asleep, but no, I have to be here with It. You pathetic piece of filth! You little bastard! You know your function. You're not a *person*, but . . . a *thing* to do with as *I* please. Do you understand? Am I making myself clear, or perhaps It needs another lesson?' Mother thunders.

Mother's words echo inside my soul. For years I've heard the same thing over and over again. For years I've been her human robot to do with as she pleases, like some toy that she can turn on and off whenever she wishes.

I break down inside. My body begins to shake. I can't take it anymore. *Go ahead*, I say to myself. *Do it! Just kill me! Come on!* Suddenly, my vision sharpens. My insides stop shaking. Rage slowly begins to fill me. I no longer feel ice cold. I shift my head from side to side as my eyes creep up Mother's robed body. The fingers of my right hand tighten around the wooden broom handle. As I slowly let out a deep breath, my eyes stare directly into Mother's. '*Leave me alone . . . you bitch!*' I hiss.

Mother becomes paralyzed. I focus every fiber of my being on piercing through her silver-framed glasses and reddened eyes. I will myself to somehow transfer every moment I had to carry for the last eight years of pain and loneliness into Mother.

Mother's face turns ash white. She knows. Mother knows exactly what I'm feeling. *It's working*, I tell myself. Mother tries to break away from my stare. She moves her head slightly to the left. I match

Mother's movement. She can't escape. Mother looks down and away. I tilt my head up and sharpen my stare. I smile. From the bottom of my soul I feel so warm. Now *I'm* the one in control.

From the back of my mind I hear a chuckle. For a moment I think it's me laughing at Mother. I lower my eyes and see Mother's crocodile smile. Her putrid breath breaks my concentration. The more Mother smiles, the more my body becomes tense. She tilts her head toward the light. *Now,* I tell myself, *now I can see it coming. Go ahead, give it to me! Come on, do it! Show me what you got!* I see the blur a split second before I feel her hand collide against my face. A moment later, warm blood seeps from my nose. I let it drip on the black-matted stairs. I refuse to give Mother the pleasure of watching me cry or reacting in any way whatsoever. I defy her by remaining numb inside and out.

'Showing a little guts, are you? Well, you're a few years too late!' Mother sneers. 'You don't have what it takes. You never have and you never will. You're such a pathetic little worm. I can kill you anytime I please. Just like *that*,' Mother says with a snap of her fingers. 'You are only alive because it pleases me. You are nothing more than . . .'

I block out Mother's words as a cold fear creeps back inside my soul. I bow my head, resuming the position of address. Dark red blood spatters the toes of my shoes. *For a fleeting moment I felt so alive.*

She's in control now.

The more that Mother babbles, the more I nod my head, acknowledging Mother is indeed almighty and God-like for allowing me to live another day in her household. 'You don't know how lucky you are. When I was your age, you wouldn't believe what *I* was put through . . .'

I let out a deep sigh and close my eyes in a vain attempt to block out the sound of her voice. How I wish she would pass out and drop dead. In my mind I fantasize Mother sprawled on the hallway floor. I would give anything to be there as she quivered helplessly on her back before taking her last breath.

Mother's voice changes in pitch. Suddenly my throat feels as if it is on fire as Mother tightens her grip around my neck. My eyes want to pop out of my head. I did not focus on Mother's attack before it came. By reflex I wrap my hands around Mother's fingers. As much as I try, I cannot pry her hands off. The more I struggle, the more Mother tightens her death grip. I try to scream, but only a gurgling sound leaks out. My head slumps forward. As my eyes roll backward, I concentrate on Mother's face. *Do it!* I shout to myself. *Come on, do it! You're so bad, you're so tough, come on! Show me, show me what you got! Kill me, you bitch!*

Mother's cheeks twitch from her intense hatred. Her nostrils flare from her rapid breathing. I want Mother to kill me. I begin to feel myself drift away. My hearing seems as if I am in the middle of a long tunnel. My arms fall to my sides. For the first time in years, my body relaxes. I'm no longer cold inside. I'm no longer frightened. I'm ready to . . .

A hard slap makes my head shake from side to side. 'Oh no, wake up! Wake up, you miserable piece of trash! I'm not through with you yet! I know exactly what you want!' Mother hisses. 'So, you think you're so smart? How about . . . instead of sending you to your Uncle Dan's this weekend, maybe I should have the boys go instead, so you and I can spend some *private time* together? Bet you didn't think of that one, did you?'

I know by the sound of her voice that I am supposed to respond, but I can't.

'Oh, what's the matter? Does the little insect have a sore throat? Oh well, that's just too bad!' Mother smiles. I can see her lips moving, but I can barely make out what she's saying. After another quick squeeze, Mother lets go of her hold. Without permission, I rub my neck, gasping for air. Somehow I know she's not done with me – not yet. A second later I nearly lose my balance as Mother snatches the broom from beside me. I automatically tighten my upper body. 'This,' she says, 'this is for cheating on your chores. I've told you a hundred times that you are to get that miserable butt of yours up and working before I get up. *Do I make myself perfectly clear?*'

I hesitate, not knowing how or if I should respond.

'I said, *is that clear?*'

'Yes . . . ah, yes, ma'am,' I stutter in a hoarse voice.

'Tell me, what is your name?' Mother asks as she tilts her head upward in a show of supremacy.

' "It," ' I answer in a sheepish tone.

'And what is "*Its*" function?'

'Ta . . . ta . . . ta do . . . do as you command and stay outta . . . outta trouble.'

'And when I say, "Jump"?'

'I ask, "How high?" ' I reply without thought.

'Not bad. Not bad at all!' Mother leers. 'But I do think It requires another lesson. Perhaps this will teach you . . . teach It . . .'

I can hear a swishing sound. I brace my arms for the impact. My upper body is rock solid, but I have no way of telling which direction the sound is coming from. A jolting thud strikes the side of my neck. My knees buckle as I turn inside the doorway and lean against Mother's body. Without thinking I reach out to Mother. Her eyes shine with pleasure. She slaps my hands away. As my feet slip, my head jerks backward. I can feel my throat collapse the same way it did when Mother had me swallow teaspoons full of ammonia. I fight to swallow a breath of air, but my brain is too slow to respond. My eyes lock on to Mother's. 'So, do you still think you can fly?'

I glance down and see Mother's hand in motion. A moment later I can feel myself floating, my arms flung above my face. Suddenly, a rush of air fills my chest as the back of my head smashes against the staircase. I reach out, but I can't stop my body from bouncing backward down the stairs. At the bottom of the staircase, my chest heaves; I want to find a bucket and throw up. At the door above me, Mother bends over with laughter. 'Look at you! You're a hoot!'

Her face becomes taut. In an ice-cold voice Mother says, 'You're not even worth the effort.' With a jerk of her hand she flings the broom at me, then slams the door shut. My only form of protection is to close my eyes. I don't even bother to turn away or cover my face. I can hear the broom topple down the stairs before missing me completely.

Alone in the garage I let go and cry like a baby. I don't care if Mother, or anyone else in the world, can hear me. I have no dignity, no self-worth. Rage slowly builds inside my soul. I clench my hands together and begin taking my frustration out on the floor. *Why, why, why? What in the hell did I ever do to you to make you hate me so much?*

With every blow I can feel my strength drain away. The whitish-yellow garage light begins to fade as I lose consciousness. Without thinking of Mother catching me, I lie on my side, pull my shirt over my face, bury my hands between my legs, and close my eyes. Before I pass out, I clasp my hands together and mutter, 'Take me.'

'Wake up! Wake up, I tell you!' My eyes flicker open. I'm trapped in a mental haze as I stand in front of Mother in the kitchen. I have no idea how I got here. And somehow I know it's almost time for me to run to school. My mind struggles to recall why I keep losing track of time.

'I said, wake up!' Mother barks. She leans over and slaps my face. I'm fascinated that I can no longer feel the pain. 'What in the hell is wrong with you?' she asks with some concern.

Forgetting who I am, I rub my face and reply, 'I dunno.' Immediately I know I've just committed a double crime of *moving* and *speaking* without Mother's permission. Before I can stop myself, I commit *another* offense by looking right at her and shaking my head. 'I don't understand . . . what's happening to me?'

'You're fine,' Mother states. I lean forward to catch what she said. I'm not sure, but I think Mother just spoke to me in a soft tone. 'Listen. Listen up. Tell 'em . . . uhm, tell them that you were . . .' I strain to pay attention to Mother's instructions, but her words seem mumbled and confusing. Mother snaps her fingers, indicating a breakthrough for her latest cover story. 'If those nosy teachers ask, you tell them that you were wrestling and you got out of control . . . so your brothers had to put you in your place. Do you understand?'

I'm trying to digest Mother's new set of instructions.

'*Do you understand?*' Mother probes, fighting to keep her anger under control.

'Ah, yes,' I chuckle. I cannot believe how easily Mother can come up with her off-the-wall lies every single day of school. I'm also amazed that I no longer care about masking my emotions in front of her: 'Tell 'em I was wrong. I was bad.'

'And . . . ?' Mother whines, trying to draw me out further.

'Tell them . . . I was . . . I was playing, I mean wrestling! I was wrestling and . . . I got out of control. Yes, I understand,' I stammer.

Mother tilts her head to one side as she inspects her latest damage. She holds her gaze for a few moments before losing her balance, stumbling toward me. In a jerking motion I flinch backward. 'Shh . . . no, it's okay. Relax,' Mother calmly says with an

269

outstretched hand as she keeps her distance, acting as if I were a stray dog. 'No one's going to hurt you. Shh . . .' Mother circles around me before backing into her kitchen chair. Bending her head down, she stares into space.

My head begins to slump forward when Mother's hacking cough makes me snap upright. 'It wasn't always like this, you know,' she whimpers in a scratchy voice. 'If you knew . . . if you only understood. I wish I could somehow make you, make *them* understand . . .' Mother stops in mid-sentence to collect herself. I can feel her eyes scan my body. 'Things just got outta control, that's all. I never meant to . . . to live like this. No one does. I tried, God knows I did – to be the good wife, the perfect mother. I did everything: den mother, this PTA, that hosting the perfect parties. I really did try.

'You, you're the only one who knows, who really knows. You're the only one I can really talk to,' Mother whispers. 'I can't trust *them*. But you, you're the perfect outlet, the perfect audience, anytime it damn well pleases *me*. You don't talk, so no one will hear your pain. You don't have any friends, and you never go outside, so you know what it's like to be all alone inside. Hell, besides school, no one knows you. It's as if you were never . . .

'No. You'll never tell anyone . . . never!' Mother brags as she nods her head up and down to reinforce her warning.

Without stealing a glance, I can hear Mother sniffle as she struggles not to let down her guard. I realize she's only using me to talk to herself. She always has. When I was younger, Mother would drag me out of bed in the middle of the night, have me stand in front of her as she poured herself glass after glass and raved on for hours. But now as I stand in front of her, I'm too numb to understand her ramblings. *What in the hell does she want?* Can she be totally smashed so early in the morning, or is she still under the effects from last night's stupor? Maybe she's testing my reaction? I hate not knowing what Mother expects of me.

'You,' she continues, 'oh, you were so cute! At parties everyone loved *you*! Everyone wanted to take you home. Always polite, always with manners. Wouldn't speak unless spoken to. Oh, I remember whenever you couldn't sleep, you'd crawl up into my lap and sing me Christmas songs, even in the middle of July. Whenever I felt bad I could always count on you to "croon a tune".' Mother smiles as she remembers the past. She can no longer control the tears that stream down her cheeks. I've never seen her like this before. 'You had the sweetest voice, David. Why is it you don't sing for me anymore? How come?' Mother stares at me as if I were a ghost.

'I don't . . . I dunno.' My grogginess vanishes. I realize this is not one of Mother's sinister games. I know, deep inside Mother, that something is different. She's reaching out. Mother's never been this emotional about her past. I wish I had a clear head to analyze what she's trying to tell me. I know it's not the booze talking, but my real mother, the one who's been trapped inside her for so many years. 'Mommy?'

Mother's head jerks up as she covers her mouth. '*Mommy?* Oh Lord, David, do you know how long it's been since I've been someone's *mommy*? My God!' She closes her eyes to hide her pain. 'You were so fragile, so timid. You don't remember, but you were always the slow one. It took you forever to tie your shoes. I thought I'd go crazy trying to teach you that damn square knot for your Cub Scouts badge. But you never gave up. I'd find you in a corner of the room trying to tie knots. No, that's one thing about you, you never gave up. Hey,' Mother asks with a wide smile, 'do you remember that summer when you were seven or eight years old, and you and I spent forever trying to catch that fish at Memorial Park?'

With perfect clarity I recall how Mommy and I sat at the far edge of a giant fallen log that hung over a small stream. I couldn't believe she had chosen me – over my younger brother Stan, who constantly fought for Mother's attention. As Stan threw a temper tantrum on the beach below us, I thought Mother would realize her mistake. But Mommy had paid no attention to Stan's commotion; she simply tightened her grip on my belt, in case I slipped, and whispered encouragement into my ear. After a few minutes of fishing, I deliberately kept the pink salmon egg bait just above the water. I never wanted my adventure with my mommy to end. Now, as I shake my head clear of the memory, my voice becomes choked up. 'I, ah, I prayed we'd never catch that fish,' I confessed to her.

'Why's that?'

'So . . . we could spend more time together . . . as mother and son.'

'Oh, your brother Stan was red with jealousy, stomping up and down beside the creek, throwing rocks into the water, trying to scare off that fish of yours. My God.' Mother tosses her hair back, revealing a rare smile.

I'm not sure if she failed to hear or understand the true meaning of what I said.

'David?' Mother pleads. 'You do remember, don't you?'

'Yes,' I cry, shaking my head, 'I do. I remember everything. Like the first day of school when the teacher had us color a picture of what we did that summer. I drew you and me sitting on that old tree with a happy-face sun shining above us. Remember, I gave it to you that day after school?'

Mother turns away from me. She clutches her coffee mug, then puts a finger to her lips. The excitement from her face drains away. 'No!' Mother states in a strict tone, as if our fishing adventure were a hoax.

'Oh, sure you do—'

'I said no, goddammit!' Mother interrupts. She clamps her eyes shut and covers her ears. 'No, no, no! I don't remember. You can't make me! No one can force me to remember the past if I don't want to. Not you or anybody else. No one tells *me* what to do! You got that, mister?'

'Yes, ma'am,' I automatically respond.

Mother's face turns beet red as the muscles in her neck tighten. Her upper body begins to shake. I'm not sure, but I think Mother is having a violent seizure. I want to yell out, but I'm too scared. I stand in front of Mother like a helpless fool. I don't know what to do.

After a few seconds the redness from her face disappears. She lets out a deep sigh. 'I just don't know anymore . . . if I'm coming or going. I don't know . . . I didn't mean for things to happen this way; no one did. You can't blame me, I did my best . . .'

The sweetness in her voice fades. I want so badly to run and hug *Mommy* before she completely slips away, but, like always, I know in a few hours *Mother* won't remember a single word of our conversation. I back away from the kitchen table and resume the position of address.

'Oh, Jesus!' Mother snaps. 'Now look what you've done! I've got to drive my boys to school! Forget the dishes; you can finish them after school. And listen up: I don't want to hear a peep from any of those nosy teachers today, so you keep that carcass of yours the hell out of trouble! You got me, mister?' Mother raises her voice to her usual evil tone.

'Yes, ma'am,' I mutter.

'Then get the hell out of my house! Run!' Mother bellows.

'What about lunch . . . ?' I ask.

'Too bad. You took my time, then I take your lousy sandwich. You'll just have to go diggin' for food today. Now get the hell out of here! Don't make me get the broom! Now run!'

In a flash I race through Mother's house. I can hear her evil laugh as I slam the front door shut before sprinting off to school.

Minutes later, after running to school at top speed, I stagger into the nurse's office with my hands slapping on my knees. With every breath I take in, the muscles around my throat tighten. An enormous pressure from behind my eyes begins to build. I slap my knees as if that will somehow make air rush into my lungs. The school nurse spins around from behind her desk. My mind fumbles to yell, but I cannot form the words. But I try again. '*C-a-n-'t b-r-e-a-t-h-e!*' I finally sputter, pointing at my neck.

The nurse leaps up with lightning speed, grabs a brown bag, turns it upside down, spilling its contents onto the floor, and kneels down in front of me. Through my tears I can see the terror in her eyes. I want to cry out, but I'm too scared. The nurse pulls on my hand, but I slap her away as I continue to pound my knees. The more I try to draw air into my lungs, the more the invisible bands tighten around my chest. 'No!' the nurse shouts. 'David, stop it! Don't fight it! You're hyperventilating!'

'Hipper ventle . . . ?' I gasp.

'Slow down. You're going to be fine. I'm just going to put this bag over your—'

'*Nooo!* I can't . . . won't be able . . . to see. I . . . have to see!'

'Shh, I'm right here. Close your eyes and concentrate on the sound of my voice. Good. Now slow down. Take tiny puffs of air. Breathe through your nose. That's it,' the nurse whispers in a soothing voice. With her I feel safe. 'That's much better; tiny breaths. Reach out, take my hand. I'm right here. I'm not going to leave you. You're going to be fine.'

I obey the nurse and shut my eyes. As the nurse places the bag over my face, I can instantly feel warm air circulate. It feels good, but after a few breaths my exhaled air becomes too hot. My legs begin to lock up. By accident I jerk the nurse's hand.

'Shh. David, trust me, you're fine. You're doing better. Much better. That's it, slow down. See? Now, lean your head back and relax.'

As I tilt my head backward, a rush of air escapes from my mouth. The pressure is so intense that I fight to keep myself from throwing up. I rip the bag from my face before my legs buckle, and I fall to the floor gasping for more air. Within seconds the bands around my chest begin to ease.

After a few minutes, the fire from inside my neck begins to cool. 'Here,' the nurse says, holding a glass of ice cubes in front of me, 'take one of these to suck on.'

I try to pick up a piece of ice, but my trembling fingers cannot grasp the cube. Without a second thought the nurse reaches into the glass and picks one out. 'Open up.'

I lower my head, trying to hide. The moment I do, the searing pain returns. 'David, what's wrong? Come on now, open up,' she instructs in a more commanding tone. I close my eyes. I know what's coming next: questions. *I'd give anything to avoid another round of questions.* All they do is make everyone at school upset and somehow Mother always finds out. Whenever the principal has called Mother, the staff at school would see the results the next day. As I continue to avoid the nurse's eyes, I fantasize about crawling into a corner so I can disappear.

I slowly open my eyes when I feel the nurse lift my head with her fingers. Her face turns chalky white.

'Oh . . . my . . . Lord! What in heaven's name happened to your neck?' the nurse exclaims as she peers from side to side.

I wring my hands, hoping she'll drop the subject. '*Please!*' I wheeze. '*Let it go.*'

'The side of your Adam's apple is so swollen!' The nurse flies away to snatch a tongue depressor from one of her glass jars. 'Let's have a look. Open up.' I let out a raspy sigh before obeying. 'I need you to open just a little bit wider. Can you do that for me?' she asks gently.

'Can't,' I whimper. 'Hurts too much.'

At last the nurse allows me to close my mouth. Again, I try to avoid her stare. I bury my trembling fingers in my lap. She shakes her head before standing up and grabbing her clipboard. Every school day, for over a year, the nurse has inspected my body from head to toe before documenting her examinations. Now she mutters to herself as she scribbles her latest findings. Kneeling back down, she delicately massages the palms of my hands. I bite my lip in anticipation. The nurse stares into my eyes as if not knowing what to say.

Now I'm really scared.

'I'm sorry, David,' she says as tears seep from behind her glasses. 'I was wrong. You weren't hyperventilating. Your, ah, your larynx . . . your epiglottis is swollen and your trachea is inflamed. What I'm saying is: this is why you are having trouble breathing. The opening to your throat was cutting off your flow of oxygen. Do you understand?'

I take a moment to visualize in my mind the nurse's meaning. I don't want her to think I'm stupid.

'When did this happen?' she asks.

I look away from the nurse's gaze and stare at my shoes. 'I was, uhm . . .' I fumble for the exact wording to Mother's cover story, but my brain still feels trapped in a fog bank. 'I was . . . I fell . . . I fell down the stairs.'

'David?' she replies, raising her eyebrows.

'It's my fault!' I snap back. 'I was wrestling and I got out of control and my brothers—'

'Poppycock!' the nurse interrupts. 'You mean your mother knew of your condition . . . and she still made you run to school? Do you realize what might have happened to you? For goodness' sakes, you could have . . .'

'Uhm, no, ma'am. Please, I'm better now. Really, I'm fine,' I say as softly and as quickly as I can, before the burning sensation returns. 'Please! It's not her fault! Let it go!'

The nurse lifts her glasses to wipe away her tears. 'No! Not this time! I won't let it go. I've had enough. This is the last straw. This has to be reported to the principal. Something has got to be done.' She stands up and slaps her clipboard against her leg as she marches for the door.

'No! Pleeze!' I beg. 'You don't understand! If you tell, she'll—'

'She'll what?' The nurse spins around. 'Tell me, David, tell me so I have something, anything, to go on! I know it's her – we know it's her – but you've got to help us, to help you,' she pleads.

In an effort to relieve the pain I stare up at the ceiling. I wring my hands and concentrate on inhaling tiny puffs of air through my nose. From the corner of my eye I can see the nurse still standing by the door. I slowly turn my head toward her. Tears run down my cheeks. 'I, ah . . . I can't.'

'Why? In heaven's name, why do you protect her? What are you waiting for?' she barks in a rattling voice. 'Something has to be done!'

The nurse's words pound through my skull. I bite down on my lip until it bleeds. My arms begin to shake. 'Dammit!' I blurt out in a squeaky voice. '*Don't you understand?* There's nothing, *nothing*, that anyone can do! It's my fault! *It's always my fault.* "Boy" this, "It" that, blah, blah, blah. Every day is a repeat of the day before. Even you,' I state with my finger thrust at the nurse, 'every day I come in, take off my clothes, you look me over, you ask me about this, about that . . . for what? Nothing changes, and nothing ever will!' The band around my throat begins to tighten, but I don't care. I can no longer control my flood of emotions. 'Miss Moss tried—'

'Miss Moss?' the nurse asks.

'My, ah, my second-grade teacher. She tried . . . she tried to help and she's gone . . .'

'David?' the nurse says in a disbelieving tone.

I bury my face in my hands. 'Father tried . . . and he's gone, too. You have to understand: everything I am, everything I do, is bad. Everything's wrong. If you get too close, she'll . . . she'll deal with you, too! No one wins!' I cry. 'No one wins against The Mother!' I bend over in a coughing fit. Whatever energy I had drains away. I lean against the nurse's examination bed. I fight to slow down my breathing. 'I, ah . . . when I sat at the bottom of the garage stairs and they'd watch TV or eat dinner, I tried to figure things out, to understand why.' I shake my head clear of the countless hours spent in the garage. 'You know the one thing I wanted the most?'

Her mouth hangs open. She's never seen me like this before. 'No,' she answers.

'I just wanted to be *real*. To be a real kid – with clothes and stuff. I don't mean just toys, but to be outside. I always wanted to play on the jungle gym after school. I'd really like to do that.' For a moment I smile at my fantasy. 'But I know I won't be able to. *Never.* I have to run to The House fast or I get into trouble. Sometimes, on really sunny days, as I'm running from school, I cheat and stop to watch the kids play.'

My vision becomes blurred as I rattle off my deepest secrets to the nurse. Because I am not allowed to speak at Mother's house and have no friends at school, I have no one to express my feelings to. 'Other times in the garage, at night, when I lay on my cot, I'd think hard to figure out what I could do. I mean, to fix things between Mother and me, to make things better. I wanted to know why, how, things became so bad. I really thought if I tried hard enough – if I prayed with all my spirit – I'd find my answers. They never came.

'I . . . I, ah, tri- tried,' I stutter. I'm holding back my tears. 'I spent so much time . . . I, ah, I just . . . I just wanted to know why. That's all. Why me, why us? I just wanted to know. Why?' I stare into the nurse's eyes. 'I don't care anymore! I just want to go to sleep! I'm tired of everything! The games, the secrets, the lies, hoping one day Mother will wake up and everything will be better again! I can't take it anymore!

'If you could just let me sleep, for just a while, please?' I beg.

She shakes her head. 'This has to end, David. Look at you. You're—'

'It's okay,' I interrupt in a calm voice. 'I'm not . . . when I'm at school, I'm not afraid. Just promise me you won't tell. *Not today, please?*'

'David, you know I can't do that,' the nurse replies in a flat tone.

'If you . . . if you tell,' I pant, 'then you know what will happen. Please, let it go!'

She nods her head in agreement. 'Just for today.'

'Promise?'

'Promise.' She takes my hand and leads me to the small bed in the corner of the room.

'Cross your heart and hope to die?' I ask, making an X mark on my chest with my finger.

'Cross my heart,' she repeats in a choked-up voice. She covers me with a thick wool blanket.

'. . . And hope to die?' I repeat. The nurse's lips part with a smile as she gently strokes my matted hair. I take her hands and cup them around mine. '. . . And hope to die?'

The nurse gives my hands a gentle squeeze. 'And hope to die.'

In the deepest part of my soul, I feel at peace. I am no longer afraid. *I am ready to die.*

chapter 2

FLY AWAY

August 24, 1979 – Thick, sticky sweat coated every pore of my skin. My stomach seized with fear. My fingers seemed fused together as they clawed the armrest. I wanted to shut my eyes, but the combination of exhilaration, fascination, and terror inside me kept them glued to the small Plexiglas window. I studied every feature of the Bay Area – my home for the last eighteen years.

'I'm flying?' I asked, to my own amazement.

My body slid from my seat, and I thought for sure I'd fall out of the plane as the Boeing 727 made a sudden sharp roll to the right. To help contain my fear, I forced my eyes shut. *I'm okay. I'm all right. I'm fine. My God, I can't believe it! I'm flying! I'm actually flying!* I could feel myself drifting off. Because of the excitement of finally enlisting in the US Air Force, saying goodbye to my foster parents, and struggling with my past, I had not slept in days. As the roar of the jet's engines began to fade, I started to unwind. The more my tension disappeared, the more I began to think of how far I had come.

As a child surviving in the garage of Mother's house, I had never dreamed of making it out alive. Somehow, I had known Mother was close to killing me, and yet I did not care. I had given up all hope. Yet on March 5, 1973, the day after Mother had thrown me down the garage stairs, my teachers called the police, who immediately placed me into protective custody. I was free. As elated as I was, I sensed that my freedom was a hollow victory. At the county's court proceedings, I felt that Mother had given me away. I felt as if *I* was not good enough for *her*. When my angel of mercy – my social worker, Ms Gold – informed me that I was never to have any contact with Mother or her children ever again, I was crushed.

It was then that I became obsessed with finding answers to my past. Even though I was still terrified of Mother, who wanted nothing to do with me, I struggled to prove that I was worthy of her love and worthy enough to be a member of her family.

As a foster child, I soon learned that I knew absolutely nothing about *living in the real world*. My former life as Mother's prisoner had been dominated by elemental needs of survival. But after my rescue I felt like a toddler – learning and growing by leaps and bounds. The simplest things taught to preschool children became major obstacles for me. Because I had spent years in the garage with my head bent backward in a POW position, I developed very bad posture. As a foster child, I had to learn to focus and walk upright. Whenever I became nervous, I stuttered or slurred every word. It would take me forever to complete one simple sentence. My foster mother, Mrs Turnbough, spent hours with me every day after school, teaching me phonics and helping me to imagine the words flowing from my mouth like water cascading over a fall. Mrs Turnbough's valiant efforts were perhaps her undoing. Within a few months, I was driving my foster parents up the wall with all I had to say. It was all they could do to shut me up. I wanted to show off my new form of communication to everyone, every minute. But my mouth soon became my Achilles' heel. Because I was so skinny and awkward, I became easy prey for others, and my only form of defense was my mouth. Whenever I felt backed in a corner, words of intense anger and hatred seemed to erupt before I could analyze what I was saying or why.

The only way I felt I could make friends was stealing for acceptance or doing whatever else I could to gain recognition. I knew that what I was doing was completely wrong, but after years of being an outcast and totally isolated, the need to fit in was too powerful to resist. My foster parents struggled to keep me on the straight and narrow, and teach me the seriousness of my decisions.

On the lighter side, they were dismayed at my naïvety and ignorance. The first few times I took a bath, I filled the tub to the rim *before* stepping into it, causing water to spill over the sides. I would then squeeze every drop I could from what I thought was 'fancy-smelling bubble bath' into the tub, then stir the water like a whirlpool trying to form as much lather as possible. As much as my foster parents laughed at my water frolics, my foster sisters were not amused and hid their bottles of Vidal Sassoon in their bedrooms. Up until then I had never heard the word 'shampoo'.

I thought that in order to survive, I had to work. Early on as a foster child, it was drummed into me that foster kids – labeled as 'F-kids' – never amounted to anything, never graduated high school, let alone went on to college. I also discovered that by the time I turned eighteen years old, I would no longer be a ward of the court – a minor that was provided for by the county – and since I didn't have parents to rely on, I would be all alone. The closer I came to reaching adulthood, the more I became terrified of being broke and homeless. Deep down I feared I would not be strong enough to make it on my own. As a frightened child living in my mother's garage, one of the promises I had made was that if I ever escaped, I would always have enough money to eat. So, as a young teenager, I abandoned my Lego and Erector sets and my Hot Wheels toy cars and focused on earning a living. By the age of fifteen I was shining shoes. I lied about my age to get work as a busboy. I did whatever I could to put in at least 40 hours a week. As a freshman in high school, I slaved six days a week to put in over 60 hours. I did anything I could to squeeze in an extra hour a week to earn an additional $2.65. Only after I'd show up to school and collapse on top of my desk and get sick from total exhaustion did I begin to slack off. On one level, thinking that I was ahead of the game, I was proud, almost to the point of being cocky. But on the inside I felt hollow and lonely. As other boys my age were dating beautiful girls with short dresses and fancy makeup, driving their parents' cars and whining about their ten-hour work weeks, I became increasingly jealous of their good fortune.

Whenever I felt a little depressed, I would bury myself even more in my work. The harder I applied myself, the more the cravings of wanting to be a normal teenager disappeared. And more important, the inner voice bubbling inside me, fighting for the answers to my past, remained quiet.

For me, work meant peace.

In the summer of 1978, at age eighteen, in order to further my career as a top-rated car salesman, I decided to drop out of high school. But months later, after a statewide recession, I found myself as a legal adult, with no diploma, no job, and my life savings quickly draining away. My worst nightmare had come true. All of my well-thought-out plans of getting ahead and sacrificing while others played vanished into thin air. Because of my lack of education, the only jobs available were at fast-food restaurants. I knew I could not make it by working those jobs for the rest of my life.

Ever since I had been Mother's prisoner, I had dreamed of making something of myself. The more she would scream, curse at me, and leave me sprawled out on the floor in my own blood, the more I would fight back and smile inside, telling myself over and over again, *One day, you'll see. One of these days I'll make you proud.* But Mother's prediction was right: I had failed. And for that I hated myself to the core. My idle time awakened my inner voice. I began to think that maybe Mother had been right all along. Maybe I was a loser, and I had been treated as such because I deserved it. I became so paranoid about my future that I could no longer sleep. I spent my free evenings trying to form any strategy I could to survive. It was during one of those endless nights that I remembered the only piece of advice my father ever gave me.

In six years as a foster child, I had seen my father less than a dozen times. At the end of my last visit, he proudly showed me one of the only possessions he had left: his badge, representing his retirement from the San Francisco Fire Department. Before loading me onto a Greyhound bus, Father mumbled in a dejected voice, 'Get out of here, David. Get as far away from here as you can. You're almost at that age. Get out.' As he looked at me with darkened circles under his eyes, Father's final words were: 'Do what you have to. Don't end up . . . don't end up like me.'

In my heart I sensed that Father was a homeless alcoholic. After spending a lifetime saving others from burning buildings, Father had been helpless to save himself. That day as the bus pulled away, I cried from the depths of my soul. Every time the bus passed someone sleeping beside a building, I'd imagine Father shivering in the night. As much as I felt sorry for him, though, I knew I did not want to – I could not – end up like him. I felt selfish thinking of myself rather than my stricken father, but his advice, *Don't end up like me*, became my personal commandment.

I decided that joining the service was my only chance. I even fantasized about serving in the air force as a fireman, then one day returning to the Bay Area and showing Father my badge. Trying to enlist proved to be an ordeal. After struggling to obtain my G.E.D., I had to fill out mounds of paperwork for every time I had been bounced from one foster home to another, then explain on separate forms why I was placed in another home. Whenever the air force recruiter pressed me about my past, I became so terrified that I stuttered like an idiot. After weeks of evading these questions, I caved in and gave the sergeant a brief explanation about why Mother and I did not get along. I waited for his reaction. I held my breath knowing that if the recruiter thought I was a troublemaker, he could refuse my application.

Every morning, for weeks, I stood outside the door, waiting for the office to open, before I hurried in to fill out more paperwork, and studied films and whatever booklets the recruiter had available. I became possessed to enlist. The air force was my ticket to a new life.

After the paperwork was filled out, double-checked, then reverified, I had to get a physical examination. During the battery of tests I was poked and prodded on every inch of my rail-thin body. At the end, as I sat nearly naked, the doctor kept circling around me as he questioned the ancient bumps on my scalp, the scars on my body, the marks on my right arm where Mother had burned me on the gas stove. I simply shrugged off the doctor's questions, telling him I had been a clumsy kid. The doctor let out a sigh and raised his eyebrows. Immediately my heart seized. I just knew I had said the wrong thing. Fearing my statement would disqualify me, I quickly added that it was a stage I had gone through when I was a kid. 'A kid?' the doctor asked, as if he were not buying my story.

'Yeah, you know, when I was six, seven years old. But' – I raised a finger to stress the importance of this point – 'I'm not clumsy now! Nope, not anymore. Not me. No sireee . . .' The doctor waved me off and told me to get dressed. I felt a surge of relief as I saw him mark the block that claimed I was medically qualified to enlist. I was on top of the world, right up until the moment I leaned too far and crashed against the table. Folders containing other recruits' paperwork exploded in every direction, and, still struggling to pull on my pants, I tried to grab the papers, only scattering them more. The doctor ordered me to stop trying to help and get out of his office as fast as humanly possible. As I hurried out the door, the doctor flashed a smile. 'Over that clumsy period, eh?'

Hours later that same day, I sat frozen in front of a computer next to an air force sergeant who typed in an endless stream of information. Finally, the sergeant paused, turned toward me, and nonchalantly asked, 'So, what day do you want to enlist?'

I shook my head, not sure I had heard what the sergeant just asked. I leaned forward and whispered, 'You mean, I'm in? I can join? You're actually asking me if I want to join?'

'Don't make a federal case out of it. Yeah, you're in – that is, unless the FBI tells us you're a criminal,' the sergeant teased.

My mind immediately flashed back to all the close calls I had had with the police for speeding tickets when I was a teenager. My heart skipped a beat. I knew that if the air force found out about my past, I was a goner. The sergeant startled me when he tapped on my shoulder. 'Hey, Pelz-ter, relax. So . . . when do you want to enlist?'

I was lost in a daze. *Now you have the chance to make something of yourself. Now is your time to build a life.* I simply could not believe that after struggling over six months, I had actually made it.

I allowed myself the reward of smiling. 'When's the soonest I can join?'

He snapped back, 'Girlfriend problems, eh?' Before I had a chance to respond, the man bowed his head and feverishly pounded on the computer keyboard. 'Well,' he began, 'if you really feel the need for speed, I can have you on a plane and in basic training by . . . tonight. Or, if that doesn't suit you, you can enlist next week. So, what will it be?'

I immediately knew what I had to do, but a wave of shame washed over me. For months I had lied to my foster parents, telling them that I was taking specialized tests and interviewing for a job, which in a way I felt I was. The Turnboughs had no idea what I was really up to. I felt a sudden urge to run off and enlist and then simply phone them from boot camp. Besides my foster parents and a handful of close friends, I had no one in my life. No girlfriends, no work buddies, no friends who picked me up to go cruising or see movies, no relatives to speak of – no one. I felt that if I fell off the face of the earth, less than half a dozen people would even notice. But deep in my heart I knew that I owed my *real* family – my foster parents and whatever friends I had – more than a long-distance phone call. Above all, it was a matter of honor. I let out a deep sigh before answering the sergeant. 'Next week.'

'All right, next week. You sure about this?' he politely asked.

Without blinking an eye, I nodded my head. 'Yes, sir!'

The sergeant pressed a button, and the computer began printing a stream of papers. 'Sign here, here, here, here and . . . here,' he informed me without a trace of emotion. I stared at the blocks with the bright red Xs. *This is it!* I told myself. I snatched the government pen and scribbled my name so hard that I nearly tore through the sheets of papers. As the sergeant took the paperwork and typed in more commands to his computer, I killed time by looking at the framed glossy photographs of the hi-tech air force fighter jets. My mouth began to water at the sleek, crisp lines of the airplanes against the endless blue sky.

'Sir, is that the F-15 jet fighter?' I asked, pointing at a photograph above his desk.

Without looking up from the computer, the sergeant replied, 'Nope . . . F-16.'

I nodded my head to the sergeant's answer, then stated before thinking, 'Excuse me, sir, but if I'm not mistaken, that's the McDonnell Douglas F-15 Eagle: first strike, air superior fighter, capable of speeds in excess of Mach 2.5, produced by a pair of G.E. F-100 after-burning engines . . .'

The sergeant turned toward me with his mouth hung open.

'Did I say something wrong, sir?' I thought for a moment of what I had just said, and even I was surprised how easy the basic technical aspects of the airplane came from my mouth. All these facts I had learned from the recruitment brochures and stream of books I had digested over the last few months.

He simply nodded for me to continue.

Immediately I thought this was part of some strange test. I closed my eyes to recall as much as I could. 'Uhm, I know it has a comple . . . dent – I mean, complement of AIM-7 Sparrow and AIM-9 Sidewinder missiles. And . . . I think . . . it was two, maybe three years ago that a modified F-15 Streak Eagle beat the time-to-climb altitude record held by a Russian MeG.' I paused to catch my breath and waited for his reaction. Craving acceptance, I didn't want the sergeant to think I was trying to show off. By the smile in his eyes I realized he was not only impressed, but interested in planes as well.

'That's "MiG" Pelz-ter, not "MeG",' he countered. 'Okay, smart guy: What base did they launch the Streak Eagle from?'

'Grand Forks, North Dakota!' I stated with confidence.

'All right, not bad. Now,' he said, 'the big one: Why Grand Forks?'

I smiled back, enjoying the game. 'Molecule compression. The colder air allows the plane to reach speeds and altitudes quicker while at the same time consuming less fuel. I mean . . . I think that's the idea.'

The sergeant responded with a wide grin and slapped me on the shoulder. 'Where in the hell did you . . . ?'

By instinct, I hesitated. For a second I thought I had just revealed military secrets. 'I read, sir.'

'You read?'

'Ah . . . yes, sir. I read a lot. I've always wanted to . . . I mean, Sergeant?' I asked in a low voice. 'You think they'd ever let me fly?'

'My Lord!' he coughed. 'You're a piece of work, aren't you? Hey, Max,' he bellowed to the next cubicle. 'I got the next Chuck Yeager over here! Wants to know if he can fly!' As a small roar of laughter erupted, I closed my eyes. I always seemed to say the wrong thing at the wrong time and make a jerk out of myself.

After I let out a deep breath, the sergeant caught my eye. I stated in a firm tone, 'Chuck Yeager was *enlisted* before he flew.'

The sergeant thumbed through my paperwork. 'Listen, Pelz, you barely made it in. You're a high school dropout, your aptitude scores are *way* below average, and you have the body of a skinny rat with the eyesight of Stevie Wonder. A fly boy? Thought you wanted to be a fireman. Listen,' he said, 'here's what you do: Learn your trade as a fireman and get some college classes under your belt. Heck, the air force will pay for your tuition. And then after a few years if you want to reenlist, you can apply for a slot. That's a major goal, but if you're serious, we'll meet you halfway. Okay?'

I swallowed hard, realizing how lucky I was even to enlist. 'Yes, sir. I understand. Thanks for the advice.'

'Hey, that's what I'm here for.' He stood up, indicating he was through with me. 'Not to worry, Pelz. You keep studying and they'll have you piloting the SR-71.' He then raised his eyebrows. 'I assume with your plethora of aeronautical knowledge, you do know about the Blackbird, *don't you?*'

My eyes lit up at the mention of my favorite plane. 'Yes, sir!' I exclaimed. 'I know about the Blackbird, like nobody's business!'

'Well then, we'll see you next week.' He extended his hand.

'Thank you, sir,' I said as I shook it. 'I'll make you proud. You'll see.'

The sergeant let out a chuckle, released my hand, then snapped to attention and gave me a crisp salute. 'See ya, *Airman Pelz-a-Yeager*!'

Later that afternoon, before I chickened out and changed my mind, I informed my foster parents, 'I enlisted in the air force! I leave next week!'

'Oh, really?' my foster father, Harold Turnbough, casually replied.

I searched their eyes for any kind of reaction to my explosive news. After what seemed like an eternity of silence, I broke the ice. 'I'm going nowhere. I've been working myself stupid. I thought I could find the answers – to my past, to Mother – trying to numb myself about my dad. And now, now it's my time. My time to make something of myself. I've already missed so much, but if I stay focused and work hard, maybe someday I can turn this around.' I stopped to gauge their response. My foster parents continued to just sit there. 'Isn't that what you've tried to teach me; I mean, to become self-reliant? Well . . . ?' I asked, frustrated.

Alice and Harold, who years ago had adopted me into their hearts, began to nod their heads before exploding with laughter. I shook my head in disgust. Because of the day's mounting tensions – the test and examinations, my fear of not being good enough to enlist, my lack of sleep, and hiding my secret for so long – I felt sick to my stomach. 'Stop it!' I shouted. 'What's so funny? This is serious! I mean it! I already signed the paperwork.'

Alice leaned over to embrace me. 'We've known for a while, David.'

Harold said with a crooked smile, 'With all those brochures layin' around and your babblin' 'bout airplanes this, airplanes that, what else would you be up to?'

'So, you're not mad? I mean . . . ?'

'Of course not, David. But answer this: Why the service? Three years is a long time,' said Alice.

'Four years; I'll be in for four,' I corrected her. 'I'm just fed up. I'm tired of living hand to mouth. Working my butt off, for what? For nothing! I've been scrimping and slaving away, and I have nothing to show for it. Check it out: in four years I can grow and learn, I can explore and see things beyond any picture in any magazine.' I stopped and lowered my head. 'Maybe getting away will help me . . . help me find my answers . . .'

Mrs Turnbough reached over to cup my hand. 'David, you may never know. Sometimes, bad things happen. For some things there are no absolutes.'

'No,' I interrupted, 'it's wrong. I have to know. I have to find out. If I don't deal with this, all I'm doing is hiding "the secret" like everyone else, and if I do that, then what's to say I don't become like her or like my dad? Something made them the way they are. Things do happen for a reason. I want to understand; I want to know. And if I don't find out and do something, who will? How many kids have you taken in who came from the same kind of homes as me? The problem's not going to go away by turning our backs or sweeping it underneath the carpet anymore. Every day *things* happen, and everyone acts as if nothing's wrong. No one wants to talk about *things*, let alone deal with the consequences afterward. It's wrong, and it's about time to take a stand. Isn't that what you and everyone else have pounded into my head since I was rescued? Be good, be honest and fair, find something I believe in, work hard and keep the faith no matter how long it takes? Well . . . ?'

My foster parents sat in front of me totally mesmerized. In all the years I had known them, they had never seen me so intense, so articulate about my past. I continued in a softer tone. 'Listen, it's going to be okay, I can handle it. I'll be fine, but please understand, I don't want to turn out like them. This is something *I've* got to do.'

I took a moment to compose my thoughts. I did not want to screw up and tell them in the wrong way what I felt in my heart. 'You know I love you both very much. You've treated me as if I were a *real* person. But while I'm in the air force, I'm gonna save every dollar I can. I want a home . . . *my home*. I want to buy a home in Guerneville, on the Russian River. Ever since kindergarten I knew that's what I wanted. That's my lifelong dream. When I lived in Mother's house, when things were really bad, I'd go inside and dream of a log home by the river with a warm fireplace and the smell of redwood trees. It made me feel safe. Mother could never get me when I thought about the river. As a kid, that dream gave me something to live for. I want *my* home.' I hesitated as my throat tightened. Tears began to trickle down the sides of my face. I tried to hold back my emotions, but the years of extreme pressure were just too much.

'David, what is it? What's wrong?' Mrs Turnbough whispered.

I closed my eyes before bursting with a flood of tears. 'All his life, all he wanted was to have something . . . And now he's alone, living on the streets, and has nothing. It's not right.'

'Who's alone? Who are you talking about?' Alice probed.

'My father!' I cried. 'I'm gonna buy a house and have Dad live with me. It's the right thing to do. And,' I said, renewing my vow, 'I'm going to find my answers, and when I'm ready, I'm going to do what I can to make a difference.' I wiped my tears away, feeling foolish.

'So, you're – joining the air force?' Harold asked with a hint of humor. 'Do you think you can manage to stay out of *the brig*?'

My smile matched Harold's. 'Yes, sir!' I said. 'I'll make you proud, you watch. One day, you'll see. I'll make you proud!'

'Well,' Alice broke in, 'now that you've made your decision, when are you going to tell your parents?'

I took a long, deep breath. As I inhaled, I felt clean. I could feel my entire body relax. I suddenly felt as if I could curl up in a big, soft bed and sleep forever. For the first time in nearly half a year I found myself at peace. In front of me the Turnboughs sat hand in hand. I gently placed my hands around theirs. 'As far as I'm concerned, *Mom*,' I said as I gazed into Alice's eyes, '*and Dad*,' I said, looking at Harold, 'I've enlisted in the United States Air Force. I leave next week. Any questions?'

The Boeing 727's sudden downward lurch shook me from my trance. I blinked, struggling to focus on the San Antonio skyline outside the airplane window. The more I stared through the Plexiglas, the more the faces and serenity of my parents faded away. I was on the threshold of my new life. I took a deep breath, then smiled. *And so it begins!*

chapter 3

LETTER FROM HOME

Air force basic training was no cakewalk, but after stumbling through the first two weeks, I began to get into the groove and felt comfortable with the expectations of my drill sergeants, which in an odd sense reminded me of living with Mother. I had sense enough to keep a low profile and never make eye contact with the instructors whenever they lashed out at my squadron. I performed my duties as quickly and precisely as possible, and, most important, I made certain to keep my stuttering mouth clamped shut. Whenever I had a free moment, I'd crank out epic letters of my *mis*adventures to my foster parents, my 'aviation mentor' Michael Marsh from my days in foster care, and my father. Every day in the late afternoon our squadron received mail call, and every day my heart pounded with excitement. But the only letters I received regularly were crumpled ones addressed to my father with RETURN TO SENDER stamped on the envelope. After a few weeks I gave up trying to reach Father through the mail, so I tried to keep close to him through my prayers.

After saying my evening prayers I would roll over, feeling relieved that I had truly escaped Mother's tangled web of hate and deceit. I knew she could no longer manipulate or harm me in any way. For the first time in my life, I was my own person. I had finally locked Mother away in the deep recesses of my mind. I felt so elated, my lifelong quest no longer seemed that important. I was free.

At night, though, I discovered, as I had in foster care, that The Mother still lived in my dreams. As always, she would stand before me like a marble statue at the end of a long hallway. I stood in front of her – in full view and helpless – but somehow thinking her sculpture could do me no harm. And then her eyes blink open. She smiles before gazing down at her bony hand and pulling out a gleaming silver carving knife. I know I should do something, anything, but my fear paralyzes any defenses. In slow motion The Mother steps toward me. Her glazed eyes pierce my soul. A split second before her foot touches the floor, I turn and flee down the hallway at full speed. As my heart races, I know I am miles ahead of The Mother, but I can somehow feel her presence inches behind me. I run forever, but there is no escape. I frantically hunt for a way out of the maze-like corridors, but I stumble and fall into a void. Above me The Mother stands poised, revealing her yellow teeth and putrid, steamy breath. As I look into her eyes for mercy, her expression seems to laugh before she raises her arm and lunges at me. I close my eyes as the shiny-silvered knife flings from The Mother's hand and flies through the air. I empty my lungs, screeching, '*Why* . . . ?'

'Hey, Pelz, wake up, man!' my air force 'bunk buddy', Randy, whispered low enough so no one else could hear. 'You havin' one of those dreams again.'

I wiped the sticky sweat from my forehead as I scanned the outline of the sleeping bay of my fellow airmen. I thanked God that I didn't wake up my squad, let alone the entire training base. I checked my chest, making certain that The Mother had not crossed over and stabbed me. I thanked Randy for his concern, then spent the remainder of the night sitting on the edge of my cot.

The next morning after inspection, my drill instructor summoned me into his office. As I stood at attention in front of his desk, I became so terrified that my body began to weave. I kept my eyes glued straight ahead and held my breath, praying the instructor had no idea of my latest anxiety attack. 'At ease, airman,' the master sergeant commanded. 'Says here,' he stated as he casually read, 'in last night's report . . . you had one of your episodes . . . again. Third time this week. *What's your problem?* You homesick for Momma?'

As my mind raced for an answer, I somehow had enough sense to evade the truth. Instead I bellowed, 'Negative, sir! I'm not homesick, not for a moment, sir!' I glanced down at the sergeant, who wasn't fazed by my off-the-cuff response. My lips trembled as I tried to make up for lost ground. 'Won't happen again, sir! Ever!' I promised in a quavering voice.

'Make certain it doesn't, *airman*. Damn sure! Understand this,' the master sergeant said as he shot up from his chair and stood inches in front of my nose, 'the United States Air Force has no room *whatsoever* for whiny little momma's boys. Our sole objective, our sole purpose, is to protect the freedom of this nation's democracy. *Is that clear?* If you can't handle the magnitude of that responsibility, then get out! If you continue on your present course, I will have no alternative but to have you undergo psychiatric evaluation for possible medical discharge. *Do I make myself clear . . .* Airman *Pelzer?'*

I swallowed hard. 'Crystal clear, sir!' But even as the words came out of my mouth, I could feel my 'master plan' evaporating. In my mind, I could see my dream – my log cabin, with Father and me sitting on the porch or fishing together on the Russian River – fading away. After being dismissed by my drill instructor, I gave a crisp salute and marched out of his office. Immediately I fled to the latrine and threw up. On my hands and knees I cursed myself for allowing Mother to continue controlling me. I became filled with shame.

After wiping away the vomit, I became furious – not at Mother but with myself. Everything I had accomplished – from studying books on big adventure in the darkness of Mother's garage to working endless hours as a teenager at fast-food restaurants – was to somehow better myself and to prepare myself to live a better life, a *real life*. If I was kicked out of the air force, it was *my* fault, not anyone else's. Therefore, as the sergeant had stressed in his underlying message: *I had to do something to change my present course.*

That morning I schemed to come up with a way to somehow save me from another *episode* and a possible lifetime of disgrace. To be booted out of the armed forces for having immature, childish dreams was not an option. Since I'd been having the nightmares in the early hours of the morning and my bunk buddy, Randy, was a light sleeper, I bribed him to wake me at the first sign of trouble. But after a couple of nights, I felt I was stretching Randy's Southern generosity to its limit. So I decided to volunteer for the guard-duty shift that began at 2:00 A.M. until reveille at 6:00 A.M. My idea was an immediate success, but days later my lack of sleep made it impossible for me to concentrate on my academics. Whenever I'd study my manuals in class, the words became blurred and ran together. I'd slump forward at my desk only to be awakened by a furious drill sergeant. During parade practice I'd misstep nearly every move and was soon abandoned to practice precision movements alone in the blistering Texas sun, so not to further embarrass my squadron. I was ridiculed by my air force instructors for my lack of concentration and never ending clumsiness.

But I refused to cave in. I didn't mind being condemned; if anything, my weakness in certain areas kept my mind off my inner struggles. As long as I kept myself out of the shrink's office, I would have gladly practiced my marching routine barefoot on the searing tarmac.

Because of my awkwardness and the spreading rumors of my nightmares, I found myself isolated from my squadron, which had begun to break into cliques. The only friends I had were the ones assigned with me for latrine duty. During the latter part of training, our class was awarded afternoon weekend passes. I refused mine and stayed behind to catch up on my studies, practice my marching movements in the long, empty hallways, starch-iron my uniforms to a razor's edge, and polish my boots with a wet cotton ball until they had a mirror finish. Hours later, groups of my squadron returned, bragging about their adventure of sneaking beers and showing off their dress-blue uniforms to the local girls. I simply counted the days until I could begin my training as a fireman. More importantly I mentally counted the money I had saved by remaining at the barracks. The more dollars I began to hoard, the more my pride grew with the fact that I was finally getting a foothold on buying my home on the Russian River.

During the last week of basic training, as I reported to the career counselor's office for my fireman position, I knew by the distant look on the sergeant's face that my goal was not meant to be. Without looking at me, the counselor rummaged through a stack of forms and mumbled, 'Airman . . . there was a slight holdup in your specialty request, and, well, by the time it was rectified, well . . . don't ask me why, but these things happen . . . so . . .' As the sergeant's words trailed off, I could feel a sense of doom hanging over me.

For a moment I thought my paperwork problems were due to my constant screw-ups and the ever-looming 'psych eval'. I shook my head clear, praying that the sergeant was somehow toying with me and that this was a trick the career counselors played on young, gullible airmen. 'Sir, I don't understand. What is it you're saying, sir?'

The sergeant cleared his throat and stated that all firefighter positions had been filled.

'That's okay,' I said. 'I can wait.'

'Negative!' the counselor shot back. 'There are no available positions. *You*,' he said, jabbing a finger in front of my plastic black-rimmed glasses, '*are not*, I repeat, *are not*, going to be a fireman!'

Breaking all rules of protocol, I blurted, 'But . . . that's what I signed up for. That's why I joined. I—'

'I am sorry,' the sergeant broke in. 'I truly am. But mission necessities come first—'

'But, sir,' I interrupted, 'it took me forever to get in . . . to fill out all that paperwork, passing the interviews . . . This can't happen. I mean, my whole life, all I wanted . . . My father!' I shrieked. 'He was a—'

'At ease! Stand down, airman,' the sergeant snapped. 'The air force couldn't care less what *you* want! Listen,' he spoke in a softer tone, 'I realize your position. I've got half a dozen other troops outside this office with the same problem. You knew when you enlisted that mission necessity has priority. So, for now, the air force dictates that it needs 62210s.'

'62210s?' I asked as I leaned closer to his desk.

The sergeant flipped through a manual, matching the coded numbers with the job description. I knew by his reaction that I was in for another shock. 'Uh, food service specialist.'

'Sir?' I asked, shaking my head.

'A cook, Airman Pelzer. You'll be a cook. Come on,' the sergeant said in a cheerful voice, 'it's a slack job. You go in for a few hours, then you go home – nine to five. Bankers' hours. It's a cakewalk. Hey, at most bases you're in charge of the civilians; they're the ones who cook, they do all the work. You'll just supervise!'

'So . . . in my off time I can go to college or get a part-time job?' I inquired. I had instantly accepted my fate and somehow was trying to formulate a plan to turn my negative setback into a positive outcome.

'Listen,' the counselor said, 'you'll have so much time on your hands, you'll be bored stiff – that is, unless you get assigned to a field unit. Then you'll work your tail off in some godforsaken boondocks. But hey, I've yet to see that happen. Don't sweat it. In three years, if you keep your nose clean, you can cross-train and then become a fireman.'

'But if I stay in, I wanna fly. That's why I gotta go to college,' I said.

'Yeah, sure, whatever. Not to worry. Just sign this paper that I briefed you in this little snafu. And don't worry, you keep pluggin' away. Things have a way of turning up. Aim high!'

Without hesitation I snatched a pen and scribbled my name, rank, and date. I found it strange that after my months of intense longing, my life's course was again heading in a direction in which I had no control. I felt completely helpless. My childhood ambitions were instantly erased with a stroke of a pen. Afterward, I stared at the cheap, black ballpoint that had US GOVERNMENT stamped on it and flung it on top of a stack of papers. I was so numb that I strolled out of the office without being dismissed, let alone saluting my superior.

Weeks after graduating basic training and being transferred to my specialty training base, the shock of serving in the air force as a mere cook began to fade away. I was so ashamed that I didn't tell my foster parents. I wrestled with the fact that I had, in a sense, failed my father. I knew being a firefighter meant the world to him, and he had seemed so proud when I phoned him days before I enlisted. I had wanted so badly to impress him, to surprise him that David Pelzer – the unwanted one, the child called 'It' – would someday be entrusted with saving the lives of others, like my once-upon-a-time hero . . . my dad.

The more I had boasted to Father on the phone that day about my worldly plans of obtaining a degree in fire science after my initial qualification training, the more happy he seemed. His violent coughing attacks, caused by a lifetime of smoking, eased for a few moments, and his voice seemed less tense and more warm. I nearly broke down and cried after he let out a strained laugh, saying how proud he was of me. 'You're going to make good, Tiger. You'll be fine.' I clutched the phone with both hands and pressed it against my ear at the mention of the word 'Tiger'. As a young boy, before my world had turned black, the highest compliment Father could pay his adoring children was the word Tiger. After I hung up the phone, I stood mesmerized. After all these years Father had still remembered a single precious word. I felt from the bottom of my soul how desperately I craved to someday make both Mother and Father proud. But more so, I had hoped that by becoming a fireman, I would somehow ease the loneliness and pain I felt that Father had lived with every day – because of a son, a wife, and a family *he could not, would not save.*

I swallowed my dreams and my dignity and focused on applying myself as best as I could. Because of my years of working in various fast-food chains, I found the training classes boring. I blazed through the study materials while maintaining a near perfect score, and my hands-on skills surpassed the entire class. Whereas some of my peers would haphazardly throw their meals together, I would analyze every measurement, every ingredient, then time each move of whatever I was assigned to prepare for that particular shift. No matter what I cooked – a fluffy omelet with cheese oozing from both ends, perfectly crisp vegetables, or BBQ ribs that melted in one's mouth – I felt I had somehow prepared the perfect entrée, and I surged with pride whenever my instructor, or anyone who came through the food line, especially an air crew member, threw me a compliment for my efforts.

During my off-duty hours, while most of my classmates partied at the Airman's Club, I maintained my vow of pinching pennies and stayed in the barracks. I buried myself in books about the history of the air force or adventures of combat flying. I soon became addicted and began to build my own aeronautical library, one book at a time. Every payday I would retrieve my crumpled shopping list of specific planes that, to me, had changed the course of history. I soon became a walking encyclopedia, and I wished that someday I, too, could make a difference in my new world of flight.

No matter what time of day or night, whenever I thought my mind would explode from the constant studying, I'd take long walks around the base. I would go to my postal box with my eyes widened. I would utter a quick prayer before speed-dialing the combination. At times I would become so frantic that I would spin past my number, and have to clasp the fingers of my right hand together to keep them from shaking. But even before I flipped open the box, I knew the outcome. It got to the point that I'd shrug my shoulders as if I didn't care. Just as I had years ago in Mother's house, in order to protect myself I'd turn off my emotions and remain tough inside. So I'd simply take a few laps around the air base and return three or four more times, hoping that someone from the post office had made a mistake, found my misplaced letter on the floor, and stuffed it in that precious box. For the most part I'd become numb, for I'd know that tomorrow was another day.

One day during my lunch break, I decided not to check my box. I dared myself to stroll past without giving it a thought. The disappointment had become too much. I got only as far as five feet before I spun around and hurried back. Seconds later my fingers trembled as I pulled out a crumpled, soiled letter. With my mouth gaping open, I focused on the childish scribbling. My heart raced as I tore open the envelope. I impatiently scanned the length of the paper but lost my grip, then stood paralyzed as I watched it flutter to the floor. The distinctive penmanship belonged to Father.

From behind, a friend woke me from my trance when he bent down and picked up my letter. 'What's wrong?'

I took forever to form the words. 'My . . . ah, my dad . . . he's not doing too well.'

My friend shook his head. 'Hey, man, don't sweat it. Parents they get old, but, hey, his old lady can take care of him. Come on . . . shit happens.'

No! I wanted to scream. *You don't understand* . . . But before I could justify my fears, my friend became lost in the crowd of other airmen retrieving their mail and letting out whoops of joy as they clutched their prizes over their heads. I lowered my head and disappeared in the opposite direction. I wished I had never received that letter.

I wandered outside, found a bench, and sat down. It took me more than half a dozen tries to comprehend the contents of the letter. The more I digested, the more my heart sank. Father had written that times were very tough for him. He could no longer find part-time work either washing dishes or filling in as a short-order cook. Feeling ashamed, Father gave up on asking friends to stay at their home for a few nights at a time. With no one to turn to and no money, society's old hero was now alone with no place to live. I wanted to mail Father some money to ease some of his pain.

Rereading both the envelope and the letter, I frantically hunted for the return address, but there was none. Father's handwriting had always been barely legible, but this letter was almost impossible to read. Nearly every sentence was incomplete or rambled on without any conclusion. Words were misspelled, jumbled, or ran off the page altogether. I concentrated so hard on Father's writing that my head began to throb with pain. Suddenly it struck me: he probably had been drunk when he scrawled out the letter. That had to be the only conclusion. That would explain the condition of the soiled envelope, his penmanship, and, more important, the reason he forgot a return address.

In the blink of an eye I became furious. I was so ashamed of the life Father was living. *How*, I wondered, *could he be so foolish to keep drinking?* He had to realize his binges – his entire lifestyle – would be the death of him. *Why?* I yelled at myself. *Why couldn't Father just quit once and for all?* He had been so courageous as a fireman; why couldn't he muster the will-power to deal with something so relatively simple? *How hard was it to throw away the bottle?*

I closed my eyes, replaying the countless times Father had nearly passed out, literally on top of me, with his eyes blood-shot and his clothes reeking from days-old perspiration and spilled drinks. Dad had always promised that he would someday, somehow, take me away from Mother's evil clutches. But even back then I realized it was the booze talking. As brave as Father had been on the job, he had no intention of crossing Mother. Sitting outside the air force barracks, I felt utterly helpless. To me, Father wasn't a bad man. *Maybe*, I justified, *Mother's fury forced him to drink.* Maybe . . . his drinking was his only outlet to deal with . . . ? 'Oh, my God!' I cried out. What if Father's boozing began as his way to escape all the hell between Mother and me? What if I was the reason for Father's drinking problem?

My body shuddered from humiliation. My thoughts swayed between the intense guilt of Father's plight and wanting him to find the determination to help himself. I thought if I was the reason for Father's alcoholic condition then I was responsible for the family's devastation, my parents' separation, and for Father's downfall at the fire station; *I was the reason for his current condition.* The sudden wave of shame was so overwhelming that I began to weep. In some sense, in the back of my mind I had always known this. As a child, I knew I was the bad seed. Somehow I had made everyone I had come into contact with miserable. As an adult, I had to make things right – buying a home for Father and me was not enough. Who knew what condition Father would be in by the time my enlistment was complete? I was the only one who could ease his pain, and I had to do it now.

I decided to wire Father some money. Even if he used the funds to buy booze, I didn't care. *Who was I,* my conscience argued, *to judge a grown man when in so many ways I was still a pitiful child?* After all the hell I had put Father through, this was the least I could do for him. If the money helped to numb his loneliness and despair for a few hours, then so be it.

After I reached a definite decision, my fingers quit shaking. I wiped my tears away and stared at the crumpled envelope. Seconds later I shook my head in disgust after remembering that Father had left no return address. 'Goddammit!' I exploded. 'Why?' I cried as I clutched the letter. 'Why is my life constantly plagued with so much bullshit!' When my own mother tried, for eight years, to kill me, I never fought back. I never ran away. I had just taken the abuse by adapting every moment of every single day to surviving. And foster care was no breeze, but I made the best of it. As a teenager I'd worked my tail off while normal kids were having the time of their lives. While scores of others waltzed into the recruiter's office to enlist, it took me forever to join the air force. When my lifelong dream of becoming a fireman was shattered because of some foul-up in the paperwork, I bit my lip and pressed on. And now I couldn't even help my father because he had no address or no phone number for me to call. I couldn't even disturb Mother and beg her for information on Father because I have been excommunicated from *her precious family* – I was not worthy of the privilege of having her unlisted phone number. As I sat and stewed at my latest predicament, I so badly wanted to be anyone other than David James Pelzer. I covered my face with my hands as if to squeeze an answer from my brain.

The only alternative I could think of was if Father by some chance wrote me again. Maybe then he would scribble his address. Whenever I was faced with overwhelming, impossible odds, I always turned to God. As a child I always felt guilty, begging for His time to help me, but now I pleaded for God to keep my father safe and warm. Mostly I begged for God to somehow ease my father's pain. 'Please,' I whispered, 'do what You can to protect my dad. And please, deliver him from all evil. Amen.' After pleading with God I discovered that a film of snow covered my fatigues, the bench I was sitting on, and the entire air base. Even though the tips of my fingers had turned purple and my ear lobes raged with pain, I somehow felt warm inside. As I stood up and walked back toward the barracks, a howling wind blew in my face. I didn't blink an eye. 'It's up to God,' I said to myself. 'Only He can save my father now.'

Days turned into weeks, which turned into months. As much as I waited, as much as I prayed, I never heard from Father.

After graduating from specialty training, I was transferred to my permanent base in the Florida panhandle. Just as my counselor in basic training had boasted, I expected to serve in a typical setting while overseeing civilians who ran the kitchen. But it was not meant to be. I was stationed with a combat engineering group, which entailed spending most of my time laboring under the cover of a tent rather than simply monitoring others in an air-conditioned building. I dreaded rolling out of bed in the early morning, before driving over an hour, in the middle of nowhere, to the field site, and working straight through without a break, then finishing the day at eight that evening, only to repeat the cycle the next day. I detested the job, and I felt as worthless and degraded as I had when I lived with Mother.

As always, I swallowed my pride and rose to the challenge. However, as much as I tried, it seemed that I could do nothing right for my two hard-nosed supervisors, who berated me every minute of the day. I refused to cave in. Because I had a hard time getting the field-burner units, which cooked the meals, up and running in time, I had to begin my day at 3:00 A.M. rather than 4:30. By the time others showed up to begin their shift, I had almost everything cooked and on the serving line and ready to be dished out. But that was not good enough for the sergeants. When I accomplished that feat, I only found myself being chewed out for something else. Every week, it seemed to me, the harder that I'd focus on my tasks, the more I'd screw up. I seemed to be in the middle of a never-ending cycle. It never failed: I always had everything under control, right up until the moment the sergeants peeked in on my progress, only to find me fighting off my latest blunder. A short time later I discovered I was the only cook preparing all the meals, while the sergeants and other airmen seemed content to watch me sweat away.

Then one afternoon, out of the blue, my supervisor, Technical Sergeant Campbell, a towering black man who always bellowed at me while his gleaming white teeth maintained a vise lock on one of his huge cigars, called me for what I thought was another lecture on my shortcomings. 'I tell you, Airman Pelt-der, you a working fool,' he stated with a wide smile.

My eyes dodged down to my splattered boots. 'I'm trying hard, Sergeant Campbell.'

'You need to understand, squadron's job's to build bases from nothin' and fix runways in the event they've been damaged after an enemy attack. Runway's not fixed, planes don't take off. Mind can't be on business of buildin' and fixin' if everyone's hungry. It's that simple. You get what I'm sayin'?' I nodded my head. 'I get you to work hard, to see if you quit. That's why I ride ya. Ride ya hard. Gets the job done, that's all that matters to me. We're in this together. You still needs to work on adjusting that attitude, though. Ain't no shame being a cook. I know you want something else; you can do whatever you like in the future. But for now you stay with us,' Sergeant Campbell said. 'You done good! No need to be ridin' on your behind no more,' he stated with a grin as he slapped me on the back.

It was then that I understood why I had been constantly harassed and forced to carry the load more than others: I was being tested. I let out a sigh. *At least,* I told myself, *I tackled a job I detested and was willing to give it my best shot.* Above all, I knew that I would never give up and with my determination I would find honor.

A short time later I found myself on my first temporary duty assignment (TDY). Because of Sergeant Campbell's faith in me, two peers and I were the sole cooks to feed a small group of pilots and support staff in a remote location. The two senior airmen and I worked from dusk to dawn, and our efforts were rewarded with praise. During my stay I began to feel a certain pride that I, in some small way, had contributed to a team effort.

That evening, while the other cooks cruised to the local bars, I stayed behind and studied one of my books. Part of the reason was that I felt enormously intimidated in front of other people. While others would tell wild stories of where they grew up and adventures in school or dating, I would become afraid, lock up like a statue and stutter. I couldn't look anyone in the face, let alone maintain eye contact long enough to tell a joke. So I had decided that I'd rather be alone than make myself out to be more of a fool than they already knew.

Hours later, after reading several chapters of my book, after filing away another written letter to Father that I would never mail, and after staring at the ceiling, I still could not fall asleep. For some reason something seemed to keep me from relaxing. I was wide awake even after my cohorts stumbled in and collapsed on their beds. As usual, whenever I'd become uptight about something, I'd doze off literally minutes before I had to begin another day.

The next day, after serving lunch, one of the cooks thrust a phone in my hand, refusing to look at me. Confused, I shook my head. My eyes darted between my friend standing a few feet away and the phone cradled in my fingers. For a moment I hesitated before pressing the receiver end against my ear. 'Hello?' I uttered.

'David?' The voice seemed to crackle from a million miles away.

My heart skipped a beat. 'Mom, is that you? What is it? What's wrong? How did you get this number? Why are you calling?' I asked my foster mother as fast as the words could spill from my mouth.

'My God!' Alice exclaimed. 'David, I'm so sorry. I beg of you, please forgive me. It took days, and I mean *days*, to reach you. Your squadron . . . in Florida . . . they weren't sure where you were . . . I tried every number they gave me. Please know that I—'

'Wait! Slow down, I can barely hear you! The line . . . it's too much static. Just tell me, what is it? What's wrong?!'

'Harold's fine. I'm fine . . . David, just believe me when I tell you how hard I tried. Honest to God, I tried . . .'

My stomach began to clench. The more my mind ran through every possible option, the more the answer became crystal clear. 'Tell me,' I said as I clamped my eyes shut and uttered a quick prayer, 'just tell me. Tell me he's not . . .'

On the other end of the line I could hear Alice lose control. 'Come home, David. Come home,' she sobbed. 'Your father's in the hospital. They say he's not going to . . . he only has a few days . . . Come home, David. Just come home.'

As the words sank in, the receiver dropped from my hand. I fell to my knees as a static shrill from the phone filled my head.

chapter 4

WISHFUL THINKING

Nothing could have prepared me for seeing my father. I had zero tolerance for the assistant at the nurses' station at Kaiser Hospital, in the heart of San Francisco, who stood in front of Alice Turnbough and me as if we were invisible, while refusing to say if Stephen Pelzer was indeed on that particular floor or even if he'd been admitted to the premises. Because of my insomnia, zigzagging across the country in the middle of the night, and the anxiety of seeing Father, I was ready to explode.

Whatever scenarios I had formulated during the flight over, dealing with the actual situation was far more stressful than I had planned. Aboard the plane, every option seemed cut and dried, but now, I strained just to lean my upper body against the counter to keep from collapsing. I could feel my resistance to stay razor sharp, to retain a crystal-clear focus, drain away. The sterile pine smell nearly caused my nose to bleed and triggered memories of being trapped in the bathroom with Mother's concoction of ammonia and Clorox. The thought of not only coming face to face but actually dealing with Mother whenever she showed up would be hellish at best. My only wish was that somehow Mother would for once find it in her heart to bury her immense hatred and permit me a few moments alone with Father without unleashing her explosive fury.

But maybe, I imagined, I was the one going too far. It was in fact Mother who had called Alice to tell her of Father's condition. Maybe there was already a crack in Mother's defensive armor. When I had spoken to her before joining the air force, she had seemed overly pleasant, even proud of my efforts. For a fleeting moment her soothing tone reminded me of the mommy I had once adored. *What if*, I thought, *Dad's condition brought them back together?* As a small child, before events turned the family upside down, I knew my parents had been deeply in love with each other. I had always heard

302

that a crisis could bring strained relationships back together. There had to be a reason why Mom and Dad never divorced after all those years of separation. So now there was hope. I knew it! The scare of Father being in the hospital could be the best thing to happen for the entire family.

The more I thought about this possible outcome, the more my anticipation of seeing Father grew. Like a lot of folks in similar situations, I, too, had initially overreacted. As my optimism grew, I pictured myself with Father, checking him out of the hospital in a few days, spending time with him one on one, then maybe . . . one day soon . . . I could return again on military leave, and all of us could sit down to a dinner. I told myself, feeling replenished with energy, that no matter what the consequences, nothing was going to be the same. The winds of change had begun to stir the moment Mother broke down and telephoned Mrs Turnbough. The entire charade would be over. Nodding my head in agreement with myself, but nodding more to the deranged woman at the nurses' station, who continued to act as if she was engaged in more important matters, it no longer fazed me. I was in control of my emotions, and I knew that everything would work out for the better.

From out of nowhere, a male nurse wearing a name tag STEVE slid behind the station and took immediate control of the situation. Before I could badger him, Steve read my name, stitched on my green air force fatigues, and let out a heavy sigh.

'My father, Stephen Pelzer, he's here? I mean, he's okay and he's *in this hospital* on *this floor*. Right?' I blurted out. I stared down the arrogant woman, who turned away after tossing her hair in disgust.

Steve began to reply but raised a hand to his mouth as if to first collect his thoughts. 'Man, we've been waiting on you. Yeah, kid, your father's here, and . . . yeah, he's on this floor. But chill for a sec. There's a few things you need to know.'

I rolled my eyes as if to say, *Yeah, yeah, come on, out with it.* 'So . . .' I nagged, 'what's the deal? What happened? He fell down, broke an arm? What is it? When does he check out?'

As Steve rapped his fingers on the countertop, wondering how to deal with me, my ears picked up the faint sound of a hacking cough. Without thinking, I spun to the right and marched into the room next to the nurses' station. It took a few seconds for my eyes to adjust. Before me, shaking like a leaf in a flimsy hospital gown, was the skeleton-like figure of my father. His arms were twitching uncontrollably as he struggled to slide his bare feet in front of him. He seemed to be using whatever strength he could muster to make it to the bathroom. By the vacant look in his eyes I could tell he had no idea of who I was, or even that someone else was in the room with him. Coming around behind him, I slung his arm around my shoulder and helped him into the bathroom. His wafer-thin body trembled against mine as he fought to stand straight while relieving himself. My mind was spinning, and I kept questioning like an idiot, 'Are you all right? Are you okay?' over and over again.

Only after helping Father to his bed did I realize how bad his appearance was. His eyes were blank. They rolled to whatever caught his attention for that split second before drifting off somewhere else. As he lay flat on his back, the only time his arms were still was when he would drag his bony hand over to the other and hold it. Looking into Father's face, I smiled, hoping to catch his darting eyes. The skin around his cheeks was crimson red and stretched thin. I noticed a large white patch taped to the right side of his neck and shoulder but paid no attention to it. Instead I reached out to cup Father's hands. 'Dad,' I gently whispered, 'it's David.'

No reaction.

'Dad,' I said in a firmer tone, 'can you hear me?'

Father's only response was a raspy exhale.

I could hear Alice sniffling from the entrance of the room. Out of frustration, I lay my body next to Father, while keeping my face just above his. 'Dad? Hey, Dad! Can you . . . do you hear me? It's me, David. *Say something*, anything. Dad?'

Studying Father's eyes, I looked for the slightest response. I thought if he couldn't speak, at least he could communicate with his eyes. Minutes crawled by with no answer. I wanted to grab the sides of his face and squeeze out some type of reply that Father indeed knew I was with him.

From the right side of my shoulder I could feel a firm but gentle squeeze. I smiled, knowing Father had snapped out of his trance. 'I'm here, Dad. I'm right here,' I said with a wave of relief. Patting the hand, I nearly jumped off the bed when I discovered it belonged not to Father but to the nurse Steve.

'We need to talk,' he said without the slightest trace of embarrassment.

'But my dad . . . ?' I asked, thinking I could not leave his side.

'I'll stay,' Mrs Turnbough said, as she now stood over my father.

When we were both outside of the room, Steve carefully closed the heavy oak door. 'What's wrong with him?' I demanded. Feeling my anxiety take hold, I pressed for hard answers. 'What type of medication do you have him on? How come he doesn't recognize me? Is it the drugs? How long will it be until he gets better and gains some weight? When do you expect him to be released?'

'Hey, man,' Steve said, raising his hand, 'give it a rest. Didn't your mother tell you . . . ? You don't know, do you?'

'Know what? If I knew, I wouldn't be bugging you!' I sarcastically shot back. 'Just tell me, what in the heck is going on? Please!' I now begged, 'I gotta know.'

Leading me down the corridor, Steve searched for a more private setting. At the end of the hallway, he stopped to offer me a chair. I refused, feeling the need to stand. 'It was about four months ago when your father was admitted—'

'Four months!' I yelled. 'Admitted? Admitted for what? Why didn't anybody call me? Why now?'

'Please,' he interjected, 'give me a chance. Your father . . . he wanted to keep things discreet. A lot of patients are like that. Anyway, it was only after we ran all the tests that our diagnosis was confirmed. David, your father has cancer. I'm afraid it's terminal. He's in the advanced stages. I'm sorry.' Steve reached out for my hands. 'There is nothing we can do.'

'Hang on!' I said, stepping away from his gesture. 'What do you mean, *terminal*? I don't get it . . .'

'David,' Steve said in a deliberate, slow voice, gripping me by the shoulders, 'your father . . . *he's not going to make it.*'

'You mean . . . you're saying he's going to die? *My dad* is going to die? No way!' I shook my head in complete denial. 'Can't you give him a shot of something . . . or I thought there's some kind of chemo treatment. If it's money you need . . . just don't let him die. Not now. Please!' I begged, as if he alone decided the fate of my father.

'David, listen, chill for a sec. I don't know, no one knows exactly how long your father has, but,' he emphasized in a strong tone, 'the thing I do know for certain is this: *your father is not going to make it.* And there is nothing, *nothing*, that you, I, or anyone else can do about it. Come on, you're not a kid. You understand these things.

It's a fact of life. Your father's lived a full life, and now it's his time.'
Steve paused to collect his thoughts. Looking at him, I realized the
immense strain he was under and how hard he was trying to help
me. For a brief moment I wondered how many times a week he
spent with others like me. I felt foolish and ashamed. 'David,' he
said, taking my hand, 'I am sorry. I truly am.'

My thoughts refused to come together. Whatever reserves of
energy I had left suddenly disappeared. Finally, at the one time I
needed to be in control, to be strong, I found myself completely,
pitifully helpless. I had so many questions, but it took everything I
had to form a single sentence. I simply stood in front of Steve like a
zombie. I wanted to release everything and cry. A heartbeat later, I
suppressed the urge. 'Four months?' I asked incoherently. 'You're
telling me my dad's been here that long? How long has he been . . .
like he is now? Why can't he talk? Is he doped up? I mean, he acts
like he doesn't even recognize me . . . I don't, I just don't understand,' I stammered. 'I just wanna know. That's all.'

'Well,' Steve began, sliding a chair for me next to his, 'as I was
saying, your father checked in a few months ago. Since then his
condition has rapidly deteriorated. The growth was primarily centered on the side of his neck, but has since spread to his throat. He is
on medication, and under the circumstances I'm sure you can
understand why. That is the reason he lacks discernment. If we take
him off the "meds", his understanding might improve, but the pain
would be unbearable.'

'So . . . he'll never be able to say anything again? Ever . . . ?' I
asked as my voice trailed off.

'That is correct. Not any longer,' Steve replied, nodding his head.

I sat on the edge of the wooden chair, rubbing my hands together,
wondering what I could do to comfort Father. For once in my life, I
was actually glad when I thought of Mother. With all her diabolical,
scheming tactics, *she* would know how to deal with Father's situation.

Breaking the silence, Steve spoke up. 'Ya know, when your dad
first checked in, I don't think he fully understood the seriousness of
his condition. A great deal of patients are like that. They won't allow
themselves to be examined until it's almost always too late. Call it
embarrassment, ignorance, ego, whatever. But please know that we
did all that we could for your father. It's important for you to know
that.'

'Yeah, I understand. Thanks, but,' I probed, 'was he able to speak when he first came in?'

Steve barely nodded his head.

'So, why didn't he call anyone?' I inquired.

'He did,' Steve frowned. 'He must have, right after he was admitted, 'cause his other son, your brother Ronald, came over to visit. They spent a few days together. I guess he's in the military, too.'

'*Ronald?*' I gasped. Ronald, the oldest of my four siblings, who I hadn't seen since my rescue in 1973, had finally escaped Mother's wrath a few years ago by joining the army as soon as he turned eighteen years old. I hadn't thought of Ron in years. 'He was able to talk? I mean, talk to Ronald?'

'Well, as much as he could. Your father was in a great deal of pain. It was soon after your brother's visit that he lost his ability to speak,' Steve gently explained.

'How long ago . . . I mean, when Ronald came to visit?'

'Uhm, I have to say about two, almost three months ago,' Steve answered.

'What about the others? Mother and my brothers, Father's firemen buddies? Were they able to talk with him? I mean, my father was coherent? He knew who came to see him?'

'Hey, man,' Steve interrupted, 'what others? Ronald was the only one who came to see him. No one else saw your father.'

'But Mother, she must have seen . . . ?'

'No one,' Steve adamantly stated. 'And I mean *no one*. We didn't even realize he was married until we rechecked his admission papers. I understand, after talking to your father, that they're not exactly in close contact. There is a chance, knowing how your father guarded his condition, that your mother doesn't even—'

'Oh, she knows,' I objected as my entire body suddenly tensed.

'I'm sure if she—' Steve countered.

'No way,' I said. 'You don't know. You don't know her.'

'And how do you know?' he asked.

'Come on, Steve, think about it. Who do you think called my brother Ron and Mrs Turnbough?' I returned.

Steve paused, then switched the focus from Mother's total lack of compassion. 'Well, right now, since you're the only relative available, you need to be thinking about your father's arrangements.'

I still refused to admit I could be losing Father. 'So . . . what can I do?' I asked. I somehow wanted to uncover something, anything that the staff had forgotten or overlooked which might be a cure for Father's disease. Everything was hitting me at once. 'So! Why doesn't he look at me? Does he know, I mean, is he capable of knowing I'm even here?'

Steve sighed as if growing tired of my endless stream of questions. 'For the most part, it's fifty-fifty at best. He seems more coherent in the morning but, for the most part, no more than a few minutes at a time. He's at the stage when he drifts off quite a bit. Part of the reason is due to his meds. Again, this is all normal for his condition.'

The more the nurse talked, the more I began to feel a crushing weight bearing down on my shoulders. My mouth hung open as I stared upward at Steve.

'I know it's a lot to deal with,' he stated, shaking his head, 'but first things first. Spend time with your father. That's priority one. I can walk you through the paperwork and all the other things you need to do when the time comes. For now, just spend time with your dad.'

'But . . . I, ah, I don't know what to say,' I replied. 'I mean, he doesn't even know that I'm with him.'

'Well, David, he's been in seclusion for nearly the entire time since he checked in. Your father doesn't show it, but he's scared. He knows he's not going to make it. Anything you can do would mean the world to him. He's all alone in there.' Steve gently scolded, 'You have to do this! Just . . . just reminisce about all those good times you spent together. Keep him "up". He'll know.'

Yeah, all those good times, I said mockingly to myself.

I thanked Steve for the umpteenth time, while he assured me that he would stay in close contact. But even as I reluctantly returned to Father's room, I somehow believed that my dad would miraculously pull through.

As I cautiously reentered the Lysol-scented room, Mrs Turnbough turned and flashed me a bright smile. 'Your father and I are having a nice chat. I'm just telling him what a fine young man you've become,' she said as she patted Father's hand.

'Oh, my God! He can talk?' I nearly screeched.

'Oh, you don't need to blabber away to hold a conversation, right, Mr Pelzer?' Alice returned in a smooth tone, as she continued to smile at Father. 'I'm gonna leave you two dashing gents alone for now.' She laid down Father's hand and eased out of the room.

Not knowing what to say or do, I felt paralyzed. For the first time in nearly two years, I finally had the chance to be with my father. As I stared at him, I suddenly realized I knew nothing about him. For as long as I could remember, my visits with Father had probably amounted to less than ten, maybe twenty hours together, so now, I wondered, had I been caught up over the last few years craving to love Dad, hoping he *may* love me in return? As a child, I so badly wanted to be with him, but watching Father's body writhe as he struggled to breathe, I so desperately wanted to flee. Without warning tears began to swell in my eyes. 'I, ah . . . I tried to write. I mean, I wrote . . . but I wasn't sure of your address.' I shook my head, knowing I sounded like a complete idiot, but I stammered on. 'I got your letter when I was stationed at the base in Colorado. I didn't – I mean, I couldn't find your address. I'm sorry. I truly am. I didn't know. I would have come sooner. I just didn't know.'

I turned away to compose myself. The last thing I wanted was to lose it in front of my father. My focus had to be his needs rather than my sorrow. After a few minutes of silence, I remembered Steve's advice about keeping Father uplifted. Out of nowhere, a memory of Father and me, when I was a preschooler, sprang from my mind. I sat on Father's bed while tucking the sheet under his frail back. 'You may not remember,' I began, 'but when I was four, maybe five, all of us went to the Russian River . . . Early one evening, after dinner, you stepped out for a walk, and I tagged along behind you . . .' The more I spoke, the more that fragment of time crystallized. 'I snuck out and walked behind you, tracing your steps. I had those little Forest Ranger boots, and I tried to keep up while being as quiet as I could. I think I made it five, maybe ten feet away from the cabin, when you heard me. You spun around so fast I thought you were going to bite my head off, but you—' I stopped for a second to smile at Father's face. 'You simply extended your giant hand and scooped my fingers into yours . . . Then, without a word, you let me walk with you.

'I have to say, as a kid that was pretty cool. At the time, between Ron, Stan, and me, to be able to hog a few minutes alone with you, well, back then that was all I talked about after our walk. It was that summer when I knew that's where I wanted to live. The trees, the river, the smell, those precious moments with you, that's when I knew. Back then, with you, I was safe. Back then you were my superhero; you were my Superman. I know it sounds kinda dumb,' I scoffed, 'but that was the only time you held my hand. When *you* wanted to be with *me*.'

I stopped for a moment to close my eyes. As I did, my vision with Father faded away. I could feel my insides swell up. As a teenager in foster care, I couldn't wait to become an adult so Father and I could work through our past. I had somehow hoped it would bring us closer together. I had no intention of making him upset or trying to use what happened to pin the blame on anyone. I simply thought if I had the answers, I would free myself from being doomed to repeat the tragedy of mindless hate and violence. Looking down at Father, I felt that Mother had deliberately manipulated this situation, calling me only *after* Father was unable to utter a single syllable.

'When I was at The House, I remember all those times you'd come home from the fire station for just a few minutes to check in on me. Mother didn't know it, but I made sure I timed your arrival when I was washing the dishes so I could actually see you. Sometimes I got too far behind with my chores and . . . well, you know Mother . . . I paid the price when you were gone. I knew she'd never allow you to go down to the basement, so I'd wash the dishes over and over until I heard you open the front door.' I paused to stare directly into Father's eyes. 'You saved me. Even though it was only for a few seconds alone in the kitchen, it made all the difference. Sometimes if you brushed against me, I'd breathe in your Old Spice cologne. You were my invisible force field. I'm just sorry you, the boys – everyone – had to deal with so much crap. I somehow thought I'd be able to make it up to you – to everyone.

'You see, Dad, I knew. I always knew you came back to The House for me. And now, no matter what happens, I'm here for you. No matter what anybody says, I'll protect your honor.'

From behind me I heard Alice close the door. Without breaking my train of thought, I nodded at Mrs Turnbough and continued talking. For the first time in my life I was actually opening up to my father.

'As a kid, I was always proud of you being a fireman. I . . . I, ah, remember when Mom was a den mother for the Cub Scouts and she drove the pack down to your fire station on Post Street. You looked so cool in your dark-blue uniform, leaning against the polished fire truck. I think I was maybe in the first grade. It was then that I knew I wanted to be a fireman. That's why I joined the air force.' I abruptly stopped. I didn't have the guts to tell him the truth: I was a pathetic 'food service specialist'. Even if I lied, I knew Father would hear it in my voice. I so badly wanted him to be proud of me. I wanted to prove to him that I was not a loser, that I would not end up like . . . like . . .

A flash of embarrassment washed over me. The more I gazed at Father, the more I saw myself as a hopeless creature that, no matter how hard I tried, would not amount to anything.

As I cleared my head, my mind flashed to Father's fireman badge. 'Dad,' I asked, 'Dad, do you . . . do . . . do you still have your badge? Your fireman's badge?'

I pictured the time he had blushed with pride as he displayed his silver badge, with his identification number stamped above the seal. 'It's the only thing he has,' I said to Alice in a soft voice, 'that showed what he did. After everything, it's all he has . . .'

'David!' Alice gently whispered. 'Your father, look!'

My head snapped back toward Father. His head continued to twitch, but now more to the right, while his eyes strained as if telling me to look in . . . 'The closet!' I exclaimed. 'You want me to look in the closet?'

I searched Father's face for any type of reaction. It seemed as if he was committing whatever strength he had on leaning toward the closet. I jumped from the bed and flung open the door. Neatly hung were a pair of worn pants, a pressed shirt, and a heavy overcoat. My eyes darted to the bottom of the closet. I searched for Father's Pan Am travel bag he had used to pack his belongings when he worked at the fire station. All I could find was a pair of scuffed shoes, brushed off and placed neatly together. An odd sense of fear began to overtake me as I flung open the drawers, only to find a pair of white socks. No clothes, papers, wallet, and no fireman's badge. I turned to Father, shaking my head. In a moment of stillness, as he kept his eyes locked onto mine, I understood what he was trying to convey.

I gave Father a slight nod before my hands patted down his coat. Part of me felt jittery for invading, of all things, my father's privacy, while a deeper side couldn't wait to find his prize. I found a set of official-looking papers that I stuffed into my back pocket without thinking. I could read them later. The only thing that mattered was Father's badge. After two attempts, I slowed down my pace. I used the tips of my fingers to trace every outline, for any opening, while I studied Father's face. I felt a small bulge. Without looking I yanked out a small, black leather casing.

'Is that your father's—?' Mrs Turnbough began to ask.

'Yeah.' I interrupted as I opened the small case, revealing the silver emblem inches in front of Father's twitching face.

Immediately his breathing eased. While holding his badge, I began to feel the magnitude of what it meant to him. The only thing that represented Father's adult life – besides his broken marriage – was what I now held in my hand. Father shut his eyes as if in concentration. I then noticed his lips quivering. I bent my head down, but much as I tried, I could not decipher any sounds escaping his mouth. When his eyes blinked open they again locked onto mine. Out of fright I shook my head. 'I don't know!' I snapped. 'I don't know what you're trying to . . .' Suddenly I felt the slightest sensation on my right hand. Glancing down, I saw Father's bony crimson fingers wrapped around my hand clutching his fireman's badge. As my hand began shaking from Father's trembling, he sealed my fingers around the black leather case. Searching his eyes, I understood. I whispered into his ear, praying he could hear me, 'As God is my witness, I will protect and keep your badge. I will carry it as a sign of honor.'

As Father's grip eased, I could tell he had fallen asleep. Before his fingers could slip away, I kissed his hand. Standing beside his bed, I gently laid Father's vibrating hand on his chest. Turning toward the door, I saw Steve standing beside Alice. 'He'll be able to rest now. You've made him very happy. He told me months ago, when he checked in, that he wanted you to have it.' We both looked down at my right hand, still clutching Father's badge. 'It's the right thing to do,' he said in a broken voice. 'Today was a good day for your father. A very good day.'

'How do you – I mean, I don't know if he can understand me. If he could just talk—'

'He is talking,' Steve replied, 'and you're learning to listen. It's hard, but as long as he knows you're there, beside him, that's all that matters.'

'He's not . . . my dad's not going to . . . to make it,' I cried, choking on the words. Staring at Father, I felt as if a sledgehammer crushed my skull. 'He's going to die,' I whispered to Alice. Instantly, out of humiliation, I gasped, slapping my hand against my mouth. I couldn't believe I had uttered those words. Up until that exact moment I had still held out for some dramatic turn. In some odd sense, I felt that by saving Father from his life of despair, I would in effect save myself.

Returning to Steve, I stood half frozen. 'So, how will I know . . . when it's time?'

'You still have some time. Someone is always watching over your father. We'll let you know if there're any changes.' Steve had returned to his official nurse's tone. 'It's going to be all right.'

After assurances that Father would be resting for some time, I found myself driving Mr Turnbough's whale-sized, oxidized blue Plymouth Fury. With Alice beside me, I slowly cruised through Golden Gate Park on John F. Kennedy Drive. At Rainbow Falls, I stopped 'The Blue Humpback' and rolled down the window. I recalled the hundreds of times both Mother and Father had driven Ron, Stan, and me through the park. With our noses pressed against the glass of our beat-up station wagon, we'd stare at the endless rows of freshly planted flowers in brilliant colors. If one of us dared to crack open a window, I'd suck in the distinctive scent of the eucalyptus trees. And if Ron, Stan, and I were lucky, we were able to catch a glimpse of the red-ear turtles basking in the sun as the silver station wagon rolled by Lloyd's Lake. Back then, as a preschooler, even though I knew Mother and I had our secret, I felt safe when all of us were together as a family. Back then I had prayed that my life could someday be as serene and as beautiful as the park.

Snapping out of my trance, I realized what I had to do. 'I have to see her,' I stated without emotion.

'I know,' Mrs Turnbough answered, nodding her head in agreement.

I was surprised. I had expected her to challenge me. When Mother had called me hours before I joined the air force, it was Alice who had rightly stopped me from seeing her. Whenever I had a question regarding Mother, I had always run it by Mrs Turnbough first. But now, I realized, Alice was giving me a wide berth, allowing me to make my own decisions.

After taking a final mental snapshot of the cascading water at Rainbow Falls, I shifted the car into drive, eased my foot off the brake, and coasted from Golden Gate Park . . . to Crestline Avenue in Daly City.

chapter 5

SLIP AWAY

I walked hesitantly up the red steps that led to Mother's house, knowing there was no turning back. For the life of me, I didn't understand why I still felt drawn to her. By choice, I left Mrs Turnbough in the Plymouth. Above all, I didn't want to drag her into my slimy world any more than I already had. At the top of the steps, before I could chicken out, I gave a strong rap on the front door. The moment I did, I saw there was no way for me to control my trembling hand. I hid it behind my back, taking up my military stance. I was thinking about straightening my hair or anything else that would make me more presentable when the front door opened.

A small boy's eyes ran up my air force fatigues. 'Hey, are you a Pelzer, too?' The child turned his head and yelled, 'Mom! There's a Pelzer here to see—'

'My God, Kevin?' The words flew out of my mouth. With perfect clarity I remembered one Saturday, years before, when Kevin was a baby crawling on the floors, dressed in his blue outfit. Back then his shrieks of joy had melted my ice-cold heart. Now, as I studied his features, I was certain Kevin had no idea who I was.

His eyes grew wide. Total shock was etched in his face. 'Mom?'

From the back another figure emerged. A taller, freckle-faced teenager shoved Kevin aside, taking an offensive stance – as if to protect his home. He put on his best tough-guy act as he stared me down. As much as Russell tried not to show it, though, I could tell by his fidgety movements that he was nervous, too. 'So . . . what do you want?'

In a deliberate tone I replied, 'I need to see her. Please?' I added, attempting to defuse my younger brother's hostile attitude.

'Yeah, right,' Russell nodded, as if I had an appointment.

Extending his arm toward the living-room, Russell permitted me to enter but followed behind me like a prison guard escorting me to the warden. Part of me felt that Russell's disposition was due to Mother's years of psychotic brainwashing, or maybe jealousy that I had escaped her wrath while he and my other brothers remained behind. I also felt in some odd sense that Russell resented me, perhaps because he might have become my replacement.

With Kevin bouncing in front of me, I scanned the living-room. In seven years nothing had changed. Every piece of furniture seemed as if it were glued to the same position, as it had for years even before I was rescued. The only thing that appeared different was how small and dark the room had become, due to the paper-thin, soiled drapes and nicotine-stained walls. An overpowering stench of urine, from what I assumed was Mother's small herd of dogs and cats over the years, nearly made my eyes water. I let out a cough and shook my head in disgust. This was a woman who when I was a tiny child had hosted elegant parties and prided herself on her home's grandeur.

Upon stepping into the kitchen and seeing Mother's silhouette, my entire body locked up – my hands fused to my sides, my chin fastened to my chest, and my eyes staring at the multicolored spots on the floor. A split second passed before I regained my senses. But it was too late. By the sickening sound of her chuckle, Mother had just witnessed my automatic response. Standing a safe distance away, putting my hands behind my back in the at-rest position, I leaned against the countertop to stabilize my dizziness.

Mother was emptying a brown paper bag full of groceries. As she grabbed a loaf of Wonder Bread, she flashed me one of her snake-like smiles, and asked, 'So . . . I can assume you've at least seen him?'

'Yes, ma'am,' I replied with no emotion.

'And how is *he*?' Mother sarcastically probed as she began folding her grocery bags for future use.

Calculating my every word, I asked, 'You haven't seen Dad, have you?'

With the speed of lightning, Mother slapped her hands on her hips and took three steps toward me. Surprisingly, I didn't back away. I stood my ground. 'That's none of your goddamn business!' she ranted. 'Listen to me, you little shit! *I'm* the one who did *you* a favor! I didn't have to phone that – that *foster* person. I didn't have to do that, you know.'

'Mrs Turnbough,' I calmly corrected her.

'Whoever.' Mother returned to the kitchen table and started to cough, emptying her lungs. She acted as if she were under an over-whelming strain. Hearing her agony, Russell slid closer to Mother, as if she might collapse at any second. With a dramatic flair Mother threw up her hands, tilted her head back, and cried, '*I'm* fine. *I'm* all right.' Only when Russell moved behind her again did Mother drop her hands. Then in a vindictive tone she hissed, '*You* of all people, you have no right. No right whatsoever to judge me.' Her face went from bright red to ghost white. 'No one knows,' Mother sobbed, 'no one knows how hard this is . . . *for me!*'

'Now look what you did!' Russell yelled.

For a moment I stood there confused. *Is my direct questioning truly setting her off?* I thought to myself. *Or perhaps my presence is too much for her?* This could also be another dramatic performance of hers, trying to shift the focus of sympathy onto Mother and not to the situation at hand. With little to lose I dug further. 'I just don't understand. How is it that Dad's been in the hospital all this time and you haven't seen him once?'

I hit pay dirt. 'The pain would be too much for me to bear. Don't you understand? I've known him longer . . . than anyone. It's just, it's all just too much.'

Outwardly I nodded at Mother, as if I agreed with her statement. But inside I was saying to myself, *And the Oscar for best performance – under fake duress – goes to . . . Catherine Roerva Pelzer!*

Interrupting my thought, Mother went on to claim, 'You have no idea. He was never there for me or his children. If he wasn't at work, he was with his pals out drinking God knows where.'

Again I nodded, knowing full well that Mother was throwing out whatever excuses she could to justify her lack of common decency and compassion.

'Boys,' Mother announced, 'excuse us,' she decreed, with a wave of her hands.

'But, Mom,' Kevin said.

'I said, leave!' she screeched. 'Before I really give you something to cry about!' Like magic, the boys scurried from the room.

As Mother rambled on about her anxiety, my head began to throb from the day's overload. I didn't know how much longer I could stay in this house. 'So,' I interrupted, 'what about Father?'

'I told you!' Mother roared.

'No, ma'am,' I said in a soothing tone. I met her gaze, and she knew I wasn't going to back down. 'He's still your husband. He's all alone. He's not doing well—' I caught myself before I lost control. In front of Mother – *in her house* – I had to maintain total composure. 'Dad's not going to . . . make it. There's not much time.' I waited for Mother to respond, to wake up and throw on her jacket and race off to see Father. Knowing that I was passing the point of no return, I stepped toward Mother and said, for her ears only, 'He's the father of your children. Don't end it like this. Please, I beg you. Do the right thing. See him.'

By the strain on Mother's face, I knew I was getting to her. Ever so slightly she nodded her head in agreement. Behind her faded silver-framed glasses I could see her eyes begin to water. The last time Mother had lowered her guard like this was the day before I was rescued in March 1973, when we had both stood in the same room, while she broke down and began talking about her past. Standing in front of her now, I prayed I didn't lose her . . . again. My sole objective was for Mother to be with Father. *Maybe, somehow*, I thought, *a few minutes alone might wash away the years of animosity.* 'Come on,' I softly pleaded, 'let's all go see Dad. Come on.' I smiled as I extended my hand to hers.

'Oh, David,' Mother cried as she stretched out her trembling arm. Without hesitation I took her hand. Mother let out a sigh as I cupped the palm of her hand.

'It's going to be fine. It's going to be okay,' I told her. Her body began to weave. Mother closed her eyes tightly, as if washing away all the pain she had kept locked in her heart. She let out another, deeper sigh, as if cleansing herself. As I looked at Mother's face, her color seemed to change. A reddened look began to take over. Before she opened her eyes, I knew what was coming. Suddenly her hand felt ice cold. 'Don't go,' I softly pleaded. 'Please, don't go.'

The same moment I released her hand, Mother jerked it away. Just as years before, I had enough sense to back away from her. By the evil smile I knew *The Mother* had returned with a vengeance. 'Oh, what a manipulating little shit you are! How I bet those foster people of yours are ever so proud! And here you come traipsing into *my* house, telling *me* what to do. Who made you the Messiah?' Mother paused to reload, while she struggled to light a cigarette. It took several attempts for her – not only to light it but to take a drag – due to her violent shakes. 'You' – she thrust a finger at my face while smoke poured from her mouth – 'of all people, have no right. You might be something to the *United States Air Force*, but you know . . .' Mother hesitated, as if to have me feel the full meaning of her words, '. . . you know what you are. Deep down, you're nothing. You don't even deserve to breathe the same air as me or my children. How could you march into my house, as if you owned the place, and tell me what I should or shouldn't do? How could you, after all I've done for you? What gives you the right to come back?'

I tried to maintain an unthreatening stance. As I had years before, I simply shut down and became a cyborg: part man, part machine. Yet her words 'after all I've done for you' caught me by total surprise.

'Done for me?' I muttered.

'You still don't get it, do you?' she sneered after taking a long drag. 'I didn't have to release you. No! *I let you go.* I was done with you. You gave me no pleasure, so you were disposed of.' It took me a few seconds to comprehend what Mother was saying. 'You were trash, and like trash I simply tossed you away.' Mother struck the pose of a refined aristocrat and said in a sarcastic voice, 'Oh, dear me, how rude. Am I bursting your bubble? And all this time I bet you thought your blessed little saviors at your school were the ones responsible for your dramatic deliverance.' Then in a tone barely audible, Mother whispered, 'You don't know how fortunate you were. I could have ended it all. Just . . . like . . . that,' Mother emphasized with a snap of her fingers. 'You know what you are, so if I were you, I'd keep that little trap of yours shut. Don't push it. You were lucky once, so don't think I haven't done anything for you.'

Behind her, Kevin popped his head in from the dining room. Seeing him, Mother assumed the role of the grieving wife. With a fresh stream of tears rolling down her face, Mother tilted her head back as if to ease the intensity of her pain. As if the effort of standing was too much for her, Mother struggled to sit down. In all, I thought it was a fair performance. I also was certain that Ron, Stan, Russell, and Kevin had seen her charades many times before.

'Care?' Mother reached out to Kevin with an exaggerated trembling hand. 'Oh, I care about your fath – about *him*,' Mother corrected herself. 'I care. That's the problem, I care too much.' Mother finished by wiping away her tears.

I deliberately remained stoic. I had already pushed her too far, so I did not want to say anything that might reignite the situation. Still, I had surprised myself by not caving in. I couldn't believe I had actually penetrated her defenses, let alone stood up and questioned her status as a wife. Either I was exceptionally lucky or Mother was losing her grasp.

Kevin broke the tension. 'So, you used to live here?'

Surely, I assumed, Mother must have told him something about me and why I no longer lived with them. She had to justify my going away. As much as she reigned over everything, snippets of the truth must have seeped out. I flashed Kevin a smile and he smiled back. 'Yes,' I stated with confidence, 'I lived here, but that was a long time ago—'

'Oh no, he didn't!' Mother retaliated. 'Don't listen to him! He's . . . he's a liar. He's not one of us.' To emphasize her point, Mother raised a finger. 'Remember what I told you? About . . . about bad people?'

I locked into Mother's eyes, thinking to myself, *You're right. You are absolutely right. I am not like you.*

Before Mother could continue, Kevin broke in, 'So, you wanna see my house?'

An overwhelming sense of curiosity took hold as I passed Mother and followed Kevin into the dining room. I walked around the table before stopping to gaze at the red towers of the Golden Gate Bridge. Distant memories from childhood began to flood my mind. I looked down at the backyard, where I had spent countless hours sitting on my hands on top of a bed of rocks – as a form of twisted punishment for whatever crime I had committed. I remembered shivering in the chilling fog, scarcely dressed, but too terrified to remove my hands and rub them together for fear of being caught. Feeling myself weaken, I turned from the sight. I remembered the good times, when Ron, Stan, and I were preschoolers and played in the sandbox, and how one summer afternoon Mother had taught us all how to catch a lifeline – just in case, she said. Back then Mother seemed so devoted about every aspect of her children's well-being. I could still picture Mother, on her hands and knees, wearing her gardening gloves, weeding her flower beds that she had taken so much pride in, and how she used to fill the home with the orchids she had meticulously cared for. Even now I could still see the remnants of what had once been.

'That's the waterfall Stan built,' Mother pointed out, breaking my trance. I was startled. I was so tired that I hadn't heard her approaching. 'He's so good with his hands. He keeps everything up and running. He's such a handyman, you know. And with Ronald serving his country, I don't know what I'd do. Stan, he's the man of the house now,' Mother boasted with pride. From behind I could hear Russell let out a sigh of frustration. By the look I stole at Russell, I knew there was a power struggle between him and Stan, who as a baby had suffered a massive fever and was never the same. In the early years Mother had always gone out of her way to shield Stan, by showering him with praise – telling him how brave, strong, and smart he was. But even as a child, Stan became jealous of Ronald, the firstborn, who had Father's confidence while Father was at work.

Continuing the tour, Kevin led me through the living-room, then down the narrow hallway. As I walked down the passage, an odor from years ago filled my senses. I glanced down at the worn carpet and paused in front of the bathroom. Kevin stopped and gave me a puzzled look, asking, 'Gotta go?' I stood transfixed at the tiny room, where I had almost died from being locked in the bathroom with Mother's lethal concoction of ammonia and Clorox. I stared at the far left side of the bathroom floor at the vent – where I had prayed that fresh air would come through before I gagged to death. Turning toward the mirror above the sink, I remembered looking at the fresh pink scars on my chin and my tongue that had skin peeled away from swallowing teaspoons of ammonia. As a child I'd usually steal time to look into the mirror and yell at myself for whatever I did wrong – that had made Mother despise me so much. I had hated everything about myself – how I looked, how I stuttered, everything. Back then I so desperately wanted to somehow transfer myself to the other side of the mirror. But as I grew and became aware of my situation as Mother's prisoner, I knew I could never rid myself of that person in the mirror. For that reason, I still refused to look at myself in a mirror.

'You gotta go to the bathroom?' Kevin again interjected.

'No, I'm fine,' I said with a trembling voice.

From behind, I caught one of Mother's snide smiles. 'Something amiss?' she said in a low tone.

Making our way forward, Kevin led me into the bedroom that I assumed he shared with Russell. The last time I had seen it was when Kevin was sleeping in his crib. Growing tired of the tour, I simply nodded and turned away. 'And this,' Kevin stated grandly, 'is Mom's room.' Still amazed at how small everything seemed, I stepped into Mother's sanctuary and gawked at her mirrored bureau, where her once cherished perfumes and figurines were coated with dust.

As I turned to leave Mother's bedroom, I noticed a set of photographs. The upper left picture was a color bust shot of Ronald in his army uniform. By the look of his expression, Ron was his own man. He looked fantastic in uniform, and I was proud of him. He had escaped. My eyes then darted to the outdated school photos of Stan, Russell, and Kevin. In the middle of the surrounding pictures was a black-and-white portrait of Mother on her wedding day. Catherine Roerva Pelzer was absolutely stunning. Her eyes glowed with love. Her complexion was flawless. She seemed to radiate the model of a young bride who couldn't wait to live a lifetime filled with happiness. As I admired Mother's portrait, I suddenly realized that Father was nowhere in the set of pictures. Looking closer, I discovered that I, too, had been excluded. I now understood why Mother refused to have anything to do with Father. How could she help Father, if, in her mind, he had already died?

I turned around to search for Mother, but she had retreated to the safety of her kitchen. I could not understand how one person could hate so much. I could only imagine how she had validated her cover story to the boys. *How easily she could make anything that troubled her completely disappear.*

'So, what d'you think of my family?' Kevin chimed. Turning away from the set of pictures, I saw Russell's face, which revealed a crocodile smile acting as if everything was exactly as it should be. *So be it*, I thought to myself.

'Fine,' I replied to Kevin with a grin before pushing myself past Russell.

At the end of the hallway Mother stood, puffing on a cigarette. 'So, I can assume you found everything you came to see?' she said in a belittling tone. Facing her, I became too distraught to reply. I knew I should leave, that it was useless to try to convince Mother to see Dad. Sensing my weakness, Mother added, 'Ronald's in the army, you know. *He's* doing quite well. He sends me all of his medals.' Mother turned away, then produced a box of assorted medals. Dumbfounded, I could only look into the box as Mother bragged on, 'This one's for sharpshooting . . . and this one's for basic training . . . ah, this . . . I'm not quite sure. There are so many of them, it's hard for me . . . anyway, he's stationed in Alaska. They don't just station *anybody* there. He won't say it, but I know better. He's one of the best military police they've ever had. I'm so proud that one of my boys is serving their country. You can't imagine how proud I am,' Mother sighed, laying it on as thick as ever.

'I'm . . . in the air force.'

Mother glanced up from her prized box in bewilderment, as if she had no idea, even though I was wearing my air force fatigues. 'Ah, yes, well, isn't that nice. Army wouldn't take your kind, eh?' she said. 'So, what is it you do to protect our country?'

I smiled triumphantly. 'I'm a cook.'

As soon as the words came out of my mouth, I felt like an idiot.

'*A cook?*' Russell broke out laughing.

'Didn't you enlist to become a firefighter?' Mother asked bitingly. 'What happened, did they boot you out of that too? I thought the air force was about jets. No one's a cook.'

The silence that followed extended into infinity. Without a word I nodded my head, as if to thank Mother for her time and for her hospitality, before seeing myself out. I could feel all eyes on my back as I closed the front door behind me, and only then did the living-room erupt into a burst of laughter. Easing back into Mr Turnbough's car, I let out a deep breath.

'Had to do it?' Mrs Turnbough asked.

'Had to. She doesn't have, nor ever did have, any intention of helping Dad,' I stated in a cold voice.

'My Lord,' Alice replied, 'how does a person like that—'

I interrupted Mrs Turnbough by raising my hand. 'I only hope she gets hers. It's just not fair.' I struggled to control my breathing. I thought my head would explode from the surge of hatred I had for my mother. Sensing that *her boys* were spying on me through their bedroom windows, I regained my composure, started the car, and coasted away. I had somehow thought things would be different. But, like always, when dealing with Mother, I had been foolishly wrong.

The next morning, I returned to Father's room. With my head slumped, I bumped into a chaplain, who simply nodded at me without a word and patted my shoulder as if I were some stray dog.

I debated what to do next. I felt the urge to do something. I wanted to kidnap Dad and take him to a baseball game, take a walk through the park, even sit in the back of a dingy bar and simply shoot the bull, go anywhere as long as we were together. But there was no way I could do anything.

Excusing myself, I reached into the back of my flimsy wallet and pulled out a crumpled note before making a telephone call to Mother's mother, to tell her about my dad.

Seemingly within moments of replacing the phone in its cradle, Uncle Dan, Mother's brother, flew out from the elevator. After a crushing hug, he pulled up a chair next to Father's bed and whispered in his ear. I stood against the door beside Alice to give the two men their time together. I knew I did the right thing. As Uncle Dan held me, he fell over himself with apologies. 'We didn't know about him. No one knew,' Dan said.

Watching Uncle Dan and Father together, I sensed the closeness they once must have shared. 'Hey, Steve,' Dan grumbled, 'come on, you gotta get dressed. I got a few good bottles and a couple of nice-looking dames in the car. Come on, we can't keep 'em waitin'.' I nearly jumped out of my skin from the audacity of what Uncle Dan said. Of all the settings, it was the most tasteless thing I could possibly imagine. But by the response from Father's eyes, I realized the true meaning of Dan's statement. I selfishly felt as if I were babying Father, protecting him from anything I deemed might be harmful. Quietly, Alice and I slipped from the room, where I found a couch, closed my eyes, and pondered what to do.

Sometime later Uncle Dan woke me with a shake, pleading for me to go home with Alice. Peeking in on Father, I felt that my weak need for rest was somehow a betrayal to him. Emotions of guilt over Father, elation at seeing Uncle Dan, and the rage I still felt about Mother swirled inside my head all the way home until I lay down again, this time on Alice's couch.

Almost the moment I fell asleep, Mrs Turnbough shook me

awake. I bolted up, thinking the worst. But before I could race into the kitchen and seize the phone, Alice gently informed me it was not Kaiser Hospital but my grandmother. Dealing with Mother's mother had never been easy. As a child, Mother and Grandmother always had an intense love-hate relationship, which my brothers and I had seen whenever one of the women had a run-in with the other. Though we were by no means close, I had always felt as a child that Grandmother was a covert ally.

Wiping my eyes, I fought to regain my focus. Knowing that Grandmother was getting older, I had made sure when I called her hours ago that I deliberately downplayed the drama of Father's condition. Because of Mother's complete lack of regard for Father, I suddenly felt like an arbitrator. I was proud. For the first time, I was truly helping 'The Family'. Reminding myself not to frighten her, I smiled and said in my most cheerful voice, 'Grandma! I'm so glad you called. Everything's fine. Father's sleeping and there's really been no change since this after—'

'What in the goddamn hell is going on down there? What in the hell are *you* doing?' Grandma blasted.

'What is it?' I said, stumbling. 'What's wrong? Father's okay. I – I just . . . left him.' With Grandmother's silence on the other end, I became seized with anxiety. 'I just left over an hour ago. I'm sorry; I only wanted to catch a quick nap. I checked with the nurse. He said it was okay and that he'd call if there was any change. I swear it. Since I've been back, I haven't had an hour's sleep. I'm so sorry,' I said as I felt a wall of guilt crashing down on top of me. I knew I shouldn't have left the hospital, so *I* could relax, while Father fought for every breath just a few miles away.

Grandmother broke in, 'What in hell's bells are you babbling about? I don't give a damn about your father at the moment. Right now all I want is an explanation. *What did you do?* How could you . . . at a time like this? Holy Mother of God . . . you've got some explaining to do, young man!'

I was totally confused. 'What?' I begged. 'Grandma, please, slow down. Did what? What are you—'

'Don't you interrupt me. Don't get too big for your britches. I'm sick and tired of you, of everyone talking over me. I'll be goddamned if I have to sit here, sit here all alone and put up with . . . with this!' I couldn't believe my ears. I slapped my hand against my forehead for the crime of committing yet another atrocity. Biting my tongue, I readied myself for the next volley.

'You know damn well what you did – storming into your mother's house this afternoon . . . ranting and raving like a mad man . . . terrorizing her and tearing up everything in sight . . . throwing things . . . demanding this and that . . . inspecting every room as if you were goddamn General Patton! You're lucky she didn't call the police. Just who in the hell do you think you are? How in the world could you act like that at a time like this? Does anybody care to think about . . . to think how I feel?' Grandmother paused to cry into the phone. 'I'm all alone here. I'm not getting any younger. If I live to be a hundred . . . I am very, very ashamed of you, David James Pelzer!'

All I could do was shake my head as Grandmother continued to berate me. I knew it was pointless to inform her that I, in fact, had not threatened Mother nor had I destroyed her house. Even the timing was off by a day. But much like Mother, no one could tell Grandmother anything. All I could do was reply with an occasional 'Yes, ma'am' or 'No, ma'am' whenever I felt a response was needed. An hour later, and after repeating herself for the umpteenth time, I broke in. 'Grandma, I saw her *yesterday*, not today. And when you talked to Mother, just before you called me, was she . . . was she drunk?'

Hundreds of miles away, I could hear Grandmother suck in a deep breath. Intentionally, I had pushed her buttons. I was in no way trying to be disrespectful, but rather calming Grandmother down before she drove herself to a frenzy. Sensing she was close to a meltdown, I thought it best to bring her back to reality with a question so startling she had to see the situation for what it was: one of Mother's futile ravings. 'Well,' she insisted, 'you know damn well she was! Drunk? She's always drunk. I'm just sick and tired of her calling me. I mind my own business, you know. I don't bother a soul, and every day it's always something about *her* that *I* have to deal with. I've told everyone and now I'm telling you: I'm not getting any younger out here. It's not easy . . . but does anyone care to think about how I feel? Do they? Well . . . ?'

Grandmother's self-pity sounded word for word like Mother's self-centered speech just one day ago. 'Grandma?' I lightly interjected. 'If Mom's drunk when she calls you, maybe you should, you know . . . not take what she says to heart.' Grandmother was by no means feebleminded; on the contrary, she was an intelligent, over-bearing individual, who seemed at times to relish demeaning her daughter. As I carefully tiptoed past Grandmother, I suddenly real-ized the problem: her attention was never on the crisis at hand, but rather on *her* and how *she felt* at the time of the problem.

Feeling drained, and before Grandmother could fire off another round, I said, 'Listen, I know it's late back there, so I'll call you later. Sorry to have disturbed you. I gotta go. I'll give Father your best. Bye.'

As I gently lowered the telephone, I could hear Grandmother erupt like a volcano. 'David James Pelzer! Don't you even think about hanging up on me! I'm sick and tired of everyone walking all over me, like some doormat. You'd think, as much as I've done, that someone would be kind enough to think about my feelings . . .'

As I dragged myself back to the living-room couch, Alice ex-claimed, 'My Lord, you look a mess!' Since I avoided mirrors as much as possible, I could only imagine my appearance. 'You haven't slept in Lord knows how long, and you eat like a bird. And now your face and neck are beet red . . .' Mrs Turnbough placed her hand on my forehead. She shook her head in dismay. '. . . and now you're burning up.'

As Alice disappeared into the bathroom, I exploded, '*Man, what is their problem?*' Returning a moment later, she presented me with some aspirin and a glass of water. With one swoop I tossed the aspirin into my mouth and gulped down the water. 'I don't get it,' I said to her. 'They don't care. Not one of them. Mother nor Grand-mother even asked about Father. And now,' I shouted as my frustration spilled over, 'it's like Father doesn't exist. It's too much for them. Or he's not important enough? I don't know. They didn't ask about him – how he's doing, what's going on, nothing. They didn't offer to lift a finger. Everything, all the time, is always *them*. How they feel their pain. Poor pitiful them. Dammit!' I swore, hit-ting my knee.

I quickly caught myself. 'I'm sorry.' I didn't want Alice to think I was upset at her. Feeling myself run out of steam, I added, 'I don't know what I'm doing . . . I mean, about Father. I just wish I had a real family who loved each other or for once could bury their hate and do what's right. That's all I wanna do.'

'David!' Alice cried. 'Wake up, we're late. It's after nine. We've overslept.' Before she could finish, I shot up from the couch, brushed my crumpled fatigues, which I had worn for the last four days, and bolted to the front door. In record time Alice and I arrived at the hospital.

Sprinting down the hallway, I met Steve at the entrance to Father's room. Extending his arm, Steve blocked me from entering. 'We need to talk,' he stated. Peeking in on Father, I noticed that except for his intensified breathing he seemed the same. But I knew by Steve's forced smile all I needed to know. 'David, you need to understand . . . sometimes they can't . . . they won't go . . . until they know the ones they love will be fine. You . . . ah, get what I'm saying, David?'

I fully understood, but the moment was too much for me. 'Hey, David,' he went on, 'your dad, he's in pain. You have to tell him you'll be fine. You have to let him go. You understand, right, David? He won't pass until you do this. Ease his suffering. It's the right thing for him. It's the proper thing to do. He won't pass until . . .'

I turned to Alice. 'Could you go in and talk to him, please?' I begged, before fleeing to the far end of the hall, where I found a wooden bench. With a million thoughts running through my mind, I became fixated with my cheap Timex watch. It showed a few minutes to ten. Clasping my hands together, I prayed. 'I've never really asked You for much. And You know what I've been through. I guess I thought I could save him . . . So, if You could grant me this . . . if there's no way that he can get better . . . then take him. Ease his pain and take my dad. Amen.'

Not knowing what to do next, I wiped away my tears, cleared my mind, and made my way to Father's room. A small legion of nurses and specialists, who had probably been Father's only contact with the outside world for the past few months, cleared a pathway as I stepped into his room. Alice turned toward me after patting Father's arm. 'You're a good man, Mr Pelzer. God be with you,' Alice said with tears swelling in her eyes, then left the room. From behind me Steve whispered, 'Let him go.' Everyone else filed out after him.

Alone now, I noticed how huge the room seemed. The drapes were wide open, and the sun poured through the windows. Besides the bed, all the other furniture and medical equipment had been removed. The sheet to Father's bed was crisp, and his gown seemed new. The only sound to be heard was Father's raspy breathing. Taking a long, hard look, I saw for the first time, below the left side of his neck, that Father's bandage had been removed. It exposed the blackened area where the cancer had literally eaten his skin. Even then, as much as I wanted to ease his pain, I could not say goodbye.

Standing by his bed, I took Father's trembling hand. From behind my eyes I could feel the pressure build, and fought to bury the pain.

'I, ah, got . . . some great news,' I lied. 'The doctor says everything's gonna be fine . . . and that . . . they can have you up and outta here real soon.' Part of me felt like a heel, and yet the more I talked, the more my fantasy seemed to take hold. Peering into Father's face, I stated with confidence, 'I didn't tell you this before, but I got a home on the Russian River.' I paused, beaming at Father, who seemed to understand. 'It's got knotty pine walls and ceilings. A stone fireplace, your own room. It's always warm and sunny. It's really nice. It's got everything. It's on the river, and when the sun goes down, the water's as smooth as glass. At night you can smell the redwood trees . . . it's a piece of heaven, Dad. Heaven.

'Remember that time when I was a kid and you let me walk with you that summer at the river . . . you said it was like heaven. You and I can live there . . . and go fishing, sit at Johnson's Beach, or do anything we want. And in the summer . . . we can go to San Fran and catch a game at Candlestick – just like you always said we'd do. We can be like a real father and son. Just the two of us.

'We made it, Dad! We really made it! Everything's gonna be fine. We can be together . . . and live at peace. We got a home, a real home. No more fighting, no more troubles, no one's gonna kick us out. We got it made! It's gonna be fine. You just relax and . . . I'll take care of you . . . I'll take care of everything . . .'

I broke off when I felt Father's trembling fingers clutch my hand. Never before in my entire life had both of us looked deep into each other. His dark eyes were perfectly clear as they bore into mine. I could somehow feel the immense shame, loneliness, sorrow, and pain in Father's gaze. 'I've always been proud of you. You've always been my hero. And as your son, I swear to God, one day I will, *I will* make you proud. I always have and always will love you, Father. Now you relax . . . and I'll meet you at the river.'

With whatever strength Father had, he strained to lift his head to mine to kiss me on the mouth. With my free hand I held him from behind his neck as delicately as possible. The two of us had finally joined as father and son. I returned the gesture by smiling at him and kissing him on the forehead. Then, like so many years ago, as he had that summer when we strolled together at the Russian River, my father winked at me before he slipped away.

I held Father's body as long as possible before I eased his head back onto the white pillow. Looking at Father's face, I felt so utterly stupid for thinking that I could have somehow saved him. Time seemed to come to a halt as I gazed at the man I had so long wanted to be with. After closing Father's eyes, I thanked God for allowing me to be with him during his last moments. With the tips of my fingers I rubbed my lips, thinking how Father had never kissed me before. No matter what void had existed between Father and me in the past, I now had the memory of being with him when it counted most. It was something I would forever cherish.

Stepping outside the room, I saw that Steve understood. With a piece of paper in his hand, he dialed the phone and gave it to me. 'What?' I asked in a daze.

Not looking at me directly, Steve muttered, 'Your mother . . . she wanted to know as soon as it happened . . . the moment he passed away.'

Closing my eyes, I could feel myself drift. At the lowest point of my life, Mother, in all her grandeur, had maintained control of the situation. As always, I wasn't even worthy of the privilege of her majesty's unlisted line, but was somehow good enough to do her dirty work. At the other end of the phone line, I could hear Mother's heaving voice. I swallowed hard and performed my function. 'This phone call is to inform you that your husband, Stephen Joseph Pelzer, has just passed away.'

I stopped for a second, surprised by my deadpan tone and lack of compassion. As much as I prided myself on manners, at that moment I didn't give a damn about Mother or her dramatic, self-centered exploits. Mother didn't even flinch. 'Well . . . yes. It's really better that way, isn't it? Uhm . . .' A moment later the line went dead.

I stared at the phone, which seemed welded to my hand. From behind the nurses' station, Steve pried the phone from my fingers. 'We need to talk,' he said with a bright smile. 'Remember, when I told you that he wouldn't go until he was ready?'

With tears now freely running down my face, it was all I could do to nod my head yes.

'Your father wasn't ready. He held on . . . he waited . . . he waited for you.'

'For me?' I repeated.

'Yes!' Steve said with conviction. 'Out of all the people he's met during his life, your father hung on so he could say goodbye to you.'

'But,' I babbled, 'he, ah . . . he couldn't even speak, not even with his eyes. He couldn't—'

'Doesn't matter,' Steve replied as he came from behind the counter. 'He knew what he was doing. David, listen carefully, your father fought as long and as hard as anyone I've ever known under those conditions. He could have given up a long time ago. He knew the outcome; he knew he wasn't going to walk out of here. He waited. He waited for *you*! You get what I'm saying?' Steve asked as he held my shoulders.

'Yeah,' I said, 'I understand now. I really do.' Wiping away my tears, I said, 'I appreciate everything you and everyone else did for him. At least' – I stopped to look at the small group of staff – 'at least he wasn't alone. For that I'm grateful. I truly am. Thank you. Thank you all.'

Shaking everyone's hand, I saved my appreciation for Steve last. All I could do was nod my head, up and down.

'It's all right, man, I understand,' he said before embracing me.

Reaching behind to my back pocket, I pulled out a faded piece of black leather. 'It's my father's badge,' I announced triumphantly.

'He wanted you to have it. He told me so,' Steve said, taking my hand.

'It's the only thing he had that was his . . . that no one could take away.' I paused to collect myself. Without warning I felt an overwhelming urge to crawl into bed, hide from everything and everyone, and sleep forever. 'One day I'm gonna make my dad proud,' I adamantly stated. 'I will!'

'David,' Steve said, shaking his head, 'not to worry. You already have. He told me himself. He's proud of you. He told me you made it . . . that you made it *out* of whatever situation you were in.

'Your father's "up there" right now. He can see you.' Steve stopped for a moment of introspection. 'Maybe he was never physically with you. But up there, he'll be with you . . . always.'

Four days later, on a foggy Monday morning, I parked Mr Turnbough's car in front of the same Catholic church Ron, Stan, and I
had briefly attended with our aunt years ago as preschoolers. Upon
entering, I thought I was late – the services were apparently under
way. Trying to be as inconspicuous as possible, in my olive-green air
force fatigues, I stepped with Alice lightly yet quickly down the left
side of the aisle before sliding into one of the front pews.

While praying on my knees, I couldn't believe that I had dis-
honored my father by being late for his service. After thanking God
for relieving Father's pain, I concentrated on the service. In an odd
sense, I was excited to hear the good things others would say about
Father. *Maybe*, I thought, *I could learn something about him. I* had
always wondered about my parents' pasts, their ideas, their outlooks
for the future, how they met, fell in love, why things turned sour,
how as a couple they seemed to have it all but lost everything. I
especially wondered about the love that I felt they had at one time
for each other. But instead the priest hastily began to run down a list
of announcements. 'This Wednesday evening's sermon will be
canceled. But the potluck dinner will still be served at the regular
time . . .' I turned to Alice in disgust.

It was then that I noticed behind the pulpit there were no
bouquets, wreaths, or even a casket for Father. 'Look.' I elbowed
Alice.

Mrs Turnbough leaned over and whispered, 'Your mother said
your father's wishes were to be cremated.'

'No way!' I erupted. 'He was a fireman! Get it, *a firefighter!*
They're paranoid of getting burned . . . No!' I said, trying to
restrain my fury, 'This is wrong. Totally wrong. Dad wouldn't want
this!'

'I know,' Alice gently replied, 'but it's too late. She already . . .'

Not wanting to hear my father's fate, I turned away and caught a
hateful glance from Mother, who sat directly across the aisle from
Alice and me. By her look she seemed outraged that I was in the
same building with her and her precious children, who for the most
part appeared to be bored of the whole affair. My concentration
returned to the priest, who cleared his throat before chanting his
final blessing, '. . . of the Father, the Son, and the Holy Spirit. May
the Lord be with you.'

'And also with you,' the congregation answered.

'Go in peace,' the priest concluded.

A surge of anger came over me. *How could I have screwed up and missed Father's service?* On my knees I cursed myself for somehow misunderstanding the time of the funeral. Alice leaned over, saying, 'I could swear that your mother said nine o'clock.' I nodded, checking my watch, which read a few minutes after the hour.

Turning from the crowd, the priest bowed before stepping away from the podium. But by the sudden change in his face, the priest must have looked at Mother. Without breaking stride, he returned to his pulpit and unfolded a paper. 'Pardon me,' he said, 'the church wishes to recognize the passing of Stephen Pelzer, who now rests in the hands of our Heavenly Father. A retired fireman of San Francisco, Stephen is survived by . . .' The priest paused to read his notes. '. . . Stephen is survived by his beloved wife, Catherine, and his four children: Ronald, Stan, Russell, and Kevin. Let us pray.'

As I bowed my head, I realized: *That was my father's entire eulogy.* Ten, twenty words. A lifespan said in a single breath. My father wasn't even worth a single flower, a prayer offering, anything. *How empty,* I thought, *his entire life spoken within a blink of an eye.* Then I recalled the words: *his four children.* 'Oh, my God!' I swore to myself. 'She did it again!'

I fired a glance at Mother, who wiped her swollen red eyes with a clean white handkerchief. As always, she didn't miss the opportunity to make herself the center of attention. Surrounded by *her children* for others to behold, the beloved Mrs Pelzer played the role of the grieving widow to the hilt.

The priest broke my trance. 'Peace be with you.'

'And also with you,' the congregation again answered.

'This mass is ended. Go in peace.'

While standing, I maintained my hard stare at Mother, who lost her footing as she struggled to get up. I could hear a series of muffled gasps from the crowd. Per her dramatic display, all eyes turned to Mother. From behind me, I could hear people rushing toward the widow. I shook my head in disgust.

'Dah-veed?' someone called. 'Dah-veed, do you remember? You remember us?'

I turned toward an elderly couple standing before me. It took me a moment to realize that they were my old next-door neighbors,

Tony and Alice. 'You remember us, yah?' Tony asked in broken English. I could remember him smoking his pipe while he pushed his wooden lawnmower across the grass when I was a preschooler. But when I was older, I also recalled that winter when Mother's game was having me skate up and down the block, nonstop in near-freezing weather, wearing only a worn-out T-shirt and a pair of shorts. Once Tony stepped outside, bundled in a thick jacket, to pick up his evening paper. All we could do was nod at each other. Somehow we both understood. The last time I had seen him was days before I was rescued. Because of the closeness of the houses, you could walk up the stairs that led to the front door and easily see into the small kitchen window of the neighbors' house, which was just a few feet away. Late in the afternoon, Mother drove her foot into my face as I lay sprawled on the kitchen floor. For a second Tony's eyes had met mine. Blood was pouring from my mouth and nose. As always, he understood, but was unable to do anything. Times were different back then.

'You be okay now. I see you in the army air corps. You be fine,' Tony said with pride as he held my shoulders. With his wife, Alice, standing beside him, he stated, 'We proud of you. Everyone knows. You a goot boy. We all, de whole neighborhood, know about you and Ronald, joining the service. You goot boys. Always goot boys.'

Out of embarrassment, all I could do was nod. 'You come to see Tony and Alice when army gives you time to come home.'

Before I could reply, a band of men in dark blue uniforms stepped forward. I swallowed in awe as the group of firemen from Father's station stopped in front of me. For a moment I thought they had mistaken me for a member of Mother's party. A man, who I assumed by his commanding presence was the captain of the station, took my hand and whispered into my ear, 'Your father was a good man and one hell of a firefighter. Don't you ever forget that, son.'

'Yes, sir, I'll remember, Captain,' I promised.

'And do you remember your favorite uncle?' a voice from the past asked.

Among the group Uncle Lee, my father's longtime partner, emerged, giving me a hug. One by one the men from the station paid their respects, in the process seeming to form a protective shield from Mother.

'Thanks, Lee,' I blurted.

'For what?'

'You know . . . for *acknowledging* me. I was there when . . . he passed away. But you guys shouldn't be with me. I don't want to do anything that may set her off,' I said, glancing over at Mother.

' "Acknowledge", my ass. Ain't nothin' can pry us away. He loved you boys. You, David, need to know that. Maybe he didn't say it, and maybe he wasn't there for ya, but he always thought about you kids. Things just . . . well, they didn't work out. And if Ronald was here, I'd tell him the same thing. You boys need to know. No one's perfect. Your father did things I didn't approve of, but,' Uncle Lee adamantly asserted, 'your father wasn't evil. Whatever his short-comings, it was never intentional. Get my meaning?'

I nodded my head. 'I understand. Thanks, Lee.'

'Listen,' Lee knelt down, 'your father gave his helmet to Ron. Do you have his badge?'

Checking behind me to ensure I was safe from prying eyes, I confided, 'Yeah, but I'm not so sure I'm supposed to have it. Am I supposed to give it to you guys? What do I do?' I swallowed hard. 'Give it to her?'

'Not on your life!' Uncle Lee cried. 'Listen up. It's your father's way of saying how much you meant to him. He wanted so much to give you kids something, instead of all the hell you boys were put through. David, you got shortchanged quite a bit and' – Lee paused to look in the direction of the pulpit – 'and I expect you're going to get the shaft before this matter is through. You keep it. To your father . . . well, that badge represents the kind of man he longed to be – on and off the job. To him it's worth more than any amount of money. Do we have an understanding? What your mother doesn't know won't hurt her. So, keep your mouth shut and keep that badge. Do your namesake proud.'

I felt as if I were ten feet tall. For a shining moment, I was a real person.

Outside the church, I shivered from the morning chill. A thick gray blanket of fog swirled above. '*Excuse me!*' Mother interrupted in her best sarcastic, pompous tone, '*Mrs Trewn-bow*, I require a moment alone to speak with *The Boy*.'

Alice – who had suffered years of Mother's psychotic 'disciplinary instructions' on what a burden I was to society in general during late-night drunken ramblings – had had her fill of Mother. Before Mrs Turnbough could give Mother a piece of her mind, I intervened and led Mother to the side of the church. Alone in the empty parking lot, Mother grabbed my shoulder and spun me around. 'Just who in the hell do you think you are? What gives you the right to show up at a function like this?'

With my resistance completely drained, I returned to my former position of address – with my head down and my arms locked to my sides. 'You called,' I interjected.

'I don't ever remember placing a call to you . . . I can't keep track of everything . . . and don't . . . don't *you* of all people contradict me . . . not today . . . you little shit! I'm not saying I called or didn't call, and if I did, I did so out of *courtesy*. You should've had enough sense to understand that you weren't welcome. But you were never that bright, were you?

'And what in hell's bells do you mean by having all those men fondle you as if you were something special?' Stealing a glance at her, I could tell that Mother was truly upset.

'You listen up! I only brought you out here, from your measly air force base, out of the kindness of my heart. I didn't have to do that, you know. So you stay the hell away from me and my boys! You know *who you are and what you are.* You don't belong. Don't you ever, ever, step foot in my house again!' Mother hissed. This time she didn't use her finger to lift my chin, as she had when I was her prisoner. I looked up on my own and into Mother's fiery-red eyes. Not backing down, Mother leaned closer to me. 'Don't you have something for me? Didn't *he* give you anything before he passed away?'

Ever so slightly, I uncoiled my fingers on my right hand and ran them across my back pocket. I became less tense when I felt the outline of Father's prized badge. Without batting an eye, I returned Mother's cold stare. 'No,' I said. 'Father did not give me a thing.'

'You're lying!' Mother shrieked. In the same instant I felt the sting of her hand slapping my face. Maintaining my stance, I let the blood from my bitten lip trickle to the pavement. Her physical assaults no longer hurt me. Mother's act of aggression was the final nail in her coffin – she had absolutely no control over me, and the only way to dominate me was to beat me. It never really worked when I was a child, and it certainly wouldn't work now. It also meant that Mother

335

must be desperate to resort to this form of treatment, especially in public.

'I called the hospital . . . and they checked his belongings. They said he had the papers when he checked in, so don't stand here and tell me those papers just up and disappeared! And what in the hell gives you the right to dispose of his clothes at his motel? I called and they said you had come by and simply gave them away. So, tell me, tell me just who in the hell gave you the right to march in and—'

'You did!' I interrupted. 'When you didn't visit him. When you deliberately went out of your way not to lift a finger. When you let the father of your children, your husband, someone you've known for years, rot away in a deathbed for months. You did *nothing* to help, but everything you could do to make him feel unworthy and isolated,' I fired back, venting my anguish over Father's treatment. 'Whatever I did, I did my best. At least *I* would have had the decency to give Father a proper burial service. I don't know why you . . . you hate everybody and everything so much!'

'You think you're the only one who's been through hell? You're the source. You made everyone's, every single person's life a *living nightmare*, and you thoroughly enjoyed it. You relished it. You had everything. You blew it. Not me, not Father, Grandma, the teachers, the neighbors, your friends, Uncle Dan, Ron, Stan, Russell, or Kevin. It's not my fault, not then as a kid, and not now! Father deserved better. No matter all the fights, his fault or yours, he deserved better!'

'Why, you pompous, filthy piece of . . .' Mother muttered under her breath. Again she raised a hand to strike me down.

'Don't you even think about it!' I shot back. 'Know this,' I stated in a low, clear voice, 'everything you've done to me, to Father, to everyone, will come back to you. The pain, the suffering, the hell . . . everything!'

'Don't you – you . . . try and change the subject,' Mother fumbled. 'One of the nurses . . . told me . . . he said he saw you . . . go through his jacket pockets stealing the papers.'

Papers? I truly had no idea what Mother had been ranting about. *Unless she was referring to when I was first searching for his badge in the hospital . . . and found a set of documents and stuffed them into my back pocket near my wallet.* My only concern had been for Father's badge. In all the chaos of dealing with Mother, Grandmother, and the lack of sleep, let alone Father's needs, I had stupidly forgotten to look over the papers. For all I knew . . .

My facial expression must have given me away. 'Yeah,' I hesitated, 'I have 'em. I didn't mean to . . . I mean, I meant to give them—'

'Shut up and give me the fuckin' papers!' Mother ordered.

I could only guess that the papers were some gigantic insurance policy that Father had taken out years ago. Part of me wanted to whip out the papers and watch Mother grovel on her hands and knees as I ripped them to shreds. After years of enduring Mother's misery, head games, and torture, I now had control over something she desperately craved. *I now called the shots.* But as I stood in front of this pitiful wreck, I realized that my passing fantasy was not the outcome Father would have intended. In all, I still had the prize of prizes. But by withholding the documents, I thought I would somehow discredit whatever dignity Father had. *No matter how many times Mother had plotted to kill me, stooping to her level was something I could not do.*

'Here,' I said as I unfolded and presented her the papers. 'It was a mistake. I forgot I had them. Really, I did. I never meant to keep anything from you. I would have given them to—'

In a flash Mother snatched the papers. The only time she ever moved with such speed was years ago when she used to beat me. Her eyes sparkled and she sighed with relief. 'And now, young man, I indeed have everything I will ever need.'

'You lose,' I smiled.

'What?' Mother asked as she leafed through the papers.

'All those years you tried your best to break me, *and I'm still here.* Father's finally free, Ron's in the service, and soon the boys will move out on their own. I'm a good person. I try my best in everything I set out to do. I make mistakes, I screw up, but I learn. I don't blame others for my problems. I stand on my own. And one day you'll see, I'm going to make something out of myself. Whether I dig ditches or flip burgers for the air force, I'll be the best, and somehow, some way, I won't waste my life away. If you taught me anything, you taught me that.' Turning, I saw Mother's boys milling around at a safe distance with a small group of adults. I took a half step forward and pointed a finger in Mother's reddened face. '*Stay away from me.* Everything you've done to others . . .' I stopped as my voice quavered. I could feel whatever energy I had fade away.

The last seven days had taken their toll on me. Taking a deep breath, I lowered my finger and backed away. 'I pray for you every night, I swear to God, I really do. You may have your papers, your money, whatever. You can hate everybody and everything on this planet, but *you* lose!'

Mother stood with her mouth gaping. Before I left her, I clasped my hands together, then made the sign of the cross and leaned toward her ear, whispering, '*May God be with you, Mrs Pelzer, for no one else will be.*'

Ten hours and three thousand miles later, I returned to Hurlburt Field, in Florida, only to discover my somber mood was no match for that of the base. After a small fleet of specially outfitted C-130 cargo aircraft landed, I learned that the air unit had been directly involved in the ill-fated rescue attempt of the American hostages held in Iran. Five of the eight men who gave their lives when a helicopter accidentally sliced into the C-130 had been assigned to Hurlburt Field. To make matters worse, I learned that the men had died the same day Father did.

I woke up in the early morning hours the next day to find I could barely breathe – the sides of my throat had swelled to the size of oranges. After a quick examination at the base's clinic, I was rushed to the hospital and admitted for severe mononucleosis. Since it was the first time I had ever been admitted as a hospital patient, and coupled with the strain of just losing my father, I was terrified. Because of my condition, I was heavily sedated. As the medicine took effect, I was finally able to lose myself and whatever problems I had through sleep.

During the night, I dreamed I was lying next to Father. I tried to stretch my arm toward him and hold his hand, but I could not budge. I fought to scream out to Father, to say something, anything. But, just like Father, I could not utter a single word.

chapter 6

REGROUP

Because of severe mononucleosis, I was heavily sedated in a hospital bed for over a week. Even after being released, I found myself without a clear-cut purpose for the first time in my life. I was devastated that I had lost my father. My sole objective for the past few years had been to push myself beyond any normal limits in order to save every penny, which would enable me to buy my home, then scour San Francisco until I found Dad. Without him, though, sharing the cabin in the serenity of the redwood trees, fishing at the river, talking over a crackling fire, or anything that might resemble an ordinary family life was a complete delusion.

As a shivering child in the garage, I had always dealt with my challenges by pushing down my feelings, thinking of what I could learn from the situation, and doing whatever it took to somehow make things better. I had always formulated the ultimate plans and broken them down to the tiniest detail. This strategy helped me prevail over Mother, served as my protective shield while I was in foster care, and propelled me into the air force. As long as I had a chance – a glimmer of hope in a tunnel of darkness – all I had to do was clear my head, rid myself of any self-pity, and forge ahead.

And yet another part of me felt that my best-laid plans of becoming a knight in shining armor to my father were nothing but an idiotic pipe dream. Since Father and I spent so little time together during his lifetime, we were obviously not that close. But I had always believed that if I could put all the large-scale pieces in place, I could smooth out the minor details of a relationship later. This delicate process had become a guilt-filled obsession. How dare I go to the beach with my air force friends, buy records or even clothes while Father was out in the cold somewhere. It had gotten to the point that I never did anything beyond waking up, working my tail off, returning to the barracks to catch a bit of sleep, then repeating the cycle the next day. Whenever I had a day off, I'd simply sleep in, watch television, or read. To do anything more meant taking money away from my goals. Yet, I had to admit to myself, it was also because of my lack of social skills, taking a chance at making a jerk of myself in front of people. Even as a young man in my early twenties, I'd continue to say the wrong things at the wrong time, and whenever I became nervous, I dug a deeper hole by stuttering uncontrollably.

By focusing on my future, I was able to reject the present.

Months dragged on, and I came to realize that I had used Father as an escape from dealing with my new life as a young adult. Now with Father's death, I had to learn to deal with myself.

I coped with Father's death the only way I knew how: working. I would get off work and rush to the barracks to change clothes before putting in a full shift as a short-order cook at the local Denny's restaurant. After an eight-hour shift I would get off from Denny's with just enough time to change back into my rumpled air force fatigues and head out to the field for a day's work. At times I went without sleep for several days. I really didn't care. I hated my jobs. I hated my life. After a while, when I'd sleep, I often had intense nightmares of being late for either my air force or restaurant job.

At least now when I slept, I no longer had nightmares of Mother trying to kill me. She always used to appear in my dreams standing at the end of a hallway surrounded by a gray mist. But now as Mother moved forward to attack me, instead of fleeing, I'd march toward her, step for step. When Mother would raise the knife above her head, I would rip open my shirt and hiss, 'Do it . . . ! C'mon, do it!' The gleaming knife would remain frozen beside Mother's red face. Stepping within inches of her, I'd whisper, 'Kill me now or let me be!' Even though I was still intimidated by Mother in real life, she no longer had control of my dreams. I had been terrified for so long, yet with Father's passing, day by day I believed I was finally releasing myself from her grasp.

Soon I found out my squadron had been chosen to fly to Egypt and build a temporary air base. Nearly all of the four hundred men assigned to the unit were tasked for the mission. I found myself desperately wanting to be a part of the extraordinary adventure. As a low-ranking airman who had been in the squadron for less than a year I was not considered, but a major officer in charge of logistics spoke with my hardhearted supervisors to give me a chance. And they did. When I was finally selected, I was so elated that I waltzed into Denny's, quit my job, and packed my duffel bag.

The exercise, dubbed 'Proud Phantom', gave me a different perspective on being part of a team. As a cook in the middle of the desert, just outside Cairo, I'd work ten to twelve hours in furnace-like heat during the day, then in bone-chilling temperatures at night, without any breaks. I was proud to sweat side by side with others who also pushed themselves beyond the norm in our combined effort to achieve a military mission. Whenever I'd steal a few moments for myself, I would step outside the sweltering dark green tent and scan the skies for the vintage American F-4 Phantom fighter jets as they raced overhead, showing off to the Egyptian pilots by either making diving passes or pushing their planes through Mach 1, shaking the ground like a volcanic eruption. The shock wave would practically demolish our cooking tent, scattering pots, pans, and every other piece of equipment in every direction. During more serene times, I'd stand outside mesmerized by the streaks of powder-blue and bright orange skies before the sun set beyond the brown-speckled dunes. At other times, just before dawn, when an eerie quietness filled the base camp, I'd gaze at the thin layer of fog, minutes before the rising sun, and watch as a blanket of purple evaporated the mist. Halfway across the world, it was a relief not to worry about my future or be locked away in my past. I had finally found some peace.

Immediately upon returning from Egypt, I called Alice. Barely giving her a chance to talk, I began recalling my adventures of putting in grueling hours at the base camp, my visit to the pyramids and the sphinx, and the loads of postcards I had mailed her and Harold. Finally she broke in, telling me that my uncle Dan had passed away. Cutting the conversation short, I phoned Grand-mother so I could get the telephone number of Uncle Dan's wife, Jane. As always, I didn't know what to expect, so I took a deep breath, waiting to see what mood she was in. I was not prepared for the frail tone of Grandmother's voice. In all my years of knowing her, even as a child in Mother's house, I had never heard her so vulnerable. 'I am truly sorry to hear about Uncle Dan,' I gently said.

Thousands of miles away, outside the limits of Salt Lake City, I could hear Grandmother whimper. After crying for a few minutes, her entire manner began to change. As much as I wanted to 'be there' for Grandmother on the phone, I knew I was just her captive audience. 'No one knows what it's like,' she began, 'to lose your children, to be all alone. No one knows.'

'What?' I exclaimed. 'Did you say she's dead? Mom's dead?'

'Well,' Grandmother sniffled, 'she sure as hell might as well be. You'd think the least she could do is visit her own mother.'

'So she's alive? I'm sorry, I misunderstood, I thought you just said . . .' My words trailed off.

'You know damn well, young man, that when your mother sold the house to some foreigner – and let me tell you, I heard she got a pretty penny for it, too. That house sold so fast it would have made your head spin. And does she offer me anything? Hell no! Not one red cent, let alone grant a kind word to her own mother . . .'

I steadied myself, trying to clear my head. I had no idea Mother had moved. And I truly did not care. All I could think about was my brothers – if they were still with her, if they were safe. Maybe they even had a new chance of happiness. Slowly I came out of my trance, wondering how the conversation had turned. I knew the unspoken rules of speaking with Grandmother: Let her rant as long as she wanted, never question her opinion, never interrupt, and, above all, never ask a question. Any questions could mean dire consequences. 'Grandma, I am sorry, but . . . could I please have the number to Aunt Jane's? I just would like to pay my respects. I've been away for a while, and I don't want her to think . . .'

'Well,' Grandmother said, 'I just don't know if I can find it. I just don't know *what* I'm going to do.' After a lengthy pause, she let out a labored sigh. 'And if that weren't enough, can you believe she settled here?' I could hear Grandmother stab her finger into the phone. 'Here of all places? She doesn't even have the decency to come see me. Not once. Well, if she's waiting for me to traipse over to her place and bow down before her holiness, well, she can wait till hell freezes over! I don't need this, you know.'

Standing in the cramped phone booth, I automatically nodded in agreement. 'Yes, Grandma,' I replied, 'I understand.' Yet, as I thought about it, Mother moving near Salt Lake City made absolutely no sense. I recalled as a small child that Mother had told stories to Ron, Stan, and me about how she despised Utah, the extreme winters, and what she dubbed, 'the inner society of "The

Church".' I would have never guessed that Mother would, of all places, move near her own mother – a person whom she treated with absolute malice.

Clutching the telephone, I recalled Mother's instantaneous change of attitude whenever Grandmother dropped by. Even when I had sat at the bottom of the stairs in the basement, I could distinctively hear Mother's unique way of being both slightly sub-missive and coldly dispassionate. Mother seemed to attempt to appease Grandmother but only to a limit. The more Grandmother tried to reach out, the more Mother refused Grandmother and whatever offers she made. Whenever Grandmother left Mother's home, there was always hell to pay, and I was usually Mother's outlet. Now, leaning against the metal ledge of the phone booth, I could not remember a single gesture of love or compassion between the two women. Straining to pick up what Grandmother was saying, I could not help but make the connection between mother and daughter – both consumed by their mutual hatred and yet they were a mirror image of each other.

From the books I was studying on psychology and human de-velopment, I could only assume that Mother's drinking, vindictive behavior, and her treatment of me were somehow linked to her past.

Grandmother's labored breathing caught my attention. 'And . . .' she huffed, 'I just don't know what to do about Stan. I give him odd jobs and I pay him, of course, but I'm not going to be around forever, you know. I've told him time and time again, he needs to finish school and get a high school diploma. I've told him over and over that I'd pay for a tutor. You'd think he'd listen to me. You'll see, when he's on his own without a pot to piss in, he'll come running to me. You'd think with all I've done . . .'

I had to jump in to keep her from belittling my younger brother, Stan, who had been mildly retarded since suffering a severe fever as a small child. 'Grandma,' I interjected, 'I'm sorry about Stan, but could I please, *please* get the phone number for Aunt Jane?' By the extended pause on her end, I knew I had pushed too hard, but I also knew that the simplest request was always met with a wall of resistance. After several more gentle nudges, Grandmother finally relented. I hung up the phone feeling completely drained. Part of me felt I should mail Grandmother a card, send her some flowers, or maybe take some military leave to visit her. I had been outside the family fold for so long that I wasn't sure what to do or how my intentions would be received. For years I had wanted to do the right thing and make up for years of loss. As always, a blanket of guilt covered me and I wasn't sure how to proceed. Stepping outside the booth, I took in a few deep breaths to clear my head. Yes, I told myself, Grandmother was obviously having a hard time, but I had gotten so wrapped up in her grief that I almost forgot about my uncle Dan.

Thinking of our conversation, I realized Grandmother had said little of Aunt Jane and how her children were coping. When I had asked about my brothers, the question was brushed aside. Like Mother, the center of attention had shifted to Grandmother and *her* anguish.

Speaking with Aunt Jane was completely different than with Grandmother just minutes before. She was more concerned about my feelings than her loss. Trying to take Aunt Jane's mind off Uncle Dan, I told her of my trip to Egypt and my hopes of going to college to make something of myself. 'You already have, David. Dan was proud of you, and all of us here are, too. Don't push too hard and just live life. Take time and enjoy a little.' As we spoke back and forth, I remembered Uncle Dan as a hard-nosed man who had lived as the ultimate outdoor sportsman, and who also drank as much as Mother and Father. I remembered as a child looking deep into his eyes, and sensing that Dan was like Mother – a person with a volatile temper that could erupt at any moment. As Aunt Jane opened up to me a little more on the phone, I felt that her marriage to Dan and the lifestyle that went with it were not smooth. 'It wasn't easy for anyone back then, David. Back then things were different . . . the drinking, everything. It was considered the norm back then: "The days of wine and roses".'

'I'm not trying to pry,' I asserted, 'I just want to know so . . . so I don't do the same as . . .'

I could almost see Aunt Jane nodding in approval. 'I understand. Don't be too judgmental. Like I said, it was a different era back then; for your parents, and their parents before them. Whatever problems we had were swept under the rug. Family skeletons were kept locked in the closet. A lot of us had high hopes that situations we dealt with or how we were raised wouldn't be passed on to our children. It was hard on all of us. If you children can break the cycle, that's all any of us as adults can ever wish for. There are no guarantees in life, so learn from others' mistakes. Enjoy what you can, while you can. Don't let it consume you like . . . well, just let go and let life happen.'

For me, Aunt Jane said it all in a nutshell. Afterward, I replayed every word in my mind, even months after we spoke. Aunt Jane did not know, but her words 'Don't let it consume you' were the last words Father had said to me before I enlisted in the air force: 'Do what you have to. Don't end up like me.' My aunt helped me to realize that whatever had happened between Mother and me had deeper causes than her drinking and abuse. I could only guess whatever anxiety Mother or even Grandmother carried within their heart of hearts. I was in no way looking to place blame on either of them; if anything, I felt a certain sadness for what it must have been like for both of them during their childhoods.

I vividly recalled as a preschooler how, when I called her Mommy, she showered Ron, Stan, and me with endless love, attention, and anything we could wish for. At times, whenever Grandmother left from one of her visits, the four of us would celebrate. It was as if Grandmother was still a parental figure in Mommy's house, and once she departed, Mom was able to do as she pleased. One time, when Grandmother was adamant about Mommy not allowing my brothers and me to play the game Twister for fear of us contorting ourselves into bone-snapping positions, Mom rolled out the plastic sheet and played with us the moment the front door closed. 'Oh, don't mind her,' Mommy cooed. 'She doesn't know how to play. Let's have some fun!' Looking back, I thought perhaps some black hole from Mommy's past had caught hold and sucked in all the goodness and any chance for her to relive her childhood. As a boy sleeping on an army cot, I had always prayed for 'Mommy' to come back and rescue me from 'The Mother'. I truly believed that 'Mommy' would someday wake up, and once she did, all of us would forever live our lives as one perfect, happy family.

In some peculiar sense, I began to feel a certain pity for Mother. Did she, I wonder, have a happy childhood? Was Mother resentful toward Grandmother because of the way she was raised? If so, perhaps Mother became a hateful person because she had not dealt with her unresolved issues? Maybe Mother turned her back on her past, while hoping for the best in her future. Barely in my twenties, I already knew that unless a drastic change is made, the way a person is raised will most likely be the way that person will raise their children. For me it was not a matter of placing blame on Mother, or pointing the finger at my grandparents, but to ensure my freedom to live a life free of misery and despair. And I had to make certain whatever pushed Mommy into the abyss would not suck me in, too. I was still confused and, strangely enough, I still craved Mother's acceptance. For now, all I could do was take Aunt Jane's advice and get on with my life.

After more than two years of being a field cook, I was reassigned to the training section of the squadron, enabling me to work a basic eight-to-five schedule. No longer having to get up at 3:00 A.M. to put in ten to fourteen hours a day, let alone the hour drive to the work site each way, I welcomed the opportunity. The timing of my assignment was perfect. Since I desperately wanted to become an air crew member, I needed to take college classes. As a field cook, there was no way I could take time off even to register. But now I had all the time I needed.

Attempting to better myself through college courses after normal duty hours was frustrating. I had never taken anything beyond basic math while in high school before I dropped out, so fundamental algebra was way beyond my comprehension. Even one of the simplest rules – negative multiplied by negative equals positive – was too hard for me to grasp; I could not understand the logic. Even after the instructor explained, 'It just is,' like a broken record, the equation still did not add up for me. Because I could not apply the most basic of rules, I would spend hours trying to solve a single problem until I would literally bang my head against the desk.

Because I'd still mispronounce words at times and stutter when I became nervous, I'd spend hours in front of the mirror, studying the way I formed my lips as the sound came out. Due to my low self-esteem, I was terrified of girls, and had a complete lack of any social finesse, so I hardly ever went out with friends. I had always known the kind of person I was and where I fit in. It was as it had always been for me: break down the situation, analyze the different scenarios, make a decision about the problem at hand, and cut my losses the moment the issue looked hopeless. My life was black and white.

I got so far behind in class that the only thing I learned was how to curse myself for my stupidity. Part of me felt as if I were trying to become someone that I knew in my heart I wasn't. I thought college classes were the big leagues. While everyone else seemed to pick up on the material, I became completely lost. I had always prided myself on knowing my limitations, and now I was in way over my head. Late one evening I asked myself out loud, 'Who am I kidding?' I threw the math book against the wall and quit the class.

Initially, I was relieved. I was free of the mind-numbing pressures from the class. I spent my free evenings consuming books like *Operation Overflight*, written by the U-2 pilot Gary Powers, who was shot down over Russia. The U-2 was the product of the same engineer who designed the SR-71, Kelly Johnson. As I studied other books that pertained to unique jets constructed by this famed aeronautical wizard – Johnson formed his own division dubbed *Skunk Works* – I realized that in order to have even a remote chance of becoming an air crew member, I needed to return to college. To reaffirm this, I phoned an air crew boom operator who in midair refueled the SR-71 Blackbird, Sergeant D. K. Smith, who told me straight out that not only did the air force require advance courses in math, but the slots to become a boom operator were few and those who applied for the position fought for them with a ferocious intensity. The issue had come down to a simple matter of how badly did I want it, and was I willing to stick it out in order to achieve my dream.

It took two more attempts, and an instructor with the patience of a saint, for me to muddle through the material, until one day something clicked and I understood the hows and whys of algebra – everything suddenly made complete sense. I actually enjoyed solving equations. I regarded math as absolute – no maybes, no ifs, no letting things be and seeing if it works out somewhere down the road. X always equaled something. In math, and as I had always lived my life, there were no gray areas.

With the first hurdle behind me, I applied my efforts to advanced algebra, then tackled trigonometry. My instructors were outstanding. I began to build upon a good foundation, helping me grasp complicated equations with relative ease. My esteem began to take root. I lived in the breathtaking state of Florida, I spoiled myself by purchasing a monstrous motorcycle I owned free and clear, went through intensive prequalifications, and officially applied for a slot as an elite air crew member. I had a fantastic job and even completed rigorous training as a paratrooper. Ever so slowly, I was doing what I could to better myself. For once my efforts were beginning to pay off. Life was great. I felt as I had when I first entered foster care – every day was a precious gift.

One day, out of the blue, at the end of May 1983, I received a letter from my brother Russell. Since I had not been in direct contact with Grandmother for nearly three years, I wondered how Russell knew where to write me. As I sped through the letter, I had to force myself to slow down, so I could digest each word. I was thrilled to hear from one of my brothers, to hear from an actual family member. But as the contents of the letter began to sink in, I could feel my stomach turn. Russell's letter confirmed what Grandmother had told me years ago, that after Father had passed away, Mother had moved and now lived just outside Salt Lake City. Russell also stated that before he died, Mother's primary focus of malice was mainly directed at Father. As evil as Mother had been when I lived in her house, she seemed to have reached new levels of hatred. With Father gone and me removed, it appeared as if Russell had become the target of Mother's rage.

I remembered one time when I was a foster child, I ran into Russell at a nearby school. By the haunted look on his face, I knew. While I was safely tucked away in the county's protective arms, Mother must have been putting my brothers through hell. As a child, I lived with Mother for only twelve years, while my brothers had to endure her vindictiveness until they were at least eighteen.

My thoughts turned to Stan. In the letter, Russell wrote that he was worried about Stan, who had become financially dependent on Mother and was now resenting his situation. He was proud and wanted to be his own person. What, I wondered, if anything happened to Mother or Grandmother? What would become of Stan? What could I do?

Even my older brother, Ron, who had recently married, was not beyond Mother's reach. The letter stated that although Ron and his wife, Linda, lived in Colorado, for Mother's benefit they were only a phone call away. It was not hard to imagine Mother in the middle of one of her drunken binges, telephoning late in the evening and ranting for hours. Knowing Ron was still a military police officer in the army, I could envision him getting only a few hours of sleep before he had to go to work. This poor man, I thought, was bombarded from both sides. When did *he* ever get a moment of peace? How in the world was Ron able to tell Linda about Mother and the history of The Family? If Mother kept to her pattern, she probably cleaned herself up for Linda, playing the role of the loving, overly gracious parental figure who lived the picture-perfect life. While Mother's act may have worked for her years ago, it hardly seemed she could carry on with the charade any longer.

Thinking ahead, I promised myself that if I ever became involved with someone, I would have to protect her from the sickening relationship between Mother and me. Even if it meant going against everything I stood for, I would have to lie. In order to have a chance of a future with anyone special, I would have to bury my past.

At least Russell's letter stated that Kevin, my youngest brother, had little idea of what had happened or what was going on around him now. For Kevin, Mother's way of life and the hell that went with it were perfectly normal. In an odd sense I felt that Ron, Russell, and even Stan did what they could to shield their younger brother. If anything happened to Kevin, perhaps Grandmother could offer him safe refuge. As I reread the letter, I began to feel a deep remorse. All in all, without a doubt, *I was the lucky one.*

The letter ended with a positive statement. Russell would soon be enlisting in the Marine Corps. He seemed proud to join the elite force, and I felt that its camaraderie and values of duty and honor would serve Russell well. At the very least, getting as far away from Mother as possible would do Russell good. I smiled at the thought. Three down, two to go.

As the weeks passed, though, the letter from Russell gnawed at me. Every night as I unfolded the papers that I kept in my Bible, I'd reread the letter. Why, after so many years, had Russell written to me? What did he really want? What, if anything, could I do? After years of working myself stupid on my hopeless quest, I was just now getting a foothold on my life. As much as I still craved answers to my past, part of me did not give a damn. After years of feeling totally worthless, I was now the guy with the fancy motorcycle, with the chance of making something of myself by becoming an air crew member. Overall, I thought I was a good person: I worked hard, was self-reliant, kept to myself, stayed out of trouble, and did whatever I could to better myself. I had all anyone could ask for. As time passed, my childhood was increasingly becoming an illusion.

During one of these evening readings of Russell's letter, I came to a realization. Though I knew my brothers were still exposed to Mother's lifestyle, I, like my father at the time, remained passive to the situation. I never wrote anyone, called, or even mailed a simple Christmas card. After years of trying to fit in, it was I who had become reclusive. I had conveniently become nonexistent. Part of me wanted to tear up the letter in the same way I almost ripped up Father's insurance papers. If I did, I would no longer have Russell's letter tugging on my conscience. I would be saving myself by not being sucked in by my past. Closing my eyes, I clutched the letter. I took a deep breath, envisioning myself shredding it into tiny pieces. Suddenly my hands began to tremble. A wave of shame crashed over me. Opening my eyes, I broke down and cried. I ran the tips of my fingers down the length of the papers. After over ten years of exile, Russell's letter was the only form of contact I had with my family. Maybe the letter was a subliminal open line to my brothers. The least I could do was keep it. For now all I could do was replace my brother's letter in my Bible, and pray for the best.

Three months later, I took military leave for the first time in years, and after a short visit to the Turnboughs, I rode my motorcycle from the Bay Area nonstop to Salt Lake City. Although I would be staying with Grandmother, my intention was to spend as much time as possible with my brothers, and if all went as planned, I would finally come face to face with Mother. Over the last few months since Russell's letter, Grandmother and I had established a fragile truce. Even though at times I was still her sounding board, Grandmother now treated me like an adult capable of making my own decisions. But before my journey, when I had told Grandmother of my intentions, I knew by her sarcastic reply that I had hit a raw nerve. I did not understand what I had said that set her off. As I drew nearer to Utah, I only hoped that Grandmother would not interfere for once. Perhaps spending time with her would not only help us grow closer, but maybe, just maybe, would shed some light on how Mother came to be the way she was. The answers were within my grasp. The only thing that was certain, as I raced my super bike toward the sun, was that I was heading into the heart of my childhood, and my life would be forever changed.

chapter 7

FOOLISH CRUSADE

By the time I found Grandmother's home in the midst of the trailer park, it was well past midnight. I repeatedly knocked on the door, but because of the late hour she had gone to bed. Being exhausted from the nonstop ride from California and frustrated from the built-up anticipation, all I could do was roll out my sleeping bag, which was strapped on the motorcycle, and sleep on one of the patio chairs on the deck.

The next morning I awoke to the sound of the sliding door opening. For years I had fantasized of greeting Grandmother with a warm embrace, as I had seen in so many movies, but before I could unzip my sleeping bag Grandmother was standing over me with her hands on her hips. 'So, I see you made it,' she stated more than asked. 'Sorry,' I yawned, rubbing my eyes, 'it was a long drive.' I smiled as I stood close to Grandmother, then awkwardly leaned forward to hug her. For a second I thought she flinched. I gently held her, wrapping my long arms around her back. Although she returned the gesture, the hug seemed mechanical to me – it had no emotional significance. As Grandmother pulled back, I let go and followed her into her mobile home. An overwhelming scent brought back to me the days when Mother would bring Ron, Stan, and me over to Grandmother's apartment in San Francisco, where we would spend the entire day decorating her artificial Christmas tree. *My God*, I thought. *I must have been five, maybe six years old*. After all those years Grandmother seemed to have the same pieces of furniture in the same perfect condition. I stood with my mouth open as my fingers ran over her piano. Grandmother's house was like stepping into a time warp.

Still a whirlwind of energy in her seventies, Grandmother took me on a trip to the local bakery to purchase a few loaves of day-old bread, then a brief but spastic tour of the city in which her stop-

and-start driving left me nauseous – pointing in one direction, while flooring the accelerator and wheeling the car in a completely different direction. Afterward we both settled outside on her patio for lunch.

For whatever reason, I could not get myself to relax. All I could think about was not saying or doing anything that might make Grandmother upset. So far my visit was nothing like I had hoped for. I couldn't even look at Grandmother's face for more than a few seconds. I found myself turning away whenever I spoke. As I picked at my food, I realized that I was intimidated. Being with Grandmother in person was completely different than our relationship on the phone. In front of her, I was a pathetic child.

The situation became unbearable. Clearing my throat, I broke the ice by asking, 'Are you still getting some good golf time in?'

By the flash in Grandmother's eyes, I knew I opened with the right question. 'Just last week I played a round with a general from Hill Air Force Base. He's a general officer, you know. I asked if he knew you and, well, I guess there are so many of you soldiers—'

'Airmen,' I corrected.

With a sandwich in her hand, Grandmother stopped cold, staring me square in the eye. After a long silence I apologized.

'Well, anyway, you should take time and visit the Air Force Academy in Colorado Springs. Yes,' Grandmother stated, 'you must go and see the chapel. I have a map here somewhere. Now, where did I leave that map?'

As she stood up to leave, I accidentally brushed against her arm. 'It's okay,' I said, 'we'll find it later.'

In a flash Grandmother pulled away and stomped into the house. From outside I could hear her going through various drawers, searching for the elusive map. Minutes later, Grandmother returned to the patio looking defeated. 'We'll just have to go to AAA. I go there all the time. The girls there are so nice.'

The thought of another drive with Grandmother made my stomach flip. 'Grandma, I'm sorry. I didn't mean to have you go through all that trouble, but I'm not going anywhere near the academy. My leave is up in a few days. I'll have just enough time to make it back to the base.'

'Then you just make time, young man,' Grandmother snapped.

I nearly dropped my sandwich. Looking into her eyes, I was met with another cold, hard stare. It took me an instant to realize my error. I was in no way trying to be impolite or disrespectful. I was only trying to make a point that to me seemed perfectly clear. Traveling over twelve hours a day on a motorcycle on the interstate for three days meant I truly did not have time for any side trips.

Trying to redeem myself, I changed the subject. 'Anyway, about two months ago I got a letter from Russell. I hear he's going to join the marines. You must be so proud – the three of your grandkids in different branches of the service.'

'Russell?' Grandmother exclaimed. 'Let me tell you something about Russell! He borrowed my metal chest. I loaned it to him . . . going off with some church group to Hawaii, picking pineapples for the harvest . . . or whatever they do over there. I don't understand why their people don't do their own work. If you ask me, it's nothing but a vacation. Back in my day, when you worked, it certainly wasn't over there among the palm trees, that I can tell you. It was hard work, all day every day.

'Anyway, ever since he came back – high and mighty, I might add – he comes over telling me that I'll get my chest next time; he forgot it or he's too busy. By the time I got the damn thing, it was in a terrible condition. That's *not* the way I had loaned it to him, I can tell you that!'

I sat with every muscle in my face frozen. I could not believe the floodgates I had opened. Grandmother was on one of her spiteful rolls. With my back against the chair, I asked myself if there was any subject, any person, safe to talk about. She went on. 'The chest is useless to me now. You'd think as much as I do, it wouldn't be too much to ask to have my chest returned in the condition I loaned it to him!'

'Grandma!' I halfheartedly interjected, 'you've traveled a lot. You know how it is. Things get banged up. You probably had that chest for what, years? I'm sure Russell didn't know how much it meant to you. Besides' – I shrugged my shoulders – 'he can't help what happens when it's loaded from plane to plane all over Hawaii.'

'Doesn't matter!' she huffed. 'I paid a great deal for that chest. He should have apologized. I may have accepted that rather than his – his treachery. I can't and won't tolerate a liar!'

I wanted to reach over and hug Grandmother's frustration away. I couldn't believe that she had become so worked up over something so petty. 'Maybe,' I said, 'Russell was embarrassed. Maybe he was afraid to bring the chest back to you after he returned from Hawaii. Do you think that might be the reason he might have avoided you?' I delicately asked, trying once again to defuse the situation.

'Doesn't matter. If you can't keep your word, then keep your mouth shut!' Grandmother replied, as if telling me a coded message.

I took the hint and sighed, trying to clear my head. 'Well,' I smiled, changing the subject, 'the place looks great. Did you say Stan keeps it up for you? He does a great—'

'Stan? Let me tell you something about Stan!' Before I could blink, Grandmother launched into another tirade. 'I've told him to finish school so he can make something of himself. I told him what he needs to do. I've offered to help with his reading. If he doesn't get some schooling, well,' she huffed, 'I don't know what will become of him. You can only be a pizza delivery boy for so long. He needs to go to school and learn a trade. I can tell you what I'm not going to do: I'm not going to be the one responsible for him.'

I had had enough. Without her knowing, I clenched my fist under the table. 'Grandma,' I coldly stated, '*Stan is mentally retarded. It's not his fault.*'

'I'm well aware of that. Doesn't mean Stan can go around life looking for a handout,' she retorted. At least she now addressed Stan as a person.

'There's a limit to his understanding, his comprehension. Can you imagine what it's like to read something and not only not understand it, but forget whatever you've read? Believe me, I know. Some of that stuff can be pretty intimidating. And quite frankly, well, I really think he's embarrassed. I think he knows he'll have to break his back and work hard for the rest of his life. I – I . . .' I stammered, 'I don't know him very well, but . . . Stan's . . . well, he's too proud to admit it.'

Grandmother's eyes flashed. 'You don't know a thing about him – or anyone else, for that matter! Like I said, if you don't know what you're talking about, then you should keep your trap shut.' She paused for a moment as if for effect. 'Besides, he needs to be humbled a peg or two.'

My emotions began to swallow me up. Even though the person in front of me was my relative, an elder whom I respected, I truly detested her vindictiveness. Before I said anything, though, I excused myself to the bathroom, where I splashed cool water on my face. Taking a rare look at myself in the mirror, I saw my eyes were still red from the spine-numbing ride of traveling six hundred miles on a motorcycle with no protection against the wind and rain. As I rubbed the back of my neck with a face cloth, my thoughts returned to Grandmother. I could not understand why nearly everything that spewed from her mouth was filled with malice. The manner in which Grandmother spoke, the tone of her words, was nearly a carbon copy of Mother's.

A heartbeat later, I made the connection. *Oh, my God!*

Outside the bathroom, I scanned Grandmother's living-room. As meticulous as it was – every item, no matter how small or how large, was placed in such a deliberate fashion – I could not find a single picture of Mother. Besides a few scattered photos of her grand-children, there were none of Grandmother's husband, who, I was told when I was a child, had passed away when I was a baby, or any other adult relative. I could not help but think the lack of portraits was just like Mother's bedroom when I had visited before Father died.

Grandmother startled me as she came through the sliding door. Her look said she did not approve of my snooping. As she sat in a chair, I could tell by her posture she was upset with me. My fingers grazed a photo of Ronald in his uniform – the same picture I had seen at Mother's years ago. 'Tell me about Mom. I mean, as a kid, when she was young. Was she ever happy?'

Grandmother's head shot up. She sputtered for a second before placing a hand under her chin. 'Happy? Well, uhm . . .' Her voice cracked as she struggled to regain control. She cleared her throat. 'No one was happy back then,' she said as if I should have known all along. 'Things were tough all over. I remember, when I was a young girl . . .'

As she went on, I patiently waited for her to finish. After her ancient clock struck twice, I broke in, 'Yes, but, what about Mom? Do you realize I know absolutely nothing about my own mother?'

'Hard to please. Never appreciative. You'd think for once she'd show an act of kindness.' Grandmother paused as she looked upward. 'I told her she'd *never* finish nursing school,' she said in her 'I told you so' attitude.

'Never finished? But I thought that's how she met Dad? I mean, as a nurse.'

355

'Hell's bells! She worked at the pharmacy across the street from the fire station. Always been that way, out to impress. Always showing off. Never accepted who she really was. Never sees things as they are,' Grandmother grumbled.

I was completely surprised. It had been ingrained in my memory that 'Mommy's' lifetime dream was becoming a nurse so she could help others in need. As a child, I recalled, whenever a kid scraped their knee or bumped an elbow, Mommy, the neighborhood nurse, was always there. My mind began to reel. *Is anything in my life real? Must everything be secrets within secrets? Why are there so many lies?*

Grandmother never broke her stride. 'I told her – over and over and over again – she would never make it as a nurse. She never listened. *Never has, never will.* Never appreciated one damn thing I did for her. Even now, all she does is call me, I don't know how many times a day, drunk as a skunk. Sometimes I just put the phone down and walk off.'

'But why, do you think?' I gently probed. 'What made Mom become the way she is? Come on, Grandma, something in her past had to—'

'Don't you even . . . !' Grandmother commanded, shaking a finger at me as she leaned forward. 'I never, *never* abused her! I might have given Roerva a good swat on the behind; she might have gone without a few meals when she didn't appreciate it, but I never, never abused her!' Grandmother slapped the back of one hand against the palm of the other with such force that I thought her hand would break. 'If you ask me, she had it too easy.

'What you people today call abuse . . . times were different back then. Anyway . . .' She began to calm down. She repositioned herself into the rear of the chair. 'I have no idea what happened back then. That's not my affair. What happens in someone's house stays in their house. It's no one else's business. I see no need to open up Pandora's box. It can't do anybody any good.' Grandmother regarded me as if I were supposed to agree obediently.

All I could do was nod my head in agreement. I heard. And more important, I *understood* Grandmother's message.

After a lapse of silence, she announced to me, 'I was the one who called the county's social services before you were removed.'

I sat dazed by the sudden change of subject. 'I don't understand. I—'

'Don't act so naïve. The woman who visited the house, when your mother dressed you up and paraded you around, I know all about it. And who do you think purchased that bike of yours that last Christmas before you were taken away? Your mother sure as hell didn't do it, I can tell you that! She had new bicycles for all the boys, except Kevin; he was too young. Your mother said she simply forgot to get one for you, and by the time she remembered, well, she was over budget. Or so she said. I didn't have to get you one, you know. I paid for it in more ways than you could know.'

I was overcome with shock. Of all people, my grandmother, who had just adamantly stated, 'What happens in someone's house should stay in their house,' was the one who initially called the authorities. As I sat in front of her, I could not believe my ears.

I remembered that bike, too. As a child in Mother's house, my only possessions were the ragged clothes that I had washed by hand in the basement sink. Even though I was allowed to ride the candy-apple-red Murray bicycle only a couple of times that winter, the thrill of freedom was still phenomenal. I had no idea; I had always thought, that Christmas of 1972, Mother, out of kindness, had broken down and purchased the bicycle.

I smiled and thanked Grandmother for calling social services. But then Grandmother, like everyone else, had always known how I was treated. On one visit Grandmother found me standing in front of the bedroom mirror yelling at myself, 'I'm a bad boy! I'm a bad boy!' over and over again. With tears streaming down my cheeks, I had confessed how sorry I was for making Mommy upset. Another time Grandmother, the overly stern disciplinarian, had cupped my face with both her hands, saying, 'You're the sorriest child I ever met! Quit feeling so sorry for yourself and do something about it!' At the time I didn't know that what was happening to me was wrong – I simply thought I was a bad boy.

Although I had an impulse to reach out and hug Grandmother for all the times she had silently helped me, I held back. Still not one word of compassion or sorrow had escaped Grandmother's lips about the past. She never showed or expressed to me any remorse about Father's death, what my brothers had been put through, or whatever I had suffered by the hands of her own daughter. *Maybe*, I thought, *from Grandmother's point of view, life was full of suffering.* You couldn't engage in self-pity, but rather had to do whatever you could to get out of bad circumstances, no matter how young. And, I guessed, you became hardened from the process.

What had made Grandmother the way she was? What was it that had hardened her heart? In her day, I assumed, she had to be rigid just to survive the times. However spiteful she may be, at least she was a self-reliant adult.

Maybe after dedicating a majority of her adult life fighting just to survive as a widow, while raising two children, she was worn down and fed up with how hard life could be. Perhaps that was one of the reasons Father advised me, before I enlisted in the air force, when I had brought up my childhood: 'You'd be better off forgetting about it. The whole thing. It never happened.' At that time I thought Father was ordering me to sweep the family secret under the rug. But maybe he was protecting me from taking on a lost cause. Maybe that's why Father had become a broken man. As much as he might have tried, his efforts were futile. That might be the reason, I assumed, why Grandmother always referred to the past as Pandora's box – once opened, uncontrollable agony of human suffering would follow. And in the end nothing would change. The back of my head began to throb from the overload. *Maybe*, I told myself, *I just think too much.*

'Well,' I announced as I stood up, stretching my legs, 'I'm off to see Russell. I should only be gone a couple of hours.'

'Oh no, you're not!' Grandmother said. 'You're not to go there. I don't want you seeing her.'

'It's okay, Grandma,' I calmly corrected, thinking she had mis-understood. 'I'm not going to see Mother. I'm only going to see Russell. It's all worked out; Mother won't know. It's okay, honest,' I reassured her.

'You're not to see her. I forbid it!' Grandmother choked up. 'You're not here. Ron's away. Nobody knows; I'm all alone. All she does is call – all the time, night and day. I'm surprised she hasn't phoned today. I don't initiate anything. She's the one who gets drunk and goes on and on and on. The hell she puts her own mother through. If she catches a whiff of you being here, there'll be hell to pay, and I'm the one who'll have to pay the price!'

All I could do was shake my head. I didn't mean to hurt anyone, but in my short visit here, every move, every intention, was being questioned and scrutinized. Once again, I was caught between pleasing Grandmother or visiting my own brother, whom I had not spoken to in ten years. A familiar wave of guilt came over me.

'Grandma,' I consoled, 'don't put yourself through it. If Mother calls and goes off like she does, hang up. It's that simple. Don't let her get your goat. Just hang up the phone and walk away. I don't mean to be disrespectful, but let Mother stay in her own little world. Go out and play golf. You'll be fine. It's only a game to Mother if you play along.'

'You don't know, *no one knows*, the hell she puts her own mother through . . .'

It was then that I felt as if I was being manipulated. As a grown, independent adult, I was growing tired of walking on eggshells with every subject that was brought up, constantly smoothing the waves while practically begging for permission to do something any normal person could do freely. 'I gave Russell my word,' I said. 'I have to see him.'

In a heartbeat Grandmother's tone changed from utter despair to cold vindictiveness. 'Russell, Russell, Russell! He's not worth the time of day. I don't see any good in it. There's no need to run off all over the place just to see him. Nothing good can come of it. If you ask me, he's not worth rubbing two pennies together. That's what I think. I'm not telling you what to do, but if you want my two cents' worth . . .'

I stood in front of Grandmother, waiting for her to order me to stay. And I would have. Without hesitation – just as I always had when faced with a confrontation that dealt with others' feelings – I appeased her by shutting up, swallowing my pride, and forgetting about it. After a lapse of silence, I grabbed my motorcycle helmet, saying, 'It's gonna be all right, Grandma. It's not the end of the world. It's only a visit with my brother.'

Minutes later I was guiding my motorcycle through a maze of road construction, freeing my mind of deserting Grandmother. I parked the Honda CBX on Mulberry Way, where, because of Mother, Russell had been recently taken in by friends from his church. I walked up the pathway not knowing what to expect. My heart raced with apprehension until a tall young man with freckles flung open the door and greeted me with a quick hug. After a fast round of introductions, Russell hopped on the back of the motor-cycle, and we sped off to find a place to get to know each other.

Less than a mile away I parked my Honda next to a pool hall. Stepping inside such a place with one of my brothers was a fantasy of mine – male bonding. I marched up to the long bar, looked the bartender in the eye, slapped the palm of my hand against the bar showing off a twenty, and bellowed, 'A beer for my brother, future marine extraordinaire. In fact, a round's on me! Set us up!'

Dead silence filled the hall. Not accustomed to social drinking, I thought the response was normal, maybe even a sign of respect. I could feel Russell tugging on the sleeve of my shirt. 'Hey, man, relax,' I stated in my 'I'm king of the world' attitude. 'It's on me.' In reality I was broke. But this was a once-in-a-lifetime opportunity. I smiled, patting Russell on the shoulder, thinking of him as another escapee from the asylum. A prisoner of war repatriated. A young man taking the plunge into adulthood. Yes, indeed, a proud moment.

'David?' my brother whispered, breaking my concentration.

'Hey, man,' I cut him off. 'Don't sweat it; you're eighteen, right? Don't worry, they'll serve ya. I know my way around these places. Tip 'em a fin and they'll keep 'em coming. Come on, man, relax, you only live twice,' I advised, jabbing Russell's shoulder. For once in my life, I threw caution to the wind and lived for the moment. I was a regular guy with no problems, living outside my shell. 'Come on, man, don't be a killjoy.'

'David, listen to me,' Russell barked, 'they don't serve beer.'

'Get the—' I responded.

'This is Salt Lake City, Utah, get it? No bars.'

As my younger brother educated me on the local customs, the look from the bartender confirmed my blunder. By the man's intense red face, I knew I had, once again, stepped out of bounds. I muttered to the older man, 'I'm sorry. I truly am. I in no way mean to be rude, sir.' Whatever adrenaline I had had moments before ebbed away. I politely asked for two Cokes, left a massive tip, and took a table in the back beyond the hard gaze of the construction workers playing pool.

'As you can see, I'm still working on my social graces,' I confessed.

'Don't get out much?' Russell chided.

'Bingo,' I said after taking a swallow. It was time to move on to something else. 'Man, I just can't get over it. You look great. So, how's things?'

'Better,' Russell sighed, 'now that I'm out of *that house!*' I instantly picked up on his meaning. 'Man, you have no idea what she's like. I don't mean to say you had it easy, but believe me, you got off pretty good. It's become a lot worse.' Russell was ready to pour out his soul. 'I tell ya, sometimes she'd chase me around the house. I told her if she ever laid a hand on me . . . I just couldn't take it anymore,' he said with a heavy sigh. 'If she's not on some rampage, then she's constantly complaining about everyone, everything, every second of the day.

'When she's done with me as a sounding board, Mom makes the rounds to Grandma and even Ron and his wife, Linda. No one's safe. Ron doesn't even take her calls, but Mom just doesn't get it.' Russell paused to collect his thoughts. 'And Stan thinks he's a he-man. I mean, what's he gonna do? He's bummed; he knows he needs Mom for financial help, and he hates it. If something ever happened to her, he'd never make it. He really thinks he's Mr Fix-it. Bob Villa Jr.' Russell smiled.

'I understand,' I replied, thinking of what Grandmother had told me.

'I'm not trying to down him, but some of his electrical wiring projects almost started a few fires in the lower part of the house. Mom, of course, used to think that Ron and I were picking on him, but Stan can't do half the things Mom thinks he can, and she's so drunk she can't tell the difference. Stan just doesn't understand. It ain't his fault, but Mom's smothered him so much.'

'What about Kevin?' I asked.

'He drinks so much Coke all the time that he's practically lost all his teeth.'

'What?' I asked. 'No way!'

'You don't get it, man. The whole setup: it's all normal to him. Kevin's a kid, he's oblivious. He doesn't know anything else.'

The more Russell described the situation, the more I realized how on the mark he was. *I was indeed the lucky one.* I had been Mother's outlet as a child, and once I was taken away, psychologically she became a wounded animal, attacking anyone who crossed her path. The main difference was that by then my brothers were older and knew better than to take Mother's physical abuse, but unfortunately they had to put up with her psychological torture and self-destructive lifestyle.

And yet it all seemed surreal to me, how Mother could turn her hatred against her other children. Part of me had always feared for them. As a young boy surviving in darkness, I had known what to expect from Mother, to the point that I could predict her moods. Thinking ahead, staying a step or two ahead of her, not only kept me alive and gave me a protective armor, but became a way of life for me. Before Kevin was born, I was never sure if Mother would suddenly strike out against Ron, Russell, or even Stan. Before I was taken away, as I sat on my hands in the basement, I would cringe whenever I heard my brothers come through the front door and walk into the house as if they were entering a minefield. With every step Mother could, without warning, detonate, spreading her shrapnel-like fury in every direction. Weeks prior to my rescue I became so cold inside, I was nearly obsessed with hatred toward Ron, Stan, and especially Russell – who used to be Mother's little brainwashed Nazi – but at the same time I'd still pray for their safety.

As I sat in front of Russell now, I could not imagine the hellish nightmare Mother had put my brothers through. All I could do now was pray that whatever they had experienced would somehow not carry over into their future. Like a broken record, all I could hear in my head was, 'Three down, two to go.' Every one of them had endured more from Mother than I ever possibly could. They were indeed the strong ones, while I was fortunate enough to be rescued.

'If this means anything,' I choked up, 'I'm sorry . . . about every-thing. That's no way to live. Maybe, maybe as a kid I drove her crazy. But,' I added with remorse, 'she wasn't always like this.' I smiled at distant memories, before Russell was born. Mommy had been the adoring parent who cherished her children, taking them on springtime picnics in the park, week-long camping adventures under the stars, glorious trips to the Russian River. Mommy had embellished her home with lights, candles, and ornaments during the Christmas season. 'There were good times,' I confessed. 'And for me, sometimes that's enough to pull me through.'

'I could never understand what you could have done that was so bad,' Russell said. 'All I could remember, since I was a kid, was . . . you were always in trouble. As if that was why she had to beat you,' Russell softly stated. 'And that one summer . . . I remember when she . . . she threw the knife at you, right in front of me . . .'

I flashed back to a memory of Russell as a small child, clamped onto Mother's leg, gently rocking as she swayed drunkenly. Mother had snatched up a knife, screaming that she would kill me if I did not finish washing the dinner dishes within the specified time. At the time, I knew she didn't mean it. Afterward, as I regained consciousness in the bathroom, while blood poured from my chest, Mother announced to my dismay that she could never take me to hospital for fear of exposing the secret. Yet I knew what she meant. 'It was an accident,' I boomed, startling the group of men around the bar.

Russell shook his head. 'No way. It didn't look like an accident to me.'

How could I tell him that I truly believed Mother never intended to stab me? I assumed, from Mother's point of view, it was just another twisted game she had played to strengthen her position over me. Mother was a control freak who tried to dominate me through threatening and forbidding tactics. Mother would threaten me any way she could, but because of the bizarre nature of her ongoing progressive 'games', she constantly had to up the ante, at times to the point that she drove me to the brink of death. I went from being no longer a member of 'The Family' to *The Boy* to a child called *It*. As an adult, I believed Mother used those labels not just to demean me, but somehow to justify her treatment, to protect her psyche from some type of traumatic meltdown, from the fact that she was a mother who was brutalizing her own son.

Russell nervously rubbed his hands. 'I asked her,' he said, 'about when you were in her bedroom . . . she was beating you bad. I peeked through the door and . . . when she marched out, I remember her wiping her hands . . . like she'd just finished washing the dishes. I asked Mom why she beat you up, and without blinking she says, "Mommy loves It and wants It to be good." '

I nearly lost my breath as I visualized the scene.

'With Dad gone,' Russell continued, 'she's worse. If Mom's not on my case, then she's on the phone with Ron and Linda, or Grandma . . . it never stops.'

Changing the subject, I interrupted. 'Can you get word to Stan and tell him I said hello? As kids, before you were born, before things were bad, we used to be tight. Ron and Stan saved my butt a few times.'

Russell merely nodded. 'Okay, it's just . . . Stan thinks he knows it all and that he's the man of the house; you can't tell him anything.'

'Well,' I said, 'tell him I said hi. And can you get word to Ron?'

Russell hesitated. 'I can give you his number.'

'I'd rather you give him a call first. I know it sounds stupid, but I'm kinda embarrassed. I don't know, I mean, I haven't seen or talked to him in years . . . with him being married and all . . . being he's in the army. I don't want to do anything that might mess with his head.' My heavy breathing made me stop for a moment to collect myself. 'Man, what a family. What a waste. At least *we* made it out alive.'

'So,' Russell said, smiling, 'the big question: You gonna see Mom?'

Swallowing hard, I muttered, 'I dunno. In some odd sense, I want to. I know it sounds kinda weird, but . . . I dunno.' I paused. 'I can't explain it.'

'Man,' Russell howled, 'you see Mom and Grandma's gonna have a cow!'

'Trust me,' I laughed. 'She's having a litter of kittens as we speak. Gram gave me so much static over seeing you. It's like . . . if something's not her idea, you shouldn't do it. I mean, I feel for Grandma and I know she did a lot for us when we were kids and all, but I just can't help but think that when it comes to dealing with Mom, she doesn't help the situation any.'

'Man, you're not there to see it,' Russell broke in. 'I'm not pointing fingers, but it's like they feed off each other. The more miserable one can make the other, the happier they think their world will be.'

Clutching my Coke, I nodded in agreement.

'So, you gonna see her?' Russell again asked.

Feeling gutless, I said, 'It ain't worth it, maybe next time . . .' My voice trailed off.

'Yeah,' Russell replied, 'I understand, maybe next time.'

We drifted to other matters, until I dropped Russell off hours later. Back at Grandmother's, she gave me the cold shoulder. The next day I aggravated our situation further when I told Grandmother that I had invited Russell on the trip Grandmother and I had planned to the border of Idaho. Hours later, I again made her upset when I was shopping at a bookstore, buying a novel for Kevin.

Grandmother became impatient, announcing she had had enough and stormed out of the mall. Part of me felt bad for her – she had driven Russell and me to Idaho and fed us a nice picnic lunch – yet I felt I was somehow being manipulated again. No matter what anyone was doing, if Grandmother wanted to go, everyone had to leave at once.

All I could do was continue to wait in line, make my purchase, and sprint after her, for I felt she would leave without me. But in a small sense I was giving Grandmother a message: I would respect her and be polite, but I was not a child whom she could snap her fingers at whenever it pleased her. As I entered Grandmother's two-door sedan – with the engine running and her clutching the steering-wheel – I proudly held Kevin's book in my hand.

My last afternoon at Grandmother's, I phoned the air force office that was handling my cross-training request of becoming an air crew member. As hectic as my military leave had been, at least I felt that I stood a good chance of fulfilling my lifelong dream. When the sergeant recognized my name, his tone seemed positive. 'Ah, yes, Sergeant Pelzer. I saw your file. I got it right here somewhere, hang on . . . Yep, ah, give me a second.' I could feel my excitement grow. 'You've been at my heels for a while now, haven't you? All righty now, here it is . . .' he triumphantly announced. 'Everything seems to be in order . . . uh . . . um . . . hang on a second.'

My heart sank. 'I don't know how to say this,' the sergeant's tone softened, 'but it seems there's been a mistake. Somehow your paperwork went to ground refueling, not midair refueling. Not to worry, this happens all the time—'

'Excuse me, sir,' I interrupted. 'What does this mean? It's fixable, right? I mean, you can correct it, especially since it's not my fault?'

'I'm sorry,' he answered. 'I know how bad you wanted it, but by the time I received your paperwork, it was too late; the slots had been filled. You just missed the cutoff. Don't sweat it. If this is any consolation, I know in about eight, maybe nine months or so, we'll have another batch of slots to fill. I can't make any promises, but as much as you check in, I can advise you when to resubmit directly to my office. I have to be fair to everyone who applies, but I can guarantee you'll get a fair shot.'

'But, Sergeant!' I pleaded, 'I don't have eight months! My enlistment is up in six, seven weeks! I don't understand; I did everything.

I took math, even trig. I studied planes inside and out. I've got good annual progress reports. I've got medals. I graduated jump school. I even got a letter from Kelly Johnson.' I was yammering like an idiot. 'I've wanted this forever. What else can I do?'

'Your package is not being questioned. It's sound. If there was a slot open, I'd give it to you. But right now that's not the issue. I am sorry. I feel for you, but there is nothing, nothing I can do.'

I stood in a frozen state, still clutching the phone. I had strongly believed I had a chance. I thought *this time* my hard work and determination would pay off. Ever since Father passed away, I had found something I could focus my efforts toward, a longtime dream that I could achieve for myself. For months, in the barracks on Friday and Saturday evenings, while the other guys would party outside on the building's ledge, I'd dangle my legs over the same ledge and absorb my latest mathematical equation. Around the squadron, I'd discovered that peers whom I didn't really know were silently rooting for me, a mere cook, to cross over and become an air crew member.

As Grandmother came toward me, I could see she was not happy. I remembered that she had lectured me to keep the phone call short. I had been speaking to the sergeant for at least ten minutes, which I assumed was nine minutes too long. Besides being overly polite and careful where to tread, I felt my visit with Grandmother was not the tender homecoming I had imagined. I genuinely did not know this relative, and she did not know me.

'The phone,' she snipped.

I looked down at my hand grasping the phone. It felt ice cold. 'Oh, yeah, sorry.' My eyes darted toward the floor as I replaced the phone in its cradle. Grandmother remained by my side, as if waiting for a report.

'So?' she asked.

I shook my head like a scolded puppy. 'Oh . . . sorry,' I said. 'It was nothing. Just air force stuff, no big deal. It's nothing, nothing at all.' I wanted to tell her. To grab her frail body and open my heart to her. Not necessarily to moan about my latest futile crusade, but rather as a way finally to come to know Grandmother as a real person – her hopes, her dreams, her anxieties. To know of her life experiences as a child, as a woman, and a single parent who raised two children during hard times. There was much I admired about her. Grandmother was one of the original 'pull yourself up by the bootstraps' people. In a way I still believed she and I were alike. The whole purpose of spending a few days with her was to get to know her better. All my life I had been led to believe that any sensitive matter was to be instantly buried. As an adult, I still knew nothing about my parents and how they came to be. Yet as I stood beside Grandmother, I knew that all we could manage was idle chitchat, at best, praying one of us didn't step into forbidden territory.

'Well, then,' Grandmother heaved, breaking the tension, 'did I tell you about the time I played golf with an officer from Hill Air Force Base? I think he's a general . . . anyway . . .' And so did Grandmother and I kill time on my last evening, until we finally went to bed.

Early the next morning, I strapped my oversized green sleeping bag, my military backpack, and, upon Grandmother's unwavering insistence, a coffee can containing her homemade snickerdoodle cookies onto my motorcycle. After an impassive departing embrace, I rode off. Hours later, in the blazing heat, as my body became numb and dehydrated from the miles of endless interstate, my sole thought was getting back to my Florida base, where I could begin my out-processing. I was quitting the air force.

chapter 8

CHANGES

I barely made it back from Utah to Hurlburt Field in Florida. The chain from my motorcycle stretched so much from the cross-country trek that nearly all the teeth from the rear sprocket sheared off, almost leaving me stranded in Texas at the height of a heat wave. By the time I limped through Mississippi, my rear tire became bald, and all I could do was disregard it. I had to spend the remainder of my funds filling up my gas tank, praying every mile I'd make it.

Hours after coasting into the base, I reported to the office that handled out-processing. As luck would have it, I no sooner came before a young airman – newly assigned, frantic, and confused – before he informed me to report to the section chief, pronto! *Great*, I thought, *now what?* I was exhausted, ready to give the next person I met a piece of my mind. As I stormed through the passageways, I felt betrayed. After four years, none of my efforts had paid off. Joining the air force to become a fireman was nothing more than a joke. I slaved away like I had years ago, but this time from the swamps of Florida to the Egyptian desert. And for what? I didn't mind paying my dues, but for once, just once, I wished I could get lucky.

The more I felt myself getting hot under the collar, the more I tried to brush aside my ego. Okay, I was a cook, but one with jump wings who had actually seen the Great Pyramid. I'd had a chance to be reassigned to work in an office where I was appreciated, enabling me, a high school dropout, to go to college. I had a couple of bucks socked away, and for four years the air force had given me a home. In all, what did I really have to complain about? So I didn't snatch the golden ring of becoming an air crew member; big deal. What truly mattered to me was that I had done my best. There was a sense of satisfaction knowing I hadn't faltered. I had taken a few hard knocks and I never quit. By the time the receptionist ushered me into a captain's office, I was back to my old self. Standing ramrod straight, I popped out a crisp salute. 'Sergeant Pelzer reporting, sir!'

A towering black gentleman rose from behind his gray metal desk. He maintained a thin smile as his eyes ran up my pressed uniform. 'Take a seat. So,' the captain paused, 'we have a situation?'

'Sir?'

'You still want to be a crew member?'

I wasn't sure what he was asking. 'Well, I do . . . I mean, I did, but that's no longer—'

'The bottom line is,' he interjected, 'the way your submission was processed, the air force made a mistake. *I* have a problem with that,' the captain stated with pride. 'So, I have a proposition for you. The air force is willing to grant an extension on your enlistment. You can use it to resubmit your paperwork. If you get accepted as a crew member, you reenlist. If you don't, you can out-process, then get out. Understand, just by getting an extension in no way means getting a slot as a crew dawg. But,' he said with a sly grin, '*you'll* be able to track your paperwork along the way. You'll be jumping through a lot of hoops, and in the end there are no guarantees, but this is a square offer.'

I had just pulled an ace out of thin air. 'I'll take the deal!'

Dashing to my supervisors, I informed them of my luck. Without hesitation, they varied my work schedule so I could indeed oversee the necessary paperwork, which had to start from scratch. The next several weeks flew by as I literally ran around the entire base collecting the right forms, dropping them off at the appropriate office or, if I was lucky, hovering over them as I collected signatures, initials, or boxes properly checked off. Then I had to collect additional forms that required further verification, again in the proper sequence, until, finally, I returned to the captain's office with a perfectly completed package.

'Got a whiff from Sergeant Blue,' the officer began, 'the guy who handles your specialty request. Says he may have some slots open pretty soon.' This time he broke into a wide smile. 'I'll QC – quality control – the paperwork, give it my blessing, and send it up the pike. You maintain tabs, and within a week you should be getting a call from Sergeant Blue.'

'Thanks . . . Cap,' I saluted.

He returned the gesture. 'Like I said, air force made a mistake. *I* had a problem with that.'

Weeks dragged by with no word. I desperately wanted to call the sergeant, but feared that pestering him would blow my opportunity. I kept myself busy any way I could, fighting to keep my mind off the package. After another week I caved in and phoned. 'Been expecting your call,' Sergeant Blue nonchalantly began. 'We had a problem . . .' I exhaled, waiting for the sky to come crashing down. 'You're not going to believe this, but it seems the paperwork ended up in the hands of ground refueling again.' As he paused, I wondered, *What do I have to do?* After all I had been through, I was not going to roll over and quit. 'Anyways, like I said, we *had* a problem,' Sergeant Blue went on.

'Say again?' I asked, catching his emphasis on the word *had*.

'Let me just say this: they've been educated on the errors of their ways. I got the paperwork in time. Now,' he added, 'we have *another* problem.' My stomach turned. Clearing his throat, Sergeant Blue stammered, 'It – it seems I won't be able to grant you your base request.'

I quickly saw my opening. 'I'll take anything you have. Anything! Even Minot!' I thundered, knowing that Minot Air Force Base was located in the far region of North Dakota and was infamous for its extreme Arctic-like winters.

'No can do,' he informed me.

In my head I calculated. I would never have a chance of resubmitting another package. I had run out of time. There were no other options. Suddenly, I thought of a different tactic. 'What do you have?'

'Well, the best I could do is . . .' – I could sense Sergeant Blue's restrained excitement, and the hairs on my arms began to rise – '. . . this base out in California, west of the Sierra Nevadas.'

'Beale!' I shouted.

'Home of the Sled. Congratulations. Once you've earned your crew wings, you'll be an in-flight boom operator for the SR-71 – known to crew dawgs as the Sled. I was just waiting for your call.'

In a swirl of emotions I profusely thanked Sergeant Blue. Hanging up the phone, I clasped my hands together. Calming down, I began praying, thanking God.

*

Ten months later, in the summer of 1984, an SR-71 Blackbird stabilized in a hovering state, flying ten feet below and forty feet behind a KC-135 Q model refueling tanker, waiting on me – a recently certified crew member – to fulfill my part of the mission. Staring out of the glass that not only protected me at an altitude of twenty-five thousand feet, but gave me an unlimited view of everything within hundreds of miles, I drew in a deep breath to collect myself. I felt the unique sensation of needing merely to reach out through the glass and touch the Blackbird, as both planes made their way south at speeds exceeding five hundred miles per hour on a specialized refueling track above Idaho's aqua-blue Salmon River. It wasn't the heavenly scenery or being lucky enough to be a part of a distinctive air force program that was important to me, but that it was my first solo flight. I was fulfilling a childhood dream. I was no longer confined to a dark, torturous environment, hopelessly wishing I could 'fly away' from danger. After years of sacrifice, my life had made a turn for the better. *For the first time in my life, I began to feel good about myself.* I always knew as a child, deep down inside, I could make it if I had the chance. And now my entire life was on track. I no longer wore a mantle of shame. I was becoming a real person. I could lower my guard, relax, and live life.

'Aspen 31, Bandit 27,' I relayed to the waiting SR-71, using his identification call sign immediately followed by mine, 'you are clear for contact!'

'Hey, Boom!' the pilot in the flight deck echoed, 'make Kelly Johnson proud!'

'Roger that!' I smiled. For me, it didn't get any better than this.

Now that I was an air crew member, every day was an adventure. Every time I zipped up my flight suit, I felt like my childhood hero, Superman, out to save the world from impending doom. My green Nomex uniform was my red cape, taking me to places I had dreamed about when I was a prisoner in Mother's war. I was appreciative that I was with a unique organization that carried a sense of honor and camaraderie. The more I became involved as a boom operator, the more I cherished my position, and a deep sense of pride was growing. I was part of a family.

My new career carried a new level of responsibility. Besides flying two, sometimes three times a week, at any hour of the day or night, my crew and I would have to spend the day before planning the most minute segments – from preflighting the aircraft before takeoff to engine shutdown after landing. I quickly learned the seriousness of the job. If there was a major political or military situation anywhere in the world, the Blackbird would be deployed to collect real-time photographs of a hot spot that could be in the hands of the President, if needed, in a period of twenty-four hours. The Q model KC-135 Stratotanker was the tanker that fed precious, one-of-a-kind JP-7 fuel to the Blackbird, enabling the SR-71 to accomplish its mission. There was a sense of excitement knowing that my bags were packed and that I could be called upon to fly off into the sunset at a moment's notice.

Because I never slept the evening prior to a flight, there were times after a late-night mission that I would be so exhausted, I'd collapse at the pool of my apartment complex. Yet still I'd be smiling. I'd gaze up at the stars that hours ago seemed close enough to cup in my hand.

I lived a grand life. I had my own apartment, *my home*, where no one could kick me out or make me feel unwanted. I could go to bed as early as I wanted without being disturbed, as I had been when I was an airman living in a dormitory. I kept my tiny one-bedroom home apartment sparkling clean. Financially, I was barely getting by, but what I was losing in salary was easily made up for in peace of mind. I was proud that my first home was fully furnished and paid for from my years of saving. My life also included two close friends that I had met as a foster child, Dave Howard and J. D. Thom. They still lived in the Bay Area, and I'd drive down to goof off with them during the weekends whenever possible. I kept close tabs with Alice and Harold as well by calling them several times a week. I felt I had more than anyone could ask for.

Although I was feeling good about myself, something continued to gnaw at me. During my rare time off at the apartment complex, whenever I would go down to the pool, I could not relax like my neighbors – working on a tan, drinking beer, swimming, or celebrating that they had survived another week of work. I was known only as 'Fly Boy': a skinny, pasty white geek in shorts and a tank top, a bookworm who absorbed mounds of technical flight manuals. Unlike the majority of those by the poolside, I was not smooth, cool, or a tough-guy with endless tattoos. I didn't drink until I passed out, smoke like a chimney, use drugs daily to escape my pain, or rant nonstop about how someone or something did me wrong. Nor was I on federal aid. Yet I didn't even feel good enough about myself to be among 'them'.

It was at the pool where I first met Patsy. Even though she hung out with a wild group of friends, she seemed different. She wasn't as rowdy or aimless as the others. I felt awkward, as I studied my work, whenever we'd make eye contact, but flattered that she would even look at me. Since I could never hold a gaze, I'd immediately snap my head back down to my papers. Within days we were greeting each other with a quick hello. One Friday afternoon, in passing, I told Patsy I was going to the Bay Area. Her eyes lit up. 'San Francisco? Can I come?'

I hesitated. No woman had ever asked to be with me. 'Well . . .' I stammered, 'I'm not going to the city, but . . .'

'You'd be doing me a favor. These guys are driving me crazy.' Patsy pointed at the small herd in the pool thrashing around, screeching at the top of their lungs. 'I'm not like them. Really,' she gently added.

'Okay,' I finally answered, 'let's go.'

The next day Patsy joined me as I drove west to see the Turnboughs. I could not believe how easy it was to talk to her. Whatever apprehension I had evaporated within minutes. She even fed off my humor, laughing at whatever spilled from my mouth. In the midst of my chattering, I realized how lonely I had become. Beyond small talk, I could hardly get over how she appeared to be *interested in me*. 'So,' Patsy asked when my mouth was still for a brief moment, 'what is it you do?'

'I'm a boomer,' I automatically replied.

'A what?'

'Oh, excuse me,' I said, translating, 'sometimes I get ahead of myself. I'm a boom operator . . . I midair-refuel jets for the air force.'

'Oh, yeah, I get it.' Patsy politely nodded, but by the look on her face I knew she did not understand. 'So what's with that green overall thing I see you in?'

'It's a flight suit.'

'Well . . . it's just,' she said, 'well, some of us were trying to figure you out. You know, you don't go out. The word is out: you don't *party.* I don't know anyone who reads or writes that much.' I began to imagine the word *dweeb* etched on my forehead as Patsy continued. 'You come and go at all hours. You're always alone. The only time I've seen you with anyone else is when you're with those other guys in those green overalls. It's just, well, some of us thought you were . . . you know.'

Not understanding, I shook my head. 'What are you getting at?'

'Oh, shit!' Patsy covered her mouth. 'I didn't mean to . . . it's just, well, some of us, not me, have had a hard time figuring you out.'

I was stunned by the thought that if I didn't party, or if I spent my time alone applying myself, that I was considered so abnormal. 'Those guys you see me with are some of the men I fly with.'

I could tell Patsy was embarrassed. She in no way meant to hurt my feelings. I could only assume that in her world I was quite the outsider, and for years, strangely enough, I had been curious to discover what it would be like to fit in.

Several quiet miles passed between us until I relieved the tension by trying to make small talk again. Even after I apologized for putting her in an odd position, I felt Patsy thought badly of me. As we regained momentum in our conversation, I discovered that Patsy, as kind as she was to me, gave no thought to the happenings of the world, politics, her local surroundings, or anything beyond the latest Indiana Jones film or the pop group Duran Duran's newest album.

A couple of hours later, when Alice saw me with Patsy, her eyes lit up. As she hugged me, Alice whispered, 'Thank God you're finally dating. I was getting worried about you.' Still holding my hand, she spun around toward Patsy. 'So, how long have you two been going together?'

Patsy stepped back. 'Oh, we just met.'

I suddenly felt like a complete idiot, bringing a woman I barely knew over to my parents' place, and it wasn't even a date. Alice, who continued to radiate happiness, plopped down between Patsy and me, snapping her head left and right to keep the conversation going. Every time she turned toward me, she would smirk and raise her eyebrows. I felt like an awkward teenager, trying to be kind to my mother while protecting Patsy from total boredom. I could only pray Alice didn't slip up and tell Patsy something from my past.

After some small talk I excused myself to spend time with Harold. Though I had seen him a few months ago, Harold suddenly looked years older. He appeared so frail, and he struggled to make simple conversation. His eyes were distant, while he did his best to hide his trembling hands. After a few minutes, I gave up and cupped his hands in mine. We spent the remainder of our time in silence. In the back of my mind, the memory of my biological father suffering came back in full force.

When Patsy and I were leaving, I whispered to Alice as I hugged her goodbye, 'What's with Pop?'

Her eyes darted toward the floor. 'Oh, it's nothing. Harold's just got a touch of the flu. He's been working too hard lately. He's got an appointment to see the doctor next week. Listen,' she said, 'don't you fret, you two have fun. And I tell you something else.' Alice looked at both Patsy and me. 'You two look good together.'

'It's not what you think,' I again whispered. 'We just met a few days ago, okay?'

'Well,' Mom said, 'if you ask me, I've got a good feeling about you two.'

'You'll have to forgive my mom,' I said to Patsy as we pulled away, 'I think she's playing matchmaker.' I did not want Patsy to get the wrong impression. 'Besides,' I added in a Yiddish voice, 'I think she's seen *Fiddler on the Roof* too many times.' I was making a reference to the movie's persistent matchmaker, but I could see Patsy did not get the joke.

'So,' Patsy asked, 'are they your real parents?'

'Well, yeah,' I immediately responded. But after a few moments of silence, I exhaled, saying, 'They are to me. They're my foster parents. My mother, my real mom, well, she had a drinking problem and sometimes used to, you know, go off on me. Sometimes . . .' I trailed off, hoping not to scare Patsy off. I had no intention of telling her about my former life. I clutched the steering-wheel, afraid Patsy would suddenly fling open the car door and bail out. I had never exposed my childhood to anyone like this before, let alone the magnitude of my mother's twisted sickness.

For some time now I had been resigned to the fact that my past would probably keep me from being with someone. Even at age twenty-three, with all I had been fortunate enough to accomplish on my own, against the odds, I had the self-esteem of an ant. I was deathly afraid of women. I felt unworthy even of looking at them for more than a few quick seconds, let alone talking with one. That's why I was so overwhelmed, confused, and yet enchanted by Patsy's interest in me.

I found myself rambling about how I came into foster care. At least I had sense enough to graze the surface. Since my past was so mired in lies and deceit, I valued honesty above everything else. I believed that if I was to have a relationship with anyone, it was important to me to be as truthful as possible, yet at the same time maintain a veil to protect that person from whatever pain or embarrassment that came from being with me. I knew I was walking a fine line and in doing so was now living a true lie. I had been doing so for some time in the air force, especially during the extensive psychological evaluations that I had to undertake to become an air crew member. I had simply deflected what I felt necessary in order to protect my security clearance. I could only pray someday it didn't backfire on me or on anyone else. The last thing I wanted was to cause anyone any pain whatsoever.

'I know what it's like . . . I was the black sheep of my family,' Patsy confessed.

She went on to explain that she was picked on as a child, felt out of place among her siblings, had trouble getting along with her overbearing mother, and as a teenager felt the only way to escape was to run away. 'I hooked up with some guy. We both worked to get by, partied a lot, ya know.' As Patsy opened up, not only could I relate to her feelings of being alienated, but to me everything seemed to fall into place on how she carried herself and why she hung out with that rambunctious crowd. I felt that Patsy, too, was looking for acceptance. 'But,' she sighed, 'when my father passed away, Mom had to sell the house and move into an apartment. I moved back in to help out; no one else will lift a finger. Hell, I'm sleeping on the couch. As much as she drives me crazy, I'm the only one who will take care of her.'

Even though I picked up on her slight resentment, I knew Patsy was grazing the surface, too. 'I am sorry,' I said. 'I truly am. No one deserves to be treated bad.' I stopped for a moment. 'My real father passed away, too—'

Patsy jumped in before I could complete my thought. 'What the hell. Shit happens! That's my motto.'

Without thinking I let out a laugh. I had never heard that expression before. And I picked up on Patsy's subliminal message of brushing off whatever problems came her way.

During the drive back home, both Patsy and I gabbed nonstop. I had never been with a woman for such an extended time in my life. I didn't want our time together to end. Late into the evening, at my apartment, I proudly showed off my new home. Patsy was the first person to step into my world. We sat down on the couch, sipping wine while listening to acoustical jazz. My mind swam between saying good night and wanting to talk longer. Without warning, Patsy leaned forward. I flinched as she wrapped her arms around my neck before kissing me. Neither of us had any premonitions. We both seemed surprised that we had fallen for each other.

The next few weeks became a whirlwind. Of all people, *I* had a girlfriend. I had everything going for me. I was enthralled with my job, and for the first time I had someone who wanted to be with me, someone who cared about me. The sensation of coming home after an exhausting flight to spend time with Patsy was beyond elation. Patsy blew me away when she would cook dinner or leave me notes inside my lunch bag that I'd discover when I'd fly. I adored the attention. I felt complete.

When I had to fly overseas for weeks at a time, Patsy volunteered to watch my place, watering my plants and feeding Chuck, my box turtle. I was slightly apprehensive because I was overly cautious and felt things were happening way too fast. I knew I was caught up with her, and yet I could hardly control myself. I had always been alone. No one had ever wanted me, let alone found me attractive enough to give me the time of day. I gave Patsy an extra key, on the condition that she simply watch over my apartment.

Weeks later when I returned home, Patsy met me at the door. As I unpacked, I noticed my closet space had been taken over by her clothes and the bathroom countertop was filled with her makeup items. As I stood at the entrance to the bedroom, Patsy rushed over, hugging me and crying, 'It's not what you think! I didn't plan to, but my mom's driving me crazy! We got into a huge argument. I'm tired of being under her thumb. You know what it's like. Besides, I'm here almost all the time anyway. I missed you so much. You're not like the others. What are we waiting for? You know how I feel about you. Please?' she sobbed.

Patsy had never been so emotional before. I wanted to sit her down and calmly, logically explain that we were now considering moving in together. This was no longer a date to the movies, a romantic dinner, or a passionate affair. While overseas, I had told myself to let things cool off between Patsy and me. But as I held her, I was tired of overanalyzing every detail in my life. Looking into her tear-stained eyes, I realized how much I missed her. As her whimpering eased, Patsy kissed me on the neck and face and said, 'Sometimes it's so hard. I'm tired of being put down, always being told what to do. And no matter what I do, it's never good enough.'

It had always troubled me how Patsy was treated at times. Her mother, Dottie Mae, had seemed overly nice when I first met her, but I could sense how closely she watched Patsy's every move or corrected her on the slightest thing. When I asked Patsy why her mother acted that way, she waved a hand at me. 'It's her way of watching over me. She's afraid I'll blow it and get into trouble again. When I was younger I was pretty wild.'

One time, before I had to fly overseas, Patsy rushed into my apartment, telling me how her mother and siblings were again berating her. Before I could console her, one by one her family barged in, without knocking, screaming at the top of their lungs at Patsy before turning on each other. I even found one person gorging on anything he could from my refrigerator and someone else rummaging through my bureau drawers in my bedroom. Only after I had kicked everyone but Patsy out did I learn how common this sort of outburst was for her family.

I knew how hard Patsy had it in her mother's cramped two-bedroom apartment. Because Patsy's mother occupied one bedroom and Patsy's brother and his girlfriend the other, Patsy slept on the living-room couch. Her brother, though, spent his time waterskiing, cruising around in his prized truck he had purchased after winning a legal dispute, or partying. Due to Dottie Mae's bad hips, Patsy felt she was the only one who had to take care of cleaning the apartment, do all the cooking, and run a multitude of daily errands for her mother. 'Now you know why I go out and party,' Patsy once explained to me.

'But why don't you get a job, save some money, and move out?' I had replied.

'Job? What jobs? I tried a couple of times, and why bother? The best I could do would be a waitress. Who wants to do that? Besides . . . I have a bad back. My mom gives me money when I need it.' Patsy shrugged, as if it was no big deal.

At the time I couldn't believe my ears. All my life I had never thought about *not* working to provide for myself. I had a hard time accepting Patsy's family dynamics and how they treated her, but, thinking about my own family, who in the hell was I to judge? At least I knew, as Patsy once pointed out to me, 'I know at times we're at each other's throats, but if someone else messes with either one of us, I tell you what: we'll kick that person's ass. Now, that's how much we love each other.' I thought at the time that maybe Patsy's family wasn't so abnormal and that, once again, my standards were too high.

As I held Patsy's quivering body, she whispered, 'If you let me move in, my mom will leave me alone; she'll have to. And then I can be happy. You'll see. We'll be so happy.' My heart ached for Patsy. I knew she deserved better. Maybe, I thought, because of our pasts we had a good chance of making a good couple. We'd be strong enough to weather any storm. Besides, I told myself, no one could ever treat me as well as Patsy.

'Okay,' I said, my voice cracking, 'let's do it. Let's move in together.'

In her excitement, Patsy nearly crushed my ribs. 'Thank you, thank you, thank you! Finally, now *I* have a home!' Her eyes again swelled with tears. Patsy swallowed hard before bursting, 'I love you, David. I have for the longest time. I really love you. You're the one, the only one for me.'

I was paralyzed. I couldn't look at her. All I could do was continue to hold her. Time sped by and I still could not open my mouth. Here was a woman in my arms, now a major part of my life, who had just opened her soul to me and I . . .

I could not say the words. And for that I despised myself. How could I allow someone into my home and not in my heart? I thought after everything Patsy had done for me and all she had been through, she deserved better. 'It's okay,' Patsy sniffed as she wiped away her tears, 'I understand, I know, I do. But one day you will, I know it. One day you'll love me.'

Later, in the early morning hours, I lay wide awake with Patsy snoring beside me. Part of the reason I could not sleep was due to the time-zone changes of flying back from England. But I knew the true reason for my lack of sleep: my guilty conscience eating at me. I was now living with someone, and as I searched my heart, I didn't know if I could ever have the same strong feelings for Patsy that she seemed to have for me. How could I be so cold when Patsy was filled with joy? Was it because after years of toughening myself to survive, I couldn't break the pattern? Or was it because I didn't want to? As much as I struggled, I could not find an answer. I only knew that I was getting myself deeper into something I did not fully understand. All I could do now was follow through with my commitment.

The next afternoon I phoned Alice. After I told her of my overseas trip, the anxiety grew too much for me. 'Mom,' I stammered, 'Patsy and I, well . . . we decided, we're living together now. If that's all right?'

I could hear Mom take a deep breath. 'Well, I guess you've both given this some serious thought.'

'Oh, yeah,' I broke in, 'we, ah, we've talked a lot.'

'And she has the same feelings for you as you do for her?'

I felt crushed. 'Yeah,' I swallowed. 'Patsy, she – she treats me great . . . and she's had some hard times, too.' I caught myself. I was saying anything I could think of that would make this easier. 'I'm sorry, Mom, I know you don't agree. I just, I just respect you and Pop too much. I didn't want to live a lie.' I paused, waiting for Alice to lay into me. I didn't even hear her breathe. 'Mom, Mom, are you there?'

'Yes, I'm here. It's just . . .' She stopped, and as she did, I hated myself. All I could do was wait for the bomb to drop. 'It's just, well . . . I took Harold to the doctor . . .'

I felt a surge of relief that the subject had shifted away from Patsy and me. 'So,' I put in, 'it's the flu, right? And all Pop has to do is stay home and rest for a while?'

'David,' Alice said, 'Harold has cancer. He's scheduled for therapy, but . . . the doctor thinks it's too advanced. He's gonna fight it, so for right now all we can do is pray. I'm happy for the two of you, but for now let's keep this between us.'

Hanging up the phone, I turned to Patsy and told her the news. What I did not tell her was how ashamed I felt. That evening I thought of how selfish I had become. My flying, my globe-trotting adventures, my apartment, my live-in girlfriend – me, me, me. The next morning after returning from work, I sat down with Patsy. 'I've given this some thought, and I think on the weekends I should go down and spend time with my parents.'

'I understand. Remember, I just lost my dad, too,' Patsy responded. I nodded in agreement. 'Listen, I've got a great idea, I can go with you! I can help out Alice, and this way we can spend time together.'

My answer was not what Patsy had hoped for. 'But I barely get to see you now, what about us?' she cried.

'When I lost my dad, he couldn't even say goodbye. No one was there for him.' I stopped, imagining my father alone in the room, covered in white hospital sheets. 'When I first came to the Turnboughs as a foster kid, no one, and I mean no one, would take me in. We'll have time together, but for now this is something I have to . . . it's the right thing to do.'

Patsy nodded. 'I understand.' She reached out to hug me, but by the time I saw it I had already stood up and walked away.

When I wasn't overseas flying, I spent nearly every free weekend I could with the Turnboughs, sometimes even showing up after a Friday afternoon mission wearing my sweaty flight suit. Whenever Harold was not taking one of his lengthy naps, we'd sit outside in the closed-in screen porch he had constructed a few months before. For a person who had never spoken to me that much as a teenager, Harold now told me stories of when he served during World War II as a driver for the officers, and upon his return home from Europe how he and other veterans cried when they saw the Statue of Liberty. While some of his army buddies stayed in New York to celebrate, Harold caught the first train back to Missouri so he could get up early at home, grab his box of carpentry tools, and go from door to door to find work. For me it didn't matter what he said, just as long as we spent time together. It was during those times, while a cool breeze blew in through the screen porch, that Harold and I accomplished something my biological father and I had never done: bond as father and son.

As the months went by, I saw Harold slowly deteriorate. Those times Patsy joined me, she had to hold back her shock at Harold's appearance. Leaving her with Alice, I'd sit with Harold as he drifted in and out of sleep. We all knew the cancer had spread too far and the chemotherapy wasn't helping. Harold somehow held on, but his strength, coordination, and eyes were failing him to the point he could no longer drive his truck or do his woodworking. That's when he knew the end was near.

'I was gonna build that home for Alice, you know, in Nevada,' Harold said during one of my Saturday visits. 'Had to wait to retire.'

I nodded my head in agreement. 'Yes.'

'No time now.' He paused, rubbing his callused hands. 'So . . . what is it you want?'

'Excuse me?' I blurted from embarrassment. In all the years I had known him, Harold had never asked such a probing question. 'Well . . .' I stuttered; 'I – I like flying. I've always wanted a home at the river. Ever since my father passed away, I was kinda hoping you and I could maybe build it together.'

'No!' His voice cracked as he clasped my hands with his. 'What is it you really want?'

Our eyes locked, just as my father's and mine had before he passed away. I bent closer to his ear. 'No matter where I'm at, or what I have, or what I'm doing, I just want to be happy.'

'Yes,' Harold said. His grip intensified. 'You've found it. You make a difference. Do good, do your best, and do it now.'

Suddenly his grip loosened. His head rolled back. For a fleeting moment I panicked. By the time Alice and Patsy raced onto the porch, Harold had regained consciousness, snapped his neck back up, and smiled before drifting off to sleep. I was never able to speak to him again.

Days later, Alice called on the verge of tears to say Harold was near death. Patsy and I jumped into my tiny Toyota Celica, weaving through the Bay Area rush-hour traffic until I came to a screeching halt in front of my old home. As I stepped through the front door, I knew I was too late by the look that was etched on everyone's face. Alice came over and simply said, 'David, I'm sorry . . . he just passed away.'

At the funeral, I received the American flag, then walked over to present it to Alice. Standing above her, I stated, 'Of all the men I have known, Harold's had the most profound effect on me.' During the eulogy I tried to remain strong, but completely lost control after Harold's light oak casket was lowered. As scores of people shuffled back to their cars, I found myself standing alone filled with rage. My body shuddered as I looked up at the deep blue sky. All I could think of was: *Why? Why Harold?* He was a man who had spent a lifetime living the theme of a 'good day's work for a good day's pay', was so close to retiring, just to lose it all? While someone like my mother, a cold, vindictive person who hated everyone and everything, whose passion seemed to be destroying anything close to her as if it were some kind of sport, lived on while never having to lift a finger. This was beyond any form of reasoning for me. Harold didn't drink, he wasn't abusive, he never even raised his voice. He led a clean life; he took in kids that other families turned away. Why? As I felt myself slump to my knees, Alice's son-in-law, Del, a man I highly respected, embraced me until my anger dissipated.

Weeks after Harold's passing, I still made a point of calling Alice several times a week. Whenever possible during the weekends, I'd make the trip down to see her. I felt drawn to Alice and wanted to be there for her. We spent time strolling through malls, or when I took her to dinner I'd make her laugh by confessing some of my wild stories she had never known while I was a teenager under her care. My motives weren't entirely altruistic, though. Being there for Alice was a way for me to hide from some of my own problems.

'You look tired,' Alice said, rubbing my head during one visit. 'Are you losing weight?'

'It's the flying. It's dehydration,' I lied. 'Sometimes it's just hard for me to get some rest before a flight, that's all.'

'And how are things with you and Patsy?' Alice pressed.

'Fine,' I nodded, 'just fine.'

'You've been with someone for . . . not even a year and things are just fine? I'm not so sure of that,' she replied.

While she was still mourning the loss of her husband, there was no way I could tell her that during that time I had discovered how vastly different Patsy and I were. Even after eleven months together, I didn't feel for her what she did me. For the life of me, I could not understand why I felt closed in. Part of me didn't trust her as much as I thought I should. I found myself becoming irritated over the smallest things. Yet when I was overseas for weeks at a time, I longed for Patsy. The question was, did I miss her for the right reasons?

Whenever I came home from my extended assignments, the first couple of days were great. We'd go out to dinner, have a few beers at her favorite bar, or see the latest movie. But within a week the elation wore off and frustrations grew. While I was away, Patsy always claimed to have just gotten a job. Yet upon my return Patsy not only 'suddenly lost her job' for no apparent reason, but was never paid. I was never able to find out what was happening with her jobs. Several times when I offered to assist Patsy by approaching her employers about the money owed to her, she somehow forgot who her employers were, or if she did remember, they had somehow fled the area. Once, when I persisted in trying to find where she had worked, Patsy broke down in tears and we had an argument.

The pattern always seemed to repeat itself. Patsy seemed surprised that I recalled her continual crises that she had forgotten over the short period of time. It seemed like an obvious lie, but I could not understand why she would concoct such elaborate stories. And I couldn't get myself to confront Patsy. Part of the reason was I so desperately wanted to believe her. I knew deep inside Patsy was a terrific person. But every time I tried to trust her, some bizarre situation would come between us.

Sometimes we'd clash because I didn't go out enough. I understood that Patsy liked to go out and party, but, as I tried to explain to her, the night life just wasn't for me. At times the disagreements ended with Patsy storming from the apartment, only to return drunk hours later. She'd stumble into the bathroom to throw up. As I tried to get her to lie down in bed, Patsy would wail that no one loved her, or that everyone was trying to take advantage of her. Several times before she passed out from the booze and exhaustion, she clutched my hand, sobbing, 'Don't leave me, please. Everybody else does . . . don't you leave me, too.'

Because I was worried, I always stood over Patsy until I was sure she was asleep. At times, because of the hour, I wouldn't get any sleep. All I could do was take a shower, zip on my flight suit, and drive off to report for a flight, praying I didn't lose my focus and make a critical mistake during a mission.

Sometimes upon returning home, either late in the afternoon or early evening, I'd find Patsy, seemingly embarrassed, looking as if she had just rolled out of bed. What was it that made her drink to the point of losing control? Something had to be eating at her. I knew part of it was me. As the pattern progressed, I sometimes became frustrated when Patsy, in all sincerity, tried to make up. I'd retreat inside myself, ignoring her for days at a time. As much as I wanted to believe the line 'It won't happen again,' the act was wearing pretty thin.

Probing only made matters worse. My only concern was to stop the cycle, as I desperately wanted to ease her pain. Having seen my parents deteriorate in front of my eyes, I couldn't allow it to happen to someone else. No matter what had upset Patsy in the first place, though, her responses were always evasive. 'Oh, it was nothing,' 'I got into an argument with my mom,' 'I met an old friend,' or 'Someone just pissed me off. It's no big deal, it's all right.'

After months with no change, one evening I lit into Patsy. 'Enough! It's not all right! We live together . . . and when you come home like that and I have to take care of you, it *is* my business. I feel like, at times, you expect it of me. Okay, I realize I have a few beers, but I know my limit, I don't lose control. Do you have any idea how many times I've broken crew rest before a flight just to take care of you? Do you realize if the air force found out I've lost sleep prior to a flight, they could pull my wings? I could be grounded!'

Patsy broke in with a vindictive tone, 'Oh, Mr Perfect, Mr Control, Mr Self-righteous—'

'No!' I cut Patsy off, fighting to explain. I was not trying to be overbearing, but after months of closing my eyes to the situation, I had to get my feelings off my chest. 'Where do you get that? I am in no way perfect. You know I'm not like that. I just don't live like this. This whole thing is a problem for me and . . . if that makes me self-righteous . . . well, so be it. I thought you knew: my parents' drinking destroyed my family.' I was breathing hard as I raised my finger. 'I cannot and will not live through that again. For some folks, like your friends, I know it's okay and a part of their everyday lives. I don't care. I'm not better than anybody else. It's simply not for me.' I began to cool down. 'That's not my way of life. You've got to get this under control. Please?' I pleaded.

'You're not my father!' Patsy fired back. 'No one, no one tells me what to do! Not you, my mother, my family, no one! All my life everyone's been bossing me around. You have no idea the shit I've been put through! I'll do what I want, when I want. Why do you care what happens to me? You can't even say the words. I know you don't love me.'

I surprised myself by responding, 'How can I love you when we live like this? I want to get close to you, but how can I if you don't tell me what's eating at you?'

My only hope was if I dug deep enough, or approached the subject in a different way, Patsy and I could find the answers to our problems. I became driven to make things right. Unfortunately, our arguments usually ended with her fleeing from the apartment. At times, late at night, I would still be wide awake when Patsy came in. She would slip into bed beside me and wrap her arms around my chest. Acting as if I were asleep, I'd shrug her off, then roll over to the far side of the bed in the fetal position. I didn't know why, but whenever she'd reach out to defuse the situation, I always seemed to push her away.

From the bits and pieces Patsy revealed to me, I could relate to her difficult childhood. I truly believed our unfortunate experiences would make us closer; our past would make us appreciate our future. I knew Patsy was in pain, and as much as I was affected, I knew she was battling with herself.

For the most part it was Patsy who tried to make amends. At times when flying at twenty-nine thousand feet, I'd open my lunch to find a note she had taken hours to say on paper what she could not tell me in person. Or I'd come home to find the apartment immaculate and an elaborate dinner waiting for me. When things were smooth between us, no one was kinder or sweeter than Patsy. I doubted if she even realized her own potential. Just as Patsy was there for me, during the rough times with Harold, I owed it to her to stick it out. I believed working through the little bumps on the road was exactly what a relationship was all about. I had thought for many years of being alone that I was not good enough to be with anyone, and now I had a chance. If these were the dues I had to pay, then so be it.

When I next saw Alice, I kept replaying everything Patsy and I had been through in my head. Since I had become an air crew member, I had lost my focus. I began to live a little too much. I went out to bars, and I spent, for the first time in my life, rather than saved for my future. I began to throw away years of self-discipline. But I thought that whatever my problems, I should have known better; I had brought them upon myself.

Sadly enough, I also knew I could not leave Patsy.

'Things are fine with you and Patsy?' Alice probed.

Turning away to avoid looking at my foster mother, I paused before nodding yes. 'Mind if I spend the night?' I yawned. 'It's a long drive and . . . I just wanted to spend some time together.'

Alice nodded. By the look in her eyes, I sensed she understood.

A weekend with my foster mother gave me a chance to catch up on some badly needed sleep and time to clear my head. But within days of returning home, another problem between Patsy and me surfaced. After living together for nearly a year, the money that had taken me years to save was almost depleted. Ever since Patsy had moved in, I was spending more than the air force paid me, and I had to draw from my savings to get by. Patsy always claimed she'd help out. I knew she meant it at the time, but the funds never materialized. After wrestling in my mind whether to bring up the subject or not, finally I did, and hell followed. I was not trying to seem like a miser, for I wanted to make Patsy happy, and would have gladly given her anything I could, but even with only rent, groceries, the very basics of utilities, and a car payment, I couldn't hold out much longer. Once we even squabbled because I could not afford to buy Patsy a television set, let alone cable, to keep her company while I was either flying for the day or out of the country for weeks at a time.

By the end of the summer of 1985, when I finally sat her down to explain my situation thoroughly, Patsy became upset. 'What's the deal?' she fumed. 'I know you fly boys make a ton of dough.'

'Say again?' I couldn't believe my ears. Was Patsy totally clueless about how hard it was for me to bring up the subject, let alone support her for as long as I had? 'What are you talking about?' I shook my head. 'A ton of money? I'm enlisted! I make seventy-five, maybe one hundred bucks extra a month!'

Confused, Patsy shook her head. '*Enlisted*, what's that?'

It was then that I understood the misconception. Patsy must have assumed because I flew for the air force, I was an officer who was paid three to four times more than enlisted personnel, as they rightly deserved for the fact that officers graduated college and had more extensive technical training. But how, I wondered, could she be so naïve about such a simple issue, especially since she had lived near the air base all her life? How could she not know?

As I began to think this through, I questioned myself. Was I being taken advantage of? Nearly two years ago, when I had first in-processed into the air base, one of the lectures I'd attended warned about the possibility of women in the local community latching on to air force personnel, particularly air crew members. I had actually laughed out loud in total disbelief. But now, as I gazed at Patsy's hardened stance . . .

I knew she was not that kind of person. She was simply upset because she must have thought I had unlimited funds. Besides, Patsy had mentioned to me before how badly off she and her family had been ever since her father's death. From our time together, I understood Patsy was an emotional person and had a hard edge whenever she felt backed into a corner. I also knew Patsy was a wonderful woman, and I was grateful for all the kindness she'd shown me, especially during Harold's illness. So, I surmised, if I could relieve whatever strain that had surfaced, we would be that much better off. I wanted, as Patsy did, to work things out. At times I knew it was I, not Patsy, who could be overly petty. I breathed with relief when Patsy assured me she would indeed pitch in. Without hesitation, I accepted her word.

Because we lived in a cramped apartment, with her mother so close by driving Patsy crazy, we decided to move a few miles to a nicer, roomier house. I felt like a heel, but I had to have Patsy's absolute assurance that she would indeed help with the rent and utilities, since I was now financially way over my head. For a couple of months everything seemed fine. When I was not flying in Asia or Europe, Patsy's stress evaporated, her drinking stopped, and our arguments were a thing of the past. She landed a job as a waitress, making her feel needed and appreciated, which in turn made her esteem flourish. To top everything, Patsy loved being out from under her mother's thumb.

But upon returning home from another overseas assignment, I discovered, after nearly interrogating Patsy to get some answer, not one but several bills now months overdue. 'What happened to the money?'

'Well . . .' Patsy hesitated. 'I spent some of it.'

'Some of it? That money was specifically for—'

Patsy deflected, 'Take a chill pill, I'll pay you back. What's the deal? Everyone gets a few months behind.'

'No,' I exploded, 'not me, not now, not ever! I gave my word!'

'Words . . . ? You can't even say it!' Patsy huffed while raising her eyebrows as if giving me a message.

What? I said to myself. My feelings toward her had nothing to do with our latest crisis.

'I really don't see why you're having such a shit fit. What's the big deal? Just take care of it. You always do. I know you've got the money, just make a withdrawal. I bet lots of your air force buddies get behind. Get over it, it's a fact of life.'

'It's called financial obligations. "They" can get drummed out of the service, and if I don't meet my obligations, I can lose my clearance. Without my clearance, I can't fly, which means I can be kicked out. I don't care what happens to them or anybody else. Don't you get it? *I* meet *my* commitments. Always have, always will.'

'Really? We'll just see about that.'

I felt I was being led down another twisted path rather than dealing with the root of the problem . . . again. My brain was spinning with emotions. I constantly had to pry everything from Patsy, figure out what had happened to our funds. I felt manipulated, as if my trust was a welcome mat she could stomp on whenever she felt the need.

Patsy continued to stand with her hands on her hips. 'You're too hard. You think you're so perfect. You're . . . you're not my father!'

I knew that last statement was coming. Whenever she became irate, she always seemed to bring up her father. I tried to calm myself and her down. 'Listen, please, I'm not trying to be your father. I'm not trying to boss you around or control you. If I have, I'm wrong. I'm sorry. I truly am. All I'm trying to do is—'

'You act as if I'm some, some leech . . . I give, too! I'm here for you. I take care of your things, feed your stupid little turtle. I cook for you, pack your lunch, write you letters. I love you. And you . . . Mr Perfect, Mr "What happened to my money" . . . you can't even say the words. Just three fuckin' words!' Patsy stepped forward, waving three fingers in my face.

'It's not like you have women beating down your door. When I met you, you were just a skinny bookworm geek, reading at the pool.' Patsy stopped for a moment. 'I'm with a geek. Me, with a geek,' she announced, as if she had discovered a revelation. '*I* can be with anyone, you know. I was with someone before you, and I can be with someone else in a heartbeat! I see your fly boy buddies lookin' at me, I know what they want. You take good care of me, but why can't you say the words?'

'Why can't you be responsible?' I fired back. To me, everything was either right or wrong. To me life was not that complicated. If I saw a problem, rather than brush it aside, hoping it would simply disappear, I addressed the situation head-on. At the same time I'd make sure I did all that I could to prevent the problem from occurring again. To me, those who kept sweeping their problems under the rug were fooling themselves. A serious, unsolved issue would *sooner or later* suck a person into a black hole. That was one of the many lessons I had learned from living with Mother.

Battling Patsy whenever I was home, I came to believe that she thought it was all simply about money and all I had to do was 'take care of it'. But our core problem was that I didn't trust her as much as I wanted. At times, in the middle of a heated argument, I wanted nothing to do with her. But while alone overseas, I'd miss Patsy dearly and feel I was being too hard on her. I knew I drove her crazy with my idiosyncrasies. *Maybe*, I thought when I played back the arguments in my head, *my standards were too high.* After all I had been through, Patsy was the only person who had ever shown me any affection. Deep inside, I knew I didn't deserve any better.

But as much as I wanted to, as deceptions and confrontations continued to mount up, I could never trust the one person I wanted to love.

Because Patsy and I were so far behind on our rent, I moved from the condominium and into a smaller apartment that was closer to the base. I tried to break up with Patsy, but I couldn't bring myself to do it. Whenever I came close to explaining that we were just two different people, Patsy and I would both cry and make up, promising each other we would indeed, this time, work things out.

By Christmas of 1985, as I drove Patsy to the house of Alice's daughter, the feeling from the year before had completely evaporated. On the way to the Bay Area, I yelled at her until she cried all over her new dress just moments before I pulled up to Mary's home. Recently I had found myself becoming petty, cold, and resentful. My feelings came from how I felt about myself, but I had begun to take them out on Patsy. Even after I erupted on her, blaming her for all my problems, she didn't say a word. After I parked the car, she took my hand, saying I worried too much and assuring me everything would work out. For all the things I disliked about Patsy, at times she carried me when I fought myself.

Hours later, as I hugged Alice goodbye, Patsy leaned close, whispering, 'Oh, I forgot to tell you, Alice is coming with us. She's gonna spend a few days with my mom. Alice has been looking forward to this for a while now.'

By the look on Alice's face, I knew it was another lie. For some reason I could not understand, I felt Patsy was beginning to manipulate, of all people, my foster mother. But after blowing up at Patsy just hours ago, I thought maybe once again I was being overly paranoid. After all, Alice and Patsy's mother Dottie Mae had been friends for some time, taking trips to Reno, and Alice had stayed at Dottie Mae's apartment for weeks at a time. My only fear was having Alice sucked into Patsy's and my bizarre world.

'My mom doesn't even have an overnight bag,' I quietly stated to Patsy while trying to read her true intentions.

'Loosen up, you worry too much. If you must know,' Patsy said, smiling, 'I've been planning a surprise birthday party for you, and, well, Alice wanted to come.' I felt like a complete idiot. Suddenly everything made sense. The last couple of weeks I had known Patsy was up to something, to the point that some of my friends at the squadron were acting strange. Now more than ever, I knew I needed to let down my guard. 'I'm gonna gain your trust,' Patsy said as she kissed me. 'You'll see.'

Two mornings later I awoke to a ringing phone. I shot up, thinking it was an emergency squadron recall. That meant I had to report to the base as soon as possible. I was relieved to discover Patsy's chipper voice on the other line. 'David,' she shouted, 'I'm at the hospital!'

'Oh, my God!' I said. 'Are you okay?' Not fully awake yet, I wasn't even aware that Patsy had left that early in the morning.

'Chill out, I'm fine. Listen,' she said with glee, 'my mom and Alice are with me . . . I've got great news . . .' In the background I could hear Alice and Dottie Mae trying to speak over Patsy. 'They're so happy to be grandparents!'

'What?' I cried, trying to shake my head clear. 'Say again!'

'David,' Patsy announced, 'I'm going to have your baby!'

chapter 9

HEAVEN SENT

There was no romantic proposal. Patsy and I became 'engaged' at a local Mexican restaurant. While there, because I felt overwhelmed with shame about the pregnancy, I spilled over with apologies to Alice at one table while Patsy chatted away with her mother, Dottie Mae, at another. After an hour of sulking in front of my foster mother, the four of us ate dinner, followed by Dottie Mae and Alice springing up and announcing our imminent marriage to strangers enjoying their dinners, who clapped feverishly while I squirmed in my seat. Since I soon was leaving to fly overseas for over a month, Patsy and I set the date for the second week in February.

Days later, on New Year's Eve, I was still consumed with a combination of guilt and rage – not against Patsy but myself. After years of self-discipline and going to great lengths to build a good life, I had thrown caution to the wind. I never had the guts to confront Patsy and sever our ties once and for all. And yet part of me began to feel maybe I had led her on. As unnerving and irresponsible as Patsy was, it was I who had held on.

It didn't really matter what I thought, how I felt, or how I analyzed the situation. The bottom line was Patsy and I – who had similar childhoods but at the same time as adults saw the world in different ways – were to become parents.

Ever since Patsy had phoned me days ago from the hospital, I had been seized with fear. It wasn't an issue of escaping parenthood; it was a matter of responsibility. For most of my life I had felt rejected and inferior, so now as an adult, how could I abandon my own child? More than that, knowing full well that children who were severely abused stood a strong chance of becoming abusers themselves made me all the more terrified. As much as I had told Patsy about my childhood, she only knew the tip of the iceberg. As I promised myself years ago, in order to protect the person I was with,

I had for the most part maintained my vow of burying the past. To compound the situation, since living with Patsy, I had come to realize how petty and argumentative I could be. If that wasn't enough, air crew members in general had an extremely high divorce rate. As these thoughts clashed in my mind, I became consumed with the single thought of doing what was right for my baby.

Here I was lying in bed, next to my future wife, a person I would spend the rest of my life with, hours before the fresh start to a new year, and yet I did not trust her, let alone have the love for Patsy that she claimed to have for me. I truly didn't mean to, but at times I displayed the affection of a statue. To the outside world, I had a great career, but on the inside, after years of pushing down my emotions in order to survive, I had become robotic. *How in the world*, I asked myself, *could I raise my baby with love and encouragement when I barely had feelings for my fiancée and far less for myself?*

Patsy was far more optimistic. 'I've always wanted to have a baby,' she cried. 'My mom's got all boys for grandkids, and maybe, maybe we'll have a girl. This is going to be so great. I can dress and bathe the baby; I'll never be alone. This baby will be the answer to my prayers. A baby will make my life whole. We are going to be so happy.'

The more Patsy prattled on, the more I felt she lacked the seriousness and all that having a baby entailed. Only days ago, we had been arguing for the umpteenth time, and now because of her pregnancy, suddenly everything was going to be roses. I couldn't help but think: How could a person who constantly scraped by in everyday life manage a baby?

Clearing my head of Patsy, my thoughts turned to the one person I had to inform of my upcoming marriage. With the phone shaking in my hand, I punched the numbers to Mother's private line. Even though I had secretly had her telephone number for years, this was the first time, since Father's funeral, I had made contact with her. Holding my breath, I asked myself why I was doing this. Nothing was going to change. Mother still hated me and always would. But I still felt a bizarre need for her approval, and I thought maybe, because of the years gone by, the holiday season coming and the good news of getting married just might soften her heart. I shook my head at the thought, but before I could hang up the phone, Mother's hacking voice came on. 'Yes, hello?' Mother coughed.

I swallowed hard. 'Mrs Pelzer?'

At the other end I could hear her gagging reply. 'Yes, and who is this?'

'Mrs Pelzer, this is David' – for a split second I panicked before completing the sentence – 'David Pelzer.'

'And how did *you* get this number?' Mother bellowed.

As calmly as possible I stated, 'I only called to wish you a Happy New Year, and . . . I, uh, wanted to tell you that, ah, I'm – I'm going to get . . . get married.'

After a few seconds of dead silence Mother replied, 'Well, yes, that's good of you.'

I wasn't sure of Mother's meaning, or if she had really heard what I had just told her. 'I said, I'm getting married . . . a little after New Year's.'

'And the same to you,' Mother chimed.

'Thank you . . . but I'm getting . . .' As I stumbled in my vain attempt to draw her out, the line clicked dead. All I could do was lean against the headboard while still clutching the phone. In the course of a few days, my life had spun out of control. With the phone still in my hand, I began to shake from anxiety. My thoughts continued to shoot off in a thousand different directions, until just a few minutes before midnight when I finally drifted off in an uneasy sleep. My last thought of 1985 was how unworthy I felt of becoming a father.

Patsy and I were married in mid-February, in a small church of the town where she had been raised. Not a single member of my squadron – my air force family – came to the wedding. After several of them had given me excuses before the ceremony, I learned through the grapevine that they did not support my decision. One of my female co-pilots was so upset that she pinned me against a wall days before the wedding. 'This is the real deal, Pelz,' the lieutenant stated. 'I know why you're doing this. We all do. There's something you should know . . . It's not easy for me to say, you're like a brother to me . . . I'm not saying your fiancée's a derelict, but I've seen her kind before.'

By then the frustration was too much for me. 'Don't you think I know? I gotta do this . . . you don't know, I mean, it's my responsibility.'

'You're wrapped pretty tight, Pelz-man. You don't have to get married. You can still be the father, see the kid and all that. You better think about that baby and what happens if things don't work out,' she warned.

Agitated, I grabbed my fellow crew member – an air force officer – by the lapels and flung her against the wall. 'Don't *you* get it? That's all I do is think about the baby? What do you and the others want me to do? I see you, all of you, looking at me, talking about me behind my back, saying what an idiot I am for doing this. You think it's like I'm trapped into this. You're wrong, you're all wrong! You don't know, you really don't. You think I can just pack my bags, hit the bricks, and flee? Ride off into the sunset or fly off into the wild blue yonder? Well, I can't do that!

'I know the odds are against me. But you don't know me. I've beaten the odds before. I'll make it work, you'll see. Besides,' I smiled, 'Patsy loves me, she does. She really does.'

My co-pilot leaned over to hug me. 'Now, who's the one you're trying to convince? You don't have to do this. You say the word, and . . . I could round up the rest of the crew and we'll kidnap you and take you to Reno. We'll make it a no-notice deployment. I've got it all planned. You think about it. We're all just a phone call away.'

'Thanks, Lisa.' I swallowed. 'That's about the kindest thing anybody ever said to me.'

I had received the same response from David Howard, my childhood friend from foster care, who was so against the marriage that he refused to attend, even after I begged him to be my best man. Out of frustration, I blurted into the phone, 'For God's sake, I'm begging you, stand with me. Please?' I groveled.

David and I had known each other for over ten years, and he was one of the first friends I ever had. He gave a deep sigh. 'I know a lot's happening really fast, but I saw this coming. Did you know that Patsy practically bragged to my girlfriend that she'd do anything she could to marry you?'

I brushed David off. 'Come on, man, you took it the wrong way. She meant it . . . in, ah, a romantic way.'

David replied, 'Get with it, man. I'm not downing Pats, but it's not like you've been "out there" when it comes to dating. I know and respect what you're trying to do with your life, but man, what's it gonna be like for the kid with the two of you going at it all the time? You know what it's like. My old man was the same way. What then?' After a few seconds of silence he went on, 'I'm sorry, man, I can't back your play on this. I love you bro, but—'

'Hey, man,' I jumped in, 'I, ah, I understand.' Thinking quickly, I tried one last time. 'I know you two don't get along that well, but Patsy's really a great lady, a class act—'

'Yo, man, hold up. Don't even go there with that one!' David interrupted. 'Are you even listening to yourself? You two are as different as oil and water. Again, I'm not downing Patsy, but I know how this whole thing's gonna end.'

Patsy, who had been straining to listen in, snatched the phone from my hand. '*We* don't need you or want you at *our* wedding. So . . . fuck off!'

David's and Lisa's warnings still rang in my ears as Patsy strolled down the aisle at the wedding. I gazed left, at the groom's side of the church. Besides Alice's daughter, Mary, and son-in-law, Del, and a handful of others, my side was virtually empty. Patsy's side spilled over with friends, relatives, and nearly every member of the town, who beamed as Patsy made her way to the minister. At least one friend from my days in foster care, J. D. Thom, stood with me as my best man. I was so nervous during the exchange of the vows, I dropped Patsy's ring. Later at the reception, one of Patsy's brothers smiled widely as he slapped me on the back, announcing to the world, 'You's family now!'

Within a short time Patsy and I were fortunate enough to move into military base housing. Before I set off for another extended overseas assignment, the two of us set our ground rules. She surprised me by adamantly stating she had given up smoking and drinking, and from that moment on, Patsy claimed, she'd do whatever she could to make things right for our baby. 'I married you, David. I can imagine what you think of me, but I married you for life. I wanna do right for our baby. Both of us had sucky childhoods, so let's do right with our own. But know this, I do love you, David. It's not the baby. I knew from the moment I saw you that you were the one for me. No more fighting, partying, running around. It's over.'

I was relieved that Patsy had become serious about being a parent.

At times when things were good between us I knew she loved me, but now as her husband, my sole concern was to ensure that I did anything I could for our child. 'I wanna make sure our baby isn't treated like we were. I just want to do what's right.'

Hugging me, she cried, 'I love you, David.'

I took a deep breath and closed my eyes before replying for the first time, 'I . . . I love you, too.'

'Thank you, David, thank you,' Patsy whispered. 'You'll see, the baby's gonna make everything different. Everything's gonna be fine, you'll see.'

When not flying overseas, I dedicated every moment to redoing our house. I spent hours rearranging furniture, placing trinkets just the right way to capture as much light as possible. I wanted our home to be open and warm. I felt proud when I purchased a lawnmower and other garden tools. I'd wake up just after sunrise on Saturday mornings to spend the better part of the day mowing, raking, trimming, and watering or planting flowers to beautify our yard. I thought of myself as a husband providing for his family. I did my best to think ahead, trying to take care of every need to alleviate any friction between Patsy and me. Once all the bills were taken care of, I made certain Patsy received the bulk of our remaining funds. With each passing day my initial fears began to fade.

On payday I'd rush to the on-base department store and scour every aisle that had anything to do with babies. As the months progressed, I picked out toys, stuffed animals, or anything I knew the baby would enjoy. When I ran out of playthings to buy, I spent time in search of the perfect stroller, carrying basket, or clothes, even though I knew the baby wouldn't be able to wear some of the shorts and tank tops for years. I couldn't control my excitement. When overseas, because money was so tight, I skipped a few meals in order to buy the baby a cute stuffed yellow alligator, which I named Wally. The more I did for my baby, the more my heart warmed.

When a member of my squadron asked if I wanted a boy or a girl, my instantaneous response was 'A healthy child with ten fingers and ten toes.' In the early spring, the air force doctors assured me that the fetus was perfectly healthy and was a boy. I was overjoyed with the news, but with my luck I had to think we weren't out of the woods yet. Not until I held my baby in my arms would I be convinced that everything was fine.

Since Patsy and I had set our rules, we got along better. Now whenever we had a disagreement, rather than argue I'd escape outside to potter in the yard until we both calmed down. I knew I had caused the disputes more than half the time, and it was Patsy who would make amends. Even though I still did not trust her as I felt I should, Patsy and I were now living together as husband and wife. All we could do was wait for our baby boy.

In June of 1986 I had to attend a six-week flight instructor school course. Patsy was due in late July, so on every flight I'd drop by the administration office to give them the plane's identifying call sign and frequency in case there was any news. On Fridays, after a lengthy day, I'd make the three-hour drive at warp speed, praying Patsy wasn't in labor yet. The weeks crawled by and still no baby. Even after flight school, when the doctor assured Patsy and me everything was normal, I worried that something was wrong. Finally, in mid-August, Patsy went into labor. For months we had known our baby was a boy, but we could not decide on a name. As Patsy was wheeled into the delivery room, I held her hand and bent down to whisper if we could name our child Stephen Joseph. 'Why?' she groggily asked. 'Isn't that your father's name?'

'Yeah, but it's another chance, *my* chance to set things right. Please?' I begged. 'It will make things clean for me.' Patsy smiled as she squeezed my hand. A short time later, I was the first person besides the doctor to hold my son, Stephen Joseph Pelzer.

Stephen was so tiny and delicate I thought for sure he'd break if I moved the wrong way. I could have held him forever, but the small group of nurses insisted I relinquish my son to their care. Hours later, in the middle of the night, I lay on my bed thankful that Stephen was indeed completely healthy. Before falling off to sleep, I began to feel an invisible weight bear down on me, for now I was a father.

Just over a week later, on a beautiful Saturday, Patsy and I made our first family trip. Before noon, with sunlight beaming through the towering redwood trees, I pulled up next to the same house where my father had taken his family on summer vacations seemingly a lifetime ago at 17426 Riverside Drive. Patsy and I had made countless trips to the Russian River, sometimes staying for only a few hours or even minutes at a time, and I had bored her to tears, constantly harping about one day living in Guerneville. And yet I could not explain to Patsy why I was so drawn to the area. With Stephen cradled in my arms, I sat on the old, decayed tree stump where my brothers and I had once played. As Stephen slept soundly, I shielded his sensitive eyes and whispered, 'One day we'll live here. We'll live here at the river.' Rocking Stephen, I couldn't help but think of my foolish pie-in-the-sky fantasy of my father and me having a relationship at the same spot my son and I now shared. 'I'm gonna make things right,' I promised Stephen. 'What I do, I do for you. As God is my witness, I'll make things right *for you.*'

That afternoon at the river was more than a family outing. After that day my anxiety began to ease. Since Stephen was born, I had become paranoid, not only as a parent sustaining him, but other fears like illnesses, late-night fevers, and getting him all the appropriate shots at the right time. Back in our home at Beale Air Force Base, I discovered a million different ways my son could accidentally hurt himself – jamming his fingers into light sockets, crashing down the stairs, or even suffocating from his baby blanket. '*How,*' I asked myself, '*can I protect him from all of this, all the time?*' It was at the river when Stephen unknowingly taught me my first lesson: Do everything I possibly could as situations arose, but ease up a little and let go. I realized I could not shield, fix, or control every aspect of my son's future, or my own.

From that point on, not a single day passed that I was not utterly amazed at Stephen. How he curled up and slept in my lap, the softness of his skin, or the gentle sounds that escaped his tiny mouth. When I returned home from a late-night flight, I would always tiptoe into his room and become lost in time as I stood over his crib to watch him sleep. Almost every time I did, after a few minutes of no movement from him, I would think Stephen was dead! My heart would seize as I reached down into the crib and snatched him up. I was always rewarded a split second later as Stephen's screeching cry became music to my ears. I would then take him into my bedroom, where I would lay him on my chest.

In the mornings while Patsy still slept, I always made sure I woke up early to spend time with Stephen, listening to him coo, watching him suck on his fingers or crawl through the sheets all over the bed.

I was captivated by his constant smile and how every little thing made him laugh. At times I played with him so much that I was late for mission planning at work. At the squadron I'd show off stacks of Polaroid photos before sticking them in my in-flight checklist, so no matter where I flew I always had Stephen with me. After work I would race home, breezing by Patsy with a quick hello before playing with Stephen. By the time he was in his walker, I would chase him throughout the house as he sped away, giggling at the top of his lungs. I laughed as he learned to build up speed by pumping his tiny legs, then lean his walker before taking a sharp turn. More than once I kept my eyes on him instead of the wall that I smashed into at the end of the hallway. At the end of an exhausting day, I'd slowly read Dr Seuss books to Stephen while he jabbed his finger at the pictures. Even though he was too young to understand, I wasn't concerned, just as long as we were together.

Before his first birthday, Stephen's room, which at one time had been vacant, had become a virtual Toys R Us warehouse. He had so many stuffed animals at one point that I would fill his entire crib to the brim and gently toss him in. He would disappear, only to resurface a few moments later, giggling for me to toss him again. To me, nothing was too much if it made Stephen happy.

With Stephen, Patsy gave her all. She always made sure he was bathed and covered with baby lotion. When she fed him she seemed happy and beamed whenever he did the smallest thing. As a couple, if we had a flare-up, all we had to do was gaze at Stephen and our anxiety disappeared. At times she'd joke that I spent more time with Stephen than I did her. I took the hint. I just didn't have the heart to confess that for the first time in my life I was filled with an emotion that I never felt before. Without a shred of hesitation, my son, Stephen, was the first and only person I adored – that I absolutely loved with all of my heart and soul.

chapter 10

THE SOURCE

By the summer of 1987, just weeks prior to Stephen's first birthday, I took time off from the service and made our family's first long-range trip. Our destination: Salt Lake City, Utah. Since Patsy was complaining of being cooped up in the house, and, surprisingly to me, got along well with Grandmother, we decided to take the journey. I carefully explained to Patsy that Grandmother could be pleasant on the phone and yet in person could be controlling and spiteful, but Patsy didn't care. She thought I was being paranoid. Once there, I knew Grandmother would drive Patsy and me crazy, but since becoming married and having Stephen, Grandmother had treated me like never before. On the phone she savored all updates of Stephen. In the back of my mind, though, I was extremely leery because of my last visit with her.

Secretly, I had another reason for traveling to Salt Lake City. For years I had had so many questions, and now I felt I was ready. With each day as Stephen grew before my eyes, I could not imagine how a person, let alone a mother, could concoct ways to dehumanize and torture their own child. As much as I craved closure to my past for myself, now as a father I felt I owed it to Stephen.

With Patsy and Stephen at Grandmother's house on a warm late morning, I drove the Toyota to Mother's and stopped a few houses away. Before getting out of the car, I stopped to collect myself. I checked my watch to make sure I wasn't late. I ensured every hair on my head was in place so to make a good impression. For the hundredth time that morning, I asked myself if I really wanted to go through with this. Part of me felt it was a hopeless quest. I knew Mother would never come out and tell me why she did all she did to me. After the countless ways Mother had made me suffer and the river of booze she had consumed over the years, she probably had no memory of it all. But, I thought, if I could walk out of there with even some information, maybe that would be enough to make me feel cleansed. As a matter of closure, if I could enter Mother's house without cowering down to her and display myself as the fair-minded, independent, responsible person that I strive to be, then by the time I left, I'd know in my heart I was no longer looked upon as a child called 'It'. After the years of self-doubt, I was beginning to feel I didn't need to prove myself to Mother anymore. Of all my tests, perhaps seeing Mother was the ultimate one for me.

Walking up to the house, I noticed how worn and lifeless the grass had become and how overgrown and unkempt the bushes were. Among the well-groomed houses on the street, Mother's gloomy, rundown home stood out. 'And years ago,' I said to myself, 'her home was the Camelot of the block.' After knocking on the door, I caught a whiff of a rancid odor. When the door opened, I almost fell over from the smell. Before I could turn my head away, Mother flashed a smile. 'Yes . . . well, right on time. Come in.' Confused, I thought Mother was acting as if my seeing her was an everyday occurrence. Before I could offer a greeting, Mother spun around and made her way up a small flight of stairs. As I followed a few steps behind, an overwhelming stench began to flood my senses. Covering my mouth, I guessed that part of the smell came from the stairs, which were worn to the point there was nothing left but the bare wood. Whatever covering that remained was on the edges, but was layered in what I assumed were cat and dog hairs. The walls gave off an eerie glow from the dark yellow-brown stains from, it seemed, Mother's constant smoking.

After my youngest brother, Kevin, who by now I guessed to be sixteen, proudly showed off his bedroom, I returned to the living-room to sit next to Mother. Kevin seemed to hover nervously as Mother and I strained to make small talk. After a few attempts, my mouth became dry. All I could do was nod my head as Mother made an occasional remark. An icy tension began to fill the room. For some odd reason, I was not afraid or even slightly intimidated by her. If anything, I could not help but stare at her. Since Father's funeral seven years ago, Mother had not only gained a great deal of weight, but her face now seemed pudgy and leathery. Her crimson features reminded me of Father's when I had found him at a bar across the street from the bus station in San Francisco during a visit before I joined the air force. Mother's fingers were swollen and twitched every few seconds. I fidgeted in my chair while trying to think of something to say. But Mother's appearance said it all. Her years of vindictiveness had left her a broken and lonely person. Whatever domination Mother once waved over others like a sword, allowing her to hurt anyone whenever she pleased, had now vanished.

Growing bored, Kevin barged out of the room, down the stairs, and from the house. Before the front door closed, Mother's head snapped upright. As if making sure the coast was clear, she murmured, 'I want you to know it was an accident.'

Realizing I was alone with Mother for the first time since that day in March before I was rescued – over fourteen years ago – made me feel weak. I couldn't believe I was actually sitting four feet away from someone who had tried to kill me. Mother's statement flew over my head. 'I'm sorry,' I apologized, 'accident?'

Mother heaved as if she were already impatient with me. Raising her voice, she stated, 'I want you to know *it* was an accident!' She nodded as if I should understand her coded message. All I could do was nod back. An eerie silence followed. Raising my eyebrows, I tried to get Mother to explain, but she simply grinned. Suddenly it hit me. Years ago, one summer when I was a child, during one of Mother's rages, she had snatched a knife and threatened to kill me. Back then I had known by her drunken condition and her flailing arms that Mother's threat was beyond the norm. Sitting in front of Mother now, I could visualize the terror in her eyes as the knife slipped from her grasp before stabbing me. I knew somehow, even back then, Mother had never meant to kill me. I had always felt it was one of her 'games' that went too far.

Collecting myself, I leaned over in the chair. 'Yes,' I exclaimed, 'an accident! I knew, I always knew you didn't mean . . . to kill me.' As the words sputtered from my mouth, I could visualize the figure of a small child unconscious on the spotted kitchen floor, with blood oozing from his chest, while Mother stood above him, wiping her hands as if nothing had happened. Back then I had believed the stabbing would jolt Mother out of her vindictive madness and make her see how insane she had become. My injury would transform the evil Mother into the beautiful, loving Mommy I had prayed for. Only then could 'The Family' somehow reunite, like a fairy-tale ending.

Now, sitting with Mother in her dingy living-room, I wondered why I was still drawn to her. Whenever I thought of Mother, I found myself constantly trying to prove that I was not the disobedient *monster child* that deserved to be *disciplined*, as Mother had drilled into my head for so many years, but that I was a human being of some self-worth. Because of my lack of self-esteem, even in foster care, I had always tried to uncover what I could do to prove myself to Mother, trying to accomplish something so phenomenal that the slate from my childhood would be wiped clean. As an adult I fully realized I was a fairly competent, independent person. I had not only gone from an almost animalistic child to a functional, married adult, an elite air crew member with the air force, but I was also the father to an incredible boy whom without a passing thought I showered with true love. I knew I had a long way to go, certainly when it came to issues of trust. The shame from my past still made me question myself. Especially in front of Mother, part of me felt that I had been the source of wrongdoing, that I was a failure. Only a wave of Mother's magical wand of acceptance would make my self-worth flourish.

Easing back into the chair, though, I realized I was not wrong. *I had not made Mother do those things to me.* I hadn't forced, let alone provoked her to stab me. And now, sixteen years since the accident, Mother still could not bring herself to apologize for nearly killing me then, or for any other abuse she had inflicted on me during all those years. Mother's statement made her look as if *she* were the victim of the situation.

The booze had not erased Mother's memory – she knew exactly what she had done. She did not display any remorse, unless Mother's bringing it up was her feeble way of seeking forgiveness. If that was the case, did Mother actually bear some form of guilt? Was her statement revealing a shred of affection? Did she care? If I could just strip through the layers of vengeance . . .

With true sincerity, I gently probed, 'What happened?' But before Mother could respond, I found myself spilling over with a list of questions. 'Why me? I mean, what was it that I did to make you hate me?'

'Well . . .' Mother cleared her throat as she raised her head. 'You have to understand, "It" was bad, David.' Mother's impassive explanation hung in the air. Shaking my head, I acted as if I had not heard her. I deliberately wanted Mother to repeat herself so she knew exactly what she had just stated. With a strained exhalation, Mother restated her justification, placing a further emphasis on 'It' and 'David', as if they were two separate entities. Still I was too dazed to respond. Mother's further elaboration only confused me more. 'David, "It" was always trying to steal food. "It" deserved to be punished. The other boys had their share of chores, too, and I would have fed "It" once "It" was done with the chores . . . but . . . "It" was always stealing food.' Mother again gestured with a nod of her head, as if I should agree with her. 'When you think about it, it's really not that difficult to understand, David.'

For years I had believed if I ever confronted Mother as an adult, she would finally have to grasp the magnitude of the problem. I never meant to be vengeful. Part of me became concerned that the moment Mother realized the depth of her actions, she'd have a heart attack. But now Mother was carefully rationalizing her actions, guarding every word, making her treatment of 'It' seem like nothing more than a parent disciplining a disobedient child; brutalizing 'It' had not only been justified, but necessary.

'But why me? Was I really that bad? What did I do that was so wrong?'

'Oh, please,' Mother said. 'You may not remember, but you were always getting into everything. You could never keep that yap of yours shut. From one end of the house to the other I could always hear you wailing, more than Ron and Stan. You may not remember, but you were a handful.'

Mother's testimony made me recall when I was four and how scared I was to speak. When my two brothers and I played in our bedroom, if I became too excited, Ron would cover my mouth so my voice didn't carry. Later on I was controlled to the point that I had to stand in front of Mother, with my chin resting on my chest, waiting for her to give me permission to speak so I could then ask her if I could go to the bathroom. More than once, with Mother towering over me, she'd contemplate aloud, 'Well, I don't know what you want from me.' Even then I felt trapped. Before I could ask her for approval, she would snap her fingers as a warning, as if I were a pet that required to be broken in. With my knees locked and my body weaving, sometimes I'd urinate on myself, which only sent Mother into a further rage.

Had that been Mother's way of disciplining me initially? Maybe I was too much for her to handle. Mother could have as easily picked on either Ron or Stan; it didn't really matter. Maybe Mother singled me out for something as simple as the irritating sound of my voice.

All I could do was think of Stephen. As I did, the outline of a child sprawled out on Mother's kitchen floor in a pool of blood suddenly became my son. Seeing my reaction, Mother's eyes flashed with pleasure. Once again I allowed her to feed off my emotions.

With my hands slid under my legs, I wanted to jump up and scream into Mother's repulsive face, *You twisted, sick bitch! I was a toy for you to play with! A slave at your command! You humiliated me, took away my name, and tortured me to the brink of death, because . . . because my voice was too loud?*

Breathing heavily, I continued to rage to myself, *Do you realize what I can do to you now, at this very moment? I could wrap my hands around that swollen neck of yours and squeeze the life out of you. Or make you suffer slowly, ever so slowly. I wouldn't kill you right away, but I'd strip away the very essence of your being. I could do it. I actually could.* I'd kidnap Mother, take her to some dingy hotel, lock her in a room, and deprive her of all the things that sustained normal life – food, water, light, heat, sleep, contact with others; I'd make her life hell. Afterward, I could tell the police that . . . I just flipped out . . . from some sort of post-traumatic stress from my treatment as a child. For once I could throw everything away and . . . become like her.

A freezing sensation crept up my spine. *Oh, my God!* I warned myself. With my wrist beginning to tremble, I wondered, *Am I insane?* Or were my thoughts normal considering what I'd been put through? Suddenly the light dawned on me: it was the chain, the chain linking me to my mother – a person who for whatever reason had become possessed with so much rage that over time the emotion grew into a cancer, passing itself on from one generation to the next . . . leading to my son in a single beat of my heart; I could become the person I despised the most.

Closing my eyes, I erased the thought of revenge and flushed away any feelings of hatred that I held against Mother. I could not believe the intensity of my rage. Taking a slow, deep breath, I cleared my head before raising my face and staring into Mother's eyes. For my own peace of mind I told myself, *I'm never gonna be like you!*

How different Mother looked to me now. To me as a child, in some ways Mommy was a princess, reminding me of Snow White. Her bright smile, her kind voice, and the way Mommy's hair smelled when she had wrapped me in her arms when I was a preschooler. I had watched Mommy glow as she laughed, as Ron, Stan, and I vied for her attention. And now, with Mother hunched over and her hips molded to her chair, her past had caught up with her, like Father's had years ago. Her life these days consisted of what she viewed from a television set. Her form of control was now a piece of plastic used to change channels to her world. Whatever light had kept her soul lit had been extinguished. *Mother had become her own prisoner.* Whatever harm I had just wished upon her moments ago could not compare to her self-created prison.

Mother's change of tone brought me out of my trance. 'You may not think it by looking at me, but you and I are very much from the same piece of cloth.'

I shook my head. 'Excuse me?'

Mother seemed to make an effort to control her sniffling. 'You think life is so easy, well . . .' she huffed, 'before I was pregnant with Ron . . . I had a miscarriage.' She stopped abruptly, as if for effect. Not knowing if she was sincere or again trying to feed off a tragedy, I wasn't sure how to react. Suddenly her face turned dark red. 'You think this entire planet revolves around you! David, David, David! That's all I've heard about for years was David this, David that, "feed the boy", "don't punish the boy", every day since the day you were born!' Building up steam, Mother pointed a finger at me. 'And let me tell you something else: it was those teachers, those teachers at school, butting into my affairs! It's no one else's damn business! What happens in someone's house should stay in that person's house! But I tell you what: I taught that – that hippie teacher of yours, Ms Moss, a thing or two when I had her little behind removed from the school. She was out of there so fast, you'd thought it made your head spin.

'You don't remember,' Mother went on, 'but when you were six, maybe seven, you were playing with matches one day and . . . you burned your arm. If I told you once,' she said, 'I told you a thousand times. Anyway, one day you showed up with a few marks on your arm. And that Moss teacher of yours had the audacity to accuse me of . . . well, we both know what happened, don't we?'

Quite well, I said to myself. Mother's recollection was off by two years. I was eight when Mother held my arm over the kitchen stove. When she sent me off to school the next day, she claimed 'The Boy' had played with a match. Even back then, early on, everyone knew the reality of my situation. Somehow Mother must have believed she could not only hide the secret, but dispose of anyone who challenged her authority.

'And that principal of yours, Pete Hanson, calling me *every single day*! It got to the point every time the phone rang, well, I just knew who it was. I dreaded picking it up. If it wasn't one thing it was another, saying that boy of yours did this or that. How the boy got into a fight, pulled somebody's hair, stole food, clothes, or whatever "It" could get "Its" hands on. *Every day*. Well, it just got to the point that it drives a person to drink. It wasn't me that was after you, it was those damn teachers! Always digging, always putting their noses in other people's business. It was them!' Mother stated as if her life depended upon it.

'You think you're the only one with troubles!' Mother continued. 'You have no idea what it's like. It's not easy raising four boys all alone, barely scraping by, having a husband just pick up and walk out on you. Believe me, I could tell you things about your father!'

'Don't!' I coldly interjected. Lowering my voice, I said, 'He was your husband, and you couldn't even step into the hospital once, just once, or have the decency to mail him a card. Of all the things—'

'Well!' Mother said. 'I'm not all *that* cold-hearted. He wanted me to . . . to take him back before he even checked into Kaiser Hospital. We even had lunch. He practically begged me.'

'You love it, don't you?' I blurted before thinking. I was so close to the edge, just a single breath away from opening up and *really* telling Mother off, but I kept myself in check. The last thing I wanted was to get sucked into one of Mother's games. 'His name was *Stephen*!' I shook my head. 'You must have known he was reaching out to you. You knew he was sick and you made him beg?'

'Oh, please! Enough with the dramatics. I told your father, and now I'm telling you: I wouldn't have taken him back for all the tea in China. You have no idea . . .' Mother wandered on.

Little did Mother know, weeks before enlisting in the air force, the day I had my records sealed, my juvenile officer, Gordon Hutchenson, allowed me a few hours to read through my files, which were in two separate folders and over ten inches thick. I spent the entire day reviewing reams of county paperwork, various forms, and even scribbled legal sheets. One report claimed that after I was removed, a social worker had made several attempts to visit Mother, to the point of pleading just to have Mother open the door. All efforts by the county were met with Mother's numerous excuses until she escalated to threats. Once, she slammed the door in the face of a social worker before laughing from the other side. Back then, as a teenager with the report in my hand, I could not believe her gall, how she seemingly got away with everything. I turned to Mr Hutchenson, asking how Mother could get off scot-free when the county should step in, rescue my brothers, and either have Mother arrested or be given some sort of psychiatric help. I wasn't out for blood, but I felt that if everyone within social services had told me how outrageous my situation was before I was placed into foster care, my brothers wouldn't have to live through the same hell.

Gordon had told me, 'I agree with you, David, but back then in 1973 things were very different; your mother was never brought up on a single charge. We couldn't get her on assault, willful harm against a minor, failure to provide, or, in my estimation, attempted murder. Understand, there weren't a great deal of PCs to protect kids back then in '73. Even now, as we enter the 1980s, there are a majority of folks who are in total denial or believe parents are doing nothing more than "disciplining" their children. Believe me, this whole thing's gonna blow up in our faces – these kids are gonna grow up, go on a rampage, wreak havoc on everything and everyone, contaminate themselves with every substance known to man, whack their kids as they were; then at the end of the day, when they face the judge, these people will either blame their deeds on society or plead that they were abused as kids, which of course made them the way they were. That's when there'll be an outcry from society to change the laws to protect children like you. Mark my words, it's gonna happen. We've come a long way, but we still have a ways to go.'

'What are PCs?' I inquired.

'Penal codes. That's why we couldn't remove your brothers or even slap your mother on the wrist with a warning. So in essence, as you say, she got off scot-free. On the flip side, because of cases like yours, there are now laws on reporting abuse, intervention, the works. A lot has happened in the last six years since you've been "placed". Nowadays your mother would be hooked, booked, cuffed, and stuffed, if you get my meaning,' Gordon had stressed.

Digging further through the file, reading a rare interview Mother had given before my court hearing, I came across an official form stating one of the reasons she 'may have' been distraught was she suspected her husband was having an affair with a woman who was one of Mother's closest friends. Her defense also included how difficult it was for her to keep up with the housework while being left alone to raise *four* boys – the report corrected that it was *five* – while she worried sick when her husband was either at work or 'God knows where', whenever Father disappeared for days at a time drinking with buddies from work. Being alone with no one to console her might have, Mother claimed in the report, made her tip the bottle and fly off the handle a little more than she normally would.

As I rubbed the dried sweat from my forehead, I still could not fathom even now as an adult, over eight years after reading the documents, that my father had had an affair. As a mature person, I fully understood that anyone was capable of anything. So, as Mother continued to play the role as the helpless victim in her neverending life tragedy, I felt the affair accusation was another sinister excuse she had strung out for so many years.

'You still have no idea of what I've been put through,' Mother repeated, but this time with reddened eyes. 'You think you had it bad? Well,' she huffed, 'back in my day, my mother, that person you're staying with, well . . . when I was a girl, she'd . . . she'd lock me in a closet for hours at a time. She did! She most certainly did!' Mother announced with a burst of tears. 'And sometimes she wouldn't feed me . . . for days. Back then it wasn't like today, when children at school have a lunch program. And if that weren't enough, not one day, a single solitary day, passed that my mother didn't berate me, boss me around, telling me what to do and when to do it; what friends I could and couldn't have over for visits. My mother!' she bellowed. 'My own mother! Can you imagine!'

With my chin resting on my hand, I nodded my head. I could in fact understand. As Mother cried, she appeared lost in time, reliving her mistreatment at the hands of my grandmother. I could not help but think *if* what Mother said was true, she had in turn done the exact same things to me, but for far longer durations and in such obsessive, vindictive ways.

As much as I wanted to believe Mother's sobbing was partly show, in an odd way her confession did make perfect sense. From what I had learned, people like Mother abused their children in the same manner they were abused; thus becoming a product of their environment.

But only a few years ago, during the summer of 1983, when I had visited Grandmother, she steadfastly maintained that she had *not* mistreated Mother in any way as a child. *Could it be,* I thought, *by Grandmother's or even society's standard during her time, it was not abuse but no more than stern discipline?*

Unless, I wondered, *Mother was devious enough to concoct a story about her childhood in order to take the blame off herself, transfer it to her mother, somehow freeing Mother from any accountability.*

'You know,' I gently inserted, 'I spoke to Grandma and . . . well, I'm not pointing fingers . . . but she was adamant that she never, under any circumstances, abused you.'

'Well,' Mother coughed as she rolled her eyes, 'look at the source. You know how she is. Who are you going to believe?'

The source, I repeated to myself. *Look at the source.* At that moment in time I wasn't sure who did what to whom and what for. *Okay,* I thought, *maybe Grandmother was overbearing.* When her husband passed away, leaving her to raise two children in the middle of a depression, Grandmother had to be stern. As a young woman, Mother might have craved her independence, tried to get out from under Grandmother's ruling thumb, then somewhere down the road became addicted to booze, got married, had kids, while still carrying some resentment . . . that ate at the core of her soul. With my fingers rubbing my temples, I was totally confused. *But,* I reflected, *in the final analysis did it truly matter?* My only concerns were that I make every day count, while trying to be the best person I could possibly be, and to make certain that my son would never be exposed to anything but a safe and loving setting. Period.

Imagining my son, Stephen, with his bright blond hair and giggling smile, made me want to recapture the essence of 'Mommy' I had always longed for. I wanted to fall on my knees, wrap my arms around Mother's waist, as if she still held a lifeline to my soul. And by my openly granting her amnesty, it would free me from being tied to my past and allow me to close that part of my life once and for all.

I stopped myself before I gave in to my foolish emotions that I always seemed to wear on my sleeve. For years I had felt I was either overly proving myself or giving myself away in the vain hope that someone would like me. As if the acceptance of other people were going to make all the difference.

Although I harbored no hate or ill feelings against Mother, breathing in the fumes from her lair, while surrounded by objects from our mutual past, made me feel nothing but pity for the person who was once my mommy.

Abruptly I stood up. 'Thank you for allowing me to visit . . . Mrs Pelzer.'

Mother's facial expression changed, as if she were deeply saddened. 'Come on now,' she said, smiling, 'for old times' sake, call me . . . call me Mom,' she nearly pleaded.

I meant no disrespect, but I had to give myself some shield of protection. All I could do was extend my hand repeating, 'Thank you, thank you for your time.'

'Please?' Mother begged while she took my hand, but this time with a hint of *Mommy*'s voice from years ago. I held my breath. I could feel the fingers from my left hand shake as I started to become light-headed. Part of me so desperately wanted to collapse in her arms, peer into her eyes, and hug her as if our lives depended on it. A moment later, although there was only an arm's length between us, I knew Mother and I were worlds apart.

With a slight nod of her head, she let go of my hand. Mother understood. And yet I couldn't move. 'If this means anything, the one thing I can give you is this: You,' I said, pointing, with tears seeping from my eyes, 'you made me strong. Because of . . . you made me want it more.'

Mother cocked her head to the side. By her expression, I knew I had hit a raw nerve. Mother sucked in a deep breath, and I could feel the pressure build inside me. But a second later she let it pass. With the slightest nod, she understood my compliment.

As I walked down the stairs leading to the door, Mother burst out, 'David!'

With my hand on the doorknob I spun around. 'Yes?'

'Do you love your son?' she asked.

Feeling choked up while a dam of pressure built up from behind my eyes, I stated, 'Yes! With every fiber of my being!'

'Just remember,' Mother cried, 'at one time I did . . . I loved mine, too.'

In the car I couldn't stop myself from shaking. A bone-chilling sensation crept up my spine. Once away from Mother's house, I pulled the car to the curb, opened the door, and threw up.

chapter 11

A PERSONAL MATTER

Not a single day passed after my visit with Mother that I did not think about her. Whenever I found myself alone, my thoughts always turned to her. Usually I ended up wondering whether if someone had stepped in early enough actually to dig at the root of the problem, then maybe things wouldn't have ended as they did. As Stephen grew from a toddler to a young boy before my eyes, I became haunted by Mother's condition. Part of me felt torn between the life I had with my son and the darkness of Mother's jail, as if someday, without warning, I could join her world. As if no matter what I did, no matter how hard I tried, I was destined to become like her. I felt, in order to protect Stephen, I had to be a better person. I had to do more.

In a sense, Stephen was slowly becoming not only my outlet but my savior. When not at work, I'd squeeze in every minute I could to be with my son. Rushing home after a flight, I'd strip off my sticky flight suit, shower, then race outside to watch Stephen splash in his tiny play pool. When he wasn't playing in the water, he'd play baseball. Dressed in his brightly colored shorts, tank top, and no shoes, Stephen would clutch his oversized plastic red Bam Bam bat and cry out that it was time for 'brasebrall'. Since I had never played ball or any other games with my father, I was in complete awe of the smallest thing Stephen and I did together. Once, as the sun was setting, with Patsy across the street gabbing with her friends, I pitched a slow underhand ball to Stephen. He whacked the ball from the middle of our yard and across the street, zooming over Patsy's head and landing a few feet behind her. As Stephen ran in quasi circles, with his hand smacking the tree, the bumper of our car, or anything that he believed resembled a base, I hollered to tell Patsy of Stephen's accomplishment.

Since Patsy had seemingly missed Stephen's monster hit, I

sprinted across the street to tell her and to pick up the ball. As I reached the sidewalk where Patsy stood, one of her friends, Debbie, grabbed her own toddler by the arm and yanked the girl toward her. 'Put the ball down, it's not yours! You stupid little shit! You'd better listen up or I'll whack ya till ya do!'

Bending down, I thanked the little girl, Katie, as she dropped the ball into my hand. I could see her holding back tears. I stroked her head, turned up to Debbie, and said, 'Katie's a real cutie!' Debbie gave me a hostile look before huffing at me, then at Patsy. Maintaining my stance, without pushing too far, all I could do was smile at Katie, stroll back to Stephen, and take him inside.

Later that night in bed, the incident with Katie continued to gnaw at me. For months I had heard Debbie lash out at Katie and then the sound of Katie's crying. At times when I played outside with Stephen, I'd catch glimpses of Debbie, between her chain-smoking puffs, screeching obscenities at Katie while the girl played. Reminding me of myself as a child, Katie always responded by slumping her shoulders. But whenever Stephen played with Katie, Debbie seemed overly kind. When I brought up the subject to Patsy, she agreed about Debbie's behavior, but brushed it off by saying, 'Debbie's just a loud person.' Since my upcoming deployment to Japan was only days away, I pleaded with Patsy to keep an eye out for Katie.

As much as my heart went out to little Katie, my mind was on my lengthy trip. As always, the evening prior to leaving, after packing, I sat down with Patsy to ensure all the bills were taken care of and she had enough money left over for anything extra. Saving the best for last, moments before heading out the door, I'd cradle Stephen in my arms while rocking him to sleep from the music of my stereo.

I didn't give Katie any thought until over six weeks later, when I flew back home from Japan. While scanning a newspaper I came across an article about a stepfather who had 'accidentally' murdered a boy, then buried the body. Years later when the family moved, both the stepfather and his wife dug up the remains before placing the child in the trunk of the car. In court the man's defense was not only did he have a problem with drugs and his temper, but *he* was a victim of abuse at the hands of his father. I muttered out loud, 'Can you believe this? This guy's getting ten years for offing his kid, which means he'll be out in . . . five, maybe six years for good behavior . . . 'cause he was abused? Man!'

Standing beside me, a senior officer from my squadron overheard my outburst. After striking up a conversation about the article, Major Wilson slid closer, telling me his wife volunteered with kids who had been abused and were now in foster care. 'These kids come from scummy backgrounds. You wouldn't believe the stories my wife tells me. I gotta tell ya, it's heartbreaking. It's obvious you don't hail from that arena, but if you ever get a chance, maybe you could do something – talk to the kids, make 'em laugh, whatever. The smallest thing would mean the world to them.' Patting my shoulder, Major Wilson added, 'These kids, they have nothing. You, David, could make a difference.'

Before Major Wilson had even finished, I had already made up my mind. In the last several months it seemed that every day I read, watched on television, or saw firsthand from my neighbor something that related to child abuse, as if there were a sudden outbreak of children being brutalized. Since Stephen's birth I had become more sensitive and aware, but as Major Wilson spoke I realized the subject matter had always swirled around me, but I had conveniently shut my eyes. 'Yeah, Major, I could do something,' I said, committing myself. 'I can imagine what it's like . . . for them.' *Besides*, I said to myself, *It's time. It's about time.*

Within a period of a few months, before Stephen's third birthday, I found myself volunteering for practically anything throughout the state of California that had to do with kids who came from troubled backgrounds. I began by speaking to older teenagers in foster care about not becoming swallowed up by their negative past, while praising them for overcoming their situations by their own determination. 'And if you can do that as a kid, without any help, without a college degree, without any training, coaching, or guidance,' I'd ask them, 'what on earth could you now, as a *young adult*, not possibly achieve?' A few times a tough-acting teen would interrupt, asking, 'Hey, man, what do you know? You ain't one of us. Man, you's a fly boy, what do you know?' I stopped for a moment to formulate my reply. 'All right, I have no right to tell you what to do. I may not know exactly what every one of you has gone through, but I do know what's it's like to walk a few miles in your shoes.' So in order to qualify my message, I felt I had to reveal parts of my childhood. I felt I owed them that much. And whenever I gave an illustration, I always told the audience what I had learned from the situation that somehow made me a stronger, better person. I had no need for bells and whistles or any other hype. I always spoke from my heart, treating every group like young adults instead of children. I always gave them total respect while challenging them to better themselves. My premise was never one of being a victim or exposing a dark secret for sympathy, but one of resilience.

Drawing further from my past, as I began working with adults who specialized with youth at risk, I offered reasons why some children who come from dysfunctional backgrounds react as they do and possible ideas to turn troubled kids around. To my horror, I discovered workers in these organizations rarely received any commendation, so as a matter of honor and respect, I would praise the individuals who struggled to make a difference with children.

Before I could give the matter much thought, I was overcoming one of my greatest anxieties. I was learning to talk to anyone, at any time, at any level. I became so consumed with my efforts that I conquered an enormous burden that had plagued me since I was a preschooler. But it didn't happen overnight. Before a presentation, alone in the car, I'd talk out loud, at various levels, paces, and tones to the point at times my voice almost gave out. At home, after tucking Stephen into bed, I'd sneak into the bathroom, close the door so not to disturb Patsy's sleep, and stand in front of the mirror for hours at a time, watching how my lips parted when I'd try to pronounce certain words. At work, I'd crack open my flight manual to learn long-syllable words; I also developed a technique to replace a word instantly if I became nervous and could not pronounce it correctly. Sometimes moments before a program, I'd become extremely nervous to the point of excusing myself and rushing to the bathroom to throw up. I quickly learned not to eat anything prior to speaking. Between my flight schedule and my present quest, I'd sometimes go without food for days. At times I'd still stutter, but somehow I'd find a calmness, tap into the audience, and let things happen. When the subject matter became too serious, I'd fire off comical impersonations, one after another, while maintaining my focus of driving my message home.

The more these individuals thanked me for my efforts, the more I'd open up and reach out with everything I had. I began to see my place in the world and the difference I could make to ease a bit of suffering, rather than turning my back as I had with little Katie. For years, in the back of my mind, I had always hoped something or someone else would fix the problem of not only children being brutalized, but the scores of individuals who blamed their current predicament on their past. As my father had years ago, I, too, had fantasized that if I swept the situation under the rug it would magically disappear. Now, as a parent, my conscience could no longer let me turn away.

My travels escalated to the point where after a night flight, I'd hop in my car at one in the morning, drive six hours without a break, to arrive just in time to spend the day at a teen conference. Other times I'd take leave to journey to the southern part of the state to speak to college students studying the psychological effects of abuse. I always relied on my own means. Whenever I was offered money for lodging or even gas, I'd refuse, asking instead that the sums be funneled back into the organization. As much as I felt the pinch, I believed it was wrong to accept payment. For me, changing a person's attitude for the better was payment enough.

As my activities increased, the problem of my childhood being exposed to the air force was becoming a reality. If discovered, I felt, I would lose my clearance. Whenever the squadron received a letter from one of the agencies I'd worked for, I'd casually reply that I was simply helping out. Even when I received an award from the governor's wife, Patsy accepted on my behalf and I never told my squadron. The extensive traveling and flurry of kudos from across the state were beginning to take their toll. I felt caught between two worlds. If I was to continue, I had to come up with a different tactic that would keep me local as well as provide a lower profile.

After assisting as a volunteer youth service worker, I was hired part-time in juvenile hall. I jumped at the opportunity to work directly with teens, who, like me at their age, were skating past the edge. Patsy liked my job because it kept me from constantly going all over the state, and working at juvenile hall added to our income. Patsy had been cross when I recently donated my award money to a local organization. 'Do you know how much money that is?' she asked.

'It doesn't matter,' I had pleaded at the time. 'It's the right thing to do. Besides, we're doing fine.'

'Oh, really? You may live in a high-horse morality world, but I live in a real one!' Patsy vented. As taken aback as I was, Patsy was right. Even though I had checked with her every step of the way, I had in fact spent family funds for my cause. Over the course of a year, besides all the traveling expenses, I had sponsored a child abuse-awareness contest, providing scores of prizes and certificates for all the kids who entered. During Christmas I ran around town, collecting mounds of candy, hundreds of comics, and even a big Christmas tree for the kids at juvenile hall. Since I knew what it was like for some of them, I wanted to brighten their world if only for a day.

As upset as Patsy was, I knew she had a soft heart. When I ran out of Christmas stockings for the kids in juvenile hall, Patsy not only sewed makeshift stockings out of cloth by hand, but spent an entire day making cookies for the kids and staff. I was fully aware of other influences on her. She hung out with other wives from the block who seemed to complain about everything in their lives and how the air force somehow owed them for all their sacrifices. Caught up in the tide, more than once Patsy had brought up the subject when she was upset. Part of me understood her frustration of being alone while I was away, but she, unlike some of her friends, had family only minutes away, as well as everything she could desire. Once, when I thought she went too far, I adamantly stated, 'Okay, it's not a mansion, but we live in a beautiful home, rent free. The only bills we have are car, gas, insurance, and food. Period. You don't work; you have a beautiful baby. So tell me; how bad can it be?'

'You don't know what it's like. Sometimes I just go crazy,' Patsy fired back. 'You're . . . you're always out there flying or doing God knows what. I support you in your little promotional things . . . helping the kids, making them laugh, or whatever . . . but I thought it would be different. I just . . . I just want something more, that's all.'

At the time I simply thought Patsy was bored. Her moods seemed to change on a daily basis, and I didn't consider she was giving me a vital message. Wanting to get away, Patsy joined me during one of my long drives to the southern part of the state for another series of volunteer presentations to college students. In my heart I believed our time together – without interruptions from the air force, juvenile hall, the scores of agencies I worked for, or from Patsy's family tearing at her – would give us time to sort through some issues that were simmering below the surface. A part of me also wanted to peel away some of the layers of my past so I could finally be honest and open to Patsy. *Maybe*, I thought, *hiding my past was interfering with my being able to trust Patsy.* Due to our leaving at three in the morning, Patsy slept until we arrived at our destination. Moments before I left the motel to go to the campus, Patsy suddenly became ill and remained behind. But by the time I returned that night, Patsy had recovered and was now ready to paint the town. Because of the lengthy drive, the exhausting day, and the prospect of a long drive back home in order to mission-plan a flight with the air force, I was a walking zombie. As much as I wanted some time off to be with Patsy, once again I knew I had disappointed her by declining a night out. Bit by bit, without meaning to, I was adding to our strained marriage.

Still fuming on the drive back to Beale Air Force Base, Patsy said, 'I don't get it! Why do you do this? This running around with the kids at "the hall", the colleges, collecting toys . . . Half the time I don't know where you are or what you're doing. I just don't understand. It's not like it's gonna change anything.'

I sighed as I rubbed my eyes. I knew, as exhausted as I was, I would most likely make the situation worse. 'Have you ever seen something that was wrong and . . . wanted to . . . to do something, anything? You know, just lend a hand and help out? I mean, I'm not trying to save the world, but if I can just—'

'Just what?' Patsy interrupted. 'Hello? Earth to David? It's not our deal. Besides, don't you know that you're being laughed at? Come on, all anybody has to do is pick up the phone and tell you some sob story and boom: you're off saving the world. The least you can do is get something out of it. I know for a fact you've been offered some money.'

My hands tightened on the steering-wheel. 'Really?' I asked. 'Who's laughing?'

'Well,' Patsy said, 'my mom, for one thing—'

'*Your mom,*' I retorted, as if she were a factor.

Losing steam, Patsy muttered, 'And there's more . . . uhm, every-one on the block thinks you're stupid. Come on, who else would be stupid enough to drive off in the middle of the night and lose sleep just to talk to some college dweebs, knowing full well whatever you say to them, they can get from a book, huh? They're laughing, David. They're all laughing at you.'

With sarcasm I said, 'Is that so? Did *they* laugh when you met the governor's wife for the ceremony?'

She shot back, 'Well, if you must know, it wasn't all that. In fact, at lunch the chicken was cold. All your work for what – a cold piece of chicken and some idiotic award? Like I said, someone gives you a call and you come runnin'. You may say it, but you don't owe anybody a damn thing. And if you do, it's me! You keep this up, and the day will come that you'll have to decide between what you're doing and me. The air force stuff I can take, but this "we are the children", "save the planet" thing is getting a bit too much.'

'But,' I defended myself, 'what if I'm on to something? I don't know what it is, but I truly believe in what I'm doing. Maybe these late-night drives don't add up to a hill of beans, but in my heart if I can go to bed knowing I took a chance and gave it my best, that's good enough for me. That's why I push myself. When I commit, I give it my all. I can't explain it right now, but I feel I have this gift. I feel I'm making a difference. You gotta trust me on this, Patsy, for our sake, for the sake of Stephen. If we don't do something, who will? And if we don't step in now, then when? I'm just trying to make it a better place. You know what it's like. I'm just trying to make it better for you and for Stephen. I can't turn away. Please,' I added, 'you just gotta trust me.'

'Making a difference? I don't see it,' Patsy said with a snap of her fingers. 'Besides, it's not like buying a kid a pair of shoes, giving them a video or a stupid Slurpie is gonna change anything,' she finished with a roll of her eyes before nodding back off to sleep.

Patsy's reference to a Slurpie struck a chord in me. When I was a foster child, people like my social worker Ms Gold had not only given me hope that I could make something of myself, but little things, like surprising me with an occasional Slurpie or Orange Julius. The sincerity of their gestures was something that I would never forget. And now seventeen years after others had made such an impact on my life, I reached out to lend a hand.

Yet with every program I did, every contest I promoted, donation I made or mile I logged in the wee hours of the night, I simply did what I believed was true and just. In the midst of my crusade I was becoming enveloped in a certain peace. Besides dedicating myself to being the best father I could, I had made a pact that I would do what I had to in order to ensure that no one became anything like my mother.

chapter 12

THE LONG FAREWELL

In the summer of 1990, subtle changes began to take a toll on our marriage. As an air crew member it began in January with the retirement of the SR-71. After years of rumors of base closings and cutbacks in personnel, the Blackbird was deemed too expensive. The retirement festivities held an emotional significance for me. After years of studying and being part of the unique program, I had the chance to actually see my favorite plane up close. Dressed in my flight suit, with Stephen cradled in my arms, together for the first and only time we ran our hands lightly across the titanium skin of the spy plane.

Before the aircraft's last flight, as some personnel from the base worried about a new mission to fill the void left by the SR-71 Blackbird, a few members of my squadron, including myself, were tasked to midair-refuel a new aircraft that was coming out from the highly shrouded world of 'black operations' – the F-117 Stealth fighter.

Working with the F-117 meant no more lengthy overseas deployments. After we had spent months apart for the last five years, my being home more seemed to amplify stresses between Patsy and me. Without meaning to, I drove her crazy. Patsy had always had the run of the house, and now I got in her way. Even after a few weeks of coming home from work every day, I still felt more like a guest. When I began to become frustrated over petty little things, Patsy bore it with the patience of a saint, but I could sense that the number of these situations, however insignificant, was forming a wedge between us.

But I knew my apprehension was due to matters of trust. After being together for nearly six years, I had grown to know by Patsy's sudden eruptions that something was brewing below the surface. During July 1990, two situations brought matters to a head. I discovered Patsy had a credit card under my name. After Patsy swore up and down that she had received the card out of the blue one day in the mail, she gave me the phone number to the company. As I dialed the number, Patsy snatched the receiver and slammed it back down. 'I already called and talked to them . . . and they said it was okay if we're a little late.'

I knew the only way to resolve this was to play out her game. When I probed for the person's name, Patsy could only come up with 'Richard'. She refused to give me a last name, position, or extension number. It seemed to be another obvious lie, but Patsy was steadfast to the point that even when I called in front of her, she acted as if everything was as she claimed. After explaining my situation to several people, finally I was able to speak to an account supervisor. He confirmed a signature on the card, and said no payments had been made since the card was activated months ago. Apologizing like a child, I informed the supervisor of what had actually happened and promised to make amends. I also begged him not to expose the issue to anyone outside his organization.

'Why?' I fumed as I hung up the phone. 'You . . . you could have told me the truth . . . You could have gotten a card under your own name. Why do you always have to drag me into your—?'

Patsy jumped in. 'Duh! I can't get a card! You know that. I had credit problems.'

I could not believe Patsy's gall. 'That's not the point. The card, the spending, calling some guy from the card company whose name you can't remember, telling you it's okay for you to be late with a payment! With you it never ends. It's always something. I'm tired of being lied to. The games, the constant deceptions. You think, you really believe I'm that stupid? Feeding me a line that if you call some guy, from some company, it's gonna wave some magic wand over what you did and make things better? It's a matter of responsibility, and I'm tired of cleaning everything up!' I turned to leave the room, wondering if I was right to be accusing her. Had Patsy really deceived me or had I signed for a credit card long ago that I had forgotten about? Things were moving too fast for me ever to get to the bottom of it. I stopped as I approached the door. I spun back toward Patsy. 'Do you know or even care that I have another security review coming up? If the air force finds out about this, they can pull me from—'

'From what?' Patsy lashed out. 'I'm tired of air force this, air force that. You're so full of it! You ain't doin' nothin' and you know it. You never did. You ain't shit; you're enlisted. You just tried to make out that you're a part of something just to keep me in line, but I'm telling you this: I can do what I want when I want, and no one is going to tell me what to do!

'You wanna be truthful? You wanna talk about honesty? Come on, let's be honest! Tell me about you! Come on, I'm waiting, tell me!'

For almost a year as the SR-71 was being phased out, I had signed paperwork swearing to absolute secrecy about my involvement with the Stealth program, even though the aircraft had already been revealed to the public. Even after our squadron's involvement with the F-117 during its debut in Panama, as part of Operation Just Cause, we had been warned again of repercussions if anyone said anything, including being threatened with imprisonment.

To compound matters, I hadn't told Patsy about some of the organizations I was working for outside the air force. When I had tried to before, she was either too bored or simply wasn't interested. In my heart I had hoped Patsy would discover for herself the feeling of assisting others in need, and then, maybe, we could work as a couple through issues that still seemed to tug at us both. But even after accepting the award from the state's first lady, Patsy still had not made the connection.

So, standing by the door with Patsy's face turning red, I knew if there was a hypocrite in the house it was me. Taking a deep breath, I meekly asked, 'Talk to me, what's going on? Do you think we are having problems with money?'

'That's your problem,' she said. 'That's all you care about is money, money, money!'

'If there's anything you want, if it really means that much to you, I'll get it for you. You know that. It may take some time, but if there's something out there that would make you happy . . .' As I searched for the elusive answer, the more guilty I began to feel. Was I saying Patsy had to spend money in order to find happiness? If Patsy had everything she desired, that would somehow fill the void of whatever troubled her? I wondered if maybe Patsy spent so much in part because I did not provide for her emotional needs.

Suddenly, I felt I was being snowed. 'Hold on! Wait up!' I said. 'No, it's not about money—'

'Bullshit!' Patsy yelled. 'Even your grandmother says so. Everybody knows that's all you care about. Money, money, money. That's all you're worried about. You need to chill out.'

'You don't get it. It's like you don't want to understand. We have a son, we need to save for Stephen's college. We owe him that, and a home, a real home, that's ours. We're not going to be in the air force forever. You may not see it, but there's a lot of changes coming down the pike, and we're spending everything we have.'

'Don't give me that "poor house" attitude,' Patsy said, shaking her head. 'I know you always have some kind of secret stash. We'll be fine. You act as if the sky is always falling.'

'Patsy,' I said, 'it's not about the money, it's about us! It's at the point you don't even care. I know you do, a lot, and I appreciate everything but . . . at times I feel like all I do is clean up after you. It's like you don't even think about the consequences of what you do. Do you really think I like battling you just to drag out a shred of information, just so I can fix something you did?

'Yeah,' I went on, 'I want a home! I want to save for our son's future! Does that really make me a bad guy? I've been working my tail off for what, since I was thirteen, and even before that as my mom's slave? A slave! And I'm tired of it. So, if having only one credit card and saving a few bucks makes me the bad guy . . . then I'm guilty. The bottom line is: I still have to fix your mess.'

'Damn straight you will!' Patsy blared as she brushed past me. 'Just fix it. Besides, what am I supposed to do? When you're home, you spend more time with Stephen than me.'

'Hang on for a moment.' I tried to stop her by grabbing her arm. But by the flash in her eyes, I knew I had pushed too far.

'Get your hand off of me, Mister Child Abuse Prevention Advocate.' Dazed by her statement, I dropped my hand. 'Got your attention, didn't I?' Patsy said. 'Just fix it and get over it.'

After Patsy stormed out of the house, I removed a piece of paper that I kept behind my checkbook. I scribbled the new bill next to the other bills that had mounted over the past several years. At least, I sighed to myself, I had my job at juvenile hall. It had started as a way to earn extra money, but had become necessary for survival. With my forehead resting on my hands, I began to shudder. All I could do was pray there weren't any more of my credit cards floating around.

It took me nearly a month to get over our latest crisis. As much as Patsy continued to say she was sorry, I brushed her off. After years of hearing the same thing over and over again, I had grown numb to anything that she did that was unrelated to Stephen. All I could do was pray every time I opened a piece of mail or answered the phone that I did not discover another catastrophe. My concern became more intense as rumors began to circulate that the air force might initiate cutbacks in my field. Fearful of the outside world and limited prospects, I worried about not being able to take care of my family.

Finally I got over my resentment. After dropping off Stephen at Dottie Mae's house for the weekend, I took Patsy out on a rare dinner date. As we ate, I held Patsy's hand and apologized for acting like a child. 'I know it's not easy, and I don't wanna come off like some hard ass . . . but I just get scared. I know what it's like to go hungry, to be without, and I can't' – I stopped, shaking my head – 'I won't allow that to happen to you and Stephen. I know you used some of that money to buy me some pants.'

'You never do anything for yourself. I was gonna surprise you,' Patsy said.

'Well,' I laughed, 'I was surprised. I also know by the credit card statement that you didn't buy a lot for yourself. I'm sorry. I feel like an ass that I can't do more for you. That's the reason why I work so hard. Someday, if we're lucky, we'll be able to do things. It's just, as of now, there's a lot of changes, and I don't know how it's gonna affect us. So, we gotta use our heads, watch our spending, and at the same time save for our future, our son's future. That's all.'

'You just take everything so seriously,' Patsy whispered with affection. 'You worry too much. You need to pull back . . . just a bit.'

'Yeah, I know. You're right,' I confessed. 'But let me say this: since the credit card thing, you've eased up. It's like you're a different person – the Patsy I knew when I first met you. That's why it tears me up. When you hang around those half-wit neighbors who bitch and moan, all they do is bring you down. You're better than that. Look at you: you don't need them messing with your head. You live a good life, and you're one hell of a mother.' I paused, aching to say the one thing that would make Patsy believe in herself once and for all. 'I just want you to be happy. With me, without me, it doesn't matter. You don't need Stephen, your family, those "friends" – anybody to make you happy. All you need is this!' I said, pointing at Patsy's heart. 'I know what a great person you are; all you have to do is make it happen.'

With tears trickling down her cheeks, she nodded. 'Thanks, David, for believing in me. Trust me, I won't let you down. Trust me.'

The next evening after returning home, minutes before midnight due to working the swing shift at juvenile hall, I found the house completely dark and Patsy missing. After searching every room, I began to fear the worst. I phoned one of her friends, who answered with music exploding in the background. After I asked for Patsy more than a dozen times, an inebriated voice screamed back that she wasn't there, before dropping the phone. Covering all bases, I was about to telephone Dottie Mae when I heard Patsy fumbling at the back door. Rushing to meet her, I was knocked into the wall when she fell on top of me. ''Unny, I'm 'ome,' she slurred. 'Like you said, gotta be me. But don't worry, *I'm happy*. This is me, and jou' – Patsy jabbed her finger at my chest – 'jou gotta love me for who I am . . .' Suddenly her head rolled back. She opened her eyes wide a split second before she threw up on me.

Hours later, after stripping off Patsy's soiled and booze-soaked clothes, and assuring her she had nothing left in her to vomit, she allowed me to put her to bed. With Patsy taken care of, I cleaned the bathroom, threw our clothes in the washer, and showered off and got dressed to work the morning shift at juvenile hall.

As I drove from the air force base to the city of Marysville, I chuckled to myself. I knew Patsy had dropped by her friend's place and obviously had one too many. It wasn't her fault. She didn't mean to. Yet as the sun began to appear in my rearview mirror, a wave of rage engulfed me. The only reason I was killing myself was to pay her bills, and, to top it off, here I was trying to earn the trust and respect of these teenagers at the 'hall' who had been through hell, so they could get on with their lives and be responsible rather than live their lives as helpless victims. All the while Patsy would spend the day in bed sleeping off another stupor. 'Godammit!' I screamed, pounding the steering-wheel. 'How could I be so stupid?' Every single time I swallowed my pride, thinking I was too hard on her, and reached out with all my heart, something always happened.

'Stupid, stupid, stupid! You're never gonna learn, Pelzer. She's never, ever going to fuckin' change, and you're an idiot for taking her shit!'

I fought to clear my head as I parked the Toyota at the juvenile hall parking lot. I didn't have time to think about Patsy, or analyze the situation I would face when I returned home, or even how exhausted I had now become. As I went up the walkway, all I knew was that it was the beginning of the end. Patsy would never again have my trust.

In August 1990, Saddam Hussein's invasion of Kuwait shifted my priorities. Whatever marital problems I was facing paled beside the prospect of fighting an actual war. For over a week every air crew at the base loaded jets with every conceivable piece of support equipment. We received countless briefings, varying from chemical warfare defense to our task of refueling the Stealth fighters. Knowing full well that the KC-135 aircraft had no defensive capabilities and since the Boeing jet was a 'force multiplier' – meaning the various fighter aircraft could not fly to their targets without our plane's fuel – the Boeing tanker had the makings of a prime target. And because it was a flying gas station in the sky, if we took a single hit from enemy aircraft, my crew and I would be vaporized from the explosion. As the days passed, and as the base waited for our orders to deploy, worrying about Patsy, the checkbook, or whatever credit cards she might have acquired was the last thing on my mind. I had to set aside my mixed emotions about my marriage and focus on doing my part and coming home alive.

After endless delays and a series of last-minute standdowns, I received official notification that our squadron would deploy the next morning at three o'clock. I spent the night before with Patsy ensuring that she had everything she might possibly desire while I was away and knew what to do 'just in case'. I knew Patsy would be fine.

But my heart went out for Stephen. As I lay beside him on his bed, he clutched his red Sony Jr Walkman I had just given him that day. Before drifting off to sleep, he whispered, 'Daddy, where you gotta go?'

'I just have to fly off for a while,' I softly said into his ear.

'You gonna bring me back something?'

'Yeah, but only if you take care of your mom.' I then caught myself repeating what my father had said to Ron, my oldest brother, years ago before he left for work. 'You be the man of the house for me. Can you do that?'

Stephen rolled over and fell asleep on my chest. As I stroked his spiky blond hair and kissed his forehead, I declared to myself that everything was going to be fine. *They won't shoot us down, Stephen. If they do, we won't blow up. I'll use my parachute. Once on the ground, I'll evade. They'll never take me prisoner. If they do, I'll escape. If I can't escape, I'll be fine. I'll come back. No matter what happens, I'll come back. I'll come back for you!*

In the midst of all the apprehension and wild sense of adventure, I felt an overwhelming calmness as I held my son. In an odd sense, it was the same feeling I had experienced as a child when I was ordered to sit on top of my hands in Mother's basement. Summoning all my willpower, I would tell myself that no matter what happened between Mother and me, I would survive. She could beat me, or do as she pleased, but God willing, I would somehow prevail. Now as the night slowly passed, I readied myself for another test. Hours later, I deployed for Operation Desert Shield on Stephen's fourth birthday.

The first few weeks in Saudi Arabia were like constantly walking on eggs. We weren't sure what to expect and when or if we were going to do anything. Whenever I spoke to Patsy on the phone, she seemed distraught, as if I somehow knew when I would be coming home.

By mid-January 1991, as the air force generals briefed us on the probable losses during the initial phase of the air campaign, the possibility of losing every third person opened my eyes. This was no longer a test of adulthood. My main concern was not to screw up on my part of the mission. As it turned out, though, after the first couple of weeks, the coalition maintained air superiority over Iraq, and the missions became routine.

Because we reported for a night flight in the afternoon and returned in the early morning hours, I found it nearly impossible to get any sleep. As I lay on my army cot, my thoughts always turned to Stephen. I became paranoid over things beyond my control. *What if he choked on food when Patsy wasn't looking? Or if he didn't look both ways before crossing the street and got hit by a car? What would I do?* At times I was so consumed by nightmares, I'd awake with my body soaked with sweat. Finally one evening after another anxiety attack, I strolled outside to marvel at the stars. In the stillness of the night, in the middle of the war, as a cool breeze blew from the desert, I somehow found serenity. What I still needed to understand was that there were so many things beyond my control. I needed to let go. After that morning, and on others to follow, I never slept as soundly as I did when I served in the Gulf War.

I returned from Saudi Arabia in March 1991. I stepped off the plane, Patsy ran up to meet me. In the middle of a swirling rain shower, I held her like never before. 'It's okay,' I said. Patsy gave me a puzzled look. 'Everything's gonna be fine. I am so sorry; I truly am, for everything. All the petty bullshit I've put you through. Worrying about things that don't mean a hill of beans. No matter what happens, I know we're gonna be all right.' I then sprinted and scooped up Stephen, who was wearing his little brown flight jacket. I crushed him to me until he cried out that he couldn't breathe. As my family and I walked through the sea of people waving flags and cheering, a surge of pride swelled within me. Not only had everyone from the base returned alive, without a scratch, I had everything anyone could ask for. I promised myself that I would do whatever it took to make things right between Patsy and me. After enduring all we had, I knew nothing could tear us apart.

After I came home, things that had seemed so critical months before were now insignificant. I continued to sleep soundly, and I no longer continually pushed myself to the limit as I had in the past. For a few weeks I felt like I was walking on a cloud. Patsy and I were closer than ever. And, for the first time, I could see changes in her attitude. She was upbeat and self-reliant; she faced her situations by herself, head on, without interference from her mother. One day while driving to nearby Sacramento, I reached over to take her hand. 'I'm so proud of you, Patsy. I know it's not easy being married to me, putting up with all that you do, but you have really come a long way. You should be proud of yourself. You've made it, you truly have. No one can boss you around anymore, turn their nose down at you, 'cause you're better than that; you always have been. Maybe the war in the Gulf was the best thing . . . for the both of us.'

The euphoric honeymoon ended when I officially received transfer orders to Offutt Air Force Base in Nebraska. On a late evening in May, I was overwhelmed with sadness as I drove off from Beale Air Force Base – my home and surrogate family for over eight years. There were no goodbye parties or squadron ceremonies, since others, too, were quietly scattered to other bases. In the process of base closures and personnel cutbacks, I was among the lucky ones. At least for now, I had a job.

A day later, while resting at Grandmother's home in Utah, I received a frantic call from Mother. Taking the phone, I wondered how she knew I was in the area, since I had no intention of visiting her. But as I listened to the sound of Mother's pleading voice, something in her tone compelled me to go see her. The next morning, after I became reaccustomed to the odor of her house, Mother and I initially chatted as we had before. Mother complained about her ailments, and this time I knew it was no longer a performance. I could not help but notice how her hands constantly shook. Even when she placed one hand on top of the other, she could not hide her tremors. Only after taking a gulp of what I guessed was vodka did Mother's shuddering ease. She went on to complain about how hard it was for her to walk and how at times she thought her feet would tear apart from the searing pain. After listening for more than an hour, I realized, even with Kevin still living with her, how desperately lonely Mother had become.

After a few moments of silence, I took a tremendous risk. 'You know,' I lightly said, 'I'm involved . . . with helping kids and others who've . . . had problems.'

'Yes,' Mother replied with a nod. 'Well . . . your grandmother . . . she ought to get a kick out of that.'

We both suddenly broke out in a burst of laughter.

For a fleeting second the sound of Mother being happy took me back in time. By her brightened eyes, she seemed to feel it as well. But I knew it was nothing more than a passing moment. I would never receive an acknowledgment of what had happened between us, let alone a sincere apology. And, after all I had been through, I felt I did need it. Yet the child within me felt a tremendous urge to wrap my mother in my arms and absorb every ounce of her anguish. In that moment I would have given my right arm to hear the sound of 'Mommy's' laugh.

In my trance, my fingers grazed the edge of Mother's once prized oak hutch. I caught my breath as my gaze became fixated on her assortment of towering red Christmas candles. I snapped my head around toward Mother. Then, looking back at the candles, I wiped off the accumulated dust from their bases. As long as I could remember, the one thing Mother had been adamant about was her treasured Christmas decorations. She always put up the decorations the day after Thanksgiving and put her ornaments away immediately after New Year's. *Why,* I asked myself – as I now discovered the sprayed-on snowflakes still in the window in the middle of May – *would Mother not tidy up the one element of her life that had meant so much to her?*

This went far beyond being lazy, I thought. *If Mother hadn't taken care of Christmas decorations with summer approaching, when would she? Unless . . . Oh, my God!* I said to myself. *Mother knew . . . she somehow knew her time was limited.*

Her hands were again shaking, and by habit Mother covered one with the other. But as her hands twitched with more intensity, she struggled to take another drink. Peering deep into her eyes, I stated, 'Don't quit. Don't try to stop drinking.'

Mother's face lit up. 'You . . . *you understand?*'

I nodded. As I stood in front of Mother, my eyes scanned her every feature, in the vain hope of finding the person I had worshiped as a tiny child – the person I had so longed to love me. Yet, as I closed my eyes, I could not give Mother the humanity I gave to total strangers. With all the compassion I could muster, I swallowed hard before saying, 'Go in peace.'

As if she did not hear me, she lifted her head.

Feeling weak, I swallowed before repeating myself in a quavering tone. 'I wish you no pain . . . Only for you to go – to go in peace.'

'Yes, well, that's nice . . .' Mother said in her old condescending tone.

'No!' I lashed out, pointing my finger in her face. Raising my voice, I could feel my legs shudder. 'Don't you even . . . don't you spoil it. Not after all you've done. This is not one of your little games that you can manipulate. You have . . . no one, nothing left. Just stop it! For once put away your bullshit and do what's right, for God's sake!' I pleaded, on the verge of tears. 'I swear to you, with all of my honor, I wish you no pain, no suffering, I only wish you peace.' I paused as my chest seemed to heave. Calming myself, I said in a controlled voice. 'That's all I can . . . that's the best I can do.'

Mother's eyes tried to bore right through me. After a few moments, her intensity softened. I slowly shook my head back and forth. Without saying the words, I mouthed, 'I can't. I can't do that.'

With a nod Mother showed that she understood. Perhaps she had thought that by calling me during her emotional state, I would rush over and anoint her with forgiveness. To my own dismay, and after a lifetime of constantly proving my worthiness to others, I did not – I could not – forgive Mother.

As I walked down the stairs to the door Mother shouted from her chair. 'David?'

'Yes, ma'am?'

'I want you to know . . .' She stopped as if to collect herself. 'I, uh, I'm proud of you. You turned out fine. I am proud of you, David Pelzer.'

I turned, looked up the staircase, and uttered a quick prayer before closing the door behind me.

Mother died of a heart attack in her sleep in January 1992.

Twenty-four hours later, on Mulberry Street just outside Salt Lake City, all five Pelzer brothers joined together. Initially it was awkward for all of us, until Ron came up and hugged me. There was so much to say, but we didn't seem to know how to begin. Over a matter of days, as the five of us talked to each other, I felt overtaken both by shame for what all of us had experienced and pity for the life Mother had lived. We spent nearly every waking moment covered with stench and grime while we gutted out Mother's dilapidated house. Just before Mother's funeral, as we cleaned out her bedroom, one of us came across Mother's wedding portrait. I had seen the photo countless times, but for the first time I realized how stunning she was. Mother's face seemed silky smooth and her hair glistened, but what took me aback were her eyes. They seemed to radiate with pure joy. Mother's expression gave me the feeling that she was about to embark on an incredible life filled with happiness. With the frame shaking in my hand, I emptied my chest. I forgave her. I forgave 'The Mother'. Over the past several years, after I had visited Mother in the summer of 1987, I had wavered on how I felt about her. When I had sat in front of Mother just a few weeks before she died, I came within a heartbeat of stating my forgiveness. But because of giving myself away so many times, for so many years, only to appease others, in hope of their acceptance, I hesitated. Then, because of Stephen, part of me detested her. But, as I became involved with others who struggled, in part due to their past, I felt I had to rid myself of any feelings of resentment.

On a wintry, overcast day, only a handful of people came to Mother's funeral to pay their respects. A gentleman whom I later learned had met Mother a few times and worked part-time as a golf pro, gave Mother's eulogy. At Mother's gravesite, with scattered clumps of snow surrounding me, I knelt down and prayed. With my hands clasped, shivering from the chilling breeze, I prayed out loud for God to grant my mother peace. 'May your soul finally be given eternal peace. And, may Almighty God protect you and deliver you from evil . . . Amen.'

As I finished, I could feel a gigantic weight lift from my soul.

Before I caught my departing flight, all five of us promised to stay in touch, but that was the last time the five Pelzer brothers would come together.

chapter 13

THE LAST DANCE

I was not looking forward to returning to Nebraska. Once again, I discovered Patsy had borrowed money. This time she had begged Grandmother nearly a year ago, while I was flying in Saudi Arabia. I would never have known had I not asked Grandmother for a loan so I could use the money to give to my youngest brother, Kevin, who in his early twenties needed the money to find his own place to live. At first Grandmother was insistent that I had borrowed the money from her. When I assured her I knew nothing about the loan, she then became more livid because I *should* have known.

All the while Patsy fidgeted in her seat, claiming her innocence until she broke down in tears, saying she had forgotten to tell me and she was now too embarrassed to say anything in front of Grandmother. As I tried to stick up for my wife, Grandmother simply raised her head in an 'I told you so' attitude, as if she enjoyed fueling the fire between Patsy and me. At the time I felt like a heel that my other brothers and I could do little to help Kevin, who eventually was able to provide for himself.

At my new air force base, even though I had been stationed there for over eight months, I was still adjusting. My job was completely different and absurd compared to Beale. I was now part of the EC-135 Looking Glass, whose mission had been to serve as an alternative airborne communication command post in the event of a nuclear war. But even though there was a refueling boom attached to the aircraft, the EC-135 rarely midair-refueled other planes. To confuse matters more, the Looking Glass was retired but continued to fly 'unofficially'.

During my in-processing I learned my biggest task as a boom operator was not learning to midair-refuel a different aircraft, but to ensure that the twenty-plus members of the crew received their lunches.

On my first qualification flight, I found out how *serious* my job was when a low-ranking radio operator actually berated me in front of the entire crew because his lunch did not receive a mustard package. Upon landing I was immediately reprimanded by my superior, who rolled his eyes in mock dismay. Within days, because of my blunder, all boom operators were mandated to check every item on every meal prior to taking off.

At home, after settling into a nice condominium we could not afford, Patsy soon became bored. Because we lived off base, she felt even more isolated. When I first found out about my reassignment, I had prayed the move would somehow force us to rely on ourselves, as a couple, without 'family' interference once and for all. During our drive to Nebraska, Patsy had even chatted about getting her G.E.D. and then taking courses in college. She had seemed so optimistic. But within weeks she complained of missing her family in California.

I had assumed with the reduced flight times, due to budget cuts, I would be able to spend more time with my family, finish my college degree, and volunteer once in a while. But because of the ever-changing flight schedule, I could not attend college or volunteer as I had in California, and I rarely saw Patsy or Stephen. To make matters worse, when I received my promotion to technical sergeant, I was assigned as the wing's senior in-flight evaluator, forcing me to work longer hours. At times I'd come home only long enough to throw a ball a few times with Stephen and give him a bath before reading to him in bed. At times I was so tired, I'd fall asleep with Stephen on his bed. As the months passed, I felt my job was completely worthless, and I began to detest myself as a father and a husband.

In the spring of 1992, rumors began to float of severe personnel cutbacks. I saw the writing on the wall. Since the Looking Glass was no longer an operational aircraft and boom operators were not allowed to perform their tasks, I believed I would be among the first to be relieved from active duty. I had always envisioned myself serving twenty years until I could retire, but now that was no longer an option. The air force was also offering early retirement bonuses but for a limited time, and after a certain cutoff, the air force claimed, they could legally dismiss anyone as they deemed necessary. Because of my years in service and my pay grade, I knew I was a prime candidate.

After months of speculating, I had a heart-to-heart with Patsy. So not to upset her, I had deliberately tried to keep her in the dark. 'We've got to make a decision,' I began. 'Uhm, the air force, is going to announce—'

'Get out!' Patsy broke in. 'Your job sucks, you're not happy. I'm miserable. I hate this place, there's nothing to do. Stephen needs . . . to be with his family. Let's take the money, bonus, separation thing, and go home before the air force gives you the boot and you have nothing to show for it.'

'Okay.' Patsy's outburst had stunned me. 'How long . . . I mean, when did you know?'

Patsy raised her eyebrows. 'I know a lot more than you think.'

'Well, hang on, there's more. *If* we do this, you need to know, I mean fully understand what this means. It's a one-time payment; we won't have medical coverage—'

'How much?' Patsy quizzed.

'Well, if we don't have any unexpected bills,' I said, 'we should be able to put some money away for Stephen's college and, well, the rest we'll use to save up for a down payment on a home. But,' I warned, 'with me being the only one working—'

'I told you, I got a bad back,' Patsy said defensively.

I waved her off. 'I'm not saying that. But listen, I'll need to get at least a full-time job with lots of overtime, if not two jobs.'

'So, they're not going to give you a lot of money?' Patsy asked, as if offended.

'The way I see it, the air force doesn't have to give me a thing.'

'What will you do?'

'I've thought about this a great deal. I can't work full-time at juvenile hall; I need a degree, and aeronautics is not what they're looking for. If I'm lucky, I could work there part-time. Jobs right now are scarce with the recession and all, but . . . there is an option . . .'

I spent the remainder of the time telling Patsy about a local speaker organization. 'They've seen me speak a couple of times, and, well, Rich and Carl, the owners, think I have what it takes to become a speaker. It's not a bureau,' I warned. 'It's like having my own business. The firm, they provide the support staff. I can work out of California, and you know me, I'll work my tail off. In a couple of years, if we get lucky, maybe we can get a house and live on the river. Think of it, Patsy.' I reached over to clasp her hand. 'It's the best of both worlds. If I do this, I'll never be laid off. I can help kids, the people who work with kids, corporations, the works. I know I'll never be one of those motivational speakers you see on TV, and I don't want to be. I can't explain it, but I believe with all my heart I have a message that could really help a lot of people. We may not get rich, but who cares? Think about the impact we can make! And,' I smiled, 'they said they'll publish the book.'

'*That* thing? You've been working on it for how long? Why is that so important to you?'

'*That book* is definitely going to change people's lives,' I stated. *Besides*, I told myself, *it's a promise I made a long time ago.*

'Listen,' I continued, 'I know I'm hitting you with a lot. We still have some time. I don't want to jump into anything without both of our heads on straight. This is only the first of many steps we have to address. Either way, it's not gonna be overnight. I love the air force, it's been like a family for me . . . but I think my time has come.

'I'll promise you this. If I have to work a dozen jobs to pay the rent and put food on the table, I'll do it. I'll never put you or Stephen at risk. I promise.'

Taking it all in, Patsy asked, 'How much? With you speaking, how much can we make?'

'Well,' I said, stumbling, 'it's like being on commission. The more programs I do, the more I can make. But there are expenses; I'll be on the road a lot, and I'm going to have to fill the pipeline giving free programs. But, like I said, after a couple of years we should be able to make a living. I just wanna do a good job, that's all.'

'One thing,' Patsy asked, 'what's the name of the book?'

'*A Child Called "It"*.'

'*That's* a depressing title. It's about you, isn't it?'

Still trying to shield her, I shrugged my shoulders. 'Let's just say it's a story about a kid who never quit.' Looking at Patsy, I could tell I had lost her. I paused slightly before restating. 'We don't need to decide now, but I just want to let you know—'

'Go for it!' Patsy grinned. 'I say fuck 'em! Take the money and don't look back. We'll be fine. I know you'll take care of us. Let's do it! Get out!'

I received an honorable discharge from the air force that August. As much as I craved to live on the Russian River, we returned to the area where I had first met Patsy, outside Marysville, so she could be close to her family. We enrolled Stephen in a fantastic school and started anew.

In the fall of 1992, while doing a series of fact checks for *A Child Called 'It'*, I contacted my elementary school to discover that one of the teachers who had notified the authorities, Mr Ziegler, was still teaching. He asked me to visit the school. There was an odd note in my teacher's voice, as if there was something he wanted to tell me.

One of the hardest things for me to confront, far more than stepping into Mother's lair, was returning to my former school. In the middle of October, on a beautiful, crisp morning, I stepped onto the schoolyard as if revisiting hallowed ground. The first thing I recognized was the scent of food from the cafeteria, where years ago I used to sneak in, run off with a handful of hotdogs, only to gobble them down behind the Dumpster.

I met Mr Ziegler as he accompanied his class into the library, where I gave my various presentations. Because we both felt a little awkward, we gave each other a half-felt handshake and a quick hello. As I spoke to his class, whenever I glanced at Mr Ziegler he seemed to avoid me by looking down and away.

At the end of the day, as hundreds of kids scurried from the school to play or run home, a young boy dressed in a worn-out, oversized down jacket politely asked if he could talk to me. In the heat of the afternoon sun, I noticed that the child was nervously tugging on the ends of his jacket sleeves. After calming the young boy down and assuring him everything would be fine, I knelt and held his hand. The boy suddenly exploded in a burst of tears, telling me how his uncle would beat him and burn his arms with lit cigarettes. As his little chest heaved, he sniffled. 'I'm sorry, Mr Pelzer, I don't mean to take your time. I don't want to get anyone in trouble. Please,' he begged, 'you can't tell. Please?'

I felt as if I had stepped into a time warp. I had met the child I once was. 'Listen,' I said, still holding the boy's hand, 'you remember what I said about what happened to me when I was a kid?' The child nodded as he wiped away his tears. 'Here's the deal. We need to get you some help. We're not here to get anyone in trouble, but that's no way to live. Am I right?' The boy again nodded. Thinking of my social worker Ms Gold and what she had said to me when I had opened up to her about my secret, I relayed, 'Listen, you're going to be fine. It takes a brave young man to tell a secret like you did, and it's the first step in making things better. You gotta be strong, but you gotta trust me.' I stopped to look him in the eye. 'You're going to be fine. I promise you' – with my finger I made an X sign on my chest – 'cross my heart and hope to die, you have my word. You don't deserve to live like that, and we're going to turn things around.'

I escorted the boy to the same room where I had waited before I was rescued nearly twenty years ago. After speaking to the school principal, Mr Rizzo, I said goodbye to the young man, again assuring him that he was doing the right thing. I then stumbled toward the parking lot in a daze. As I watched a group of children in the playground, screeching with laughter – the same place I had once so desperately longed to be – I started hyperventilating. I couldn't stop myself. At last, with my hands on my knees, I recovered just before a group of children strolled past. I took a moment to pray for the young boy. I then thanked God for the strange twist of fate of having the privilege of returning to the school that meant so much to me, and how I had played a small part in helping a child in need.

Behind me the voice of my fifth-grade teacher startled me. 'Just heard what you did. The kid's gonna be fine. You certainly have a way with them – the kids, I mean.' Mr Ziegler held out a hand. 'Listen, I know you have a long drive ahead of you, but if you can spare the time . . . ?' A lump began to creep up my throat. All I could do was nod yes.

That evening, during supper in a local restaurant, both of us stumbled to keep the conversation going. I noticed that we made little to no eye contact. I was simply too ashamed. From across the table Mr Ziegler turned away when I looked up from my food and spoke. Clearing his throat as he finished dinner, Mr Ziegler said, 'It's really good to see you . . . It's been on my mind for a while, and I need to get this off my chest. I'm not sure if you even know, but . . . that day, when you came to my class, that day in March when you were taken away . . .'

I suddenly became paralyzed with fear. I had never known why my teachers finally intervened and called the police. I became so anxious that I thought my eyes would pop out of my head. With my left hand under the table, I squeezed my thigh. I almost raised my hand to stop Mr Ziegler. I got as far as running my fingers through my hair.

'You . . . came to school that day . . . you were so small. But, uh – I've just got to get this out – you came to school that day in March, with, uh . . . with no skin on your arms,' Mr Ziegler finished, then took a gulp of wine.

I dropped the fork that I was using. I sucked in a deep breath, staring at my right arm. 'I, uh, I remember. I remember . . .' I felt almost in a trance-like state. 'Yes, I remember, grayish flakes, dark grayish flakes, like patches, on my arms and . . . and my fingers . . . Right?'

Looking as if he had seen a ghost himself, Mr Ziegler stated, 'Yes.'

'I forgot – I mean, I never knew why. It's stupid, but I never thought it was anything she did different . . . I mean, at times she, Mother, she was so careful . . .' I was sputtering as I struggled to find that one thing Mother had done to me that . . . 'Holy shit! Excuse me.' I shook my head. 'That's it. The day – the morning you, all of you, called the police, I remember!' My eyes welled up. 'I remember,' I repeated, 'my fingers and arms . . . they itched. I couldn't stop scratching . . . and uh, I didn't finish my chores on time. That Friday morning when you called the police . . . Mother had to drop me off at school that day. She never did before, but . . . I was so late, late with my chores. Without skin . . . I couldn't grip anything . . . I couldn't get them done on time . . .'

I emptied my lungs in one deep breath. I could feel the tips of my fingers beginning to twitch. 'But . . . it was the afternoon, before Friday, she made me stick my arms in a bucket that had . . . the mixture . . . ammonia and Clorox. That's it. That's what did it.' I closed my eyes and shuddered from the cold that crept up my spine. When I opened my eyes, I could feel a small tear running down my cheek. 'I'm sorry,' I apologized to my teacher. 'I, uh, always had to think ahead, I mean to survive, to outsmart her, and I remember Mother tried, I think, to force my head into the bucket, so, stupid me, all I could do was . . . to think of . . . getting any air I could in case . . . in case she put my head into the bucket.' I stopped for a moment. 'I just forgot, the whole thing. My God. I remember everything she did, every word she said, but, I just, I dunno. For the life of me, I never knew what made all of you call the police that morning. So much happened to me on a given day . . .' I looked down at my hands, which were now shaking. 'I know it sounds lame, but you . . . all of you . . . saved my life.'

'All we did was . . .' Mr Ziegler said, downplaying the situation. 'Anyway, anybody could see what she was doing. Back then there was nothing we could have done, or were allowed to do. Back then it was considered discipline, parental rights, but we had to do something. Any one of us could see what was going on. It's something you don't forget. Ever.'

Afterward, in the parking lot we hugged each other goodbye. 'Thanks, Mr Z.'

'Call me Steven.' He smiled.

'Thanks, but I can't,' I said. 'You mean that much to me. You're my teacher.'

Months later, the week of the twentieth anniversary of my rescue, I returned to present Mr Ziegler with the first signed copy of *A Child Called 'It'*. The second signed copy I kept for my son, and the others were given to Mrs Konstan, my fourth-grade teacher who still taught at the school, and Mrs Woodworth, my English teacher who, because I had stuttered in class so badly, had encouraged me to communicate through writing. By dedicating and presenting the book to my saviors, I felt I was able to fulfill my vow of honoring them that I had made the day I was rescued.

Weeks following, I received a framed picture of my teachers taken the day of my visit. Engraved on the frame was WITH LOVE AND PRIDE. Like a child with a prized toy, I rushed to show Patsy, but she didn't seem too interested. For some time her patience with my new profession had been wearing thin. I tried to tell her, but I could not get her to understand how hard it was to start anew, especially since for years I had given programs for gratis, for organizations that had little to no funds. Somehow, it made it that much more difficult to make a living. To calm Patsy, I told her that because I had not received many bookings, the firm was kind enough to loan me advances. But in order to pay the rent and other bills, when not on the road I worked part-time at juvenile hall and took another job sanding kitchen cabinet doors. It seemed no matter how hard I fought to convince Patsy, for some reason she thought I was going to be an overnight success.

I knew there was something wrong back in the Lincoln office. By now I should have received more bookings. But I felt too intimidated to say anything to the owners, Carl and Rich, especially since they were helping to feed my family. I hated myself for the position I was in. For the first time I was receiving money without earning it beforehand. Since my time in foster care, I always had pulled my own weight. For the most part I kept my apprehension to myself. A part of me felt I was being overly paranoid. I believed if I worked hard enough, somehow, someday, with a little luck, I would succeed.

My only concern was for Stephen. At times I would rush home after flying, driving throughout the night, working at juvenile hall, or putting in a full shift at the cabinet shop to greet Patsy, jump in the shower, then race off to take Stephen to the latest Disney movie or spend the afternoon at the park playing baseball. Whenever Stephen came home from school, I always put aside my work so I could be with him; then later, after tucking him into bed, I'd return to complete my tasks. As much as I struggled to take care of my family, I didn't want to lose my son in the process.

For Patsy, the final straw came in July 1994. After waiting for me to break through, she had had enough. 'It's been nearly two years,' she said. 'It shouldn't take this long. And you're still not making any—'

'I told you, it takes time.'

'Two years, you promised. You said two years and you ain't made it yet. What about me? I had to wait around while you flew for the air force, and now, after two years, what do I have to show for it? We can't even afford to heat the house.' Before I could defend myself, she went off in a different direction. 'You're such a wimp. I know you're getting screwed from those – those speakers in Nebraska. They have no idea what the hell they're doing. They can't pitch you. For God's sake, they plug you as the child-abuse guy, and who wants to hear about that? Whatever happened to you giving those motivational-responsibility programs you gave before?' I shook my head, indicating I didn't have an answer. 'You're so smart on some things but completely stupid on others. I don't trust them. Think about it: If you're such a *great speaker* and if your book is *so good*, tell me, how come you can't get any paid bookings?'

'Well, we got more than last year . . .'

'Oh, no, don't you even go there with that. Even after your little outstanding-American-person thing, you got nothing.'

'Ten Outstanding Young Americans Award,' I proudly corrected.

'Excuse me! Whatever!' Patsy rolled her eyes. 'If your revered little award was all that, why didn't you get anything out of it? It's been, what, a year and a half since you got that thing, and I don't see anybody beating down your door. Huh, come on, tell me.'

If I had a lifetime, I could never explain to Patsy the mix of unworthiness and absolute honor I had felt receiving the recognition on the eve of the twentieth anniversary of my rescue. The Ten Outstanding Young Americans trophy was the same award presented to my childhood idols Chuck Yeager, Orson Welles, the actor who played my all-time hero, Superman: Christopher Reeve, along with a league of others.

'Hello?' Patsy snapped her fingers, bringing me back to the present. 'The point is, you still didn't make it. You may have been hot then, but you're nothing now. Those buttheads in Lincoln should have handled you better. We could have been rich!' Patsy cried. 'After all you've done, after all these years, *you don't get it*. It ain't happening! You ain't got it. You can act all high and mighty saying whatever it is you say, but it don't pay the rent. And,' Patsy amplified, 'if you want to know something, I think you're full of shit. I read your book, if you can call it that. They made it look more like a pamphlet, and, it still didn't happen. Ain't no way no one could live through all that. I should know. Think about it; if you were *that* abused, if you didn't die . . . you'd be psycho, messed up on drugs, an alcoholic, or whatever. I've been living in Marysville and Yuba City all my life, and if what you claim is true, I know the air force sure as hell wouldn't let you enlist, let alone be involved with those jet planes. *If* you didn't lie about that, too. No way!' Patsy shook her head. 'No way! You're too clean, everything's too perfect. What'd you do, pay off those teachers so they could say you were abused? Oh, yeah, you tried to hide it, but I found out. The only reason why you wanted to hide your past from me is because it ain't true. That's why you can't get paid bookings. That's why that piece of shit book of yours ain't in any, I repeat, *any* bookstores. So why you doing this? You wanna talk about trust? Come on, come clean, tell me, tell me the truth! After all the shit you put me through, I deserve to know!'

I had reached my boiling point. 'You want to know what I do? Do you? Do you *really* want to know? I work with kids, begging them that no matter what happened to them, they can turn it around. At the "hall" I restrain teenage girls who have so much meth in them, they want to kill themselves, 'cause they're tired of their fat, sick pimp stepdad hooking them out. Oh, it gets better! I have to stand in front of police officers and social workers, whose jobs are to find kids, babies, locked in cages, beaten to death, chained to toilets, and convince them to put on their jacket and tie, blouse and blazer, every single fuckin' day, and go out, eat shit, and see things that no one in our society wants to acknowledge. And these, these people are treated like the enemy!

'When I'm lucky enough to speak at the corporate gigs, I swear to you, I pray, I pray on my knees I don't speak too fast, come off the wall with my humor and give *them* something, just one thing they can use to better themselves. To tell them that if I can swallow ammonia and learn to speak after stuttering for years . . . if I could bandage myself up after being stabbed . . . if I didn't turn out, as you put it, *psycho* after all the shit I went through, what on God's green earth is stopping them? And you want to know the damned of it all? I pray to God that they – all those people – never see . . . how I feel on the inside. I can't even look into their eyes. Some of them think I'm all that, and I don't feel worthy enough to look them in the eye. Ever! I know I'm not smart. I know I ain't all that. I feel like such a fake. Even now, after all the awards, flying for the air force, getting a letter from the President . . . I feel so guilty . . . and I rack my brain and I don't know why, after all of these years . . .

'I know I'll never be a motivational speaker – I'm not cool, smooth, I'm not polished – but I'm the real deal. I try. With every ounce, every breath, I try to give my best. That's why I land in Omaha, Nebraska, make the ten-hour drive to Bismarck, North Dakota, hit a deer that crashes through the windshield, so I can work all day and into the night, with a concussion, do a program for the kids in a youth jail, all the time hoping my insides don't bleed 'cause I swallowed shards of glass, just so I can save my client $33 on the airfare! Why? 'Cause I feel guilty, that's why! You wanna know why I do this: reliving my past in front of my eyes *every single day*?' I fumed. 'I work so you don't have to. I get up from fleabag motels with no hot water to shower with, praying my underwear I just washed in the sink three hours ago before I went to bed is dry, so I have a chance of giving my son a better life! I eat shit every single day, praying I can plant a seed – just one, that's all. I know I'm a joke, but I give it my all. I just want people to feel good about themselves. That's it. I know what it's like to be less than zero, and I want everyone I meet to feel they're the one. The one person who can go out there and make it better. And sometimes in the midst of all this crap, I can make 'em laugh. I have a gift, and if I can use it to better people's lives so they won't have to go through the hell my brothers and I went through, well . . . I'll do what I have to do,' I concluded.

Not even a heartbeat later Patsy retorted, 'It doesn't change the fact. You . . . you had your chance. You can pass off that Mister "High and mighty, holier-than-thou, give my word" shit to others, but *you're a liar.* No matter how you slice it, you promised two years. I'm getting tired of waiting. What about me? I'm tired of waiting for something better to come along. Don't *you* get it? You're a loser! You ain't ever gonna make it. You're a loser with a big L,' Patsy said, making an L sign with her hand. 'That's it. I've waited and I've had enough. So here it is. Do you love me?'

Still angry, I hesitated to clear my head. After a few seconds I slowly nodded.

'No,' Patsy insisted, 'I want to hear it. After all the shit you've put me through, I deserve to hear the words. Say it!' she demanded.

Again, I exhaled before nodding. 'I . . . I . . . love you.'

Cocking her head to one side, Patsy sneered. 'Well, then, do you trust me?'

Without a moment's hesitation, I replied, 'No!'

After years of hiding it, gently treading around the smallest detail that might explode in my face at any second since I had known her, I said it. I finally spoke the truth that had weighed so heavily on my heart since I first knew Patsy. As much as I was astounded by my revelation right in front of her, I felt cleansed even more.

Patsy was paralyzed. As I waited for her to slap me across the face, she continued to stare at me. 'I'm sorry,' I stuttered, 'I love you . . . and I always will . . . I'm sorry, but . . . I just don't . . .'

'Well, if that don't . . . I can't believe it! After all I've put up with. The sacrifices I've made. That's it! I've had enough. I can't live with anyone who . . . You broke your word!' she exclaimed. 'Two years! You said two years. Trust? I don't trust *you.* And I will not live with any man I can't trust. That's it!' Patsy shrieked, 'I want a divorce!'

chapter 14

RESOLVE

After eight years of marriage, Patsy and I separated late July 1994. We sat down with Stephen to tell him the news. Even though he seemed to take it in his stride, my heart went out to him. Above everything, I never wanted Stephen to experience the loss and suffering that I had felt when my parents split up. Since the day I was married, I had fought so hard to protect my son from every conceivable source of harm, and now I had failed at the most basic element of my role as a father – keeping my family together.

After several private conversations with Stephen, I realized he seemed more comfortable about the separation than I was. I promised him that no matter what happened between his mother and me, our devotion for him would never change.

It took a broken marriage and nearly thirty years for me to fulfill my childhood dream of living on the Russian River. Even though Patsy hinted that our current state of separation might be temporary, I couldn't bring myself to tell her that once I moved out, there was no turning back for me.

Because I was on the road, working when Patsy and I had decided our fate, she surprised me by taking the time to find me a one-bedroom summer home near the Russian River. The day I moved to Guerneville, Patsy graciously drove the U-Haul truck over one hundred and eighty miles to my new home. Later that day, as we hugged goodbye and wiped away our tears, I thought we both felt the frustration and anxiety that had built up over the years begin to fade.

Due to the small size of the house and only a desk, bookshelf, and bureau for furniture, it took me less than two days to arrange my new home. Soon Stephen came to stay with me for two weeks. We were inseparable, spending our time stacking wood, fishing at the river, playing catch in the middle of the quiet street, or at nighttime, after we barbecued hot dogs, I'd hold him in my lap as we gazed up at the stars. When Patsy picked Stephen up, the magnitude of our separation exploded like a bomb in the pit of my stomach. As Patsy and Stephen drove off, part of me ached to race down the street, tear open the car door, clutch Stephen in my arms, and plead with Patsy that every problem we had could be worked out. But I could not, and would not, move a muscle to chase after them. All I did was try to capture the slightest trace of sound from Patsy's car, long after it disappeared from sight.

I stood in the middle of the street for what seemed like hours. After I began to tremble, I returned home, closed the door behind me, and cried for days. For nearly a week I shut myself off completely from the outside world. My days consisted of waking up at four or five in the morning, so I could scour every inch of every object within my surroundings. Every day, after more than nine hours of cleaning the house, I'd remove, wash, and restack the virtually empty refrigerator shelves; then on my hands and knees I'd scrub the baseboards until the paint nearly rubbed off. I thought if everything around me was perfectly immaculate, somehow my life, too, would be in order. I wouldn't stop until late into the evening and only after I'd scrubbed the telephone. With my body layered with sweat, I'd collapse in my chair with the sanitized telephone glued to my hand, as if I phoned Patsy she'd somehow take me back. Many times I dialed her number, but I always hung up before the number could ring through.

If I felt good about myself and felt I deserved it, late at night after a long shower I'd open the door to stand on the deck for a few minutes and search for the group of stars Stephen and I had found together. Sometimes as I listened as the tops of the redwoods swayed, I'd catch a whiff of someone's fireplace or the sweet scent from the trees before passing out on my leaky air mattress. On a good day that was enough to get me through.

After a week of solitude, I called the Lincoln office in the vain hope that I had some upcoming work so I could somehow get away from my life. With each call my manager, Jerry, assured me he was only days away from being flooded with work. All I could do was thank him for believing in me and pray for a breakthrough.

Then in the afternoon I'd sit and wait for Stephen to return from school so I could call him and talk about his day. I thanked God that with each conversation, he seemed upbeat and happy. As Patsy had promised, she kept Stephen busy, while letting me see or talk to him at any time.

Every time I hung up the phone with him, I could not help but feel like a traitor – that somehow I had abandoned my son. Even though my home was plastered with photos of Stephen and reams of his artwork from school covered the refrigerator and every inch of the kitchen cabinets, I still felt I had deserted him. My guilt consumed me to the point that several times when I dared myself to see a movie, I'd instead return home, as if I could not allow myself to escape my reality for just a few hours. Somehow I thought the pleasure of seeing a movie took something away from Stephen.

My saving grace was the Rio Villa Resort in nearby Monte Rio. For years after getting out of the service, Patsy, Stephen, and I had been guests there, and I became close friends with the owners, Ric and Don. Since my first visit, Ric and Don knew of my passion of wanting to live on the Russian River. And now, rather than keeping myself in a self-imposed exile, they were kind enough to allow me to work on their grounds. Whenever Stephen was not with me, I now felt some form of purpose. After completing whatever assignment I had with the speaking firm, I'd throw on a set of work clothes and race over to the Rio Villa, where I'd pull weeds, trim the rose-bushes, or spend hours watering the grass in the late-afternoon sun. Slowly, with the passing of summer, I began to feel a sense of worth and accomplishment.

But my shame never escaped me. Since my separation, whenever I spoke at a program and gave suggestions about facing issues and overcoming adversity, I felt like a hypocrite. The only time I felt halfway decent about myself was when I made the audience laugh. In humor I could forget about my pitiful life.

But when alone, even right after speaking, from deep within I felt as I had as a child – no matter how hard I worked, no matter how much effort I applied, I would never be good enough. I couldn't make my marriage work. I threw away a career with the air force so I could chase my tail trying to prove myself as a speaker, just to end up being labeled as a victim of abuse rather than a person with an inspirational message. And I had hurt the one true love of my life: Stephen. No matter what the future had in store for me, I could only pray my inadequacies would not come back to haunt my son.

As the days passed, some were better than others. On rare nights, I'd be able to sleep for more than three hours at a time. I'd ration myself with a yogurt in the morning and a Cup-O-Soup with a piece of French bread in the evening for dinner – so I could save money for whenever I was with Stephen – and for the most part I was beginning to keep my food down. Although I had lost a great deal of weight, I kept telling myself things were getting better. Besides being with my son, I was prepared to live my life alone. The last thing I wanted was to screw up another person's life, as I had with Patsy and Stephen.

During the late fall of that year, while on the road, I checked in with Jerry. He told me that the International Junior Chamber of Commerce had selected me as one of the Ten Outstanding Young Persons of the World. Before I could relish the moment, Jerry dropped his voice to a whisper and informed me the firm was in serious trouble. Immediately I thought about the advances the firm had initially provided me, that by now I should have paid back in full. But for some time now, whenever I had checked with Jerry on my accounting or other matters involving specifics, he would become frustrated and at times fiercely upset. Just being out of the military and because I was still adapting to dealing with the civilian world, and due to Jerry's position as the former vice-president of the company, I always felt I was pushing too hard. All I could do was remain patient. But after months of promises, I still could not get answers to my questions, and whenever I'd probe, I felt belittled and I'd back down. As I had with Patsy before our separation, to spare myself any headaches I'd simply go along with things to avoid any confrontations. Before hanging up the phone, Jerry repeated his assurance for me not to worry and that he'd continue to stick his neck out for me.

Later that day, after I spoke to Stephen about his day, I told Patsy of the good news. Lately on the phone and whenever I had seen her in person, she seemed like a new woman. She was holding down a job she loved and raved about things she wanted to accomplish. Her attitude was one of confidence and independence. Even though I knew she was seeing someone else, I never let on. After the years of being with me, I simply desired that Patsy be happy. I felt I had dragged her down all those years. Before I flew to Japan to accept the TOYPW award, Patsy was kind enough to write, thanking me for all that I had done for her and restating her newfound happiness. Patsy had moved on with her life.

I was on the road for over a week before arriving in Kobe, Japan, staying for just over twenty-four hours, then making several flights back and landing in Nebraska to drive several hours and speak at a school. Jerry had been insistent about my returning to Lincoln on Saturday afternoon so that he could finally answer the concerns I had face to face. When I showed up at the high school, though, the principal was reluctant to have me speak to her students – I looked like I would faint from exhaustion. The principal also stated that she knew of my recent return from Japan, and she had told Jerry to have me come back to her school at another time. Jerry had joked with the principal, stating, 'Don't worry about David; he won't mind.' The stress, multiple time-zone changes, and lack of sleep had caught up with me. Assuring the principal that I wouldn't let her down, I stayed the entire day with the students and later made the four-hour drive back to Lincoln. After falling asleep behind the wheel and nearly crashing the car, I pulled over at a rest stop to catch a nap. Late that Friday evening I finally checked into a hotel, collapsing on top of the bed with my clothes still on. Before passing out, I felt a sense of pride – as tired as I was, I gave it my best and hopefully made an impact. Thinking about the day to come, I felt everything would fall into place.

Early the next morning, Carl, the senior partner of the firm, woke me with a phone call, asking me to come over to the office right away. I thought the reason was some surprise party for the award I had just received. The entire staff knew how hard I had worked to prove my worthiness, and since my separation they had gone out of their way to show me kindness.

With my award clutched in my hand, I nearly dropped it when I saw the look on everyone's face. I thought someone had died. Sitting down, I swallowed hard as I was told that Jerry had stolen funds from the organization. As I was presented with reams of paperwork and canceled checks made out to himself, everything suddenly made sense.

I didn't want anyone to think I had violated their trust, so I confessed to the group the advances that Jerry had instructed me to keep to myself, and that I felt Jerry was deliberately isolating me from the staff. When they looked at each other, then back at me, I thought I was doomed. The last thing I wanted was for anyone to think I, too, had cheated on them. With the award on the table in full view, I felt like a heel. I should have come forward months ago when I felt something was wrong. But when Rich, the co-founder, told me that the advances were not only legitimate but paid in full, only then did I feel a sense of relief. 'Besides,' Rich said to me later in private, 'you're too Jimmy Olsen. Oh, yeah, by the way, congrats on the award.'

I alone had to address Jerry. As much as I hated to, I phoned him, and for the first time as a businessman, I showed a little backbone when he made excuses. Jerry tried to blame it on the firm, and told me to trust him, but I didn't want to get into finger pointing or blaming. Without disrespect or emotion, I simply stated, 'I can never see you or talk to you again. Ever.'

Days later, upon returning to Guerneville, I hated everything about myself. I felt like a joke. Because my place was a summer home, it had no insulation or heating unit except for an ancient wood stove, and the temperature inside the house was literally just above freezing. From the constant traveling and other roller-coaster-like events, I was emotionally drained. With a clean cloth I wiped off the statuette made of a pair of golden hands that held a silver globe, with my name engraved on the wooden base. In a flash of rage I almost threw the award – which I had received days ago in front of thousands of delegates from throughout the world who showered me with praise I felt I did not deserve – into the fireplace. I shook my head with disgust. Here I was, an Outstanding Young Person of the World, separated from my wife and son because I had chased a dream, only to have my trust violated again, and if I didn't freeze to death due to my firewood being soaked from the rain, I could celebrate with a Cup-O-Soup for dinner. After pumping air back into my leaky mattress, I covered myself with layers of worn-out sleeping bags. If I was lucky I'd fall asleep before hunger took over, so I could save my dinner for another time.

When I awoke the next day, I walked for miles in a cold drizzle. I reflected on the last few years and how within a short period of time I had tossed away my air force career and my marriage. Patsy was right: she had given me two years and the result was I was now living like an Eskimo. By taking a chance and blindly charging ahead, I had put at risk all that I held sacred. As much as I thought my message was helping others, the personal results were obvious.

It was Patsy who had the guts to call it quits. I never had the nerve to walk away, and I felt she had worked on our relationship far more than I had. In the final analysis, we were simply two different people. Maybe in my desire to protect Patsy, I had unintentionally smothered her until my pettiness drove her away.

I didn't deserve to be with Patsy, or anyone else. But as much as I still cared for her, I could never trust her or, because of Jerry, anyone else. Maybe my ice-cold environment was the perfect penance for my stupidity. One thing I knew: I was meant to be alone. Because of the tangled feelings of unworthiness and self-preservation, I could never allow anyone, besides my son, into my hardened heart.

Within months, I rid myself of my self-pity, took stock of myself, and said goodbye to the Lincoln firm. I had heard Jerry and the firm had settled their issues, and I wished them the best of luck. I decided to run my own business. This way I could be independent and in control of my own destiny. If I was going to fall on my face, I wanted it to be from my doing. And for me, the bonus of being self-employed was seeing Stephen. Since he lived nearly two hundred miles away, I could take time off that I normally could not in a regular job. I could make the three-hour drive to watch him play a late-night game of baseball, spend long weekends with him, or schedule my work around his time off from school. With each day, as scared as I was, the long hours were good therapy. Because Jerry had rarely returned clients' calls who were interested in my programs, I now found myself with just enough work to survive. I knew things would work out, especially by the time I had saved enough money to purchase a cheap pedestal bed and a heating blanket. With each day I began to feel better about myself. But there was still one issue that needed closure.

One morning after returning home from church, I prayed for guidance before calling Patsy. We met hours later. After being separated for over a year, I owed it to her to get everything off my chest. Patsy arrived wearing a nice outfit and had obviously spent extra time making up her face and hair. Her appearance reminded me of the Patsy I had known when we had first met. I exhaled deeply as I began to speak, but when I opened my mouth nothing came out. After several attempts I finally blurted, 'I want you to know . . . how sorry I am.' Patsy's eyes lit up. 'I was wrong . . . in so many ways, and I beg for your forgiveness.'

Patsy reached out to seize my hand. 'Does this mean you're ready to come back to . . . ?'

'No,' I whispered. I turned my head down and away. 'I'm sorry. I didn't mean to call you and give you the wrong impression.' I shook my head. 'I can't do that to you, to Stephen. I mean, we'd be okay for a while, but . . . I'd end up screwing everything up . . .' Without warning, my chest started to shudder. I felt light-headed, and I could feel myself about to slide off the chair.

'David? David?' Patsy said. 'Are you okay, what are . . . what are you saying?'

Again with my head hung low, I shook my head.

While Patsy and I sat in silence, around us people came in and out of the hotel lounge, ordering drinks, laughing, or watching the big-screen television.

After several minutes an overwhelming pressure built up behind my eyes. Patsy's expression told me not to say anything. 'I owe you this much,' I wept. 'I could have . . . I *should* have treated you better. I – I was scared, all the time, of what might happen next. It wasn't your fault . . . I just couldn't let you in, and for that I am truly sorry. I swear to God, I know what an ass I was, and I beg for your forgiveness. I drove you crazy, and every time you reached out . . . I shut you out. How *could* I love you? I mean really love you, when I hated myself?' I said, pounding my hand. 'There are so many things I did wrong, and for that I can never forgive myself. I should have stopped and listened to what you were really trying to say. As much as I provided for you, I was never there for you.'

'Well,' Patsy asked as she wiped her eyes, 'I guess this means we're through?'

I bit my lip, and nodded.

'Just say it,' Patsy pleaded. 'Just tell me so I can go on. I can take it, be a man and tell me.'

'Patsy,' I swallowed as I gazed into her eyes, 'I'm not good enough to be your husband and I think we should . . . should divorce.'

Patsy closed her eyes before nodding that she agreed. After dabbing a tissue to her eyes and adjusting her blouse, she smiled. 'Well, you can't blame a girl for trying.'

'I'm flattered.' I laughed. 'Really I am.'

We spent the remainder of the afternoon addressing every issue we could think of. 'You realize Stephen will live with me. I'm a homebody and you're on the road too much. You can see or talk to him anytime you want. I'll never use him as a pawn. I think you and I both know what that's like. I won't do that to our son.

'The thing is,' Patsy went on, 'for both of us Stephen was the best thing in our lives. I just wanted something more, that's all.'

'No matter what, I want to be friends,' I said. Patsy immediately nodded. 'I mean it. I don't have many friends, and I think we deserve to give each other that.' I stopped to take in a deep breath. 'One more thing . . .'

'Oh, my God!' Patsy gasped. 'You're not going to tell me you're gay?'

I coughed before I could reply. 'No! What made you think that?'

'Well,' Patsy said, recovering, 'I just thought, I mean, you live in Guerneville and all. You don't go out. What's a wife to think? You leave me to go live down there . . .'

I brushed off the statement. 'Listen, please. I just want you to know, you were right about the office in Lincoln. I found out a few months ago. I was mismanaged. That's why I couldn't get enough gigs. And the books, they were "printed", they were never published. They weren't even copyrighted! That's why they weren't in the stores.'

'*The Lost Boy*, too?' Patsy inquired, my second book, which Jerry had about insisted that I write. I nodded. 'Jesus,' Patsy scolded, 'how could you be that stupid and allow so many people to take advantage of you like that? As smart as you are, I'll never understand you.'

I thought of myself from years ago. 'I dunno,' I replied. 'Ever since I was a kid . . . I never had the guts really to speak up for myself. I was always too intimidated. Even now as an adult, whether it was Jerry at the Lincoln office, buying a car, sticking up for myself so no one could walk over me or, no offense, even with you, I couldn't do it. I . . . it was easy for me to do for others, but not for myself.'

'David,' Patsy sighed, 'it's different with me . . . I'm your wife.'

I nodded, but more to myself. 'All that changes now.'

'So, what are you going to do? Sue 'em?' Patsy had a gleam in her eye.

'No.' I shook my head. 'It's not the money, it never was. I don't want a dime of something I didn't earn first. It's a matter of honor. The worst thing I could do to them – to anyone who screws me – is have nothing to do with them.'

'I think you're stupid. I'd stick it to them but good. So, what are you going to do to protect yourself?'

'Simple,' I said, smiling, 'trust no one.'

'You do that, and you'll be a lonely old man, David Pelzer.'

'I know,' I sighed. 'But I just can't allow myself to be hurt again.'

'I don't know what you think of me; I know I've burned a lot of bridges with you, but I'd never screw you, David,' she stated.

'I know. It's going to be okay. I swear, I just want you to be happy, that's all.'

'Well,' Patsy gushed. 'I am. I mean—'

'I know,' I interrupted. 'I've known for a while. Are you happy? Is he good to you? To Stephen?'

'Yeah.' Patsy beamed. 'Guess you can say I finally got myself a real cowboy.'

'And please,' I begged, 'be careful. We're adults, but I don't want Stephen to get hurt any more than he has.'

'So, what are you gonna do?'

Without hesitation I said, 'Be a good father and carry on. I'm not going to quit. I'm going to work hard and see it through.'

'David,' Patsy snapped, 'I'm not talking about work, or Stephen. I know you'll be a good father for him. For once in your life, what about *you*? What are you going to do for you?'

For a moment I felt the magnitude of Patsy's question. I sat hunched over, stymied. 'I don't . . . I don't know. Just live my life day by day. That's all I can do. I just don't want to repeat the same mistakes all over again.'

Patsy shook her head in disbelief. 'My God, after all these years . . . you're still carrying her shame.'

I had no response. I truly felt like a leper when it came to being close to anyone besides my son.

As we got up to leave, Patsy and I embraced. 'I'll always hold a place in my heart for you, David Pelzer. You're a good man, and for God's sake go out there and live a little!'

'Thanks, Patsy, you have no idea what that means to me. I pray for you every day. Godspeed, Patsy,' I stated.

'Goodbye, David.'

'Goodbye, Patsy.'

We soon filed for divorce. Less than thirty days after our divorce was finalized, Patsy remarried.

Between Stephen and my work, I deliberately stayed to myself. Overall I was content. On a good week, when I felt I earned it, I would venture 'out there' and treat myself to a movie. Working for myself proved more difficult than I had expected, yet I loved every minute of it. After purchasing the rights to my books from the Lincoln firm, I quickly found two publishers who wanted to publish the books. Even though I knew I could receive a better deal with a New York publishing house, I signed with a smaller publisher in Florida, partly because for years I had admired the works of their authors John Bradshaw and Jack Canfield. I assumed a smaller publisher would be able to spend more time marketing and promoting my books.

Within a few weeks I received a call from an assistant editor who introduced herself as Marsha Donohoe. We spoke about the changes she wished to make and the schedule of publishing my first book. After hanging up the phone, I could not help but think what an incredible voice she had. Before my mind began to wander, I pushed Marsha out of my mind by burying myself in my work.

Months passed. The more Marsha and I discussed every page, every paragraph, analyzing every word of the book, the more I found myself becoming enthralled by her. Besides having the sweetest voice I ever heard, I respected the passion she had for her work. I understood that editors could not afford to spend much time on any particular project due to the overwhelming amount of deadlines within the publishing world, yet because Marsha and I cared so much about the story, we would spend more than an hour wrangling over a single sentence. 'I don't want to get you in trouble,' I told her one day. 'I don't understand; I usually catch a lot of flak for trying to do my best. Why are *you* doing this?'

'I may be new here,' Marsha confided, 'but I've been involved with books all my life. And I gotta tell you, this book is one in a million. I swear to God, I couldn't put it down. Before I even called you, I believed in this book. With all my heart, I believe in what you are doing.' Raising her voice with excitement, Marsha said, 'Do you know how many lives you're going to change with this? I don't know you that well, Dave, but I think you're one incredible person.'

I pressed the phone so hard against my ear that I thought it would bleed. Not being used to compliments, I immediately mocked her. 'I bet you say that to all the authors!' A second later, I said, 'You believe, I mean, you truly believe I'm doing the right thing?'

After our conversation I sat frozen in my chair. I couldn't believe my luck. After all these years and endless battles, I was working with someone who had the same values as I did. 'She believes!' I said out loud. 'Marsha actually believes in me!'

I never intended to cross the relationship between editor and author, but I lost myself as I savored every second of every minute Marsha and I spent on the phone. It was easy for me to become fascinated with her. At the end of editing each page, we would reward ourselves by telling stories and exchanging jokes. I soon became caught up not only in Marsha's sense of humor, but in her work ethic and her honor. Over time, as she began to tell me about her struggles and disappointments in life, I realized the incredible willpower she had. Marsha never quit. Whenever she applied herself, she gave it her all. We made a pact that we could talk to each other about anything at any time. Marsha became my one true friend.

Unexpectedly, weeks later, after the end of one of our editing sessions, I leaned back in my chair, slowly exhaled as I closed my eyes, and imagined Marsha's smile and the way she might toss her hair when she laughed. Before I could allow myself any sense of pleasure, I buried my affections. I knew Marsha was way out of my league. She was by far the kindest, most sensitive person I knew, while I was a hyperkinetic geek boy with baggage, hiding my insecurities behind my work and manic sense of humor.

Marsha never gave up on me. Because of the graphic nature of some parts of the book, more than once she broke down and cried on the phone. One day, without thinking, I nearly swallowed the phone as if to get closer to her. 'Mar, it's okay, honey, it's all right. That was a long time ago. It's over; it's over now.' A second after the words slipped out, I backtracked, 'Mar, listen, I'm sorry. I didn't mean to . . . I'm sorry, I didn't mean to seem forward . . . please forget what I just said. Please?'

'It's okay. Precious,' Marsha sighed, 'your book has become my baby. And when someone holds a place in my heart, I protect them. I just wish I could have been there for you. You're just so precious to me. Please don't apologize, we're friends. I've been waiting for you to say something to me.'

'I, uh . . .' I paused, thinking of her. 'I, uh, just don't want to hear you cry,' I stammered, still holding back. 'I just don't want you to be sad. Believe me, I'm fine. I don't want to hurt you, that's all.'

'Dave, we've been working together for some time now. I know what you look like from the back cover of your book, but . . . can you see me?' Marsha whispered.

Hang up the phone! my brain screamed. *Before you screw up and say something, hang up!* As my grip tightened against the phone, a surge of energy seeped through my heart. 'Yeah,' I gasped into the phone – my only lifeline to Marsha. 'Sometimes, at night, when everything is still, I'll walk outside and look up at the stars . . . I'll close my eyes . . .' I stopped.

'Dave, please, go on. I know it's hard. I know you've been through a lot with your childhood, all you're trying to do, your divorce, your son . . . but just say something, say anything. I won't hurt you. I promise, it's okay.'

Closing my eyes, I prayed for Marsha to keep talking. Letting out a deep sigh, I said, 'Sometimes, at night, before I go to sleep . . . I can see your face . . .'

We stayed on the phone from nine that evening until three in the morning. Afterward, I strolled out into a swirl of gray fog that had begun to settle in the trees. I knew everything about Marsha, down to how she breathed. Looking up, I thanked God.

Maybe, I thought to myself, *maybe*.

Marsha and I began dating on the phone. Four months later, as our friendship and our personal feelings for each other grew stronger, we decided it was time to meet.

I was a nervous wreck the day Marsha was scheduled to fly in. I almost crashed my 4-Runner as I daydreamed about Marsha on the way. Hours later at the airport, I kept readjusting my clothes to look absolutely perfect for her. I felt like a schoolboy on a blind date, fearing she might think I was ugly, or laugh at me if I said the wrong thing. But by far my biggest anxiety was what if, after all our late-night conversations, romantic courtship, and reams of letters and cards we had exchanged, I freeze up and never let her get close, just as I had with Patsy? What if I could not break through to how I wanted to feel? For me it was as it always had been: what if I could not open my heart and let Marsha in? I started to panic, and imagined myself fleeing before things became too deep. Part of me wanted to drop the yellow rose I was holding behind my back and run out of the airport terminal. *For God's sake,* I said to myself, *who are you trying to kid?* With my head bent down, I found myself taking a step backward, then another step. I swallowed hard, thinking that in the end Marsha would understand – she was just too good for me.

As I turned away a sudden shimmer caught my eyes. As the passengers streamed from the terminal gate, one person stood out among the throng of people. Marsha's alluring eyes and shiny auburn hair almost made me faint. With my mind racing, I imagined myself strolling over to extend my hand to introduce myself properly. I didn't want to seem too desperate or too forward.

But I threw away my apprehension. To hell with that, I thought to myself.

We awkwardly ran into each other's open arms. Holding her tight, I could feel Marsha's heart race. 'I can't believe it,' she cried as tears fell down her face.

Lowering my defenses, I whispered, 'Hello, princess.' For a few moments the world stood still. When I finally took a long look at Marsha's face, rather than kissing her, I closed my eyes and ran my fingers along the side of her face to the base of her neck.

Leaning her face into my hand, she sighed, 'Whatever you do, don't let go.'

'Hardly a chance,' I replied.

Wiping her tears away, Marsha shook her head. 'Dave, I've dreamed about this day for a long time. Don't let me go.'

The next several days Marsha and I were inseparable. We spent every waking moment together. While clutching our mugs of coffee, we'd chat outside for hours at a time. As I grew fascinated with her, Marsha seemed to absorb every detail of my life, to the point of insisting to see the summer cabin where I had stayed as a child. Trying to recapture the magic that had captivated me so many years ago as a child, we stood holding each other, watching the sun set beneath the redwood trees as the sky turned from blue to orange. With every passing hour, I found myself stripping away layers of armor that I had worn as my defense from years of internal battle. Marsha became the only person to whom I could bare my soul.

The days passed by too quickly. The day before Marsha had to return home, I began to pull back. For me, the cold reality was that Marsha lived thousands of miles away – with a job, a great family, and a real life. I didn't want her to become any more entangled in my warped world. As much as every fiber of my being craved to be with her, the only way to keep her as a close friend, I thought, was to set her free.

After sitting outside, stirring our coffees that had grown cold in silence, Marsha tossed her hair and asked, 'Dave, is it me? Did I get too close?'

With tears beginning to build, I shook my head. 'No, it's not you. It's just, it's me,' I stammered before swallowing hard. 'I don't want to hurt you, that's all.'

Reaching out to hold my hand, Marsha probed, 'What is it, Dave? What are you so afraid of?'

I clamped my eyes shut. The pressure inside of me was too much for me to hold in any longer. 'You!' I fired back. 'I'm scared to death of you! I can't, I can't even look at you! I can't do it. I mean, you're too good, too good for me.' Marsha sat back in her chair, dumbstruck. 'For God's sake, look at you. You're perfect, a china doll. You're drop-dead gorgeous! You don't lie, cheat, or steal. You have no vices. You don't have a mean streak in your body. You believe in God and in doing your best. You're educated, you don't complain or blame others if things don't turn out. You have no baggage from your past, no skeletons in your closet. Come on. I'm waiting for you to peel off your mask . . . You're just too perfect. I know who I am and where I belong. You're way too good for me. I'm sorry, but I don't . . . I don't deserve to be with you.'

'Don't say that!' Marsha pleaded. 'All your life you've carried this guilt. Don't you understand? It's not your fault! You're not to blame. I'm an adult. I can take it. I know everything, everything about you, and I'm still here.'

Turning away, I raised my voice at Marsha for the first time. 'Don't you get it? My grandmother hates me, my mother tried to kill me. I drove Patsy to the brink . . . If you get too close . . . I'll somehow screw things up for you, too.' With my chest beginning to heave, I murmured, 'I'd rather stop before things get too serious and keep you as a friend. I'm just trying to save what we have. You mean that much to me. You're too important for me to lose. You deserve to be happy, and if you become involved with me—'

'It's too late. I'm already involved. I know what I'm getting into. I've been around the block; I've dated plenty of creeps. I've never met anyone out there like you. Don't you see how precious you are to me?'

I shook my head.

'And what about you, Dave? What do *you* deserve?' Marsha asked me. 'My God, all your life you've worked your butt off, been taken advantage of; you've gotten truckloads of manure thrown at you and you get up, wipe yourself off, and carry on as if nothing happened. You never quit! What about you? You deserve to live a better life. I've never seen anybody work as hard as you. Look at how you sacrifice everything for your son. I've never seen any parent smother his child with as much love as you do. Okay, you had a bad marriage; but it takes two, *two* people to ruin something. You were not the only one responsible for the divorce. Maybe you couldn't love her because she broke your trust. I'm not even going to tell you what I think about her! You've been more honorable, forgiving, and self-blaming than you should have. You're the most broken person I know. What about Dave? When is Dave going to be happy? You deserve, Dave, *you* deserve to be happy. When is it going to be time for *Dave*?'

I continued to shake my head. 'Some mistakes . . . can never be paid for.'

'It's her, isn't it?' Marsha asked. 'You can't stop thinking about her, can you?'

I nodded in agreement. 'Every day,' I began, 'I try, I really do, but it's like something pulls me back and I can't break free – no matter what I do or how hard I try. Sometimes when I'm out there speaking, explaining what happened between Mother and me, it's like I'm searching, crawling for a fragment of something I could have done, anything to change all that . . . besides Stephen. It's like, it's one of the reasons why I'm out there. If I could just find—'

'No!' Marsha broke in. 'You've got to let her go, it wasn't your fault that—'

'No. I could have—'

'My God!' Marsha now yelled. 'Your mother was nuts! There's nothing you could have done to stop her!'

With my heart continuing to race, I frantically shook my head. 'You're wrong. I could have . . .'

'Could have done what?' Marsha countered.

'Please,' I begged, 'don't push it. I really don't want to go there.'

'No! We're going to confront it!' Marsha demanded. 'All you do is give. You'd slit your wrists if you thought it would help someone. Just take a moment and help yourself. I'm here. I'm here for you, honey. There was nothing you could have done.' Marsha leaned closer, to hold me, but before her fingers could touch my shoulders, I pulled away.

'You don't know, you weren't there. I could have done something! That's the worst part of it all. I never said no. I never stood up for myself. Don't you get it? I could have stopped it. I let it go too far. The day she – she stabbed me, I just stood there, like I was begging for it. My brothers would have never let anything like that happen to them, I could tell by the look in their eyes. But I did. I always did. I swallowed ammonia in front of my dad. When I cleaned the bathroom with that mixture of ammonia and Clorox my throat was on fire, and all I had to do was dump that stuff down the toilet. I even ate the dog shit when she was in the other room. All I had to do was throw it down the disposal and she'd never know, but I did it, I did everything she wanted. I never stood up for myself. All I had to do was stop her, just one time. Maybe once and that could have changed everything.' A stream of tears began to spatter the wooden deck. 'I could have stopped her. I never . . . never said no.'

Marsha began to cry as well. As I covered my face to hide my shame, a wave of anxiety made me slip from my chair and fall forward to the deck. I stayed on my knees as my body shook. 'Everyone thinks I'm – I'm so damn courageous for telling my pathetic little tale. Part of me feels like a whore. The truth is, if I'm so brave, why didn't I have the guts to stop her? I could have left. I had hundreds of chances.' In my mind I envisioned Mother parking her gray station wagon at the local Serramonte Mall. 'Whenever she went shopping, when she kept me in the car, my hand would wrap around that door handle . . . sometimes my grip was so tight my entire arm would vibrate. All I had to do was turn the handle, open the door, and walk, just walk away. I could have ended it. It would have all been over. I could have stopped it.' With my eyes clamped shut, I shook my head from side to side, so much so that I could feel myself beginning to pass out.

'Dave,' Marsha cut in, 'when you were with Patsy, did you work on your marriage?'

Stopping to look up at her, I shook my head. 'Now that I've had time to think about it, it was Patsy who really put forth the effort—'

'No!' Marsha boomed, 'it's not just your fault. So, I'm asking: when you were married, did you give it your best?'

'Yeah, I guess so.' I stopped to collect myself. 'Sure, I guess so.'

'As a writer, how long did you say it takes you to construct a paragraph?'

'Anywhere from four to maybe six hours. Why?' I asked, feeling intimidated.

Marsha dug further. 'Now, don't think, just answer: Why does it take you so long?'

'Because I can't type, I have no mechanics, because I'm stupid? What are you getting at?'

'No,' Marsha calmly interjected. 'Shh, slow down. Tell me, just open up and tell me, Dave. Why?'

I could feel myself about to erupt. 'Because . . . I want to do my best, my best in everything I am and do! That's why!' I shouted.

'As a father, a husband when you were married . . . ?'

'I did my best!' I fired back.

'Flying for the air force, your volunteer work, the way you stack your firewood, fold your shirts, arrange your table when you barbecue dinner . . . ?'

'I try. I try to give everything my all. Stop it!' I begged. 'Just let it go.'

'Everything?' Marsha asked in a hushed tone. 'You've always given everything your all?'

I nodded yes.

'As a son, did you give it your best?'

'Damn straight I did! I always did. The chores, trying to impress her with my work at school, praying every day that I wouldn't piss her off.'

'And you didn't quit?' Marsha raised her eyebrows.

'No! I never quit!' I stated with conviction. 'I never quit.'

'You told me that when you were in foster care and the air force didn't want you that it took you years of proving to them that you wanted to fly for them . . . When you were scammed by that man from Lincoln and left with nothing, you walked away . . . After everything you've been through, why in heaven's name, why do you push yourself? As a child, Dave, you were a child; why did you . . . ?'

'Because that's all I had!' I cried. 'I got nothing else! It's all I am! It's all I've ever known. If I quit back then, once, for just a second . . . it could have been all over. I got nothing else, all my life . . .'

Falling to the deck, Marsha said, 'I know, I know, baby, I know.' Reaching over to cradle my head against her chest, she whispered, 'You made that choice. Your mother made hers. It's not your fault. It wasn't your doing. She gave up on herself a long, long time ago. She quit – on her son, her family, everything she had, *she* quit. No one could have saved her, least of all her own baby that she treated like an animal. She was a broken woman long before you came into her life. You've got to give her up. It's not your doing. You deserve, Dave, you deserve to be free.'

'I could have—' I protested.

'No!' Marsha shouted. 'Tell me, tell yourself, what was the one thing you could have possibly done to prevent her self-destruction?'

'Been a better son? I dunno.' I shook my head. 'I just don't know.'

'You're a good son now, and you always have been. No matter what happens to us, for your own peace of mind, after all your years of searching, you need to understand, it wasn't your doing.'

Feeling the pressure beginning to ease, I stammered, 'It's just, I feel my entire – and I mean my *entire* – life, since I was a kid – it's like I saw everything swirling around me, and somehow I allowed things to take over, to take control of me because I never felt I deserved anything but that. My marriage, the firm in Lincoln, I deserve what I got. That's why I couldn't tell Patsy or anyone else. That's why I tried to bury the dirt; that's why I eat crap every day of my life. I don't deserve any better.

'I know there's nothing I could have done to stop her, but that doesn't help, doesn't stop it from gnawing at me every day. And because of that I feel so undeserving, especially when it comes to you. You're too pure.' I let out a deep breath. 'I can't do it anymore. I'm just tired, tired of swimming against the tide, proving myself . . . I'm tired.'

'After all you've been through, no matter what happens to us, Dave, you deserve everything life has to offer. I'm so proud of you, I could just bust. You're the most inspirational person I know. You're my Robin Williams and Jimmy Stewart rolled into one. And I'm not saying that because I've got some schoolgirl crush on you. No matter what, you're precious to me. No matter what, with all my heart, I believe. I believe in you, Dave Pelzer. You're my best friend. Okay,' Marsha sighed, 'I can see where you can drive people crazy, only because you want to do your best. But, Dave, you deserve, *we* deserve to give each other a chance. I'm not going to smother you or trick you into anything. With my hand on the Bible, if I live to be a hundred, if I know one thing, it's that we deserve – we deserve to be together.'

Wiping away my tears, I locked on to Marsha's tear-filled eyes. 'I'm your best friend?'

'Why do you think I came to see you?' she asked.

Closing my eyes, I shook off my fear of intimacy, and I stripped away my last protective layer. 'When I'm with you, Marsha . . . I feel clean. You ease my shame.'

'And you're my white knight. Together, back to back, we can do anything, Dave,' Marsha cried. 'Can't you see that all I want is to be with you?'

My insides became unglued. As much as I had tried to drive Marsha away, my heart ached for her to stay. With my anxiety spent and my heart bursting, I wrapped my arms around Marsha's waist with my head bent in her lap. 'I'll never deserve you. You're my best friend. I love you. You're the one, Marsha. The only one . . . the only one I trust.'

chapter 15

ALL GOOD THINGS

Now, this was completely different. Marsha stood with her back toward my chest, venting about the demands placed on her from the day, while I tried to calm her down by pleading for her not to take work so seriously. I had my reasons to get her mind off work, but whenever I tried to veer Marsha off the subject, it only seemed to intensify her passion.

But that was one of the many things I loved about Marsha: her steadfast commitment. Months after meeting in California, Marsha had given up her job as an editor and moved to Guerneville – not only to be close to me, but to take over and manage my business. Since Marsha knew me like no other, and because of the respect we had for each other, she was the perfect choice. While some scoffed at her decision, thinking that she would play the role of a mere secretary, answering phones and filing paperwork, Marsha faced many demands: arranging continuous media interviews, strategizing every aspect of the strenuous travel logistics, and keeping my calendar packed with engagements. At times when I was away, Marsha slaved twelve to sixteen hours, only to end her day by fighting to keep up with paperwork correspondence, which began as a trickle but soon flooded to the point she was answering thousands of pieces of mail a month from all over the world.

Since our lives were so crazy, we worked hard on our personal relationship. With Marsha I learned to listen and not father her, to offer advice when I thought it was needed. When we'd have a disagreement, we'd talk things through. When we'd have a heated discussion, we'd try our best to resolve the issue, learn from it, and move forward. Throughout every situation, every obstacle we faced together, Marsha remained sincere and dedicated and never broke my trust.

Allowing Marsha into the deepest recesses of my heart, and, more important, introducing her to Stephen, was the highest compliment I could give to her. I was learning from my past mistakes and respecting her as a lady. Marsha resided in a cozy cottage near the Russian River across from me. After work we'd curl up on her futon to watch a movie or read well into the late evening, until I left after kissing her good night.

With Marsha I didn't have to spend my time worrying about when the sky would come crashing down. In business, she protected me in so many ways. She taught me the fine line between helping others and being taken advantage of. There were ways to help others, provide for my son, and maintain my own self-worth – instead of constantly neglecting and sabotaging myself just to please others.

Marsha also helped me to grow as an individual, in ways I never thought possible. For years I had felt I was swimming against the tide, with lead weights cuffed to my ankles. But somehow Marsha seemed to part the waters, while coaching me along the way. She not only made me believe there was little I could not accomplish, but that I was indeed deserving and was destined to succeed. With Marsha I was invincible.

As a couple we went through a great many peaks and valleys. Marsha was in a completely different world. Since I was on the road so much, being pulled in every direction, combined with her getting to know Stephen, and a few difficult situations she encountered with Patsy, life for Marsha sometimes became too much. When times were tough and we could barely scrape together enough money to pay our bills, Marsha would huddle with me in my bone-chilling cabin and share a Cup-O-Soup and a loaf of day-old French bread. Yet somehow, together, we found a way to help others who we knew were worse off. For a while it seemed everything was against us. We'd question our business wisdom to the point that we'd break into tears. It seemed we were both working our tails off, but only just keeping our heads above water. But together, we never lost faith, for Marsha and I knew tomorrow was indeed another day.

Over time, as we made solid progress, Marsha insisted that I move out of my moldy 'icebox', into a warm, modern two-bedroom home among the redwood trees. It looked like a tree-house for grown-ups. After years of sacrificing and pinching every penny, Marsha basically kicked me in the behind, saying that I deserved to live like a normal human being. My proudest moment after moving into my new home was holding Stephen by the shoulders as I walked him into *his* bedroom – that was filled with brand-new furniture, toys, and video games that he had wanted. For years after the divorce, when Stephen would visit me at my old house, we'd shiver in bed – at first on my air mattress, then later on my cardboard-like pedestal bed. When I could not afford to make Stephen an elaborate meal, we simply heated up a frozen dinner. Because I did not have a dining-room table then, Stephen would sit on a wobbly bar stool while I stood beside him. Stephen never complained. In an odd sense, maybe having him watch me struggle was good for his character. For only Marsha knew the extent of the sacrifices I placed upon myself, to provide for and protect my son.

As with everything in my life, ever so slowly things began to fall into place. When I was on the road, after going over an endless stream of business matters, Marsha and I would steal time to chat aimlessly. As before, when the phone had been our lifeline, I'd sit back and begin to ponder our future together.

Once back in town, as El Niño began to bear down on the Russian River, Marsha was standing in front of me, describing her day in every detail. Without her realizing, I had basically kidnapped her away from our office to the Rio Villa – to ask her the most important question of my life. For some time now I had planned to ask Marsha on Valentine's Day. I'd take her to her favorite city in the world – Carmel – and present her with a bouquet of yellow roses on the beach as the sun set. But that was over four weeks away. Like a child at Christmas, I could no longer hold back my excitement. When it came to Marsha, my willpower was as strong as jelly. I was a man possessed.

As Marsha chatted about her day, I kept trying to sidetrack her. But she was clueless as to my intentions. After a half-hour of standing outside under the canopy, I nearly gave up all hope. My timing was completely off. I wanted everything to be perfectly magical for her. Yet deep inside I was terrified she would say no. I discovered, to my own horror, that I could not think of how to ask her. Here I was – a person who spoke for a living, and with a quick wit to take people's minds off their troubles – and I could not form the most important words of my life.

As Marsha slowly began to unwind, I stepped closer to her. I wrapped my arms around her waist. In a slow, deep voice I said, 'Close your eyes. Take a deep breath.' From the bottom of her chest I could feel Marsha's tension ease. With my mind spinning, I didn't know what to say next. Whispering into her ear, I asked, 'What do you think of . . . of the Russian River?' Marsha's soothing response seemed to calm my shaking legs. 'What do you think of . . . Stephen?' I continued, as my right hand cautiously retrieved the black velvet box from my pocket and stuck it between my thighs.

A swirl of mist coupled with the freezing rain made Marsha shiver. As she said how much she loved Stephen and how proud she was of him, I closed my eyes. Uttering a quick prayer, I reached for the box. As tears began to trickle from my eyes, I came around in front of Marsha and knelt down as I sprung open the box, asking, 'What do you think of . . . spending the rest of your life with me?'

I thought by Marsha's scream that she was furious with me. She jumped up and down on the wooden deck for what seemed like an eternity. Only when she nearly snapped my neck off as she hugged me did I realize she was accepting my proposal.

A few hours later, in the middle of the worst series of storms to hit California, Marsha and I drove west toward the setting sun. We were putting away the world's problems for a day. Our only ambition was to spend the remainder of our lives together . . . happily ever after.

Another rare moment in time occurred during Stephen's summer vacation. In July 1998, after celebrating a beautiful day, topped off with a barbecue dinner, I went outside for my evening walk. As usual, Stephen joined me. For years, since he was able to walk, we had strolled together, and since moving to the Russian River, we had practically worn out pairs of shoes watching dusk turn into night as we held hands, taking in the majestic beauty around us. Now, as he approached adolescence, Stephen at times seemed apprehensive about his place in the world.

That evening the air held a certain crispness as the clouds above us seemed to melt away to streaks of orange as the sun vanished below the ridge. Taking a turn by a familiar road, Stephen looked up and asked, 'Back then . . . was it hard?' Not understanding the question, I asked what he meant. Stephen ducked his head down. 'You know, back then?'

'Oh,' I lightly replied. As a parent, I always had felt my first obligation was to protect my son from the atrocities of the world, especially the horrors from my past. And yet in order to prepare him for adulthood, I felt I had to inform Stephen of the realities of life. As early as age six, he had begun inquiring about my past. Rather than break his trust by lying to him, I had skirted the issue by claiming 'my mommy' was sick and sometimes said or did bad things. Back then a simple answer had seemed enough for Stephen's inquisitive mind. I never had any intention of revealing the magnitude of what had happened to me out of fear of scaring him. But now, after I had appeared on numerous television talk shows, with two books about my life on international best-seller lists, it was impossible to shield my past from him. 'You know, Stephen, I never thought of it as being hard. It was just something I had to get through, that's all.'

'But were you scared?' he probed.

Addressing the very topic I had fought so hard to protect him from, I said, 'Sometimes, yeah. But . . . aren't you scared sometimes when you're in the batter's box . . . when you're facing a pitcher?'

His eyes lit up. 'Oh yeah; I mean, sometimes.'

'Well,' I asked, 'what do *you* do?'

'You know.' Stephen shrugged.

'No, I don't,' I claimed. 'I never really played baseball. I never experienced what it's like to stare down a pitcher and have a ball coming at you in the blink of an eye. To tell you the truth, I don't see how you do it.'

Shaking his head, Stephen said, 'It ain't much. Just practice, that's all. I've been doing it all my life. You just do it; that's all there is to it.'

'Even when you're behind on the count, with two strikes against you, and you can feel all the pressure, don't you ever think about quitting?' I inquired.

'No,' Stephen stated, 'I just do what I have to do.'

'And that's all I did as a kid, Stephen. I dug in and made the best of things. Just like you and I did at the cabin when we didn't have enough wood to heat the house. You adjust, that's all.'

'But your dad, didn't he know?'

'Yes and no. I think he didn't realize or want to understand what was going on, and by the time he did . . . it was too late. You see, my dad, like my mom, was an alcoholic. Back then things were very different. A lot of things happened, but they were kept in the closet. A secret, like cancer, AIDS, equal rights, and lots of other things were not supposed to be discussed, out of embarrassment, shame, or whatever the reason. Hopefully, as a society, things are better now. We can openly talk about things that we would never speak of when I was your age. In fact, did you know,' I asked, taking Stephen away from our subject matter, 'the one thing you never said to a parent?'

His eyes grew wide. 'What?'

'*No*. You never said the word no. As a kid, when a parent said, "Jump," you asked, "How high?" '

'That's kinda stupid. I say no all the time. I wouldn't let anyone treat me like that.'

'Yes.' I raised my finger. 'Because of the changes within society. Things . . . things were very different back then.'

Stopping in front of me, Stephen asked, 'Do you forgive her? I mean, your mom?'

Kneeling down, I held him by his shoulders. 'Absolutely. Somehow, some way, something made my mom the way she was. Back then, when she was raised, she was not allowed to talk about things that might appear to be negative. I don't think she had anyone to turn to, really to help her deal with whatever it was that troubled her. From what I know, I don't believe anyone wakes up one day and wants to be bad, hurt others, or get high on drugs, but something leads them to that decision because of something they haven't dealt with. In a weird sense, as much as my mom did to me, I learned from her what *not* to do.' Stephen nodded that he understood. 'That's why I'm always on you for facing things as they come up. If you learn anything from my past, it's to hate no one. If you do, you'll become that person who did you wrong. As you grow older, you're going to face a lot of issues. If you have a problem, don't go to bed upset; talk to your mom, call me in the middle of the night, whatever. It's important because if you let things build up inside you, whatever the situation is, little by little it will eat away at you, like it did my mom. And that would be a waste, especially for all that you have going for yourself. Hate no one!'

'Did your dad and you ever spend time together?'

'Not a lot of time. But like I said, things were different back then.

I'm sure part of him wanted to, but I don't know . . .' My voice trailed off as I thought about Father and me.

'Did you two have a special time together?' Stephen asked, tilting his head.

Realizing where I was at that moment, I slowly turned Stephen to the right. 'Well, as a matter of fact . . .' I choked for a split second, 'I was maybe a little younger than you when one evening, on a night just like this, my dad was out for his evening smoke and I followed his footsteps to this exact spot, where my family and I would spend our summers together.'

'Right here, at that cabin?' Stephen pointed as he asked in amazement.

'Yep, right here. We walked around the block, and that one time with Dad I felt like I was ten feet tall. I was a somebody. It's something I never forgot. Back then it meant the world to me. That's why I love walking with you; it's something I can pass on.' I smiled.

Together in silence Stephen and I retraced a journey that had begun a lifetime ago. Only this time we held hands, and I kept my son close to my side. At the end of the block Stephen stopped to hug me around the waist. 'Thanks, Dad.'

'No.' I again choked up. 'Thank you, Stephen. You mean the world to me, and well, I know it hasn't been easy for you, but I try. I want you to know how much I love you. I truly do.'

On the block near our house, Stephen shyly asked, 'Dad . . . am I going to make it?'

I could only stroke his short blond hair in wonderment. That same question had plagued me for so many years.

'It's okay, Dad. I know it's a stupid question. I don't want to waste your time.'

'Stephen, take all the time you want. Here, sit down,' I instructed.

'Here, in the middle of the street?' he asked, looking around.

I sat down, folding my legs on the pavement. 'Right here, right now, nothing else is more important. Relax, you're too young to be so serious. You're going to make it. Not a doubt in my mind. Absolutely!'

'How do you know? I mean . . .'

'I know.' I nodded my head. 'I know you. You're a terrific young man. You're kind, you're sensitive. You know right from wrong and, most important, you've got a good heart.' Switching topics for a moment, I admitted, 'I know our divorce wasn't easy, and I am sorry. I truly am. I know school isn't always easy, or dealing with other kids, or things you have to face on a daily basis. No offense, but that's life. Everybody has problems. Everyone.

'But you're different: you deal with things. It's not always easy, but that's the way it is. I'm not trying to be a tough guy about this, but no matter what happens to you, it doesn't give you an excuse to blame others or wallow in self-pity. Your mother, your teachers, others who love you, or even myself: we can only help you so far. It's going to be up to you to make it happen. No one's perfect. There are no sets of perfect parents; no one has a perfect life. Your mother and I tried to make it work out. But it didn't. And as you grow older, maybe you can learn something positive from our mistakes.

'You're going to be fine. You've got a strong heart. In life you're going to make mistakes, you're going to fall down, but it's getting up that counts. Just like in baseball: you'll get a few hits, but most likely, you'll strike out more than you'll get on base. But don't quit. Find your focus, relax, take a deep breath, and give it a good swing. I beg of you, Stephen, don't quit. There are so many people who cave in at the first sign of trouble. They quit school, they act like they know it all, and develop a habit of quitting on everything. You're better than that. If you quit, everything you fought for – your grades, baseball, your self-respect – would have been in vain. The thing is, at the end of the day you still have to face yourself. I know it's a lot to digest at your age, but I'm here to help you. Like I said, I can't do it all for you, but my job as a parent is to make you a responsible, functional, productive adult. I'm not here to raise a child, but a happy, caring, nurturing man. I see greatness within you. You have your whole life ahead of you. If I've learned anything from my past, the one thing I can teach you as a father is this: Stephen, there is nothing, and I mean nothing, *you* cannot accomplish if you want it bad enough. The choice is yours. Always has been, always will be. Stay on your course. Be true to yourself, and you'll be fine.'

Smiling, Stephen asked, 'You think so?'

Taking his hand, I stated, 'I know so. You're going to be fine. I'm here for you. Even when I'm not physically with you, not a single day passes that I don't think about you and pray for you. Come on,'

I joked, 'don't do what I did and be so serious all the time. Have fun! Relax, seize the day. Take a breath. "In da nose . . . out da mouth,"' I said in my Schwarzenegger voice. As we gazed up at the stars that filled the black sky, everything seemed within reach. Both Stephen and I filled our lungs. 'Feel better?' I asked.

Wiping a tear from his eye, Stephen nodded. Leaning over, I brought him to my chest. 'Love you, Dad.'

'I love you, too, son, I truly do. Trust me, it's gonna be fine,' I whispered.

'I'm sorry you had to go through that,' Stephen said as he looked up at me.

'Well . . .' I deflected as another tear trickled down my cheek. 'To, ah . . . to tell you the truth,' I stumbled, 'as I sit here with you, it's like it never happened. Just as long as I can look at you and know you're okay, for me that's all that matters. It's times like these . . . that's what I live for. I'll always remember this, our time right now, as one of my happy thoughts.'

'Me, too.' Stephen sprang up to walk over to the nearby fence. Taking a few seconds longer to work the cramp out from my leg, I followed him, wondering what he was up to. 'Remember, Dad, how you always told me about you smelling the redwood trees, how it makes you feel good even when you're feeling down?' Still feeling emotional, all I could do was nod my head. 'Well, this is going to be my smell. When I smell this, I'll think of us and our time together. It's going to be my happy thought.'

'Good for you,' I replied, walking over to pluck off a few strands of sweet jasmine from the vine. 'So be it.'

Later, after tucking Stephen in to bed and kissing him good night, with his beloved Wally, the stuffed alligator, cradled in his arm, I stood over him long after he drifted off to sleep. Before turning off the light, I closed my eyes and took in a deep breath from the jasmine, whose fragrance filled Stephen's room. 'Happy thoughts,' I prayed as I closed the door behind me.

Returning outside, I looked down at my watch. During our walk Stephen and I had become closer in four hours than I had with my parents in twelve years. Strolling in the early morning hours of the new day, beneath a canopy of towering redwoods, I felt more fortunate than ever before. After years of intense struggles and personal battles, everything seemed to be coming together. I was a father to a terrific young man who never had a childhood like I did, I had broken the shackles of my past and was fortunate enough to help others, and I finally had a lady in my life whom I loved and adored. I was happy, in every sense of the word. And fulfilling a lifetime fantasy, I was now living yards away from the cabin where my childhood desires first took root.

Before returning to my home, I stopped suddenly when I caught a scent of the redwoods' sweet aroma. Turning up to gaze at the silvery-white stars that twinkled far above the tops of the trees, I closed my eyes, thinking of the first time I breathed in that same smell that continued to possess me. As a five-year-old boy, as Ron, Stan, and I stood with Father by the Russian River, I had strained my neck to look up as the deep blue sky gave way to bright orange and purple streaks – as if someone had taken a paintbrush to heaven's canvas. I had shuddered when I felt someone brush up against me. I thought it was Father, but glanced up to see Mother's face beaming down at me as she wrapped me in her arms. 'Take it in,' she had said. 'Take a deep breath, hold it, and never forget. Never forget this moment.' And as I did, it was as if nature's aroma was Mother's perfume and the gentle rustling of the trees was Mother whispering to me. For an instant Mom, Dad, Ron, Stan, and I were the perfect family. I had never felt that safe or as loved by Mother as I did at that moment in time. Years later, in the depths of my despair, replaying the vision in my head over and over again had been enough to wash away my pain and loneliness.

Now, standing alone beneath God's creation, I closed my eyes, relaxed my body, and inhaled as much air as my lungs could hold. I could almost recapture the scent of Mother's perfume and Father's shiny jet-black hair and beaming smile, as I recalled that evening so long ago. Opening my eyes, I found the north star and muttered, 'Rest in peace. May God Almighty grant you both eternal peace. Amen.'

EPILOGUE
June 1999,
Carmel Beach, California

Without a care in the world, I sip champagne as I gaze at the clear blue ocean. On the beach, dogs run back and forth into the water, chasing the ocean's foam or each other, or fetching sticks. A blanket of fog begins to overtake the bay. I can feel the hairs on my body spring up from the sudden drop in temperature. I erase the mere thought of fighting the chill and throwing on a jacket or scurrying away in search of shelter if the sky suddenly opened up and poured down rain. All I do is lean back on the wooden bench, take another sip, and soak in the purple overcast sky. I'm learning simply to be still.

I still can't stop myself from smiling. The last few days have been a whirlwind. Even now as I close my eyes, I can recapture only tiny, vibrant, burst-like fragments of a day that was taken from a fairy tale. Hours ago, I had stood with my back facing the Russian River – on the same ground that I had asked Marsha for her hand in marriage. With my son, Stephen, standing beside me as my best man, Marsha strolled down a red velvet runner as if she were an angel walking on water. We stood together beneath a white arch that was practically dripping with an array of vibrant flowers – bright orange lilies, turquoise-blue orchids, and porcelain-white gardenias. I caressed Marsha's trembling hand. My mind wandered as the minister spoke of the wonder of life, love, and commitment. All I could do was gaze out and make eye contact with those who were sharing our private ceremony. Mrs Woodworth – my fifth-grade English teacher who had told me when I was a child not to worry about my nervous stuttering because I was destined to communicate through writing – wiped the tears from her eyes as I gave her a slight bow. Then, looking behind her, I smiled at my childhood friends from foster care, Paul Brazell and Dave Howard, and Dave's lovely wife, Kelly.

When the minister had asked if I would take Marsha's hand, I leaned over and whispered into her ear part of a letter I had written her when we dated on the phone years ago. I then knelt down on one knee and placed the ring on Marsha's delicate finger. Within moments, the minister presented Marsha and me to the world as Mr and Mrs Pelzer.

Now opening my eyes, I can still feel my heart pound from the excitement, not only because I am committed to sharing my life with Marsha, but also with how everything has unfolded in my life. I am now happy, healthy, and no longer terrified of what the future may hold. My son is an outstanding, caring young man who has his entire life before him. I want for nothing. I have a terrific career, a small band of close friends, and a personal relationship with God.

With all the mistakes I've made, I am now my own person. One of the only links to my dark past is my father's badge, which I keep to honor him. I flew with it on every mission while serving in the United States Air Force, and I carried it in my back pocket when I had the honor of meeting President Reagan. When I was selected as a torch-bearer for the centennial Olympic Games, I carried the badge. And as I stated, 'I most certainly do!' when asked if I would take Marsha as my wife, Father's sacred badge was in my tuxedo pocket.

As a responsible adult, I am now old enough and wise enough to understand that no one's life is perfect or even normal. Everyone has a past, everyone has issues. Life is what we make of it. I am only concerned about being a kind, humble person, a caring, guiding father, and a loving husband. With each and every day, I simply apply myself as best as I can.

Above me, streaks of maroon and purple begin to spread across the horizon. A cold breeze strikes my face as my fingers find a piece of paper in my shirt pocket. Unfolding the paper, I replay every word in my mind before my eyes scan the letter, that I had in part whispered to Marsha only hours before:

Flying at 28,000 feet westbound, somewhere over Nevada, thinking of you. It is at times extremely difficult for me to open up and talk to a woman like you. Until recently, I never had.

Getting close to someone, anyone, is very, very hard for me.

It is easier, safer for me to watch from a distance. Sometimes I feel so lost. I've never been able to experience things like normal people; like being held as the sun goes down or feeling safe and 'carefree' with a woman. A sensation I have yet to experience. So, I watch others and smile for their joy. Sometimes that's enough. I'll make eye contact, bow my head in respect, and stroll off feeling a little warmer inside, thinking I would never be able to share moments in time like other couples.

Somehow lately I believe this is the springtime of my life. I've worked hard, planted many things, and soon they will blossom and grow before my eyes. I'm still scared, but no longer terrified. I can live with that. In an odd sense, being on the constant mental defensive is a comfort zone of its own. But one day I would like to be a real person. A person who is able to let down his guard and let someone in. Before I die I would like to experience that. I want to shelve my former life's mistakes. I would like to live in total peace, in every sense of the word.

If I have to remain alone, I will. Above all I know not only can I survive, but I can trust myself. And I feel secure with that premise, as well as knowing I will not cause anyone else anguish.

I still dream of a home – my home: clean and fresh and open. The scent of flowers while Pat Metheny plays on the stereo. As always, I dream. I always will. I'm trying to give up control, but it's hard because for so long I was controlled by so many. But maybe if I surrender, I'll find my answer. I'll find peace.

Maybe, one day, I'll have a home. Then maybe one day I can come home . . . home to you.

After replacing Marsha's letter, I wipe away a tear, while staring outward where the swirl of water collides against the beach. I realize how far I've come.

'Here's to my husband,' my wife, who was silently sitting beside me, suddenly announces.

'And here's to you, princess,' I reply, wrapping my arm around Marsha's shoulders, while an elderly couple strolls by, smiles, and nods at the newlyweds.

Within the recesses of my heart, I know with hope, effort, and a little luck that anything is possible.

I am living a fantastic life.

PERSPECTIVES

Dave Pelzer

Husband, father, author, and advocate

As I enter midlife, even to this day it is difficult for me fully to understand the magnitude of what happened to me as a child. Because of the life I am able to live today, it is as if my past experiences never happened. Every one of us has situations from their past. On a daily basis all of us are faced with dilemmas. I am no different, then or now. As a child I believed with all of my heart that if I could survive my ordeal, then not only could I accomplish what I set my mind to, but anything else I would encounter had to be easier. This is why my story is *not* about my being a victim of child abuse, but of the indomitable human spirit within us all.

I lived through an extraordinary experience, yet I was fortunate enough to learn from it and walk away a better person. I can't change my past, and it does not grant me the right to use it as a crutch, nor am I destined to become a prisoner because of it. For years I have lived by the philosophy: that which does not kill you can only make you stronger. I simply had to learn to pick myself up at an earlier age.

It seems all of my life I have been put down, taken advantage of, and at times fallen flat on my face. But, by the grace of God, I have somehow found myself being able to stand up, repair any damage, and forge ahead.

Years ago, a dear friend once told me a great deal of people mature in their thirties. As much as I have been through in my life, I am now a believer. With every day I soak in something previously unknown to me the day before. Like any adult, I carry regrets, one of which is Patsy. With time, hindsight, and maturity, no matter what others may say, I realize we were simply two different people and that she in fact applied herself to our union more than I. That is why I call Patsy my former wife rather than my 'ex'. I know what it's like to be a non-person, and I refuse to treat anyone as such. I can only pray my mistakes as a parent do not reverberate to my son. Strangely, because of my failed relationship, I have committed myself to be a better husband to Marsha, and this makes me appreciate her all the more. I am now fortunate enough to share my life with a person who truly makes me whole.

But as I look back, I fully realize I made a fair amount of mistakes. Like many individuals who suffer from low self-esteem, I, too, allowed myself to become associated with others who mistook my kindness or generosity as a sign of weakness and attempted to exploit that for their own agenda. At the time, part of me felt as though I were a schoolboy willing to do anything just to gain acceptance so others would approve of or believe in me. I never even thought about protecting my interests, or maintaining the standards I had fought so hard for – even though I had fully realized how grave my situations were – because of fear of rejection and being all alone. But now time, experience, and maturity have become valuable allies for me.

Because of all that was stacked against me, I should have never made it. Not a single day passes that, no matter how strenuous, hair-pulling, or defeating the day may have been, I do not thank my lucky stars. I appreciate everything – from a soggy, cold hamburger that has been sitting in the car for hours as I make my way to the airport in the middle of the night, to struggling to find the precise answer to someone's problem even after speaking nonstop for the entire day. I cherish every breath, spend hours staring at the delicate, vibrantly colored petals of flowers, become excited at the touch of my lover's fingers, or love to hear the sound of my son's laugh. Perhaps because of my past, the most important things for me are still the simplest – feeling the sun's warm rays upon my back or gazing up at the clear blue sky. Even to this day, I would not change one moment of my life. If it all ends now, I have lived, I have learned, and I have been loved. The greatest lesson is the gift of life, and no matter what, tomorrow is always another day.

There are still times when I am overwhelmed by immense feelings of hollowness, guilt, and fear of anyone becoming too close to me. It is something I will have to stand up to on a daily basis. All I can do is maintain my vow that I took years ago when I was eight years old, immediately after my mother had burned my arm on the gas stove. From this day forward I will never give up. From this day forward I will give everything my all. As an adult I expect nothing less from myself.

When my time comes, I would like to know that I have repaid my debt to those who have made a difference in my life. And to be at peace knowing that I stopped the cancer from spreading to those I love.

Claire Frazier-Yzaguirre, M. Div., MFCC
Marriage and family therapist

As a full-time marriage and family therapist, I have been involved for many years with people who've suffered childhood trauma and its tremendous impact in their lives as adults. Together with my husband, Dr John Yzaguirre, we are passionate about empowering people to overcome this cycle of hurting themselves and others, and create dynamic and healthy families. We believe that relationships, where priority is given to cooperation and unity, are at the very heart of not only preventing the hurt, but will create in us the ability to become a *culture of caring* that will renew our society from the devastating effects of the indifference, domination, and submission that characterize toxic relationships.

I love reading and sharing stories about people who've experienced triumph over tragedy. And the *best part*, for me always, is how someone can reclaim their power through pain and inspire others with hope and healing. It was on just such a day of story gathering in a nearby bookstore that I came across Dave Pelzer's poignant and heartbreaking story. As I devoured his incredible story in *A Child Called 'It'* and *The Lost Boy*, I knew I had to talk with Dave about how he was able to transform his immense suffering into a life of helping others.

As I read *A Man Named Dave*, I found myself reading from all my own experiential perspectives – as a woman, wife, mother, daughter, friend, minister, and therapist – and wept most during his tender and so-long-awaited reunion with his father, his excruciating confrontation with his mother, his joyous discovery of Marsha as his life mate, and later his heart-to-heart talk with his precious son, Stephen. At long last I, along with countless of you reading, could understand how Dave answered the many questions of his life. How he came to forgive his brutal mother for the years of torture through the life-restoring skill of empathy. How he came to forgive his passive father, who died in his arms, for not stopping the abuse, finding a way of giving up hateful lies that bind, and commending each of these wounded and incompetent parents to God. And ultimately how he, equipped with empathy, forgiveness, and the love of supportive relationships, could help others find the way, too.

It is exciting to witness Dave's triumph over tragedy through the power of forgiveness and love! Dave's whole story can be seen as a testament to the endurance of the human spirit. I rejoice with and for him, and for all who will be touched by this tender yet powerful trilogy. I am also sobered and motivated (you, too?) by the fact that there is much for all of us to do to help others and ourselves.

We've come a long way in understanding the dynamics of pain, survival, and healing. Some of the best research about the effects of trauma on the human psyche comes, not surprisingly, from war victims and victims of domestic violence. Children and adults *who do survive* use creative and powerful defenses of denial, dissociation, repression, and fantasy, which keep them alive (and for many, sane) until they can escape and hopefully find the necessary support and resources to heal. The lucky ones are not only those who get out, but those who heal, while others fall into a private hell, an abyss of mental illness, die, or propagate their horrific legacy by hurting others.

Survival, yes, but there is a huge cost to the soul and mind as important parts of one's self are buried. These survival skills provide the needed road map for healing later, tracing, as it were, the path to the *buried treasure* that all survivors, along with their skilled helpers, must find to heal – encountering and conquering the dreaded monsters of their past and liberating all the *precious bits of self* – innocence, the capacity to play, laugh, trust, love, and belief in one's intrinsic value – that were buried in the time of war.

It is not enough to survive. We can see, as in Dave's life, that when people are left unprotected at length, as he was, the situation can become frightfully ritualistic, as it did between him and his mother. Fueling this dynamic, often, is addiction, poor self-esteem and -worth, secret-keeping, denial, fear, or indifference by those who can make a difference (Dave's father, relatives, neighbors, even society at this time in the seventies). The powerful 'shame rules' – don't feel, talk about, or stop the shameful and abusive behavior – that exist in these families, and to an alarming degree still in our society, leave members, especially children, vulnerable to attack. It's as if the alarm system in a house has been disconnected, allowing any intruder easy access to burglarize.

And we can see this in Dave's life, as his attachment disorder was his 'protective barrier' that kept him from being hurt, but also kept him from getting close to anyone – even more so to people he felt he couldn't trust. His very low self-esteem made him the perfect target to be taken advantage of. And what is very common to many people, Dave ended up having a relationship with someone from a similar background. In fact, individuals with problematic pasts seem to be magnetized to each other. But these two negatives did not equal a positive, but rather created and fueled more problems, barriers, and isolations. Ultimately Dave's misery was endured only because of the absolute love and devotion he had for his son. He felt an obligation to make the marriage last.

The good news is how many people are now mobilizing and joining hands from across many fields to create a world where not only intervention occurs, as in Dave's life, but *prevention* as well. How do we create such a world? By creating relationships where the first priority is mutual love and concern for all, we overcome the indifference, domination, and submission that create problems in the first place. Dave and others like him are saved when people care and take action.

When we see how the consistent love of several people in Dave's life helped to transform his great suffering into even greater loving service to others, we witness a miracle. We see then how love can redeem every suffering, and how embracing another's suffering can work a miracle of unity in all of our relationships. When we forgive, we free ourselves from the bitter ties that bind us to the one who hurt us.

I will always remember the questions that prompted my call to Dave: 'How long does it take to forgive?' 'Can suffering be transformed into love?' And I will remember that the answers to these questions are largely determined by how well and how long we love and are loved. Through healing and forgiveness we get better, not bitter. Dave, thanks so much for your inspiring and courageous role-modeling to grow and help others to help themselves. We, along with all who are forever touched by your story, join you in this mighty work of hope and healing!

Marsha Pelzer
Wife and executive director

This man named Dave, where do I begin? There's so much to say about him. There is so much I feel for him. He's a man of virtue, an individual of countless accomplishments, and has a heart of gold. A man so dedicated, energetic, and adorably wholesome. Yet he's the most haunted person I know, constantly swimming upstream. What I admire most about him is he's the most genuine of souls and gives his *all* to everything he does. Whether he's working in his garden perfecting his impatiens, or living his life of 'Planes, Trains, and Automobiles' while performing programs back-to-back, Dave gives it his all. When writing a letter to uplift the defeated spirit of a young fan, or driving over eight hours on weekends to see his son play baseball, Dave gives every ounce of himself. While giving a soul-stirring interview on TV, or holding me at night as we drift off to sleep, Dave never holds back. In everything he does, Dave willingly offers his heart and soul. He maps out every detail, predicts every scenario, and handles everything gracefully. He does because he is. No ulterior motives. No disguises. Nothing is expected in return. To give it his all with every fiber of his being is for Dave to be Dave. Nothing else will do.

Dave has a gift – and a curse, for that matter – of making things look effortless. The passerby sees Dave ease into his daily routine of traveling, speaking, writing, and being a loving father and husband. They interpret his life as exciting, enterprising, and predestined. People feed off Dave's energy and outlook, and some expect him to solve their problems with his magic wand. His label as a *New York Times* best-selling author usually implies an overnight success and the lap of luxury lifestyle. But only a small handful knows how grueling, disturbing, belittling, and erratic Dave's life truly can be. How his sacrifices are far greater than the rewards. And only those behind the scenes of his world can understand the consequences of his struggles. Dave's life is indicative of the fact that you can't have roses without thorns. And he welcomes both without reservation. So why does he do it? Where does he muster up the fortitude? How does he sustain the dedication to what he considers responsibility? To relive his horrific past every day in his quest to help others, and do it with such passion, humor, and honesty? As close as I am to the fire, I don't completely know. Sharing a life with him, inside and outside of his heart, I catch glimpses of what inspires him. I can tell you that the indebtedness he has for those who saved his life and the compassion he has for helping others are his cause, while the love he has for Stephen and me fuels the fire. He most certainly is a man on a mission. Dave is Batman, Indiana Jones, and James Bond all rolled into one. Like these characters, Dave possesses a dark side, a haunted past, a life on the run, only to expose the light; and he will do whatever it takes to bring peace to a dying world.

Dave is such an admirable human being. I know and understand him more than anyone who's ever been honored to know him, and I consider myself blessed because of it. But it's so difficult to know of the sacrifices required – past and present – just to be Dave Pelzer. God love 'im, he's been through so much and has always been the 'bigger person' in spite of the wrong done to him. Concerning Dave's mother and father, his distorted nine-year marriage, the deceptions from his former speaking firm, not to mention his inept business relations in his career, I can simply say: Dave was way too kind! I do not mean to sound harsh and don't intend to encourage hatred and resentment, but please understand that based on what I know and what I personally have witnessed, I feel these individuals were not worthy of his understanding, much less his kindness and patience for them. To Dave, the worst thing you can do is to break his trust. He feels that is the ultimate dishonor. And that's exactly what these people did. Although I consider myself a very kind, well-grounded, and compassionate individual, I could have never endured a fraction of what Dave did in these relationships. No offense to anyone, but I would have kicked their butts (really hard), then run as fast and as far away from them as I could! I can testify that the events that have happened in Dave's life he has given to the readers in bite-sized pieces; although the reality was and is much more crude. But if it was revealed to people in full strength, it would blow their minds and the message Dave is trying so desperately to convey. This is why God has bestowed on him all the well-deserved blessings: because Dave did the right thing; he was the bigger person; he turned the other cheek. Dave has endured and accomplished things that neither I nor a lot of other people ever could. I liken him to Job in the Bible. He lived a good life only after he lived a hell on earth and remained steadfast amid it all. And I'm sure the story told of Job cannot justly describe his reality. The same for Dave's life.

Dave is simply precious. In fact, this is the nickname I gave him years ago, and I don't hesitate to call him Precious whenever I can (much to his embarrassment!). And Dave is *very* modest! If you think he is a great individual, then you don't know how great he really is. Dave is – without ego – the most compassionate, level-headed, unselfish, and devoted individual I've ever known. He is one of the Ten Outstanding Young Americans, the Outstanding Young Persons of the World, and a torchbearer for the centennial Olympic Games, just to name a few. They don't grant awards like these every day or for just any reason. These are distinguished commendations for unparalleled individuals who've made a difference in this world. But Dave would rather have you think it's no big deal! And even when his first two books were officially published and only a few believed in their potential, while many folks predicted them as 'fillers' in a book catalog and some went out of their way to sabotage the books and even laugh at Dave in the process, the books wouldn't die. They not only became *New York Times* best-sellers, but Dave is the first author to have two books simultaneously on the trade paperback list. (Of course, this was when those doubting Thomases gave him the old 'we were behind you all the way' routine!) Again, Dave remained humble and appreciative amid such a great feat.

As his wife, I want the world to know how adorable, loving, and dependable he is. How strong yet fragile his heart is. How brave yet vulnerable. How wonderful a provider and friend. My ally. My greatest fan and my biggest critic. Dave spoils me rotten. He says I'm his best friend, his princess, and his kryptonite. He jokes that on my good days I'm Bambi, on bad days I'm the Terminator. He's the only one who can make me laugh or cry just by looking at me, and makes me feel like I can conquer the world. His unyielding persistence and impatience wear me out, but he's my knight in shining armor, my soul mate, the most handsome man I know. I always feel the need to stick up for him, protect him, and defeat the enemy for him – when all the while he's protecting and defending me.

The greatest day in my life, besides being born into a wonderful family, and my beautiful Cinderella wedding, was picking up the phone years ago and introducing myself to a man named Dave. When I was assigned as his editor for *A Child Called 'It'*, my life was forever changed. Soon I would ride the most frightening and blissful roller coaster of all time. From swimming in the depths of despair to dropping to my knees every day thanking God for the air in my lungs, my life with Dave Pelzer was destined to be. Because of Dave I have learned to appreciate *life* – with all its ups and downs. I've learned to love flowers, the Russian River, and the color of the sky. The smell of jasmine and the softness of silk. Because of Dave I've learned to forgive and to forget. To see the brighter side of life. He has shown me how important it is to walk the talk and to be an example to others. And most important, he has helped me to see how broken lives can mend from hearts and hands that care.

My precious Dave, I love you so. I'm proud to know you, blessed to love you, unworthy to be loved by you. And to be your wife and friend . . . no words under heaven could ever describe.

ABOUT THE AUTHOR

A retired air force air crew member, Dave played a major role in Operations Just Cause, Desert Shield, and Desert Storm. Dave was selected for the unique task of midair-refueling the once highly secretive SR-71 Blackbird and the F-117 Stealth fighter. While serving in the air force, Dave worked in juvenile hall and other programs involving youths at risk throughout California.

Dave's exceptional accomplishments include commendations from Presidents Reagan, Bush, and Clinton, as well as various other heads of state. While maintaining an international active-duty flight schedule, Dave was the recipient of the 1990 J. C. Penny Golden Rule Award, making him the California Volunteer of the Year. In 1993, Dave was honored as one of the Ten Outstanding Young Americans (TOYA), joining a distinguished group of alumni that includes Chuck Yeager, Christopher Reeve, Anne Bancroft, John F. Kennedy, Orson Welles, and Walt Disney. In 1994, Dave was the only American to be selected as one of the Outstanding Young Persons of the World (TOYPW) for his efforts involving child abuse awareness and prevention, as well as for instilling resilience in others. During the centennial Olympic Games, Dave was a torchbearer, carrying the coveted flame.

When not on the road or with his wife, Marsha, or son, Stephen, Dave is either traipsing through Carmel or lives a quiet life on the Russian River with his box turtle named Chuck.

You can visit Dave's website at www.davepelzer.com for more on Dave.